# Inner empire

Manchester University Press

STUDIES IN IMPERIALISM

When the 'Studies in Imperialism' series was founded by Professor John M. MacKenzie more than thirty years ago, emphasis was laid upon the conviction that 'imperialism as a cultural phenomenon had as significant an effect on the dominant as on the subordinate societies'. With well over a hundred titles now published, this remains the prime concern of the series. Cross-disciplinary work has indeed appeared covering the full spectrum of cultural phenomena, as well as examining aspects of gender and sex, frontiers and law, science and the environment, language and literature, migration and patriotic societies, and much else. Moreover, the series has always wished to present comparative work on European and American imperialism, and particularly welcomes the submission of books in these areas. The fascination with imperialism, in all its aspects, shows no sign of abating, and this series will continue to lead the way in encouraging the widest possible range of studies in the field. 'Studies in Imperialism' is fully organic in its development, always seeking to be at the cutting edge, responding to the latest interests of scholars and the needs of this ever-expanding area of scholarship.

General editors:
Andrew Thompson, Professor of Global and Imperial History at Nuffield College, Oxford
Alan Lester, Professor of Historical Geography at University of Sussex and LaTrobe University

Founding editor:
Emeritus Professor John MacKenzie

Robert Bickers, University of Bristol
Christopher L. Brown, Columbia University
Pratik Chakrabarti, University of Houston
Elizabeth Elbourne, McGill University
Bronwen Everill, University of Cambridge
Kate Fullagar, Australian Catholic University
Chandrika Kaul, University of St Andrews
Dane Kennedy, George Washington University
Shino Konishi, Australian Catholic University
Philippa Levine, University of Texas at Austin
Kirsten McKenzie, University of Sydney
Tinashe Nyamunda, University of Pretoria
Dexnell Peters, University of the West Indies
Sujit Sivasundaram, University of Cambridge
Angela Wanhalla, University of Otago
Stuart Ward, University of Copenhagen

To buy or to find out more about the books currently available in this series, please go to: https://manchesteruniversitypress.co.uk/series/studies-in-imperialism/

# Inner empire

## Architecture and Imperialism in the British Isles, 1550–1950

*Edited by*

G. A. Bremner and Daniel Maudlin

MANCHESTER UNIVERSITY PRESS

Copyright © Manchester University Press 2024

While copyright in the volume as a whole is vested in Manchester University Press, copyright in individual chapters belongs to their respective authors, and no chapter may be reproduced wholly or in part without the express permission in writing of both author and publisher.

Published by Manchester University Press
Oxford Road, Manchester, M13 9PL

www.manchesteruniversitypress.co.uk

British Library Cataloguing-in-Publication Data
A catalogue record for this book is available from the British Library

ISBN 978 1 5261 4266 5 hardback

First published 2024

The publisher has no responsibility for the persistence or accuracy of URLs for any external or third-party internet websites referred to in this book, and does not guarantee that any content on such websites is, or will remain, accurate or appropriate.

Typeset
by Cheshire Typesetting Ltd, Cuddington, Cheshire
Printed in Great Britain
by TJ Books Limited, Padstow

# Contents

List of plates     vii
List of figures     ix
List of contributors     xiv
Acknowledgements     xvii

Introduction: The architectural historiography of 'inner empire'
*G. A. Bremner and Daniel Maudlin*     1

## Part I: The inner empire

1. Cultivation, constructed environments, and cultural conflict: Plantations and the inner empire     29
*John Patrick Montaño*

2. Making North Britain: infrastructure projects and the forcible integration of the Scottish Highlands     53
*Daniel Maudlin*

3. 'Housing the poorest poor': the Irish other in nineteenth-century Liverpool     78
*John Belchem*

4. Architecture of the state in Ireland: the colonial question, 1800–1922     100
*Richard J. Butler*

5. Studied indifference: eighteenth-century Irish architecture in modern British architectural histories     128
*Conor Lucey*

## Part II: Empire building in Britain

6. An empire under construction: the view from inside East India House — 155
   *Emily Mann*

7. Foreign mud, home comforts: Taipans, opium, and the remitted wealth of Jardine, Matheson & Co. in Scotland — 193
   *G. A. Bremner*

8. Spaces of empire in Victorian and Edwardian London — 218
   *Richard Dennis*

9. Australia House: shaping Dominion status in the imperial capital, 1907–63 — 248
   *Eileen Chanin*

10. Empire timbers: architecture, trade, and forestry, 1920–50 — 273
    *Neal Shasore*

11. How to live in Britain: the Indian YMCA in Fitzroy Square — 305
    *Mark Crinson*

*Index* — 332

# Plates

1 'A Plott of the Cittie of London Derry' (c. 1610).
2 'A generall plat of the lands belonging to the Cittie of London ...' from Thomas Stafford's *Pacata Hibernia, Ireland Appeased and Reduced; or, An Historie of the Late Warres of Ireland* (1633).
3 Interior, Officer's Mess, Fort George.
4 Located on the former workhouse site, the proposed cathedral was an extravagant prestige project amidst the depression of the 1930s planned to symbolise the Catholic contribution to Liverpool, the very centre of a futuristic townscape with 'slumdom' eradicated.
5 Trim gaol, Co. Meath, by John Hargrave, built 1828–34. After many years of inactivity, the state's prison inspectors convinced the County Meath grand jurors to commit to a new county gaol; the result was a powerful essay in the abstract propaganda of prison design.
6 Sir Edward Lovett Pearce, façade of Parliament House (now Bank of Ireland), Dublin, 1729–39.
7 Agostino Carlini, 'Friendly Union of Great Britain and Ireland with Neptune driving away Famine and Despair', pediment sculpture (detail), Custom House, Dublin, 1781–91. ©
8 Thomas Hosmer Shepherd, directors' court room, East India House, c. 1820, watercolour, 15.9 × 22.2 cm.
9 George Lambert and Samuel Scott, Bombay, c. 1731, oil on canvas, 81 × 132 cm.
10 Lews Castle, Stornoway, Scotland.
11 Fredrick Marlett Bell-Smith, *The Heart of the Empire* (1909).
12 'Australian Building' (1907), drawing of a concept proposed by Alfred Burr, as drawn by Charles William English.
13 Poster for the Empire Timber Exhibition (1920), by MacDonald Gill.

14 Ba Nyan, 'Timber Stacking' for the Empire Marketing Board.
15 Indian YMCA and adjacent Robert Adam terraces in Fitzroy Square.
16 Ralph Tubbs and Stefan Buzas, design for the interior of the Dome of Discovery. Drawing by Stefan Buzas (1949?).

# Figures

| | | |
|---|---|---|
| 1.1 | Portrait of John Dee, British School, c. 1594. | 30 |
| 1.2 | Title page to John Norden's *A Description of Ireland* (1600). | 32 |
| 1.3 | 'The Plott of Black Water' (Blackwater fort), County Armagh (1587). | 34 |
| 1.4 | Castle of Cahir, 1599, from Thomas Stafford's *Pacata Hibernia: or, A History of the Wars in Ireland, During the Reign of Queen Elizabeth ... First Published in 1633* (reprint 1810). | 36 |
| 1.5 | Detail image, 'Wilde' Irish man and woman, from John Speed's, *Theatre of the Empire of Great Britaine* (1627). | 38 |
| 1.6 | Francis Jobson, Map of Ulster Counties (c. 1598). | 40 |
| 2.1 | The Tay Bridge, Aberfeldy, Perthshire. | 60 |
| 2.2 | The Weem Inn, Weem, Aberfeldy, Perthshire. | 62 |
| 2.3 | Fort George, Ardersier, Inverness | 64 |
| 2.4 | Governor's Residence and Officer's Lodgings, Fort George. | 67 |
| 2.5 | Ullapool, Lochbroom, Wester Ross. | 71 |
| 3.1 | 2 Court, Mount View, Liverpool, early twentieth century (c. 1913). This image is part of a series of slum photographs taken by Richard Brown. On one of the doors on the distant wall it is just possible to discern a slogan proclaiming the allegiance of the court: 'God Bless the Pope'. | 81 |
| 3.2 | Before and after plans of the pioneering Bevington Street scheme, promoted by Harford and Irish nationalist councillors, with its 'self-contained' cottages and flats and open spaces. | 92 |
| 3.3 | Early photograph of the pioneering Bevington Street scheme, view from Titchfield Street (c. 1912). | 93 |
| 3.4 | Early photograph of the pioneering Bevington Street scheme, view from Limekiln Lane (c. 1912). The new buildings facing Limekiln Lane were in tenement form but with | |

design modifications (individual front doors opening on to balconies) to ensure single defensible space. 94

4.1 The *tête de pont* (or bridgehead) fortifications at Shannonbridge, Co. Offaly, built c. 1815. Military fortifications along the crossings of the River Shannon mark some of the clearest examples of an architecture that represented the hegemonic power of the British imperial state in nineteenth-century Ireland . 106

4.2 Perspective sketch of an Irish Poor Law workhouse. Over 130 such institutions, to the designs of the British architect George Wilkinson, were built in Ireland around 1840, marking the beginning of a new top-down British experiment in 'solving' Irish social problems. 107

4.3 Dundalk courthouse, by John Bowden and Edward Parke, built 1813–21. The County Louth grand jurors, who commissioned this landmark public building, insisted that it rigorously adhered to every detail of Stewart and Revett's *Antiquities of Athens* (1762). 109

4.4 Tralee courthouse, Co. Kerry, by William Vitruvius Morrison, built 1830–33. Morrison's elegant and creative design was a favourite among Irish grand jurors in the late 1820s who rushed to secure funding for replacing their principal administrative building. Photograph taken c. 1900. 111

4.5 Dundalk county gaol, by John Neville, built 1849–54. Neville's careful use of massing and rustication gave his Italianate façade a uniquely severe and repressive character, but the Louth grand jurors took many years to commit funding to the new building. 115

4.6 The Four Courts, Dublin, on fire, 30 June 1922. Occupied by anti-Treaty IRA rebels in April 1922 and shelled by the Free State army two months later, the retreat of the rebels was marked by explosions that destroyed much of one of Dublin's greatest Georgian buildings and the adjacent Public Record Office. 117

4.7 Tullamore county gaol, Co. Offaly, in ruins, c. 1930s. Surpassing even the most romantic nineteenth-century Gothick ruin, the gaol was burned by anti-Treaty IRA forces in 1922 and later mostly demolished. Its erasure from the urban landscape of Tullamore signified to people at the time the retreat not solely of the anti-Treaty rebels but more substantially of the British imperial presence in Ireland. 118

## List of figures

| | | |
|---|---|---|
| 4.8 | Men hoisting an Irish tricolour atop the ruins of Tullamore gaol, 1937. This posed photograph captured a historic moment in the history of the town as the nineteenth-century prison gave way to a factory. | 119 |
| 5.1 | Bernard Scalé after Rowland Omer, 'The Geometrical Elevation of the Parliament House Dublin', engraving, 1767. | 129 |
| 5.2 | Sir Edward Lovett Pearce, colonnade of Parliament House, Dublin, 1729–39. | 131 |
| 5.3 | Sir Edward Lovett Pearce, House of Lords, Parliament House, Dublin, 1729–39. | 136 |
| 5.4 | Sir Edward Lovett Pearce's annotated edition of Andrea Palladio, *I quattro libri dell'architettura*, Venice, 1601. | 137 |
| 5.5 | Bernard Scalé after Rowland Omer, 'A Section of the House of Commons Dublin', engraving, 1767. | 143 |
| 5.6 | John Dixon, *The Oracle, Representing Britannia, Hibernia, Scotia and America*, mezzotint, 1774. | 144 |
| 6.1 | Samuel Wale, East India House, c. 1760, wash drawing, 7.6 × 15.2 cm. | 158 |
| 6.2 | *The House Occupied by the East India Company in Leadenhall Street, as Refaced in 1726*, chromolithograph by William Griggs after a watercolour by Thomas Malton, c. 1800. | 159 |
| 6.3 | Old and new East India House illustrated in *The Mirror of Literature, Amusement and Instruction*, 13 April 1833. | 160 |
| 6.4 | George Lambert and Samuel Scott, St Helena, c. 1731, oil on canvas, 78.5 × 117 cm. | 162 |
| 6.5 | George Lambert and Samuel Scott, Fort St George, Madras, c. 1731, oil on canvas, 81 × 132 cm. | 165 |
| 6.6 | Michael Rysbrack, marble relief from the chimneypiece made for the court room in East India House, c. 1729, showing 'Britannia receiving the riches of the East'. | 174 |
| 6.7 | Thomas Rowlandson, *Billy Lackbeard and Charley Blackbeard Playing at Football*, 1784, hand-coloured etching, 26.3 × 37.3 cm. | 175 |
| 6.8 | Herman Moll, *A Map of the East Indies and the Adjacent Countries; with the Settlements, Factories and Territories, explaining what belongs to England, Spain, France, Holland, Denmark, Portugal &c*, c. 1715, 66 × 104 cm. | 179 |
| 7.1 | Portrait of James Matheson, by Henry Cousins (after James Lonsdale), 1837. | 195 |
| 7.2 | Portrait of William Jardine, by Thomas Goff Lupton (after George Chinnery), c. 1830s. | 196 |

## List of figures

| | | |
|---|---|---|
| 7.3 | Jardine, Matheson & Co., headquarters, East Point, Hong Kong. Photograph by John Thomson, 1868/1871. | 197 |
| 7.4 | Duncraig Castle, Scotland, from Mackenzie, *History of the Mathesons, with Genealogies of the Various Families* (1900). | 203 |
| 7.5 | Lanrick Castle, Perthshire, Scotland. | 205 |
| 7.6 | Ardross Castle, Ross and Cromarty, Scotland. | 210 |
| 7.7 | Castlemilk estate house, Dumfriesshire, Scotland. | 211 |
| 8.1 | Map of Colonial and Foreign Banks in City of London. | 225 |
| 8.2 | Photograph of Bank of New Zealand building, Queen Victoria Street, London (c. 1876). | 226 |
| 8.3 | Photograph of Sussex Place, Regent's Park. | 230 |
| 8.4 | Map of Colonial & Foreign-Born in North Bayswater, 1891. | 232 |
| 8.5 | Map of Imperial Street Names in Selected London Suburbs. | 234 |
| 8.6 | Lipton's Letterhead (1903). | 237 |
| 8.7 | Map of Victoria Street, Westminster, c. 1895 (drawn by Miles Irving, Drawing Office, Department of Geography, University College London). | 241 |
| 9.1 | Australia Pavilion (Entrance), Franco-British Exhibition, London, 1908. Photographed by H. W. Mobsby. | 253 |
| 9.2 | 'Victoria House', New London Offices for the Government of Victoria (Australia), Strand, 1909. | 254 |
| 9.3 | Floor plan for 'Victoria House', London (1909). | 255 |
| 9.4 | Canadian Government Offices in London, 1907, as proposed by A. Marshall Mackenzie & Son, as illustrated in *The Builder*, 17 August 1907. | 258 |
| 9.5 | Australia House, London, Strand Elevation (1918). | 260 |
| 9.6 | Interior, Australia House, Exhibition Hall, in Buchan (Victorian) marble, looking towards entrance. | 262 |
| 9.7 | Australia House, ground floor plan (1918). | 266 |
| 9.8 | Herbert Baker, South Africa House, Trafalgar Square, London (1933), from *The Builder* (14 April 1933). | 268 |
| 10.1 | The Henry Florence Memorial Hall, 66 Portland Place (George Grey Wornum, 1934). | 274 |
| 10.2 | View of the Dominion Screen, designed by Denis Cheyne Dunlop (carved by Green & Vardy). | 275 |
| 10.3 | Details of the Dominion Screen showing the industry of South Africa (a *left*, b *right*). | 276 |
| 10.4 | Empire timbers exhibit on the first floor of the Building Centre, photographer unknown (c. 1932). | 288 |
| 10.5 | The Timber Development Association's Pavilion, British Empire Exhibition, Glasgow (1938). | 293 |

| 10.6 | A plan of the Glasgow British Empire Exhibition showing timber use across the exhibition site. | 294 |
| 10.7 | The Imperial Forestry Institute, Oxford (Hubert Worthington, 1950). | 296 |
| 10.8 | 'Logging scenes in Nigeria'. | 297 |
| 11.1 | Destroyed houses at 106–112 Gower Street, London. Photographic vignette from *Commemorating … Hostel*, 1953. | 311 |
| 11.2 | Ralph Tubbs, 'Future college quad', site plan (including first floor plan of Indian YMCA), 1949. | 314 |
| 11.3 | Indian YMCA – rear elevation. Photograph by Reginald Galway, 1953. | 318 |
| 11.4 | Indian YMCA – student room. Photograph by Reginald Galway, 1953. | 319 |
| 11.5 | Stair hall, Indian YMCA – section. | 321 |
| 11.6 | Stair hall, Indian YMCA. Photograph by Reginald Galway, 1953. | 322 |
| 11.7 | Plan of basement, Indian YMCA. *Architectural Design*, July 1953. | 323 |
| 11.8 | Assembly hall, Indian YMCA. Photograph by Reginald Galway, 1953. | 324 |
| 11.9 | Plan of ground floor, Indian YMCA. *Architectural Design*, July 1953. | 325 |

# Contributors

**John Belchem** is Emeritus Professor of History, University of Liverpool. Having published extensively on the city's history, he is now much involved in promoting and protecting its heritage as Trustee of National Museums, Liverpool; Chair of Merseyside Civic Society; Trustee of Merseyside Buildings Preservation Trust; and Vice-President of the Historic Society of Lancashire and Cheshire.

**G. A. Bremner** is Professor of Architectural History at the University of Edinburgh. His research focuses on the history of British imperial and colonial architecture and urbanism. His books include: *Imperial Gothic: Religious Architecture and High Anglican Culture in the British Empire, c.1840–70* (2013), *Architecture and Urbanism in the British Empire* (2016), and *Building Greater Britain: Architecture, Imperialism, and the Edwardian Baroque Revival, c. 1885–1920* (2022).

**Richard Butler** is Director of Research at Mary Immaculate College, Limerick. He was formerly Associate Professor of Urban History at the University of Leicester. He holds a PhD from the University of Cambridge. His publications include *Building the Irish Courthouse and Prison: A Political History, 1750–1850* (2020) and *Dreams of the Future in Nineteenth-Century Ireland* (2021). He is the current President of the Society for the Study of Nineteenth-Century Ireland.

**Eileen Chanin** is a historian at the Australian National University, Canberra, and Visiting Fellow of King's College London. She writes and lectures widely on cultural philanthropy, the arts, and the built environment. Her books include *Capital Designs: Australia House and Visions for an Imperial Capital* (2018). She is presently writing a biography of London's famed street, the Strand.

**Mark Crinson** is Emeritus Professor of Architectural History at Birkbeck, University of London. He was Vice-President and President of the European

Architectural History Network (2016–20), and he is a Fellow of the British Academy. His books include: *Shock City: Image and Architecture in Industrial Manchester* (2022), *Rebuilding Babel: Modern Architecture and Internationalism* (2017), *The Architecture of Art History – A Historiography* (2019, co-authored with Richard J. Williams), and *Modern Architecture and the End of Empire* (2003, reissued 2019). He is currently researching a Leverhulme-funded book, *Heathrow's Genius Loci*.

**Richard Dennis** is Emeritus Professor of Geography, University College London. His books include *Cities in Modernity: Representations and Productions of Metropolitan Space, 1840–1930* (2008) and, as co-editor, *Architectures of Hurry – Mobilities, Cities and Modernity* (2018). He has published widely on housing, transport, and literary representations of nineteenth- and early twentieth-century cities, especially London and Toronto.

**Conor Lucey** is Associate Professor in Architectural History at University College Dublin. His research focuses on domestic architecture, interior design and decoration, and the building industry in eighteenth-century Britain and Ireland. Recent publications include *Building Reputations: Architecture and the Artisan, 1750–1830* (2018), for which he was awarded the Alice Davis Hitchcock Medallion by the Society of Architectural Historians of Great Britain in 2019; and, as editor, *House and Home in Georgian Ireland: Spaces and Cultures of Domestic Life* (2022).

**Emily Mann** is an Associate Professor of Architectural History, Race, and Spatial Justice at The Bartlett School of Architecture, UCL, where she is a member of the Survey of London research unit. Publications include essays in *Building the British Atlantic World* (2016) and *Ireland, Slavery and the Caribbean* (2023). She previously taught and studied at the Courtauld Institute of Art, and is currently Editor of the journal *Architectural History*.

**Daniel Maudlin** is Professor of Architectural History and Heritage at the University of Plymouth. His research focuses on the British Atlantic World and the social history of buildings, especially the everyday spaces, places, and material culture from cottages, farms, and inns to planned towns. His publications include *Building the British Atlantic World* (2016), with Bernard L. Herman, and *The Highland House Transformed: Architecture and Identity on the edge of Britain* (2009).

**John Patrick Montaño** is Professor of History and the Head of Irish Studies at the University of Delaware. He has contributed books and articles on

Restoration England's political culture and Tudor Ireland. His most recent book was *The Roots of English Colonialism in Ireland* (2011). He is currently working on a book about the role of violence in cultural conflict.

**Neal Shasore** is Head of School at the London School of Architecture. An architectural historian by background, his research has focused on architectural culture in the interwar decades. His first book, *Designs on Democracy: Architecture and the Public in Interwar London* was published in 2022. An edited volume (with Jessica Kelly), *Reconstruction: Architecture, Society and the Aftermath of the First World War*, was published in 2023.

# Acknowledgements

The editors wish to acknowledge the generous financial support of the Marc Fitch Fund in assisting with the production of this book.

# Introduction: the architectural historiography of 'inner empire'

G. A. Bremner and Daniel Maudlin

Recent events have shown how issues relating to the legacies of modern European empire, colonialism, and slavery are as present and urgent today as they ever were. Wider social movements, such as Black Lives Matter, or efforts at 'decolonising' the curriculum in schools and universities, indicate that recognition of and debate over these legacies remains live. These concerns naturally affect the way we view our historic built environment, both at former imperial 'centres' and in postcolonial nation states. To be sure, scholars who work on the history of the built environment in former colonial contexts have been interrogating the intersections between architecture, race, and the cultures of colonialism for some time. But current grievances have broached new and more challenging questions. These questions will no doubt continue to shape the field of architectural history for the foreseeable future.

But this poses its own question: what do we really know about the architectural inflections of empire in its former metropolitan heartlands? After all, the great bulk of the literature that exists on the relationship between architecture and empire is focused on the former European colonial world. The contours of the field as initially defined were shaped appreciably under the impetus of cognate disciplines such as colonial and imperial history and area studies, albeit inflected through the analytical lens of postcolonial theory and its associated modes of inquiry. Considering the imposition of built form on the ground, in the colonial world, was understood as the primary locus of investigation, and gave scholars opening up this field more than enough to contend with. However, recent developments in New Imperial history, as well as World, Global, and Transnational/ Transcolonial histories, have helped in breaking down traditional geographic and historiographic binaries, both within colonial worlds and beyond, enabling a greater understanding of the integrated, networked nature of modern imperialism and its forms of cultural production, including architecture.

In helping us better appreciate architecture and the built environment as embedded practices within wider systems of circulation, transmission, and control (between metropole and colony, and vice versa; and around colonies and/or colonial regions), these methodological and historiographic developments have assisted in foregrounding the impact of empire on the metropolis itself. Although the ways in which Britain was affected by its imperial experience found expression in more general historical scholarship from the 1980s, such as that by John MacKenzie, or in the reassessment of what 'British' history even meant by J. G. A. Pocock before that, the study of architecture has lagged.[1] Pocock's insights, in particular, shifted the historiographic dial by emphasising a 'British world' as opposed to a domestic versus colonial interpretation of British history. This was a way of looking at the history of Britain that dated back at least to J. R. Seeley in the late nineteenth century, before falling away in the twentieth following decolonisation and Britain's turn to Europe. Although increasing attention has been paid to two-way architectural exchanges in the context of empire in recent times, the fact remains that comparatively little work has been carried out on the 'imperial' architectures and landscapes of the British Isles themselves, especially on the island of Britain.

Yet it was partly through the built environment that Britons both persuaded and prided themselves on their evolving status as a global power. As much recent research has shown, the British imperial enterprise required its own forms of 'home-grown' inducement, stimulus, and even incitement to facilitate continued public and political engagement with Britain's ever expanding imperial project. Although prestigious and profitable, empire was also very costly. Buildings and public spaces, both urban and rural, revealed not only the nation's growing wealth from colonialism but also its rising power, politically and militarily. After all, few human-made objects are as conspicuous as buildings, and these were activated to varying degrees (and in different ways) as part of a much larger programme of techniques concerning communal persuasion and manipulation. Whether intentionally or incidentally, buildings of this kind suggested that Britain was indeed 'Great', and that it was fast becoming not merely *a* but *the* world power.

The history of the British Isles can therefore be understood, in part at least, as embedded in the historic building stock left by different peoples in different periods. Unlike archival sources that must be sought out, buildings are the history all around us, the legacies of the past we experience every day. Accordingly, the impact of the British empire within the British Isles can be identified, read, and interpreted through the buildings built to serve it. It is our contention that the built fabric of the British Isles warrants still closer scrutiny for what it can tell us about these 'internal' and reflexive processes of imperialism. We believe this will assist in substantiating the

# Introduction

wider proposition that this archipelago of islands was itself a contested domain of imperial intent and practice (what some scholars term 'internal colonialism') using the built environment as evidence. The volume will show how forms of internalised state violence, claims to dominion, the repatriation of colonial wealth, and representations of imperial identity and power, including post-imperial identities, shaped the British Isles through the built environment. It is this that we consider to be the hitherto rather obscured 'inner empire' of Britain's architectural history.

## Scope of volume and intellectual context

As designed objects, buildings were not only built to contain activities but also to communicate messages, ideas, and values. This included projecting carefully constructed images of British commercial and political expansion through empire to anyone who encountered them. Most obviously this was achieved through a widely understood iconography of Classical and later Gothic architectural décor, but it was also conveyed through the implications of building form, use, and materials. The latter of these concerned what might be called the 'thingness' of the building itself. In other words, that a large stone-built fort, for instance, equated to well-armed intent. Equally, buildings were consumed. Occupied and understood in multiple, often unintended, ways, their meanings have constantly been revaluated, lost, and reinvented over time. Drawing out the richness of architectural evidence, *Inner Empire* presents the British Isles over four centuries as a locale of constant change, consistently formed, reformed, and defined by its relationship with empire.

Offering an alternative perspective on the imperial implications of British history, *Inner Empire* therefore harnesses the power of the historic built environment to identify and locate imperial activity within the British Isles – social, economic, political, cultural – from the early modern period to the mid-twentieth century. The 'inner empire' motif is designed to capture in a single phrase the concept behind the volume. It embodies two basic parameters of analysis. The first of these concerns the enforcement of what can be considered 'imperial practices' across the British Isles themselves, including English and Scottish colonialism in Ireland, Stuart endeavours to govern the Highlands, and Hanoverian attempts to head-off and crush Jacobitism in Scotland. The second concerns how society in Britain intersected with and absorbed its wider imperial experience, both importing and re-presenting this experience back to itself through forms of cultural production. The second of these included not only using architecture and the built environment to signal Britain as the metropolitan centre of a global empire, but also how reinvested colonial wealth transformed the landscape of the British Isles, both urban and rural.

Considering these two analytical registers, the volume is divided into two parts: the first deals with those landscapes of colonial and imperial practice within the British Isles, primarily encompassing early modern Ireland and Scotland, while the second deals with the impact of the wider British empire on the built environment of modern Britain. These two sections are understood as different sides of the same historiographic coin.

The rationale for the volume is that, despite considerable scholarly progress over the past two decades in assessing the impact of empire on the British Isles, including on its built environment, no single volume has appeared that addresses architecture's place in this assessment. This volume therefore takes a holistic and inclusive approach to the study of the built environment, looking for the connective tissues that link country houses and canals, government buildings and slum dwellings. The individual chapters will consider collectively the role of built space in the making of imperial Britain from the intentions of those who commissioned and designed buildings, to the experiences of those who used, occupied, and spent their lives in and around them.

The volume's intellectual context is rooted firmly in New Imperial and Four Nations approaches to the study of history and the British Isles. In this respect, it endeavours to take account of the latest developments in the field, situating itself both within these developments and as an extension of them. Rather than being an orthodox 'architectural history', the volume will endorse a more cross-disciplinary approach by considering the built environment from an anthropological and material culture perspective, allowing buildings and infrastructure to become the loci through which new insights on the phenomenon of empire can be explored and explained. In so doing, it will make the implicit claim that the built environment is an important form of historical evidence, and one that is essential to any proper understanding of the cultural history of modern Britain vis-à-vis empire; a claim increasingly recognised by historians of empire working in fields outside of architecture and art history, such as John MacKenzie and Duncan Bell, both of whom have turned to architecture and the built environment in recent work.[2]

In taking this approach the volume builds upon methodological and historiographic innovations in modern British studies pioneered by scholars such as J. G. A. Pocock, Linda Colley, Michael Hechter, Catherine Hall, Kathleen Wilson, David Armitage, and Duncan Bell in thinking not only about the 'planetary' and 'archipelagic' registers of British history, but also the social and intellectual imaginaries that comprised the concept of modern Britain.[3] Considering the early modern British empire, the prevalent consensus – taken loosely as prior to American Independence – has been that significant actions, events, and thoughts took place or emerged on its edges, and that empire was moulded, maintained, and deconstructed in the contested spaces furthest from its centre. This was itself a counter thrust against the previous consensus in which the process of empire was seen as an outward ripple of action and influence from its centre, as argued by the first generation of Atlantic historians. In the case of the British empire, this amounted to England, and London especially, as the metropolitan capital.[4] But as second-generation Atlantic historians, such as Armitage and Michael Braddick have observed, nodes of empire were located throughout the British Atlantic world and, to a lesser extent, the Indian subcontinent, interconnected through transoceanic mobilisation enacted by imperial military campaigns, trade, and migration.[5] Scholarship on the nature of the British empire continues to shift. On the one hand, as seen in more recent work by Armitage and others, there is an increased global focus on seas and oceans as the location of imperial activity.[6] On the other hand, in the field of critical heritage, for scholars considering the legacies of empire such as John G. Beech, there has for some time been a growing movement against what they view as the 'maritimisation' of imperial history. These divergent viewpoints for course depend upon what one is attempting to reveal through the lens of 'imperial' history. In focusing on the sea, it is claimed, historians of empire are distracted from the significance of imperial activity inland, not least in the British Isles. Beech argues that the cotton mills of nineteenth-century Manchester and the cotton plantations of the American South are of equal, if not greater, importance than the ocean and oceanic rim when identifying sites of the Atlantic slave trade, for instance. After all, whether growing, processing, or benefiting from the profits of cotton, many activities connected to the slave trade took place far inland.[7] Using the historic built environment as evidence of our imperial past, this heritage perspective, learning from the remnants of the past that surround us today, has much in common with the aims of this book.

Whether considering the relationships between Britain and Britain's overseas territories, or the relationships between the different parts of the British Isles, New Imperial historians increasingly contend that 'centre' and 'periphery' are equally significant sites in the lifecycle of empire. Moreover, the activities of empire flowed in many directions: outward from the centre, inward from the peripheries towards the centre, and between 'peripheral' sites, bypassing the centre altogether. In this view different peoples in different places interacted at times in harmony and at times in conflict in both the production and the consumption of what was ultimately a shared history.[8] However, the centre–periphery debate at the heart of New Imperial history has been somewhat marginalised by the rise of settler colonialism as a new paradigm in colonial histories. Where the centre–periphery debate has reflected a scholarly project to better understand the inner workings of empire, settler colonialism takes a step back to see empires like that of the British from the outside, from the perspective of the colonised, from where they do not seem varied and complex but monolithic.[9] By focusing on terms such as 'replaced' and 'eliminate', this approach has attempted to change how we think about the British empire overseas, even reinvigorating the notion of the dominant outward ripple put forward by the first generation of Atlantic historians in the 1980s. It also affects how we think about the British Isles themselves as a site of English, later British, colonial activity. For instance, can the Ulster Plantations of the seventeenth century, or the civilising mission of the British Fisheries Society in the eighteenth-century Scottish Highlands, be read as indigenous histories? This also influences how we interpret the buildings, monuments, and public spaces that facilitated and/or represented Britain's overseas empire within Britain.[10]

As Armitage has shown, conceptions of 'Empyre' and 'Imperium' dating from Roman times, and inflected through Arthurian legend, were applied with reference to claims of sovereignty by English monarchs over parts of the British Isles in the sixteenth and seventeenth centuries, most notably Scotland and Ireland. On the one hand, there was Nicholas Bodrugan's notion of 'great Briteigne' (1548), understood by Tudor monarchs as including Scotland; on the other, there was John Dee's 'Brytish Empire' of the 1570s, which bundled in Ireland among other territories, including a nascent maritime empire.[11] In the succeeding centuries, these conceptions were honed and developed to further English, and later British, monarchical claims over territories and people across the British Isles. Thus, by the close of the eighteenth century we find the British Isles, at the threshold of the 'modern' industrial world and Britain's extended global empire of the nineteenth century, as a group of islands already significantly changed by the experience of more than 200 years of imperial activity at home and abroad.[12]

In the nineteenth century, following certain technological innovations, such as steam locomotion and telegraphy, both the spatial extents and intellectual horizons of the empire shrank considerably. Mass migration, in conjunction with faster and cheaper travel and communication links, enabled a new and 'connected' kind of 'Greater Britain' to emerge. As MacKenzie, Thompson, and Bell, among others, have shown, this had significant effects on how Britain, the metropolis of empire, imagined itself as an imperial polity.[13] In terms of material culture, this impacted upon architecture and urbanism in various ways, as architects and city authorities looked to signify Britain's global status through set-piece projects, monuments, and urban renewal schemes.[14] *Inner Empire* contends that architecture, as a most conspicuous and substantial cultural practice, speaks to these political and ideological shifts in ways that were both unique and significant, if not always obvious.

Shifting concepts of identity were central to this transformative process. In recognising this, *Inner Empire* seeks to position itself in the context of scholarship that has reconfigured the study of identity and nationhood within the British Isles by those such as Hugh Kearney, Colin Kidd, Nicholas Canny, John MacKenzie, and Tom Devine, among others, including Peter Borsay and Rosemary Sweet in the field of urban history and Silke Stroh in literary studies.[15] Dating back to the 1970s, this scholarship emerged not as an attempt to disentangle and disintegrate the history of the British Isles along national and ethnic lines, but to highlight the very complexity of its entanglement and to recentre the history of Britain in recognition of its own cultural and ethnic diversity.[16] This naturally extended to considering not only how these various national cultures and ethnicities were activated throughout the wider British imperial world through family, social, and business connections, but also how they led to forms of 'internal' conflict.[17] This approach has been a major factor in British historiography ever since, transforming the way we think, write, and teach British history. These approaches provide a critical frame of reference by which to understand how the British Isles and its constituent nations (and their interactions) can be identified and discussed as a site of imperial action, performance, and consumption.

In terms of what it meant to live in Great Britain at this point in history, New Imperial and Four Nations history, as reconfigured through the work of Philippa Levine and re-examined through the lens of settler colonialism, suggests a place (or places) populated by various peoples who, just like their contemporaries in Nova Scotia, New England or the Carolinas, or later Australasia and parts of Africa, felt – for good or ill – that they both belonged to a small, local place and to a larger, expanded one: the British empire.[18] With this in mind, *Inner Empire* considers Britain and Ireland as something of an interstitial zone between these two polar registers, as a collection of connected places, an 'inner empire' of home nations, not just influenced and changed by each other but connected to and influenced by experiences of empire further afield.

## State of the discipline

### *The wider field: positioning 'innerness'*

Any concept of *inner* empire necessarily establishes its resonance in relation to something *outer*. As mentioned, there is a long and distinguished pedigree of scholarship dealing with the myriad ways in which the expansion of Britain has transformed the landscapes, cities, and cultures of the non-European world through historic building practices. This includes broader studies on urbanism and the city, as well as tightly focused accounts of individual buildings and architectural design strategies. Noteworthy here is the decisive postcolonial 'turn' reflected in this scholarship from the late 1970s onwards, drawing inspiration from poststructuralist methodologies such as Foucauldian discourse analysis, and from related modes of critical inquiry, including the influential 'Orientalism' thesis of Edward Said and the spatial sociology of Henri Lefebvre.[19] For instance, in her analysis of the concepts, theories, and practices of imperialism and postcolonialism, Barbara Bush cites architecture and urbanism, visual and spatial definitions of power, as one of the key strategies used by empires for cultural oppression and the legitimisation of power.[20] We might go further in observing that scholarship on the British colonial built environment has benefited from methodologies of this kind employed in studies dealing with other European imperial powers, including those on the Spanish, Portuguese, French, German, and Italian empires.[21] Seen together, these literatures make for a formidable historiographic tradition.

There are of course too many such studies on the colonial built environment to mention here, and the field is continually expanding. But it is worth reflecting on how this body of scholarship has set the intellectual conditions for the idea of 'innerness' that we propose here, making it possible in the first place. The authors in this volume turn many of the same critical perspectives developed in this scholarship on the British Isles themselves, thus establishing a type of analytical correspondence through intellectual synergy that begins to cement the 'inner' and 'outer' domains of British building practice – indeed, to fuse them as something of a continuous field of endeavour. This is not to conflate them, nor to privilege one over the other. Rather, it is to show that these domains – again, what were once referred to in differing contexts as 'centre' and 'periphery' – can be seen as functioning in tandem, as co-productive. Thus, we employ the term 'inner' here not as a point of distinction for its own sake, but for the purpose of throwing light on one side of what is evidently a complex, entangled, and tortured interrelationship. In other words, the wider, established body of literature mentioned above has created the register that gives the concept 'inner' is expository legitimacy and power. In turn, we hope that in further highlighting and developing the *inner* side of this literature we lend additional weight and legibility to the conclusions reached in the wider field. The outer had always implied something inner, even if only tacitly.

It is important to note, of course, that the current enterprise is itself a continuation of a relatively small but growing body of literature on the 'inner' side of the historiography of what we may call the imperial built environment. As will be outlined in more detail below, pioneering works by those such as Rodney Mace, Felix Driver, David Gilbert, Mark Crinson, Dana Arnold, and Iain Black, not to mention the editors of this volume, have set a rigorous standard to follow. We hope this volume can augment and inflect this work in new and interesting ways.

### A narrower domain: architecture and empire in the British Isles

As interest in the British Isles as a site of imperial action and representation grew through the latter part of the twentieth century into the twenty-first, scholars of architecture and urbanism responded. Although slower to react to these shifting historiographic trends, study of the built environment has since made much progress, especially within the past two decades. The premise of this volume may be that more can be done, and that no single volume dedicated to the subject yet exists, but this is not to say that nothing has been achieved. On the contrary, some significant work has been carried out that has opened the field and set the tone for future developments.

Considering the early modern period in architectural history first, there has been a persistent shift away from the English narratives that dominated major studies as recently as the 1990s towards something more decentred and polyphonic. As further scrutinised by Conor Lucey in this volume, Giles Worsley's *Classical Architecture in Britain: The Heroic Age* (1995), for example, is in fact a study of English architecture with one chapter (of fifteen) allocated to the 'Peripheries: Scotland, Ireland and the Americas'.[22] Although largely overlooked as a study of building and construction, a quietly transatlantic perspective is followed throughout in James Ayres' 1998 study *Building the Georgian City*.[23] A good example of this shift is the repositioning of James Stevens Curl's widely read *Georgian Architecture*, first published in 1993, which, revised and repackaged, emerged as *Georgian Architecture in the British Isles* in its second edition published by English Heritage in 2011. However, the Four Nations and the centre–periphery debate within the British Isles has been most directly and critically addressed by Elizabeth McKellar and Barbara Arciszwekas' decentred analysis, *Articulating British Classicism* (2004).[24]

Subsequent early modern and eighteenth-century studies have continued to place British architectural production in this context, as well as looking increasingly out to the wider Atlantic world. For instance, *The Highland House Transformed: Architecture and Identity on the Edge of Britain 1700–1850* (2009), by an editor of this volume (Maudlin), considers the architecture of agricultural improvement in the eighteenth-century Scottish Highlands in a British context, but follows Scottish Gaels forced out of the Highlands to their new homes in North America.[25] While Patricia McCarthy's *Life in the Irish Georgian Country House* (2016) looks at the everyday lives of the Anglo-Irish elite, providing a welcome counterpoint to Mark Girouard's canonical *Life in the English Country House* (1978).[26] Here we can also look to the ongoing work of Emily Mann, who, in this volume and elsewhere, considers British architecture in the seventeenth century from multiple transatlantic perspectives including, most recently, the connections between fortifications in Ireland and the Caribbean.[27] Essays by Mann (on forts) and Maudlin (on the Scottish 'blackhouse') can also be found in Olivia Horsfall Turner's landmark survey of national identity in seventeenth-century British architecture, *'The Mirror of Great Britain'* (2012), based on the proceedings of the 2010 Annual Symposium of the Society of Architectural Historians of Great Britain.[28]

Influenced by the pioneering work of Bernard L. Herman, there is also a growing group of scholars of Early American architecture, design, and material culture including Stephen Hague, Zara Anishanslin, and Jennifer Van Horn (and indirectly Emma Hart in urban history) who place their work in a transatlantic context that approaches British America and the early United States within the same cultural framework as the British Isles.[29] Contributions by British scholars to this transatlantic field include John Brewer and Amanda Vickery's edited collection *Gender, Taste, and Material Culture in Britain and North America, 1700–1830* (2007) and *Building the British Atlantic World: Spaces, Places and Material Culture 1600–1850* (2016), itself a transatlantic collaboration between Bernard L. Herman and Daniel Maudlin.[30]

In part the inspiration for this volume, it is harder to identify a significant number of early modern and eighteenth-century architectural histories that focus on the impact of the overseas empire on the built environment of the British Isles. For the seventeenth century we can cite Christine Stevenson's work on the Second Royal Exchange in which she analyses the Exchange's inner courtyard as a spatial 'model of the globe presided over by a statue of an imperial Charles' II.[31] For the eighteenth and early nineteenth centuries, we might highlight studies of the Picturesque by Geoffrey Tyack, Roger White, and Maudlin, among others.[32] There is also the University of Warwick and University College London joint project, 'The East India Company at Home', which, besides highlighting the influx of wealth into Britain from the Indian Subcontinent, explored the influence of empire in the 'Hindoo style' made famous by Brighton Pavilion and popular with the returning East India Company 'Nabobs' in the design of their villa retreats.[33] Mention should also be made of English Heritage's agenda-setting publication *Slavery and the British Country House* (2016), whose significant multidisciplinary contribution to the field has allowed the editors of this volume to avoid dwelling overly on the country house as a site of imperialism.[34] Outside of academic publishing, the National Trust has also recently (2020) undertaken a detailed investigation of the historic links to the slave trade within its portfolio of country houses and other properties.[35] However, the most extensive and coherent analysis to date of inner empire in this early period, perhaps counterintuitively, is Louis Nelson's *Architecture and Empire in Jamaica* (2016), the final chapter of which sets out the extent of Jamaica's direct and indirect impacts on the seventeenth- and eighteenth-century British built environment from warehouses and townhouses to country houses and city halls.[36]

The built environment in nineteenth- and twentieth-century Britain, encompassing the 'great age of empire' and its aftermath, has naturally drawn more attention from scholars, with London attracting the lion's share of interest. Serious work on this period first appeared with Rodney Mace's ground-breaking study on Trafalgar Square, published in 1976 and simply titled *Trafalgar Square: Emblem of Empire*. In it he argued how Nelson's Column, appealing as it did to the 'hero' status of the great naval officer it memorialised, became something of a lightning rod for the inverse grievances of the masses in whose name the nation and empire had been both established and defended. In this sense, the causes of empire were both overt and implied, for better or worse – omnipresent, whether consciously invoked or not. But it was Felix Driver and David Gilbert's 1998 article 'Heart of Empire? Landscape, Space and Performance in Imperial London', with its focus on the cultural, representational, and experiential dimensions of the city, that really set the tone for developments in the field as we have come to know and understand them today.[37] Soon after came important interventions by Iain Black and Mark Crinson, especially Crinson's landmark book *Modern Architecture and the End of Empire* (2003), which took the story through to decolonisation.[38] Although not focused entirely on the metropolis, Crinson's book nonetheless had much to say about the inflections of late imperialism through built form at empire's metropolitan core, providing valuable insights for those studying the relationship between architecture and empire, whether at 'home' or abroad. Indeed, Black's contribution, which considered Herbert Baker's rebuilding of the bank of England in the 1920s and 1930s, was part of a volume edited by Driver and Gilbert entitled *Imperial Cities: Landscape, Display and Identity*, which appeared as part of the Manchester University Press 'Studies in Imperialism' series in 1999. Like Crinson's later book, this volume was not dedicated wholly to London, but did include a number of essays looking at various monuments and spaces in that city, as well as other locations around Britain such as Glasgow, so-called 'second city' of empire.[39]

Building on these foundations, detailed studies of individual buildings and settings in London were carried out by one of the editors of this volume (Bremner) as part of his PhD dissertation, the findings of which were published as a series of journal articles between 2003 and 2009.[40] These considered structures such as the new Foreign and India Office, the Albert Memorial, Admiralty Arch, the Imperial Institute, and schemes for extending Westminster Abbey in the early twentieth century.[41] Other studies, such as that by Federico Freschi, considered the evolving dynamic between colony and metropole through the study of High Commission buildings in London, in his case South Africa House on Trafalgar Square by Herbert Baker (1931–33).[42] In addition to these more focused interventions, other scholars writing on the history of particular events and institutions in Britain also began to foreground the multiple imperial connotations associated with material culture and its spatial impositions.[43] Key here were new interpretations of exhibition culture in Britain, looking at where and how themes of empire (and the dynamics of imperial power) worked their way through spatial strategies of display. The Great Exhibition of 1851 and its afterlife at the Crystal Palace necessarily came in for scrutiny, as did events such as the Colonial and Indian Exhibition of 1886, where certain objects and exhibits were interrogated for their direct or veiled references to empire, commercial exploitation, and/or the supposed inferiority of non-European peoples (racism), among other imperialist tropes.[44] Memorials to figures associated with war and slavery also began to be viewed through this analytical lens, especially those in significant sites of national memory such as Westminster Abbey and St Paul's Cathedral.[45] This included statues of British monarchs, whether in London or in centres of proxy administration, such as Dublin.[46]

The distinguishing characteristic of this new wave of scholarship was not just its attempt to identify key buildings and spaces, thus enlarging our understanding of what might be considered significant in that regard, but also to frame architecture as a form of cultural production, and to analyse it in terms of its discursive relationship to Britain's wider imperial experience. Taking on board insights from cultural history, material culture studies, anthropology and geography, New Imperial studies, and the broader thrust of postcolonial modes of analysis, this scholarship has transformed the way we view Britain's historic built environment. At the foundation of this scholarship was the by now pervasive influence of Continental post-structuralist theory, with the Foucauldian power–knowledge relationship being particularly prominent, as well as Lefebvre's ideas concerning the production of space. In this respect, such scholarship differed in terms of its theoretical ambition from slightly earlier studies, such as Michael Port's monumental *Imperial London: Civil Government Building in London,*

*1850–1915* (1995), which, despite its principal title, was more a documentary history of government architecture in Whitehall than an analysis of those buildings from the perspective of London as the governmental capital of a global empire.

Since these initial studies, additional interventions have augmented and further nuanced our understanding of the impact of empire on the built environment in the British Isles. In recent years there has appeared, among others, Eileen Chanin's book on Australia House, London; Ashley Jackson's account of the British Empire Exhibition at Wembley (1924); and Sarah Longair and John McAleer's volume on museum culture in Britain and the wider British world, not to mention Bremner's *Building Greater Britain: Architecture, Imperialism, and the Edwardian Baroque Revival, c.1885–1920* (2022).[47] Most recently, Neal Shasore and Jessica Kelly's edited volume *Reconstruction: Architecture, Society, and the Aftermath of the First World War* (2023) has offered reflections on aspects of Britain's imperial legacy, including essays on specific buildings, such as Geoffrey Tyack's on Rhodes House in Oxford; while Miel Gorten's new book has given us an insightful essay on Glasgow City Chambers.[48] The re-examination of British country houses mentioned above has also extended into this period, beyond the era of slavery, considering the reinvestment of colonial wealth in general. The remittance economy generated from colonial trade often ended up being used to increase wealth and social prestige through the acquisition of property back in Britain, whether through legitimate or illegitimate forms of commerce. For instance, Stephanie Barczewski has shown in her book *Country Houses and the British Empire, 1700–1930* (2014) the extent to which this phenomenon was prevalent among the military and merchant classes of Britain, shaping the British landscape in significant ways.[49] To this may be added Terence Dooley's *Burning the Big House: The Story of the Irish Country House in a Time of War and Revolution*, which connects themes of architecture, identity, war, and empire through the early and late modern periods.[50] Others would go so far as to suggest that it is impossible to think of a 'British' or 'English' landscape at all outside racialised categories, with its 'structural' links to imperial exploitation and violence.[51]

## Contents and structure of the volume

The chapters in the first part of the volume, 'The inner empire', deal with issues of violence, discrimination, dispossession, and social control, and their legacies. This concerns primarily the idea of 'internal colonisation' across the 'Celtic fringe' of the British Isles, on the island of Ireland and in the Scottish Highlands, but also the plight of Irish immigrants in parts of England during the nineteenth century. In Chapter 1, John Montaño traces how Tudor and Stuart officials in Ireland formulated strategies for ordering, settling, and 'civilising' Ireland. He shows how at the heart of nearly every one of these strategies was the assumption that introducing agriculture and a cultivated landscape was an essential first step. Amidst the confiscations and Plantations that ensued was a consistent effort to transform the landscape and to create a contrived environment that emphasised human control over nature. The alteration of the Irish built environment that resulted reveals an ideology of colonialism that can be read in the landscape and through its material culture. Considering constructions such as fences, bridges, barns, houses, and forts, as both signifiers of civility and as targeted markers of a colonial strategy, Montaño demonstrates how a need to replace one culture with another, and to supplant a natural environment with an engineered one (an uncultivated landscape with a civilised, rational one) provided a focus, a battleground, even a language for the conflict associated with the policy of Plantation.

Moving from Ireland to Scotland, Daniel Maudlin's Chapter 2 considers this idea of internal colonisation in relation to North Britain. Its starting point is the bridge crossing the River Tay at Aberfeldy, in Perthshire, which connected southern Scotland to the Highlands. Built in the 1730s by British military engineers serving under General Wade, to a design by leading Scottish architect William Adam, it marked the beginning of a process that through the next century transformed the Highlands from a geographically and culturally distinct place into the northern part of 'North Britain'. It is argued that this was a function of a much wider and even brutal process of political, economic, and cultural colonisation, from military pacification brought by forts, roads, bridges, and inns; land clearances that removed indigenous peoples and introduced new settlement patterns and forms of domestic housing; to cultural tourism in the form of hotels and shooting lodges. Drawing comparisons with colonial activities in Ireland and North America, Maudlin presents the architectural and infrastructural processes of change in the Scottish Highlands as interconnected acts in the expansion of the British frontier to the northern edge of the British Isles.

In Chapter 3 John Belchem explores the ever-increasing numbers of 'low Irish' who emigrated to Liverpool in the nineteenth century. Clustered in court housing and cellar dwellings near the waterfront, they were viewed with disdain and alarm, embodying the pathologies of violence, unreason, and contagion that obsessed early Victorians. Here Belchem shows that even before the famine influx of the 1840s, there were calls for interventionist social engineering, justified through ethnic denigration of the Irish 'other', seen as a 'contaminating' presence within the unreformed and unprotected 'social body'. In examining the socio-spatial implications of this 'problem', it is argued that pioneer public health initiatives, followed by compulsory demolition and displacement, added to social tensions as Irish nationalist politicians – a growing force in the north end – came to condemn the actions of the Insanitary Property Committee as a form of political gerrymandering. Irish councillors are shown to have led the way in promoting community-based housing provision, insisting on rehousing within demolition areas and advocating alternatives to 'workhouse-like' tenement blocks. Thanks to their input, Liverpool became 'a mecca for housing experts' by the beginning of the twentieth century.

Chapter 4 takes us back to Ireland, to the contested terrain of the 'colonial' built environment of the nineteenth century. Here Richard Butler first analyses the processes of production of state architecture, focusing on the network of courthouses, prisons, asylums, and workhouses that were erected during the early part of the century. Specific attention is paid to the Irish grand jury system of local administration, considering the effects of this in relation to a number of specific case studies. The colonial question is framed here through a Four Nations approach, highlighting the tensions and conflicts within and between Westminster, Dublin Castle, and Irish local government. Butler then considers the legacy of this built environment in the early twentieth century: how political events shaped representations of these buildings, and how processes of destruction and demolition during revolutionary warfare codified interpretations and meanings of the colonial question. Moving beyond the high-profile destruction of Dublin's Four Courts and General Post Office during the revolutionary period, the analysis looks at the fate of lesser-known public buildings in provincial towns into the early 1920s.

Part 1 of the volume is concluded with some historiographic reflection on writing about Irish architecture within the 'British' context. Here, in Chapter 5, Conor Lucey proposes how Georgian Dublin may be considered a locus of architectural innovation within newly constituted histories of Britain's 'inner empire'. He reflects on the reduced significance ascribed to eighteenth-century Dublin's built heritage in much modern British architectural history, in the process problematising received wisdom concerning the intellectual exchange between a supposed centre (Britain) and its periphery (Ireland). It is argued that efforts to maintain the centrality of London in histories of British Palladianism have proved problematic. The principal symptom of this subjective bias has been the deliberate diminishment, or even entire omission, of Irish buildings from the teleological narrative of this historiography. Focusing on Dublin's celebrated parliament house (1729–39), Lucey analyses the myriad problems posed by a building with conflicting national and cultural identities: at once a symbol of an emerging political confidence in Ireland during the early Georgian era, while standing simultaneously as a paradigmatic example of enlightened British architectural tastes in the wake of the Hanoverian Succession.

Part 2 of the volume, 'Empire building in Britain', in contrast to the first, is concerned with the impact of the wider British empire and imperialism on modern Britain. It opens with Chapter 6, being an examination by Emily Mann of the East India Company's headquarters in London. We are reminded that where Richard Rogers's much celebrated Lloyds building now rises, on the south side of Leadenhall Street, stood once the impressive stone countenance of East India House, the result of a major three-year refurbishment project completed in 1729 by the architect Thomas Jacobsen. Here Mann traces the development of this building and its imperial connections. Focusing on its interior spaces, she recovers the building's decorative programme, offering a reading as its early viewers would have done. The cue to her analysis is the shifting viewpoints (in both space and time) implied in eighteenth-century travel guides and accounts, which invoke the opening frames of the imperial capital's streetscape, the building's contemporary façade, and the specific commercial and political concerns of the day. This analysis is presented in the context of the changing concepts of nation and empire at the time. Reuniting building, painting, and other furnishings in a single visual field, the chapter situates and studies them as part of the integrated architectural setting of company, city, and colonial settlement.

Staying with Asian concerns, Chapter 7 by Alex Bremner deals with the directors of the (in)famous Scottish China Trade firm Jardine, Matheson & Co., and how a considerable amount of its commercial empire was reinvested in Britain. It is observed that although a growing literature on the Indian Nabob and West-Indian absentee planter has sought to reveal the effects of remitted colonial wealth in relation to 'imperial landscapes' in England, very little has been done on the impact of China Trade 'Taipans', especially in Scotland, from where many of them came. Indeed, the sojourning type represented by the Jardines and Mathesons in this regard was relatively common in eighteenth- and nineteenth-century Scotland. Family ties and business networks facilitated a system of patronage and investment that deliberately promoted Scottish interests and fealty across the globe. Returnees, many of whom had amassed immense fortunes, were often eager to plough their profits into purchasing and improving estates in Scotland. Here Bremner shows, by way of example, how this reinvestment of colonial wealth in land and infrastructure had a marked impact on the Scottish landscape, revealing in visually conspicuous ways the wider effects of empire and imperial trade on the metropolitan scene. Issues of cultural and familial obligation and identity are seen to have played a leading role in fashioning a particularly Scottish response to this imperial encounter as represented in architecture and the wider built environment.

In Chapter 8 Richard Dennis takes us on a tour of Victorian and Edwardian London showing the various ways in which Britain's imperial experience affected that city's urban morphology, in particular its domestic housing arrangements. It is noted that employment in London to a large extent involved either the processing of colonial raw materials or the servicing of imperial interests. The housing and provisioning of all who were employed in these ways generated multiplier effects for the everyday domestic economy. Here attention is focused on the building of luxurious mansion flats which provided a suitably grand backcloth for some forms of imperial display; London pieds à terre for politicians and members of the professions administering and servicing the empire, and for colonial servants returning on furlough or retirement; the layout of suburbs with street and house names redolent of empire; some architectural types and details attributable to colonial experience; and public and private gardens planted with exotic species originating in colonial exploration and trade. Even slums are explored as a means by which migrants and transients were accommodated, as well as dockworkers and their families. Considering the idea of knowledge exchange through imperial networks, comparison is made between planning concepts associated with the segregation of different land uses and socioeconomic (and, in practice, ethnic) groups in London and exclusionary practices first employed in Asia and Africa.

Moving from domestic architecture and the urban realm to buildings of state, Eileen Chanin provides a biographical history of Australia House, London, in Chapter 9. Australia House was the first of London's Dominion Houses, which were constructed by the British empire's self-governing Dominions between 1913 and 1959. Chanin shows how this singular and impressive work of architecture conveyed a host of different meanings as it evolved, from conception to construction, occupation and reception. Through this analysis she interrogates the motives of the architect responsible, the client, the building's occupants, and its reception by contemporaries and subsequent critics, providing evidence about its immediate environment, wider culture, and historic context. Australia House gave impetus to the idea of an imperial precinct and of a style of building that expressed an 'imperial' presence that was understood as adding to London's architectural vocabulary. Chanin provides new insights on how the phenomenon of empire can be explored and explained through consideration of architecture that sprang from the wider imperial experiences of 'Greater Britain', and the mark this left on the built environment of the modern metropolis.

In Chapter 10, Neal Shasore considers the material implications of the 'Empire Timber' exhibition at the first Imperial Forestry Conference, held in London in 1920. Organised by the recently formed Department of Overseas Trade, its object was to raise awareness of little-known timbers throughout Britain's empire, reflecting a postwar commitment to fostering greater trade and cooperation with colonies and dominions rich in forestry resources. Here Shasore charts how, from the late 1920s, the Empire Marketing Board took a more active role in promoting imperial timbers. This included hosting a permanent display at the newly established Building Centre in New Bond Street (1932), making it easier for architects to specify these materials for projects. We see, for instance, how imperial timbers were employed extensively at the heart of the architectural establishment, in the building of the Royal Institute of British Architect's new headquarters at 66 Portland Place in 1934, especially those from the Dominions and India, revealing the extent to which the profession acted as an imperial confraternity of interconnected practitioners. Other buildings discussed include Hubert Worthington's Imperial Forestry Institute in Oxford (1939–51), which was also replete with specimens of imperial timber, 'donated' by colonial forestry associations in a context of timber supply shortage following the war. It is argued that these exhibitions and projects highlight how the architectural profession conceived of its role in a global imperial supply chain critical to design reform in early twentieth-century Britain.

Part 2, and the entire volume, concludes with Chapter 11 by Mark Crinson on student housing in postwar Britain. Colonial students, and postcolonial students in India's case, were a source of anxiety to the British state in the immediate post-1945 period. Students were to survive and hopefully flourish, studying hard and returning to their home countries once finished. In the process, it was supposed, they would have become a friend of Britain, and both citizens and members of the newly forming 'commonwealth'. Considering the Indian YMCA building in Fitzroy Square, London, by Ralph Tubbs, Crinson explores the tension between how students both perceived themselves and behaved in this context, and how government expected them to see themselves and behave, including issues relating to sex and postcolonial politics. But, as Crinson shows, despite this anxiety, and a considerable amount of surveillance, the actual provision of colonial students' housing was left almost entirely in the hands of charities, religious groups, and philanthropists, or to the whims of the market (and prejudices of landlords). With its open-plan ground floor, cellular rooms above, multifaith prayer hall, basement auditorium, and other spaces housing cultural activities, Tubbs's YMCA building, it is argued, was less about compromise than coexistence. In short, the Indian YMCA building was concerned with making accommodations and being accommodated, about showing how to be Indian in Britain and how the British might be a little more Indian.

Together, these chapters not only add substantially to the relatively sparse and disparate existing literature on this subject, but enable us to gain a better understanding of how and where to locate notions of 'inner empire' within the architectural history of the British Isles. Presented as they are here, in a single volume, the hope is that further awareness will be raised about the importance of considering Britain as a field of imperial practice, exchange, and representation, including the idea of the British Isles as a space of not just imagined but 'lived' imperial experience.

## Notes

1 John M. MacKenzie, *Propaganda and Empire* (Manchester: Manchester University Press, 1984); J. G. A. Pocock, 'British History: A Plea for a New Subject', *New Zealand Journal of History* 8, no. 1 (1974): 3–21.
2 John M. MacKenzie, *The British Empire Through Buildings: Structure, Function and Meaning* (Manchester: Manchester University Press, 2020); *Political Theory and Architecture*, eds D. Bell and B. Zacka (London: Bloomsbury, 2020).
3 For Pocock's essays dating back to the 1970s, see the collection J. G. A. Pocock, *The Discovery of Islands: Essays in British History* (Cambridge: Cambridge University Press, 2005); Linda Colley, *Britons: Forging the Nation, 1707–1837* (New Haven and London: Yale University Press, 1992), idem, *Acts of Union and Disunion* (London: Profile Books, 2014); Michael Hechter, *Internal Colonialism: The Celtic Fringe in British National Development, 1536–1966* (London: Routledge & Kegan Paul, 1975); Catherine Hall, *Civilising Subjects: Metropole and Colony in the English Imagination, 1830–1867* (Cambridge: Polity Press, 2002); Kathleen Wilson, *The Island Race: Englishness, Empire and Gender in the Eighteenth Century* (London: Routledge, 2003); David Armitage, *The Ideological Origins of the British Empire* (Cambridge: Cambridge University Press, 2000); Duncan Bell, *The Idea of Greater Britain: Empire and the Future of World Order, 1860–1900* (Princeton: Princeton University Press, 2007).
4 *Colonial British America: Essays in the New History of the Early Modern Era*, eds J. Greene and J. R. Pole (Baltimore: Johns Hopkins University Press, 1984); *Colonial Identity in the Atlantic World, 1500–1800*, eds N. Canny and A. Pagden (Princeton: Princeton University Press, 1987); *Strangers within the Realm; Cultural Margins of the First British Empire*, eds B. Bailyn and P. D. Morgan (Chapel Hill: University of North Carolina Press, 1991).
5 *The British Atlantic World, 1500–1800*, eds D. Armitage and M. J. Braddick (Basingstoke: Palgrave Macmillan, 2nd edn, 2009).
6 *Oceanic Histories*, eds D. Armitage, A. Bashford, and S. Sivasundaram (Cambridge: Cambridge University Press, 2017). *Oceanic Histories* is part of the Cambridge Oceanic Histories series of titles that place global histories of trade and empire within a maritime perspective. For instance, see J. Mulich, *In a Sea of Empires: Networks and Crossings in the Revolutionary Caribbean* (Cambridge:

Cambridge University Press, 2020); R. C. Po, *The Blue Frontier, Maritime Vision and Power in the Qing Empire* (Cambridge: Cambridge University Press, 2018).

7 John G. Beech, 'The Marketing of Slavery Heritage in the United Kingdom', *International Journal of Hospitality & Tourism Administration* 2, no. 3–4 (2001): 85–106.

8 *A New Imperial History: Culture, Identity and Modernity in Britain and the Empire 1660–1840*, ed. K. Wilson (Cambridge; Cambridge University Press, 2004); S. Pincus, 'Empires', in *The Princeton Companion to Atlantic History*, ed. J. C. Miller (Princeton: Princeton University Press, 2015), 185–6; *Contested Spaces of Early America*, eds J. Barr and E. Countryman (Philadelphia: University of Pennsylvania Press, 2014); S. J. Hornsby, *British Atlantic, American Frontier: Spaces of Power in Early Modern British America* (Hanover: University Press of New England, 2005); *British North America in the Seventeenth and Eighteenth Centuries*, ed. S. Foster (Oxford: Oxford University Press, 2013). See also S. Aron and J. Adelman, 'From Borderlands to Borders: Empires, Nation States and the Peoples in Between in North American History', *American Historical Review* 103, no. 3 (1999): 814–41.

9 For a historiography of scholarship in Settler Colonial Studies, see S. Konishi (2019) 'First Nations Scholars, Settler Colonial Studies, and Indigenous History', *Australian Historical Studies* 50, no. 3 (2019): 285–304. See also *The Routledge Handbook of the History of Settler Colonialism*, eds E. Cavanagh and L. Veracini (London: Routledge, 2017).

10 See, for instance, S. J. Connolly, 'Settler Colonialism in Ireland from the English Conquest to the Nineteenth Century', in Cavanagh and Veracini, *The Routledge Handbook of the History of Settler Colonialism*, 49–65.

11 Armitage, *The Ideological Origins*, 24–60.

12 *The Global Eighteenth Century*, ed. F. A. Nussbaum (Baltimore: Johns Hopkins University Press, 2003); M. Ogborn and C. W. J. Withers, *Georgian Geographies: Essays on Space, Place and Landscape in the Eighteenth Century* (Manchester: Manchester University Press, 2004).

13 *Popular Culture and Empire*, ed. J. M. MacKenzie (Manchester: Manchester University Press, 1989); A. S. Thompson, *The Empire Strikes Back?: The Impact of Imperialism on Britain from the Mid-Nineteenth Century* (London: Routledge, 2005); Bell, *The Idea of Greater Britain*.

14 For example, see G. A. Bremner, *Building Greater Britain: Architecture, Imperialism, and the Edwardian Baroque Revival, c.1885–1920* (London and New Haven: Paul Mellon Centre/Yale University Press, 2022).

15 Hugh Kearney, *The British Isles: A History of Four Nations* (Cambridge: Cambridge University Press, 1989); Colin Kidd, *Union and Unionism: Political Thought in Scotland, 1500–2000* (Cambridge: Cambridge University Press, 2008); Nicholas Canny, *Making Ireland British, 1580–1680* (Oxford: Oxford University Press, 2001); *Scotland and the British Empire*, eds John M. MacKenzie and T. M. Devine (Oxford: Oxford University Press, 2011); T. M. Devine, *Scotland's Empire, 1160–1815* (London: Allen Lane, 2003);

S. Stroh, *Gaelic Scotland in the Colonial Imagination: Anglophone Writing from 1600–1900* (Evanston: Northwestern University Press, 2017).

16 For example, see essays in *Three Nations – A Common History? England, Scotland, Ireland and British History, c.1600–1920*, ed. R. G. Asch (Bochum: Brockmeyer, 1993). See also Kearney, *The British Isles*. For urban history in the English context, see P. Borsay, *The Eighteenth-Century Town: A Reader in English Urban History, 1688–1820* (London: Routledge, 1990); P. Borsay, *The English Urban Renaissance: Culture and Society in the Provincial Town, 1660–1770* (Oxford: Oxford University Press, 1991); R. Sweet, *The English Town 1680–1840: Government, Society and Culture* (London: Routledge, 1999); *Women and Urban Life in Eighteenth-Century England: 'On the Town'*, eds P. Lane and R. Sweet (London: Routledge, 2017). For urbanism in Scotland, see *The New Town Phenomenon*, ed. John Frew (St Andrews: St Andrews University Press, 2000).

17 MacKenzie, 'Irish, Scottish, Welsh and English'. See also David Armitage, 'Making the Empire British: Scotland in the Atlantic World 1542–1707', *Past and Present* 155 (1997): 34–63; D. J. Hamilton, *Scotland, the Caribbean and the Atlantic World, 1750–1820* (Manchester: Manchester University Press, 2005); and, more recently, the extraordinary exhibition catalogue *For Auld Lang Syne: Images of Scottish Australia from First Fleet to Federation* (Ballarat: Art Gallery of Ballarat, 2014). The same observation is made by Gary Magee and Andrew Thompson in their book *Empire and Globalisation: Networks of People, Goods and Capital in the British World, c.1850–1914* (Cambridge: Cambridge University Press, 2010), 85–6.

18 See *The British Empire: Sunrise to Sunset*, ed. P. Levine (London: Routledge, 2nd edn, 2013); Nancy Christie, *Transatlantic Subjects: Ideas, Institutions and Social Experience in Post-Revolutionary British North America* (Montreal: McGill-Queens University Press, 2008).

19 Among the highlights of this literature, we single out the following works: Anthony D. King, *Colonial Urban Development: Culture, Social Power and Environment* (London: Routledge, 1976); Thomas R. Metcalf, *An Imperial Vision: Indian Architecture and the British Raj* (London: Faber & Faber, 1989); *Forms of Dominance: On the Architecture and Urbanism of the Colonial Enterprise*, ed. Nezar AlSayyad (Aldershot: Ashgate, 1992); Mark Crinson, *Empire Building: Orientalism & Victorian Architecture* (London: Routledge, 1996); Robert Home, *Of Planting and Planning: The Making of British Colonial Cities* (London: Routledge, 1996); Brenda S. A. Yeoh, *Contesting Space: Power Relations and the Urban Built Environment in Colonial Singapore* (Oxford: Oxford University Press, 1996); Garth Myers, *Verandahs of Power: Colonialism and Space in Urban Africa* (Syracuse: Syracuse University Press, 2003).

20 B. Bush, *Imperialism and Postcolonialism* (Harlow: Pearson Education, 2007), 122.

21 Paul Rabinow, *French Modern: Norms and Forms of the Social Environment* (Cambridge MA: MIT Press, 1989); Gwendolyn Wright, *The Politics of Design in French Colonial Urbanism* (Chicago: Chicago University Press, 1991);

Brian L. McLaren, *Architecture and Tourism in Italian Colonial Libya: An Ambivalent Modernism* (Seattle: University of Washington Press, 2006); Mia Fuller, *Moderns Abroad: Architecture, Cities, and Italian Imperialism* (London: Routledge, 2007); Liora Bigon, *French Colonial Dakar: The Morphogenesis of an African Regional Capital* (Manchester: Manchester University Press, 2016); Itohan Osayimwese, *Colonialism and Modern Architecture in Germany* (Pittsburgh: University of Pittsburgh Press, 2017).
22 G. Worsley, *Classical Architecture in Britain: The Heroic Age* (New Haven: Yale University Press, 1995).
23 James Ayres, *Building the Georgian City* (New Haven: Yale University Press, 1995).
24 Elizabeth McKellar and Barbara Arciszwekas, *Articulating British Classicism: New Approaches to Eighteenth-Century Architecture (Reinterpreting Classicism: Culture, Reaction and Appropriation)* (Oxford: Ashgate, 2004).
25 D. Maudlin, *The Highland House Transformed: Architecture and Identity on the Edge of Britain, 1700–1850* (Edinburgh: Edinburgh University Press, 2009).
26 Patricia McCarthy, *Life in the Georgian Irish Country House* (New Haven: Yale University Press, 2016); Mark Girouard, *Life in the English Country House* (New Haven: Yale University Press, 1978).
27 E. Mann, 'Two Islands, Many Forts: Ireland and Bermuda in 1624', in *Ireland, Slavery and the Caribbean: Comparative Perspectives*, eds F. O'Kane Crimmins and C. O'Neill (Manchester: Manchester University Press, 2023), 215–39.
28 *'The Mirror of Great Britain': National Identity in Seventeenth-Century British Architecture*, ed. Olivia Horsfall Turner (Reading: Spire Books, 2012).
29 For example, see B. L. Herman, *Townhouse: Architecture and Material Life in the Early American City, 1780–1830* (Chapel Hill: University of North Carolina Press, 2006); S. G. Hague, *The Gentleman's House in the British Atlantic World 1680–1780* (London: Palgrave Macmillan, 2015); Z. Anishanslin, *A Portrait of a Woman in Silk: Hidden Histories of the British Atlantic World* (New Haven: Yale University Press, 2016); J. Van Horn, *The Power of Objects in Eighteenth-Century British America* (Chapel Hill: University of North Carolina Press, 2017); E. Hart, *Building Charleston: Town and Society in the British Atlantic World* (Charlottesville: University of Virginia Press, 2009). See also *A Material World: Culture, Society, and the Life of Things in Early Anglo-America*, eds G. W. Boudreau and M. M. Lovel (University Park: Penn State University Press, 2019).
30 *Gender Taste and Material Culture in Britain and North America, 1700–1830*, eds J. Brewer and A. Vickery (New Haven: Yale University Press, 2007); *Building the British Atlantic World: Spaces, Places and Material Culture 1600–1850*, eds D. Maudlin and Bernard L Herman (Chapel Hill: University of North Carolina Press, 2016).
31 Christine Stevenson, 'Making Empire Visible at the Second Royal Exchange, London', in *Court, Country, City: British Art and Architecture, 1660–1735*, eds M. Hallett, N. Llewellyn, and M. Myrone (New Haven: Yale University Press, 2016), 51–72. See also first part of 'The Metropolis', in *Architecture and*

*Urbanism in the British Empire*, ed. G. A. Bremner (Oxford: Oxford University Press, 2016), 123–42.
32. M. H. Port, 'John Nash and the Royal Places', in *John Nash: Architect of the Picturesque*, ed. G. Tyack (Swindon: English Heritage, 2013), 129–32; Daniel Maudlin, *The Idea of the Cottage in English Architecture 1760–1860* (London: Routledge, 2015), 95; R. White, *Cottages Ornes: The Charms of the Simple Life* (New Haven: Yale University Press, 2016).
33. *The East India Company at Home, 1757–1857*, eds M. C. Finn and K. Smith (London: UCL Press, 2018). For further references, see Mann's Chapter 6 in this volume.
34. *Slavery and the British Country House*, eds M. Dresser and A. Hann (Swindon: English Heritage, 2016).
35. 'Interim Report on the Connections between Colonialism and Properties now in the Care of the National Trust, Including Links with Historic Slavery', eds S-A Huxtable, C. Fowler, C. Kefalas, and E. Slocomb (Swindon: National Trust, 2020).
36. Louis P. Nelson, *Architecture and Empire in Jamaica* (New Haven: Yale University Press, 2016), 235–68.
37. Felix Driver and David Gilbert, 'Heart of Empire? Landscape, Space and Performance in Imperial London', *Environment and Planning D: Society and Space* 16, no. 1 (1998); 11–28.
38. Iain S. Black, 'Imperial Visions: Rebuilding the Bank of England, 1919–39', in *Imperial Cities: Landscape, Display and Identity*, eds F. Driver and D. Gilbert (Manchester: Manchester University Press, 1999), 96–113. See also 'Rebuilding "The Heart of the Empire": Bank Headquarters in the City of London, 1919–1939', in *The Metropolis and its Image: Constructing Identities for London, c.1750–1950*, ed. D. Arnold (Oxford: Blackwell, 1999), 127–52; Mark Crinson, *Modern Architecture and the End of Empire* (Aldershot: Ashgate, 2003).
39. Driver and Gilbert, *Imperial Cities*. Contemporaneous with this was Jonathan Schneer's book *London 1900: The Imperial Metropolis* (New Haven: Yale University Press, 1999), which, although not about architecture per se, nonetheless attempted to explore, in parts, the idea of London as an imperial capital through its buildings and spaces.
40. G. A. Bremner, 'Imagining London: five studies on architecture, national identity, and Britain's first city of empire, 1856–1911' (PhD thesis, University of Cambridge, 2004). Another, earlier important PhD dissertation focusing on government buildings in Whitehall is Neil R. Bingham, 'Victorian and Edwardian Whitehall: architecture and planning, 1865–1918' (PhD thesis, University of London, 1985).
41. G. A. Bremner, '"Some Imperial Institute": Architecture, Symbolism, and the Ideal of Empire in Late Victorian Britain, 1887–93', *Journal of the Society of Architectural Historians* 62, no. 1 (2003): 50–73; 'Nation and Empire in the Government Architecture of Mid-Victorian London: the Foreign and India Office Reconsidered', *Historical Journal* 48, no. 3 (2005): 703–42; '"Imperial

Peace Memorial": the Second Anglo-Boer War and the Origins of Admiralty Arch, 1900–1905', *British Art Journal* 5, no. 3 (2004): 62–6; '"Imperial Monumental Halls and Tower": Westminster Abbey and the Commemoration of Empire, 1854–1904', *Architectural History* 47 (2004): 251–82; '"The 'Great Obelisk" and Other Schemes: the Origins and Limits of Nationalist Sentiment in the Making of the Albert Memorial 1861–63', *Nineteenth-Century Contexts* 31, no. 3 (2009): 225–49.

42 Federico Freschi, '"The fine art of fusion": Race, Gender and the Politics of South Africanism as Reflected in the Decorative Programme of South Africa House, London (1933)', *De Arte* 71 (2005): 14–34.

43 An early intervention on this front was Tim Barringer's article 'Re-presenting the Imperial Archive: South Kensington and its Museums', *Journal of Victorian Culture* 3, no. 2 (1998): 357–73.

44 For instance, see Deborah Swallow, 'Colonial Architecture, International Exhibitions, and Official Patronage of the Indian Artisan: The Case of a Gateway from Gwalior in the Victorian and Albert Museum', in *Colonialism and the Object: Empire, Material Culture and the Museum*, eds T. Barringer and T. Flynn (London: Routledge, 1998), 52–67; Jeffery A. Auerbach, *The Great Exhibition of 1851: A Nation on Display* (New Haven: Yale University Press, 1999); Peter H. Hoffenberg, *An Empire on Display: English, Indian, and Australian Exhibitions from the Crystal Palace to the Great War* (Berkeley: University of California Press, 2001); Lara Kriegel, 'Narrating the Subcontinent in 1851: India at the Crystal Palace', in *The Great Exhibition of 1851: New Interdisciplinary Essays*, ed. L. Purbrick (Manchester:Manchester University Press, 2001), 147–78; R. Windsor-Liscombe, 'Refabricating the Imperial Image on the Isle of Dogs: Modernist Design, British State Exhibitions and Colonial Policy 1924–51', *Architectural History* 49 (2006): 317–48; and essays in *Britain, the Empire, and the World at the Great Exhibition of 1851*, eds Jeffrey A. Auerbach and Peter H. Hoffenberg (Aldershot: Ashgate, 2008). For an early example of this critique, see 'Imperial display' in Paul Greenhalgh, *Ephemeral Vistas: The* Expositions Universelles, *Great Exhibitions and World's Fairs, 1851–1939* (Manchester: Manchester University Press, 1988), 52–81.

45 Douglas Fordham, 'Scalping: Social Rites in Westminster Abbey', in *Art and the British Empire*, eds T. Barringer, G. Quilley, and D. Fordham (Manchester: Manchester University Press, 2007), 99–119; Madge Dresser, 'Set in Stone? Statues and Slavery in London', *History Workshop Journal* 64 (2007): 163–99. For St Paul's, see Holger Hoock, *Empires of the Imagination: Politics, War, and the Arts in the British World, 1750–1850* (London: Profile Books, 2010), 132–61, 188–202.

46 Tori Smith, '"A grand work of noble conception": The Victoria Memorial and Imperial London', in Driver and Gilbert, *Imperial Cities*, 21–39; Yvonne Whelan, 'The Construction and Destruction of a Colonial Landscape: Monuments to British Monarchs in Dublin before and after Independence', *Journal of Historical Geography* 28, no. 4 (2002): 508–33.

47 Eileen Chanin, *Capital Designs: Australia House and Visions of Imperial London* (North Melbourne: Australian Scholarly Publishing, 2019); 'British Empire Stadium, Wembley', in Ashley Jackson, *Buildings of Empire* (Oxford: Oxford University Press, 2013), 235–58; *Curating Empire: Museums and the British Imperial Experience*, eds Sarah Longair and John McAleer (Manchester: Manchester University Press, 2016); G. A. Bremner, *Building Greater Britain: Architecture, Imperialism, and the Edwardian Baroque Revival, c. 1885–1920* (London and New Haven: Paul Mellon Centre/Yale University Press, 2022).

48 *Reconstruction: Architecture, Society, and the Aftermath of the First World War*, eds Neal Shasore and Jessica Kelly (London: Bloomsbury, 2023); Miel Groten, *The Architecture of Empire in Modern Europe: Space, Place, and the Construction of an Imperial Environment, 1860–1960* (Amsterdam: Amsterdam University Press, 2022), 98–130. See also, Miel Groten, 'Glasgow's New Town Hall: Imperialism, Nationalism and Civic Pride, 1877–1889', *Urban History* 47, no. 4 (2020): 1–19.

49 Stephanie Barczewski, *Country Houses and the British Empire, 1700–1930* (Manchester: Manchester University Press, 2014).

50 Terence Dooley, *Burning the Big House: The Story of the Irish Country House in a Time of War and Revolution* (New Haven: Yale University Press, 2022).

51 For instance, see Corinne Fowler, *Green Unpleasant Land: Creative Responses to Rural England's Colonial Connections* (Leeds: Peepal Tree Press, 2020).

# Part I

## The inner empire

# 1

# Cultivation, constructed environments, and cultural conflict: Plantations and the inner empire

*John Patrick Montaño*

John Dee is often credited with inventing the concept of a British Imperialism, advocating the founding of English colonies in the New World to form a *British empire* that might rival and then surpass the brutal and inhumane settlements of the Spanish (Figure 1.1).[1] From the outset, the idea behind empire and colonies was to expand the nation's territory and to gain riches. Dee even asserted that King Arthur had established a British empire and Geoffrey of Monmouth was careful to include Ireland as part of Arthur's imperial conquests. Geoffrey took the opportunity to condemn Irish barbarity and record them, 'naked and utterly unarmed', fleeing from the battle with Arthur.[2] But even from these earliest days the theorists of empire and colonies sought a *rebirth* of the models from antiquity: the ambitions of Alexander the Great that aimed to export a superior Hellenic culture and freedoms to those trammelled by the despotic emperors of Persia; the commitment of Aeneas and the Romans to introducing and defending civility to the territories they absorbed into the empire. Even the aspirations of Boniface and Charlemagne to bring Christianity and salvation to the dark corners of Europe were adopted as fit patterns both to inspire and to justify the expansion of English influence to Ireland and beyond. In fact, all three of these paragons of the civilising mission relied on the conversion, assimilation, or at least the collaboration of indigenous leaders to further the acceptance of the *new world* on offer, providing the archetypes for the Surrender and Regrant policies followed in various permutations throughout the efforts to civilise Ireland and the Irish.

The outpouring of treatises on reforming, improving, settling, and civilising Ireland throughout the 1500s were fairly consistent in their claims that reforms and the spread of civility in Ireland justified the conquests, confiscations, and settlements that began to appear by the middle of the century.[3] Ending the disorder in Ireland and making it yield revenue to the crown rather than serving as a constant drain on the Exchequer proved an irresistible allure for Henry VIII and his successors. Moreover, when Henry's break with Rome added religious differences to Anglo-Irish relations the

**Figure 1.1** Portrait of John Dee, British School, c.1594 (courtesy Ashmolean Museum, Oxford).

prospect – the duty even – of bringing true religion and a real path to salvation became a more urgent calling for many hoping to reform, to civilise, and to settle Ireland.[4] Yet, while bringing the gospels and the saving of souls remained an emotive and persuasive justification for the strategies adopted in Ireland, other than some devoted members of the clergy and a very few others, religious reform was not much of a draw for the settlers and ambitious colonists on the make. Indeed, religious goals mattered to few of the adventurous settlers in Ireland, unless they took the form of discipline, order, and the extirpation of heresy.[5] Indeed, throughout the years to be examined here, the linkage between civility and religion became a dangerous concoction that led to increasing hostility to Protestants in general and to Protestant clergy in particular.

The introduction of civility to displace the savagery and barbarism of the *wilde Irishe* remained a central justification for official policies during the period of Plantations in Ireland. Thanks to the growing valorisation of Virgil and the *Georgics* and the growing demographic demands for food, civility was regularly associated with cultivated land, urban settlements, and a landscape characterised by neatly divided farms demarcated by fences with permanent stone dwellings at the centre.[6] Not only were these signifiers to become the clearest symbols of the transforming power of civility, but they also served to represent a familiar landscape that could welcome and reassure potential settlers from England.[7] In short, a familiar built environment looking appropriately like the landscape of the world left behind would prove a key element in the creation of an empire, no matter the proximity to the metropole.

By the time of the Plantation in Ulster official strategies were determined to transform the economy, legal system, and landscape in Ireland. The resistance faced throughout Elizabeth's reign and particularly in the Nine Years War convinced many that native culture, in the broadest sense, was the inspiration for the rejection of civility being offered and exemplified by English (and soon, Scottish) settlers.[8] Frustrations over the inability to civilise the Irish and the unremitting defiance and chronic violence in Ireland meant theorists like Edmund Spenser condemned the barbarous savagery of native culture and argued that the road to civility in Ireland must be paved with the ruins of Irish traditions and culture.[9] But the more civility and reform were attached to cultural transformation in Ireland, the more culture in all its forms became a site of contestation. The ordered landscape and built environment gave dispossession a veneer of civility, but the unmistakable transformations would bring all aspects of cultural differences into play. By examining the violence directed at cultural symbols of difference, it will be clear that the meaning of violence was not always planned and plotted in advance – but that does not mean most of the violence was not filled with meaning.

≈

As Tudor officials were searching for both a strategy and a justification for subduing the wild Irish, new thinking about cultivation, about order, and about civility emerged to provide English ministers and administrators in Dublin with the means to tame the 'barbarous' natives who continued to resist the civilising influence of English culture (Figure 1.2). Moreover,

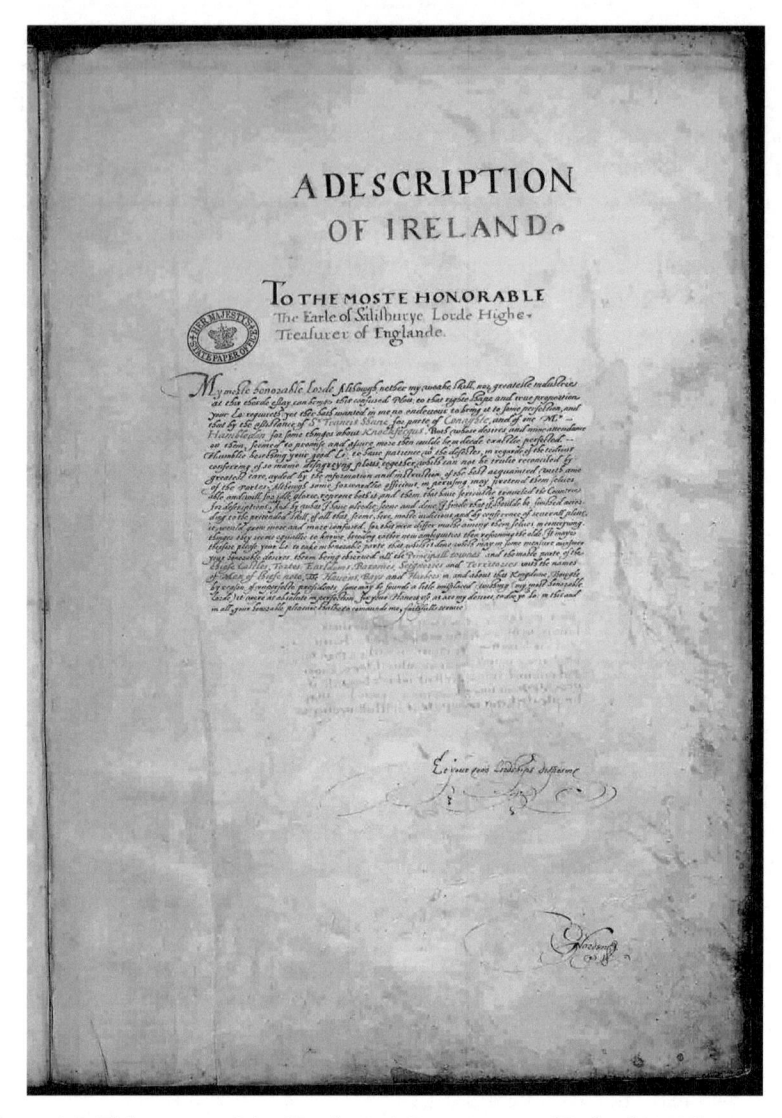

Figure 1.2 Title page to John Norden's *A Description of Ireland* (1600), courtesy National Archives, Kew.

the conflicts over land, landscape, and land use would soon provide the most important theatre for symbolic and ritualised communication: in a centuries-old struggle between adversaries with little or no common language, actions often spoke in place of words. Indeed, in the Ulster Plantation, landscape, architecture, and objects would reveal themselves in a web of performances and activities as well as meanings.

One of the most important contributions of Renaissance thought is the way notions of civility were associated with cultivation and land use. Brian Graham writes of landscape as 'a medium in expressing feelings, ideas and values and also an arena of political discourse and action where culture is contested'. If land use in fact transforms nature into a cultural realm of meaning, then it is also a place where cultures come into conflict.[10] So, if we choose to concentrate on the various meanings of land and landscape in Ireland, a new instrument will emerge which helps to clarify our understanding of English policies in Ireland, and the strategies of early English colonialism. From 1515, the way in which the transformation of land use, the contrived environment, and the emphasis on human control over nature reveals an ideology of colonialism that can be read in the landscape that resulted.

In addition, the cultural changes and signifiers assumed to be attendant upon a newly settled landscape became identified and recognised as objects of an alien culture, as artefacts to express English cultural norms and consequently as targets of cultural conflict. In short, the altered landscape and material culture of the plantations emerged as a powerful medium for communication and conflict. For many reasons, the civilising mission assumed that a remodelled Ireland ought to look distinctly like England, with the necessary precursor to the introduction of civility the division of the landscape into an ordered, recognisably English space. A space characterised by cultivated fields, fences, houses, towns, roads, and various other symbolic borders. Indeed, it would become clear to the English settler that civilisation was to be found where he was, and that he was always and everywhere surrounded by primitive and barbarous culture manifested most clearly in the fragmented, untamed wilderness of Irish land (Figure 1.3). The untamed landscape was to be carefully divided and settled with fences, roads, bridges, orchards, and deer parks that would allow settlers to find their own image in the transformed landscape.[11]

Each official settlement from the 1540s onward had specific demands for the types and numbers of houses, barns, and castles to be built, each intended to embody visually the control over nature and the previously waste land of Ireland. The cities would have carefully designed plans, stone buildings, and an emphasis on geometric regularity meant to embody a newfound order similar to that envisioned for the landscape: each of these in itself an expression of an ideology with a civilised and ordered landscape

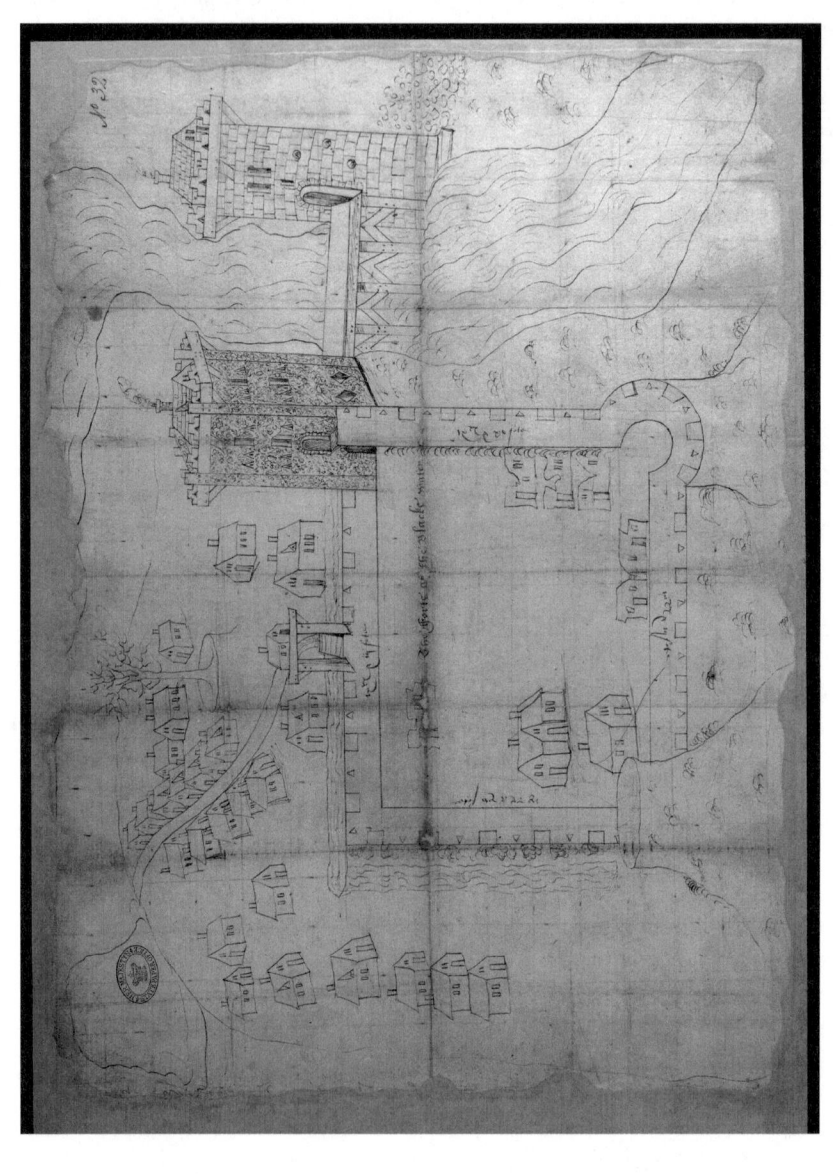

**Figure 1.3** 'The Plott of Black Water' (Blackwater fort), County Armagh (1587), courtesy National Archives, Kew.

at its heart, exemplifying the only route to civility and order. The material culture surrounded by carefully constructed and controlled natural elements of gardens, meadows, trees, and enclosed pastures: these were the essential manifestations of the settled landscape. If we can see landscape as having social, economic, and political meaning, then we might also see these aspects of the land as nonverbal documents or texts; walls, cultivated fields, fences, roads, and bridges can be powerful signs and convey a forceful message – especially in a society unaccustomed to seeing them. The hedges, walls, fences, and bounds which materialised in the Plantations were crucial markers of the transformed landscape as well as tangible borders separating the natives from the planters. Furthermore, they served a dual function as visible barriers as well as regular reminders of the landscape left behind (Plate 1). But the natives saw from the very beginning that this order, civility, and cultivation was a symbol of their dispossession. Rightfully seen as an attack on their culture and way of life, these clearly defined borders, altered landscapes, and other aspects of material culture emerged as the locus of resistance and the perfect means to offer a response. Indeed, their permanence offered conveniently sedentary targets for burning and destruction, each providing a kind of parchment on which to communicate resistance.

By extending the frontier and demanding the creation of a cultivated landscape, the erection of forts, villages, houses, walls, ditches, and the like, the new officials began unwittingly to convert what was in essence a natural space, a concept, into a cultural border. Unlike a frontier, a border is something that is defined, and by being defined, it can also be assaulted or violated. A border becomes an object, an object like a house that can be used to thwart authority, something to be defied or even destroyed. Like so many other objects in the transformed landscape and material culture that accompanied the Plantations, the creation of a border is simultaneously the creation of an object, a place to be contested, even granting objects a sort of agency in the clash of cultures. What the English saw as a marker of a right to possession, as a symbol of their intention to remain, the Irish saw as a site for resistance, an opportunity to reject the reconstruction of nature. As objects came to communicate a superior culture or to justify a particular form of civility, the response often took the shape of resistance to the more concrete nontextual expressions of the culture being promoted. In that light it is possible to read cultural confrontations as texts, or a form of communication that demonstrate the awareness – on both sides of the divide – of the essential distinctions situated in cultural differences.[12] In this way, the confiscations, the reconstructed landscape evoked by the very word *plantations*, and the many buildings associated with them will provide a ready location for a frank exchange of views between the hostile cultures (Figure 1.4).

≈

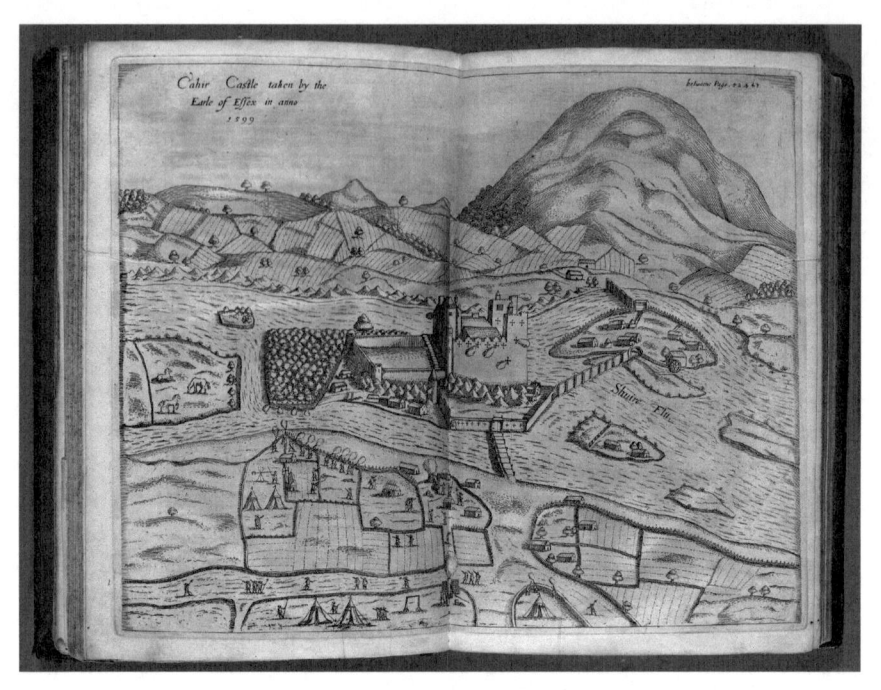

**Figure 1.4** Castle of Cahir, 1599, from Thomas Stafford's *Pacata Hibernia: or, A History of the Wars in Ireland, During the Reign of Queen Elizabeth ... First Published in 1633* (reprint 1810), courtesy Huntington Library, Pasadena, California.

The emphasis in the Plantation Papers on the architectural iconography that represented the emergence of a colonial and early imperial presence in Ulster did not spare the nearby or *inner* empire from the resistance so familiar to colonial settlers throughout history. The careful specifications demanding permanent stone houses, defensible bawns, walled gardens, fenced and cultivated fields, fortified towns and markets, roads, bridges, gaols, and record offices were meant to demonstrate a very English intention to occupy and to remain on the land.[13] But this colonial mentality was very much part of Fanon's naked violence, and the Irish early on recognised that it could only be countered when confronted with greater violence. The built environment and the wide array of objects that symbolised the transformative presence of civility became easy targets for resistance.[14] The artefacts of English culture were intended to provide visible signs of superiority and the advantages of civil society, and the Irish were well aware that these signs were designed to supplant their own culture and customs. By the time of the Ulster Plantation the message was well understood, and the responses made plain that the colonised were prepared to respond and resist in defence of their own cultural traditions.

Early on it was apparent that the Irish recognised the centrality of cultural differences as sites of contestation. The Butlers had attacked and pillaged a market fair in Enniscorthy in 1569. Burkes had repeatedly assaulted the gates and walls of Athenry in the 1580s, determined to drive off the masons and destroy Elizabeth's Arms to make certain 'to sett the newe gates on fier … BETT [beat] away the masons and other laboreres wch were working on the walls [and] sought for the stones where upon the [queens] Armes were cutt, to have broken them, swearing that none such should stande in any wall there.'[15] In Ulster, successive O'Neills demonstrated their awareness of the importance tied to symbols of English culture, forbidding English-style houses and even restricting native diets: Conn Bacach, 'on his deathbed, left his curse to any of his posterity, that would sow wheat or make any building in Ulster, for in building, they should do but as the crow doth, make her nest to be beaten out by the hawk'; and Seán an Díomais was said to murder followers for eating wheaten loaves.[16] Sir John Perrot declared that no one could appear before English officials of any kind 'without first having to cut their glybbez, which we do thinke the ffyrs token of obedience'. Similarly, he insisted that native lords attend the parliament in 1584 wearing English habit, causing one lord to ask Perrot if 'one of his Chaplaines … might goe with him along through the Streetes, clad in his Irish Trouses: for then (quoth he) the Boyes will laugh as fast at him, as they now doe at me' (Figure 1.5).[17] It was these sorts of actions that led thinkers like Edmund Spencer to denounce Irish culture as the root of the problem and to argue that it needed to be eradicated before the civilised reforms on offer could take hold. John Derricke and Henry Sidney helped establish a narrative of the obstinate Irish, choosing the dark side over civility and consequently needing to be swept away like a scythe through crops before they could ripen and mature.[18] Patricia Palmer reveals how officials were busy translating violent epics, the genre of the victors, 'exploring how violence gets written and atrocity gets translated into art'.[19] Violence and dispossession were legitimated by a cultural discourse that located civility and savagery (and the different land uses associated with each) as irreconcilable and extolled the benefits for Ireland and the Irish in replacing one with the other. Following the Nine Years War, the Flight of the Earls, and Cahir O'Docherty's revolt, officials like Spenser were convinced that the violence emanated only from the Irish and that the land needed to be emptied of inconvenient inhabitants.[20]

≈

Relying on experience gained from earlier Plantations, the officials charged with planting Ulster were careful to demand 'stone or bricke' buildings and to require English or Scots tenants be involved in agricultural pursuits.

**Figure 1.5** Detail image, 'Wilde' Irish man and woman, from John Speed's, *Theatre of the Empire of Great Britaine* (1627), courtesy Huntington Library, Pasadena, California.

However, it was quickly apparent that insufficient settlers were arriving and that driving out Irish 'Tenants who are now fullie prepared for tillage' would precipitate a 'gen'all dearth throughout the whole Countye'.[21] This meant that from the outset the Plantation in Ulster would be dependent on Irish tenants and labour, ensuring that while the owners of the land had changed, the occupiers had not. Nonetheless, the plans for Ulster committed settlers and native tenants alike to a remodelled landscape, one with tillage as its focus and with the attendant material culture proliferating alongside it. It was these markers of civility that would serve as symbols of the reformed and transformed society in Ulster. Indeed, the efficacy of these signs was apparent in how readily they were identified by both settlers and natives in previous settlements. For the former, cultivated fields, permanent structures, fences, bridges, roads, towns, walls, and markets were just the sort of reassuringly familiar built environment and landscape that would evoke the civil land of their upbringing. Conversely, these same objects provided 'outward and visible signs of the arrival of a new order'.[22] And not only were these objects often unwelcome; they were also visible, stationary, potential targets.

Consequently, the settler culture would provide the foci for later resistance and violence directed at the embodiments of the inner empire.

As in earlier Plantation efforts, the organisation of space and the transformation of the landscape and land use was accepted as the necessary first step to the creation of civility and order (Figure 1.6). Cultivation and an arable economy were tools intended to regulate not just landholding, but social structures and other relationships as well.[23] A new landlord class, valuing fashionable gardens and enclosed parks, helped facilitate the transformation of agriculture away from the disordered state of native farming and the devotion to the mobile pastoral economy condemned as barbaric. The desire finally to bring Ulster into line with the rest of Ireland by eliminating its powerful lords and removing most natives was not new but the planned severity of the Plantation was mitigated in practice, leaving the reality on the ground a long way from best laid plans of officials.[24] That said, the changes to the landscape and the push for cultivation created real concerns about 'ecological alienation' and the threat to native traditions and customs. If, as Andy Wood argues, landscapes are embedded in communal memory, then the destruction of the old order and the alterations in the land were certain to be evident to the existing inhabitants. Poets took note of the changing landscape, with Lochlainn Ó Dálaigh lamenting 'the mountain all in fenced fields; fairs are held in places of the chase; the green is crossed by girdles of twisted fences'.[25] Fields dividing the former open space, fairs breaking up the freedom of the chase, and girdles of fences compressing and confining the occupants were some of the more obvious consequences of the emerging civility. More importantly, these first hints of the materiality of colonialism were examples of how people might use objects as texts, texts meant to produce and transform and that might well be used in both the projection of and resistance to a colonising power. The emergence of a construct in which things stood for people and culture opened the door to the violent treatment of the material world as an arena for performative communication.[26]

From the outset the enclosed fields of the planters drew the unwanted attention of the locals. The exasperation of one Ulster settler stems from the very pointed and no doubt infuriating japes of his neighbours:

> For an instance of theire malice to the Englishe, an English man did strongly inclose a peece of ground for meadowe, and hee pitched out from thence an exceeding number of stones, and when he came to mowe his grounds he found more stones then he tooke out (for the Irish never went that way, day or night) but threwe in stones from under their mantles.[27]

Here we see an example of the type of the quotidian resistance and symbolic confrontation that avoids open defiance of the new order while rejecting

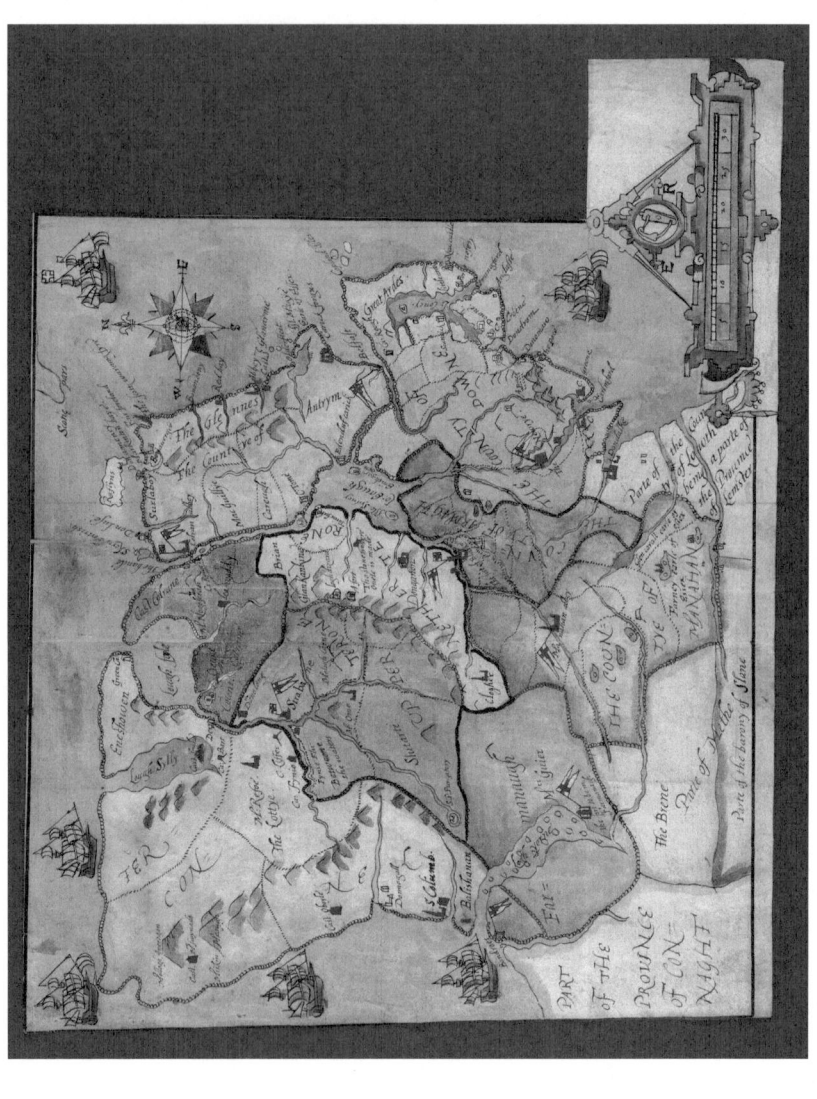

Figure 1.6 Francis Jobson, Map of Ulster Counties (c. 1598), courtesy Archives Research Library, Trinity College Dublin.

the newly created borders defining the landscape and erasing native cultural norms. The cultivated and demarcated landscape were changes designed to communicate and underpin a cultural message about civility through a material reflection of the intended cultural reforms (Plate 2). The creation and imposition of a new landscape was intended to replace the existing Gaelic definition of space and landscape, introducing the orderly arrangement of private property in lieu of the fluid and disorderly native system. Gaelic poets continued to explicate the divergent priorities between Gaelic and settler cultures, a cleavage produced from within a contested geographic space.[28] But it is important to note how readily natives defied the emergence of a new cultural landscape through simple and often amusing ways. The rock throwing resistance to cultivation can provide a fuller transcript of noncompliance and defiance too often ignored in favour of risings and rebellions.[29] Often the successful reordering of the land served to benefit the local Irish: One farmer complained that he lost

> his corne and grasse at night (for like the devell they alwaies wake when wee slept) & when they feede their Cattell on our groundes, a light-footed churle watcheth at our doores, who when he spieth any body comminge forth he runeth away crying wth a barbarous noyse, wch his Cattell understanding also runn away, so that the poore Englishe findes his grasse or his corne eaten, but findes no eaters.[30]

Increasingly the material world of settler culture was used to signify the settlers themselves. The focus on cultural conflict allowed objects and things to take the place of people, a cultural construct that would highlight the violent treatment of the very material world created to give the illusion of home, of order, and security. The attacks aimed at the artefacts of settler culture were themselves a 'form of cultural affirmation and expression of identity in the face of loss of tradition and dislocation'.[31]

≈

The material culture and built environment of the settlers served both a symbolic and utilitarian purpose. Intended as a new world in the making, the emerging villages and towns with schools, markets, almshouses, churches, and gaols were markers of a remodelled landscape as well as manifestations of settler achievements in introducing civility to savage Ulster. The display of different and better values was an important aspect in the ways architecture made manifest the aims of the settlers.[32] In parts of Ulster castles, defensive works and mansions were appearing, signalling the 'new order'. One positive report from Belfast gloated that it was full of settlers who had 'buylt good tymber houses with chimneys after the fashion of the English pale, and one Inn with very good Lodginge which is a great comforte to the travellers in those partes'. While the inn provided the actual comfort, the architecture of the Plantation went further by providing a reassuringly familiar built environment offering a welcome reminder that civility was feasible.[33] A key factor in the successful expansion of colonies and empire was attracting sufficient numbers of civilised settlers and it was apparent by the time of the Ulster Plantation that those recruited to settle the lands were reassured by finding the same architecture, diet, taste, and values upon arrival.[34] For nearly a century, officials recognised the importance of the built environment in increasing civil life in Ireland, aware that the material world could be used to construct the legitimacy of their rule. But the condemnation of temporary cabins and native mobility soon added the built environment to the cultural differences emerging as primary sites of contestation. Prior to the outbreak in 1641, there was considerable quotidian resistance, theft, sabotage, arson, and other activities that required neither planning or coordination.[35] Much of this resistance involved symbolic responses to the symbolic markers and monuments of civil culture.

The last year of Elizabeth's reign saw assaults on the products of settler culture. Domhnall Spáinneach (Donnel Spainagh) was condemned for he 'suffereth us to enjoy nothing in the parts to him adioyning, but taketh our Cattayle, moweth our medowes, spoyleth our howses'.[36] During periods of disorder, the Irish were quick to lash out at the symbols of the new colonial order. The material culture of civility – fields, fences, houses, and the like – were the first objects to be rejected, with reformed churches and English-style houses the primary targets of those looking to strike at the manifestations of colonial power. Destroying the changes in the landscape and built environment offered an obvious means of expressing popular discontent with the emerging colonial order in Ireland as well as demonstrating loyalty to the old order rooted in Gaelic traditions and culture.[37]

Recent work on environmental history has added considerable nuance to accounts of the years before 1641. Though many officials in Ireland were careful to relate how well the civilising mission was advancing and how peace, comity, and the happy fruits of civility were transforming both Ireland and the wild Irish, Arlene Crampsie and Francis Ludlow have made clear how the devastation of earlier conflicts created opportunities for settlers. Land was readily available and the aggression directed against Irish woodlands meant an ancient symbol of Irish uncivilised culture was erased. The assertiveness of the new occupiers was visible in the alterations to landscapes and the built environments. The symbolism of main streets designed to lead from demesne gates directly to the Protestant church signified a new dominance – more than a physical entity these changes were 'a tool and canvas in the ongoing campaign to anglicize and civilize Ireland'.[38] The expanding culture of civility was represented by a built environment and objects intended to convey a determination to remain; over time, the resolve to remove the very same signifiers of a new order demonstrate the loyalty to an old order, to native traditions, and to Irish culture in general.

Giving a speech at the sentencing of Sir Phelim O'Neill the Lord President called attention to O'Neill's hostility to the English and their architecture. He denounced the 'title wanting (to you) *Phelimy Totane*, the last and most affecting, as sung by your Bards, none of them singing of any of your titles but (this of) *Phelimy Totane* (the incendiary) ... [for] you burn all the Londoner's plantations in one morning'.[39] Sir Phelim had been given an appropriate English title and granted lands during the Plantation, but he had fallen hopelessly in debt while trying to adopt a civil form of living. His rejection of the benefits of civil culture made him a particular villain to officials and his burning of the buildings meant to convey the benefits of the settler culture made clear the irredeemable nature of the Irish.[40] The Lord President elaborated on ways in which the rejection of all things English and 'their hatred of the English nation' informed native violence. 'They destroy even the cattle because they are English. They destroy all the English habitations. When asked, can you not keep them for yourselves? No! that would make the English think of returning here again, and so we will burn all to the ground.' Still, Sir Phelim's hatred of all things English was not the whole story. The Lord President was careful to remind his audience that the rejection of English culture was in fact hereditary, for his ancestor had 'cursed any of his posterity who would (take to) building houses, sowing corn, or wearing English apparel or speaking the tongue of the English nation'. This is an inherited hatred, we see it in Shane O'Neill, he built a fort which he called Fagh na Gall or 'to the hate (or scorn) of the English'.[41] Once again one can see the effectiveness of the materiality of the built environment and its undeniable legibility to the native community, but also how readily contestation could be derived from the same objects. The settlers may well have felt that the primary symbolism of the English conception of sovereignty was architectural, but the colonised felt no need to accept the perpetuity of their constructions.[42]

≈

The targeting of the material culture of civility was a deliberate assault on English notions of order: with towns overrun, houses, farms, and livestock destroyed, and the tamed landscape made wild once again. Absent the symmetrical and divided fields there remained only the 'scars on a landscape once marked with fences and barns and fields of hay'.[43] Surely settlers comprehended that the violence was a dagger aimed at the very Englishness of the landscape. As the violence increased at the end of 1641, it was often intended to convey specific messages with destructive and brutal acts filled with meaning and intentions.[44] The rejection of a remodelled landscape and built environment can be read as a repudiation of English culture in general. Joan Redmond has clarified how Protestant civility created an interdependence of religion, civility, and plantation; settlements underpinned the true church by promoting civility and improvement. The linkage meant that the peaceful cultivators and civilisers were ruthlessly attacked, 'colonial martyrs' persecuted for their attempts to civilise and improve Ireland. Looked at another way, 1641 could be understood as an attack on England in Ireland, an obstinate refusal to take advantage of the superior culture on offer from the burgeoning empire.[45] Cultural conflict can easily consume social, economic, and even religious differences and the defence and preservation of culture can take many forms.

At a time when the people producing – and reading – documents remained limited, objects can tell a different story than that told by texts. Caroline Bynum shows how the 'materiality of objects carries forward the experience of people', so it should come as no surprise that all sorts of objects became the focus of the divisions in Ulster. Writing in the 1640s, Gerard Boate decried the Irish efforts to extirpate the very memory of all examples of English culture:

> the whole land, where the English did dwell, or had any thing to doe, was filled with as goodly beasts, both cows and Sheep ... the greatest part whereof hath been destroyed by those barbarians, the naturall inhabitants of Ireland, who not content to have murthered or expelled their English neighbours ... endeavoured quite to extinguish the memory of them, and of all the civility and good things by them introduced amongst that wild Nation; and consequently in most places they did not only demolish the houses built by the English, the Gardens and Enclosures made by them, the Orchards and Hedges by them planted, but destroyed whole droves and flocks at once of English Cowes and Sheep.[46]

Anything that evoked that 'civility and good things' introduced by the English was met with hostility and acts of defiance that occurred as the natives sought to make an 'expressive statement by acting on the materiality of the intruder's former presence'.[47] Material culture, alterations in the landscape, and the elimination of English animals were obvious targets, but the ways in which objects represented culture and how religion accompanied civility made certain that religious objects and the clergy associated with them would also find themselves artefacts to be eliminated in the regenerative violence aimed at restoring an ancient culture subjected to centuries of humiliation and abuse.

If objects indeed function as symbols and signs, as 'the visible part of culture', then their role in a communicative process is undeniable. Not surprisingly, the church's inherent symbolism as an alien religion displacing native beliefs offered the Irish a rich theatre for what can only be described as 'blunt symbolic expression'.[48] From the outset, in October 1641, Protestant clergy were a major target of the insurgents. While there was a considerable variety of reasons for this, many would later admit that hatred of the settlers and clergy was not really about religion but abhorrence of the English way of life being forced upon them. Civility and improvement proved unworthy challengers to the devotion to Irish culture.[49] The appropriation of churches by the settler community deprived the Irish of traditional sacred spaces and drove many to seek spiritual sustenance among the regular clergy. Furthermore, Protestant emphasis on the Word meant that churches looked remarkably changed, with whitewashed walls and much unadorned empty space with altars removed and furniture reorganised to focus attention on the pulpit. Worse still, many of the most revered objects of Irish Catholicism had been publicly destroyed in rituals meant to degrade them as little more than stone and wood.[50] But these very pressures to cast out idolatry and superstition led to demands that churches and the English settlers revert to the old religion. Protestants were pushed to 'turn to Mass' for salvation, the Catholics 'reciprocating for decades of pressure to conform'. As with the erasure of the material culture of the English, these actions are informed with a deep symbolic motive, 'namely the wiping out of the cultural capital of the colonizer'.[51] The stripping of the altars described so eloquently by Eamon Duffy was equalled by the ripping apart of English Bibles, the sign and symbol of Protestant belief, the source of their salvation, and the substantiation of their superiority. There are countless depositions recounting Bibles abused, dragged through dirty water, used for wiping bums, and strewn throughout the churchyard as so many sacred objects of Catholic worship before them. Protestants were appalled at the tales of pipers playing and people dancing on the degraded symbols on these occasions – one cultural tradition celebrating the inversion and disgrace of another.[52]

It is clear that Protestant clerics were targeted in part owing to their role as moneylenders, landowners, and agents of the expanding colonial presence.[53] Their religious identity combined with their role as symbols of an alien religion and rule, guaranteeing that the artefacts associated with them would become the focus of ritualised violence. A case can be made that much of the violence was not really about the clerics themselves but rather about breaking down the cultural boundaries they represented. There were mental, material, and cultural landscapes to be broken down: rejecting Protestantism involved the wholesale rejection of its signs, symbols, and tangible markers, ranging from buildings to human bodies.[54] Boundaries between groups are regularly asserted through symbolism and customs, what Clodagh Tait deems carving confessionalised space out of sacralised landscapes. But the ability to live together and to share conflicted locations during times of heightened tensions often evaporated, leading to the resurrection of suppressed grievances.[55] In 1641, religion may have been less of a marker of difference than other loyalties like ethnicity, community, and culture. Furthermore, aggrieved natives used artefacts to express identity, what Woolf describes as the agency of things rather than people.[56] The violence aimed at churches reveals a keen awareness of the defining differences of worship and the use of space. The regenerative – rather than destructive – power of violence informs the desecration of churches and Protestant notions of worship, with interiors ransacked, seats incinerated, and the pulpits, the central priority of heretic worship, cast outside.[57] John Walter offers persuasive evidence that the cultural patterning of violence indicates that all thing English became targets for hostility. The Depositions were organised and compiled by clergymen, guaranteeing that attacks on clergy remained in the foreground. But 'what observers separate out for analysis the participants regularly put together for action'.[58] Indeed, the bloodthirsty papist genocide designed to extirpate godly Protestants might just as well be read as part of a continuum of resistance to the imposition of English civility and culture through dispossession and Plantation. Regenerative violence aimed at the restoration of an old order rooted in Gaelic customs may provide a unifying theme more inclusive than religious bigotry and conflict.

Nicholas Canny has argued that desecration and humiliations 'were manifestations of a cultural detestation of an English presence in the community that did not enjoy the approval of the Catholic clergy'. Here again the killing of English breeds and attacks on the symbols of English influence is identified as 'essentially a struggle between cultures'. Gaelic leaders wanted a return to Gaelic order, with most hoping for a regeneration of traditions and culture; but for too long people have adopted the views of Temple and others that portrayed the violence and the changes sought after only in terms of religion. Canny claims that the prime factor was 'a sense of grievance over the loss of property or status', but the argument here is that a much wider cultural conflict was at play, one that can comprehend, social, economic, and religious elements.[59] The transformed landscape, the built environment, and the tension related to sacred spaces are all part of the visible symbols of a civility to be introduced alongside English culture. In the end, the statements made through performative violence were central to the cultural contestation at the heart of the Ulster Plantation and a recurring theme in the development of empire.[60]

## Notes

1 Gwyn A. Williams, *Welsh Wizard and British Empire: Dr. J. Dee and a Welsh Identity* (Cardiff: University College Cardiff Press, 1980), 124.
2 Dee's ideas are laid out most fully in John Dee, *General and Rare Memorials Pertayning to the Perfect Arte of Navigation* (London: Iohn Daye, 1577); Geoffrey of Monmouth, *History of the Kings of Britain* (New York: E. P. Dutton, 1958), Book 9: 10.
3 See David Heffernan, *Debating Tudor Policy in Sixteenth-Century Ireland: 'Reform' Treatises and Political Discourse*, Studies in Early Modern Irish History (Manchester: Manchester University Press, 2018), ch. 1; Ciarán Brady, *The Chief Governors: The Rise and Fall of Reform Government in Tudor Ireland, 1536–1588*, Cambridge Studies in Early Modern British History (Cambridge: Cambridge University Press, 2002); John Patrick Montaño, *The Roots of English Colonialism in Ireland* (Cambridge: Cambridge University Press, 2011), chs 1–2.
4 Heffernan, *'Reform' Treatises*, chs 2–3.
5 Joan Redmond, 'Memories of Violence and New English Identities in Early Modern Ireland', *BIHR* 89, no. 246 (2016): 708–29.
6 See Anthony Low, *The Georgic Revolution* (Princeton: Princeton University Press, 1985); John Patrick Montaño, '"Dycheyng and Hegeying": The Material Culture of the Tudor Plantations in Ireland', in *Studies in Settler Colonialism: Politics, Iidentity and Culture*, eds Fiona Bateman and Lionel Pilkington (Basingstoke: Palgrave Macmillan, 2011); Montaño, *The Roots of Colonialism*, 63–102, 213–81; Alexandra Walsham, *The Reformation of the Landscape: Religion, Identity, and Memory in Early Modern Britain and Ireland* (Oxford: Oxford University Press, 2011). Annaleigh Margey, 'Representing Colonial Landscapes: Early English Maps of Ulster and Virginia, 1580–1612', in *Reshaping Ireland 1550–1700*, ed. Brian Mac Cuarta SJ (Dublin: Four Courts Press, 2011); 'From Gaelic Outpost to Colonial Society: Donegal and the Plantation of Ulster', in *An Historical, Environmntal and Cultural Atlas of County Donegal*, eds Jim MacLaughlin and Seán Beattie (Cork: Cork University Press, 2013); 'After the Flight: The Impact of Plantation on The Ulster Landscape', in *Flight of the Earls*, eds Éamonn Ó Ciardha, David Finnegan, and Marie-Claire Peters (Derry: Guildhall Press, 2010).
7 See *Plantation Ireland: Settlement and Material Culture, C. 1550-C.1700*, eds Colin Rynne and James Lyttleton (Dublin: Four Courts Press, 2009); Alan MacInnes, 'Making the Plantations British', in *Frontiers and the Writing of History, 1500–1850*, eds Steven and Raingard Esser Ellis (Hanover: Wehrhahn, 2006).
8 Heffernan, *'Reform' Treatises*, ch. 4.
9 See Thomas Herron, *Spenser's Irish Work: Poetry, Plantation and Colonial Reformation* (Burlington: Ashgate, 2007); Willy Maley, 'Something Quite Atrocious: English Colonialism Beyond the Pale and the License to Violence', *Eolas: The Journal of the American Society of Irish Medieval Studies* 3 (2009): 82–111;

'"Barbarisme and Obdurate Wilfulnesses": Agricultural Materialism, Animal Welfare, and Irish Studies', in *Early Modern Ireland: New Sources, Methods and Perspectives*, ed. Sarah Covington (London: Taylor & Francis Group, 2018); Vincent Carey, 'What Pen Can Paint or Tears Atone? Mountjoy's Scorched Earth Campaign', in *The Battle of Kinsale*, ed. Hiram Morgan (Bray: Wordwell, 2004); David Edwards, 'Tudor Ireland: Anglicisation, Mass Killing and Security', in *The Routledge History of Genocide*, eds Cathie Carmichael and Richard C. Maguire (Oxford: Routledge, 2015); Margaret Rose Jaster, 'Breeding Dissoluteness and Disobedience: Clothing Laws as Tudor Colonialist Discourse', *Critical Survey* 13, no. 3 (2001) 61–77; Kathleen Rabl, 'Taming the "Wild Irish" in English Renaissance Drama', in *Literary Interrelations: Ireland, England and the World*, ed. Heinz Kosok Wolfgang Zach (Tubingen: G. Narr, 1987); Redmond, 'Memories of Violence', 708–29.

10 Although concerned with a later period, there is much to be drawn from Andrew McRae, *God Speed the Plough: The Representation of Agrarian England, 1500–1660*, Past and Present Publications (Cambridge: Cambridge University Press, 1996); Brian Graham, 'Ireland and Irishness: Place, Culture and Identity', in *In Search of Ireland: A Cultural Geography*, ed. Brian Graham (London: Routledge, 1997), 3. On Irish geography, see William. J. Smyth, 'A Plurality of Irelands: Regions, Societies and Mentalities', in Graham, *In Search of Ireland*, 19–42; Annaleigh Margey, 'Representing Plantation Landscapes: The Mapping of Ulster, C. 1560–1640', in Lyttleton and Rynne, *Plantation Ireland: Settlement and Material Culture*.

11 BL, Cotton MSS Titus B XIII/1, Cecil's Instructions to Sussex, May 1560; J. S. Brewer, W. Bullen, G. Carew, eds, *Calendar of the Carew Manuscripts, Preserved in the Archepiscopal Library at Lambeth, 1589–1600*, 6 vols (London: Longman & Co., 1867–73), 1: 292. For the role of Virgil in establishing the importance of introducing husbandry to savage lands, see Richard Waswo, *The Founding Legend of Western Civilization: From Virgil to Vietnam* (Hanover: University Press of New England [for] Wesleyan University Press, 1997), chs 2–5.

12 Based on ideas, expressed far more eloquently, by Patrick J. Wolfe in his Plenary Lecture, 'Beyond the Pale(stine) of Settlement: Settler Colonialism, Its Barriers and Its Contradictions', Fifth Galway Conference on Colonialism, 27 June 2007.

13 T. W. Moody, 'Ulster Plantation Papers 1600–13', *Analecta Hibernica* 8 (1938): 180–297; 'The Revised Articles of the Ulster Plantation, 1610', *BIHR* 12 (1934–35): 178–83.

14 Mary C. Beaudry, Cook, Lauren J., and Mrozowski, Stephen A., 'Artifacts and Active Voices: Material Culture as a Social Discourse', in *The Archaeology of Inequality*, Randall H. McGuire and Robert Paynter, eds (Oxford: Oxford University Press, 1991), 153.

15 David Edwards, 'The Butler Revolt of 1569', *IHS* 28 (1993): 250; PRO SP 63/56/6, printed in; Arthur Collins, ed. *Letters and Memorials of State in the Reigns of Queen Mary, Queen Elizabeth, King James, King Charles the First,*

*Part of King Charles the Second and Oliver's Usurpation*, 2 Vols (London: T. Osborne, 1746), 1: 119.

16 Camden claimed that 'Shane boiled in Hatred against the English, in such sort, that he named a Castle which he built in the Lake Eaugh [*sic*], Feoghnegall, that is, The hatred of the English, and strangled some of his own men for that they fed on English bread', William Camden, *Annales: The True and Royall History of the Famous Empresse Elizabeth* (London, 1625), 167.
17 E. C. S., *The Government of Ireland under the Honorable, Just and Wise Governour Sir John Perrot … . 1584–88* (London, 1626), 58. *Calendar of State Papers, Ireland*, 1609–73, 359, 18 June 1673, John Perrot; Collins, *Letters*, 1: 48–50, Instructions for L. P. Perrot, 14 December 1570.
18 Sara Covington, '"Realms So Barbarous and Cruell": Writing Violence and Early Modern Ireland', *History* 99, no. 336 (2014): 488–90; Patricia Palmer, 'Hungry Eyes and the Rhetoric of Dispossession: English Writing from Early Modern Ireland', in *A Companion to Irish Literature*, ed. Julia Wright (Oxford: Blackwell Publishing, 2010), 95–7. On the *View* as a plea for the extermination of native culture, see Brendan O'Leary, *A Treatise on Northern Ireland*, vol. 1. The Shackles of the State & Hereditary Colonialism in the Interpretation of Irish History (Oxford: Oxford University Press, 2019), 156–60.
19 Patricia Palmer, *The Severed Head and the Grafted Tongue* (Cambridge: Cambridge University Press, 2014), 2.
20 Cole Harris, 'How Did Colonialism Dispossess? Comments from an Edge of Empire', *Annals of the Association of American Geographers* 94, no. 1 (2004): 174–9. The harsh consequences for natives after 1608 and the need to clear territories of native architecture and leadership are discussed in Thomas Bartlett, *Ireland: A History* (Cambridge: Cambridge University Press, 2010), 99–105.
21 Moody, 'Plantation Papers', 196–8; For decades the percentage of Irish remained at 25 per cent or greater, Raymond Gillespie, 'Success and Failure in the Ulster Plantation', in *The Plantation of Ulster: Ideology and Practice*, eds Eamonn Ó Ciardha and Micheál Ó Siochrú (Manchester: Manchester University Press, 2012), 106–9. With the Ironmongers there was no real effort to recruit English or Scots, with locals given thirty-one-year leases so long as they built 'house of brick, stone or timber after the English manner and enclosed a garden or orchard', Ian W. Archer, 'The City of London and the Ulster Plantation', in Ó Ciardha and Ó Siochrú, *The Plantation of Ulster*, 84–90.
22 Jonathan Bardon, *The Plantation of Ulster: The British Colonisation of the North of Ireland in the Seventeenth Century* (Dublin: Gill and Macmillan, 2011), 210, 17–34.
23 Gillespie, 'Success and Failure', 106–07; Montaño, *Roots of Colonialism*, c.. 7; James Lyttleton, 'Natives and Newcomers: Plantation-Era Archaeology on Irish Roads Schemes', *Archaeology and National Roads Authority Monograph Series* 9 (2012): 77.
24 R. J. Hunter, 'The Fishmongers' Company of London and the Londonderry Plantation, 1609–41', in *Ulster Transformed: Essay on Plantation and Print*

*Culture C 1590–1641*, ed. John Morrill (Belfast: Ulster Historical Foundation, 2012), 178–82.
25 Colin Breen, 'Randal Macdonnell and Early Seventeenth-Century Settlement in Northeast Ulster, 1603–30', in Ó Ciardha and Ó Siochrü, *The Plantation of Ulster,* 151.
26 D. J. Mattingly, *Imperialism, Power, and Identity* (Princeton: Princeton University Press, 2011), 28. Zara Anishanslin, '"This Is the Skin of a White Man": Material Memories of Violence in Sullivan's Campaign', in *The American Revolution Reborn*, eds Patrick Spero and Michael Zuckerman (Philadelphia: University of Pennsylvania Press, 2016), 198–9.
27 Huntington Library, Ellesmere MSS, 1746, fol. 12.
28 Marc Caball, 'Cultures in Conflict in Late Sixteenth-Century Kerry: The Parallel Worlds of a Tudor Intellectual and Gaelic Poets', *IHS* 36, no. 144 (2009): 492, 500; James A. Delle, '"As Good and Easy Speculation" Spatial Conflict, Collusion and Resistance in Late C16 Munster, Ireland', *International Journal of Historical Archaeology* 3, no. 1 (1999): 16–18.
29 Robert Paynter and Randall McGuire, 'The Archaeology of Inequality: Material Culture, Domination and Resistance', in Paynter and McGuire, *The Archaeology of Inequality*, 12–15.
30 Huntington Library, Ellesmere MSS, 1746, fos 12v–13.
31 Neil L. Whitehead, 'Introduction:', in *Violence*, ed. Neil L. Whitehead (Santa Fe: School for Advanced Research Press, 2004), 6.
32 Toby C. Barnard, 'The Political, Material and Mental Culture of the Cork Settlers,. C. 1650–1700', in *Cork: History and Society*, eds Patrick O'Flanagan and Cornelius Buttimer (Dublin: Geography Publications, 1993), 309–10. Barnard goes on to say that that the classical symmetry of the architecture was rich in qualitative judgements, 'a vital assertion of English superiority' and a fastidious display of arrogance.
33 Bardon, *Plantation of Ulster*, 225, 17. William Brereton, 'Sir William Breeton's Travels in Ireland, 1635', in *Illustrations of Irish History and Topography, Mainly of the Seventeenth Century*, ed. C. Litton Falkiner (London: Longmans, Green, and Co., 1904), reports houses with 'dainty orchard, gardens and walks planted'.
34 Greg Woolf, *Becoming Roman: The Origins of Provincial Civilization in Gaul* (Cambridge: Cambridge University Press, 1998), 2–19; Bill Frazer, 'Reconceptualizing Resistance in the Historical Archaeology of the British Isles: An Editorial', *International Journal of Historical Archaeology* 3, no. 1 (1999): 6–8.
35 McGuire, 'Inequality', 4.
36 Philip H. Hore, *The History of the Town and County of Wexford*, 6 vols (London: Elliot Stock, 1899–1911), 6: 454.
37 Eamon Darcy, *The Irish Rebellion of 1641 and the Wars of the Three Kingdoms, Studies in History: New Series* (Suffolk: The Boydell Press, 2015), 63–7. Removing the symbols of the colonising culture can also carry overtones of purification of the landscape and purging of the new social order and settler culture, see David Frankfurter, '"Things Unbefitting Christians": Violence and

Christianization in Fifth-Century Panopolis', *Journal of Early Christian Studies* 6, no. 2 (2000): 290.
38 Arlene Crampsie and Francis Ludlow, 'Environmental History of Ireland, 1550–1730', in *The Cambridge History of Ireland*, ed. Jane Ohlmeyer (Cambridge: Cambridge University Press, 2018), 614–17.
39 Quoted in Mary Hickson, *Ireland in the Seventeenth Century, or the Irish Massacres of 1641-2, Their Causes and Results* (Longmans, Green and Co.1884), 184–87.
40 John T. Marshall, 'Sir Phelim O'Neill', *UJA* 2nd series, 10, no. 4 (1904): 146–7; Joan Redmond, 'Religion, Civility and the 'British' of Ireland in the 1641 Irish Rebellion', *IHS* 45, no. 167 (2021): 1–21.
41 Hickson, *Irish Massacres*, 188. The importance of the semiotic ideology of the material world in Peru is discussed in Steven A. Wernke, 'Convergences: Producing Early Colonial Hybridity at a *Doctrina* in Highalnd Peru', in *Enduring Conquests: Rethinking the Arcaheology of Resistance to Spanish Colonialism in The Americas*, eds Matthew Liebmann and Melissa S. Murphy (Santa Fe: School for Advanced Research Press, 2011).
42 Patricia Seed, 'Taking Possession and Reading Texts: Establishing the Authority of Overseas Empires', *WMQ* 49, no. 2 (1992): 200.
43 Jill Lepore, *The Name of War: King Philip's War and the Origins of American Identity* (New York: Alfred A. Knopf, 1998), 72.
44 Wayne E. Lee, *Barbarians and Brothers: Anglo-American Warfare, 1500–1865* (Oxford: Oxford University Press, 2011), 2.
45 Redmond, 'Memories of Violence', 724–9; '(Re)Making Ireland British: Religion, Ethnicity and Conversion in the 1641 Irish Rebellion', *The Seventeenth Century* 35, no. 6 (2020): 3–7, 17.
46 Gerard Boate, *Irelands Naturall History* (London, 1652), 89. For the importance of animals and cows and how they served as evidence of the civilising mission in this period, see Keith Pluymers, 'Cow Trials, Climate Change, and the Causes of Violence', *Environmental History* 25 (2020): 287–309.
47 Jeffrey Quilter, 'Cultural Encounters at Magdalena De Cao Viejo in the Early Colonial Period', in Liebmann and Murphy, *Enduring Conquests*, 111. Quilter adds that objecs were used to define, repress, and subjugate native people but they soon learned to use the system that repressed them, 19.
48 Beaudry et al., 'Artifacts and Active Voices', 154; Nicholas A. Robins, *Native Insurgencies and the Genocidal Impulse in the Americas* (Bloomington: Indiana University Press, 2005), 143.
49 Inga Jones, '"Holy War"? Religion, Ethnicity and Massacre During the Irish Rebellion 1641–2', in *The 1641 Depositions and the Irish Rebellion*, eds Analeigh Margey, Eamon Darcy, and Elaine Murphy (London: Pickering and Chatto, 2012), 140.
50 Brian Mac Cuarta SJ, *Catholic Revival in the North of Ireland, 1603–41* (Dublin: Four Courts Press, 2007), 71–89. Mac Cuarta notes that the Franciscans became leaders of the revanchist Catholics in Ulster, seeking restoration of the old lords, 87; Bridget Heal, 'Visual and Material Culture', in *The Oxford Handbook of*

the *Protestant Reformations*, ed. Ulinka Rublack (Oxford: Oxford University Press, 2017), 612, 5; Alexandra Walsham, 'Recycling the Sacred: Material Culture and Cultural Memory after the English Reformation', *Church History* 86, no. 4 (2017): 1122–6; Margaret Aston, 'Iconoclasm in England: Official and Clandestine', in *Iconoclasm vs. Art and Drama*, eds Clifford Davidson and Ann Eljenholm Nichols (Kalamazoo: Medieval Institute Publications, 1989), 58 for the symbolism of casting images out of consecrtaed space and into the streeet.

51 William J. Smyth, 'Towards a Cultural Geography of the 1641 Rising / Rebellion', in *1641: Contexts and Reactions*, eds Jane Ohlmeyer and Micheál Ó Siochrú (Manchester: Manchester University Press, 2013), 78–79, 74.

52 TCD 818, 88; 831, 175; 831, 190; 833, 4; 839, 10, 836, 63, 820,50, 835, 170.

53 Mark S. Sweetman, '"Sheep in the Midst of Wolves?" The Protestant Ministry in the 1641 Depositions', *Journal of Irish and Scottish Studies* 6, no. 2 (2013): 78–86, 91–92. John Walter, 'Performative Violence and the Politics of Violence in the 1641 Depositions', in Ohlmeyer and Ó Siochrú, *1641: Contexts and Reactions*, 139.

54 Redmond, 'Conversion in 1641', 9–14.

55 Clodagh Tait, 'Wandering Graveyards, Jumping Churches and Rogue-Corpses: Tolerance and Intloerance in Irish Folklore', in *Death and Dying in Ireland, Britain and Europe*, eds James Kelly and Mary Ann Lyons (Kildare: Irish Academic Press, 2013), 285–88.

56 Mattingly, *Imperialism, Power*, 235.

57 Kathleen M. Noonan, '"Martyrs in Flames": Sir John Temple and the Conception of the Irish in English Martyrologies', *Albion* 36, no. 2 (2004): 240; '"The Cruell Pressure of an Enraged Barbarous People": Irish and English Identity in Seventeenth-Century Policy and Propaganda', *The Historical Journal* 41, no. 1 (1998): 162–5.

58 Walter, 'Performative Violence and the Politics of Violence', 144–6.

59 Nicholas Canny, 'Religion and Politics and the Irish Rising of 1641', in *Religion and Rebellion: Papers Read before the 22nd Irish Conference of Historians*, eds Judith Devlin and Ronan Fanning (Dublin: University College Dublin Press, 1997), 57–66.

60 My thanks to the University of Delaware's General University Research Grant Program and the Department of History Research funds for making this research possible. As always the support of John Brewer, Kathleen Wilson, Fiona Bateman and the late Patrick Wolfe was essential and also friends and family, with Joanne, Carolina and Hektor serving as the key midfielders.

# 2

# Making North Britain: infrastructure projects and the forcible integration of the Scottish Highlands

*Daniel Maudlin*

This chapter turns to the role of infrastructure projects in a process of internal colonialism that transformed the Scottish Highlands through the course of the eighteenth century. Here, the practical and psychological intentions of state-sponsored building programmes in the Highlands are, in the context of the British Atlantic empire, considered collectively as the strategic tools of an expansionist, imperialist state steeped in the idea of Rome and the Roman empire. Framed around the Jacobite Rebellions (1715, 1719, 1745), the Seven Years War in Canada (1756–63), and the American Revolutionary War (1775–83), eighteenth-century events in the Highlands and overseas brought to a boil political, economic, and cultural tensions between England and Scotland, the Lowlands and the Highlands, that had simmered for centuries. Focusing on three key sites, the chapter follows three phases of 'forcible integration' – conquest, pacification, and civilising missions – through which the British government used infrastructure projects to assimilate the Highlands and its people into the British state and 'civilised' society and culture: making North Britain.[1] First, the Tay Bridge at Aberfeldy as a monument to conquest and the creation of the military roads under General Wade at the height of the Jacobite rebellions. Second, the building of Fort George and its role as the crown jewel of a network of permanent, military fortifications built to secure the peace after the failed, final, rebellion in 1745–46. Third, the planned town of Ullapool, established by the government-backed British Fisheries Society in the later eighteenth century; using urbanism, making towns – the *civitas* at the heart of the post-Roman idea of civilisation – to complete the process of forcible integration. From bridge to fort to town, this chapter makes the case for the importance of infrastructure projects in government-led 'colonialism' within the British Isles.

## Internal colonialism?

When we examine the forcible integration of the Scottish Highlands into Britain, are we looking at a process of nation building – 'forging the nation', as coined by Linda Colley – or imperialism and a process of colonisation?[2] The answer is both: the creation of the nation state of Great Britain can be interpreted as an act of colonialism in a much longer history of English colonialism within the British Isles throughout which Gaeldom represented an unacceptable alternate society and culture which had held out with relative autonomy for too long.[3]

As set out in the introduction to this volume, and discussed in different ways by Butler, Lucey, and Montaño in this volume (in chapters 4, 5, and 1, respectively) in relation to Ireland, the term 'inner empire' implies two distinct yet interwoven ways of thinking about the British Isles in relation to the wider British empire. First, drawing on the idea of internal colonialism, it considers the impact of British state-sponsored imperialism within the British Isles. Second, it assesses the impact of overseas territories on the British Isles by looking at the buildings created to manage, process, profit from, and celebrate the activities, resources, and peoples of Britain's overseas colonies. This chapter focuses on the colonisation of the Highlands in the long eighteenth century, a process that can be seen as a joint 'British' venture between England and Lowland Scotland; the final stage in England's historic gaol to absorb Scotland; and, as a continuation of the historic Lowland Scottish goal to absorb the Highlands.[4] It also sets British government activities in the eighteenth-century Highlands in the context of a wider global empire.

Colonialism implies the conquest and settlement of a place by the state-actors of another place. Following the Act of Union, the Highlands were part of the United Kingdom, but the idea of Internal Colonialism posited by Michael Hechter in the 1970s has become widely accepted as a lens through which to consider the history of the British Isles.[5] Hechter argues it is colonialism if Union is based on an unequal balance of power. He also connects the internal colonisation of the British Isles directly to the development of the overseas empire and compares Britain in the eighteenth century with early modern Spain and France and the assimilation of the periphery territories – and cultures – of Granada and Brittany taking place in parallel to the conquest of territories in the Americas.[6]

Writing what became the New British History, J. G. A. Pocock is also clear that while not colonies per se, the term 'empire' is applicable to England's dominion over the other nations of the British Isles; that is, English hegemony over three other kingdoms and not sharing its own sovereignty as would be the case in a union of equals. Like Hechter,

Pocock proposes a history of the British Isles in which the 'English showed themselves incapable of imagining Union as other than an annexation of the Scottish dimension'.[7] Pocock argues the 1707 Act of Union was 'one of incorporation not confederation ...They acquired empire [through] extension of the system to which they were accustomed.'[8] To the eighteenth-century English worldview, the Act of Union left something of an ambiguity: was Britain a nation that included Scotland or North Britain or was Scotland, like Ireland, part of the wider empire? As recounted by Linda Colley, eighteenth-century opinions on this were varied and vociferous in both England and Scotland.[9] Equally, some scholars of Irish and Scottish history have resisted the idea of a New British History, arguing that it is not so much a new British history but more an integrated study of English, Irish, and Scottish History which, while a welcome corrective from English-centric histories of the British Isles, runs the risk of losing sight of the distinctiveness of national histories.[10]

Pocock also points out that the Act of Union came at a time when the expanding overseas empire was changing the historic view of empire from the English conquest of the British Isles, as understood by the Plantagenets and Tudors, to the beginnings of a British global empire that would reach its zenith in the late nineteenth century. Accordingly, part of his vision for a New British History was to look outward as well as within, to see the history of the British Isles in the wider context of Atlantic History.[11] Pioneered in the late 1980s by historians such as Bernard Bailyn and Jack P. Greene in the United States, Nicholas Canny in Ireland, and British historian David Armitage, the British Atlantic world has since become a well-established subfield within the wider field of Atlantic history and the study of the shifting, overlapping transatlantic empires of the European powers.[12] Expanding from its origins in political history to encompass a diversity of thematic approaches and perspectives – from commodities and trade, to migration, race, religion, and material culture – British Atlantic history has successfully crossed the boundaries of national history in Britain and the United States in order to, as Simon Gunn puts it, understand the British Isles and the British overseas empire within a 'single analytical framework'.[13] One of the limitations of Atlantic history is, as identified by David Armitage, that due to the practical limitations of individual scholarship most monographic studies are what he terms 'Cis Atlantic'; by this, he means studies of one geographic region in the Atlantic context rather than holistic transnational studies that consider a historical phenomenon from a pan-Atlantic perspective.[14]

Recent studies of the eighteenth-century Scottish Highlands by scholars such as Silke Stroh can, in this light, be thought of as Cis Atlantic. For Stroh the idea of internal colonialism in the British Isles within the framework of the British Atlantic world is accepted and unremarkable.[15] In the attempt to understand the workings of nation and empire, scholars of eighteenth-century Scotland like Stroh also work within the wider intellectual framework of New Imperial History as informed by postcolonial theory: a complex, diverse, hybrid, and decentred – if essentially Eurocentric – approach to the history of European imperialism and its global impact.[16] Postcolonial theory has enabled historians of the British Isles and wider British Atlantic to explore how empire can be understood as exchanges not only between the metropole – the home nation state – and the colonies, but also between colonies: empire understood as the flows of 'goods, persons, books and ideas' through complex networks of interrelated sites, rather than as a single outward ripple of influence from the metropole.[17] Stroh argues unequivocally that the Scottish Gaels were 'victims of internal colonialism' and that the colonialism of the British government in the Highlands is directly 'comparable to its attitude towards Ireland and overseas territories'.[18] For Stroh, like Hechter and Pocock, Union was 'nominally consensual': an English hegemonic project that created a 'quasi-colonised country' within the nation state of Great Britain.[19] Within that political framework, Stroh argues, 'if Scotland resembled a conquered territory the Highlands were doubly colonized'.[20]

## British imperialism and the idea of Rome

If the British government acted as a colonial power in the Scottish Highlands, its imperial policies and practices were shaped by the idea of Rome and the Roman empire. Indeed, comparisons with Rome in the conquest and government of colonial territories is evident throughout early modern British history.[21] David Armitage identifies the deep-rooted and profound influence of Rome on British political thought in his analysis of the ideological origins of the British empire, wherein 'appeals to *imperium* and *coloniae*, throughout the Three Kingdoms, in the late medieval and early-modern period, indicate the Roman roots of British political ideology'.[22] As Armitage sets out, the idea of Rome denoted authority, described a territorial unit, and gave an 'historical foundation' to claims to both. In his analysis of the influence of European classical humanism on early modern political thought within the British Isles, Armitage argues that English thinking about Anglo-Scottish union, Scottish thinking about the Highlands, and, later, British thinking about the Highlands, was not only fundamentally imperialist but specifically and explicitly drawn from the model of the Rome and the Roman *impero*. English and Scottish humanists working in the European tradition, like Machiavelli, saw history as a source of power. Machiavelli 'recommended the Roman model' arguing that 'taking the course of Rome' – the course of constant imperial expansion – not only satisfied state pride and ambition but was the only way to secure the future of the state itself.[23] Freeman highlights the false assumption often made by scholars of empires that imperialism is consistent; that one empire is/was much like another in terms of both its ideologies and its actions: essentially territorial conquest and governance based on inequality not mutual compromise. However, he also notes that, while often inaccurate, ideologues of a particular empire often invoke former empires, 'extracting their own meaning' to justify their own ends; as is the case with the British in the eighteenth century and their obsessive comparison between themselves and the Roman empire based principally on the plundering of classical literary sources – Tacitus for the example of history, Virgil for a sense of mythic destiny – but also through the archaeological excavation of Roman sites in Britain.[24]

The idea of Rome saturates British thinking throughout the historical process of unification-cum-colonisation that started before the Union of Crowns in 1603 and continued in the Highlands through the decades that followed the 1745 Jacobite Uprising. Importantly, however, the lessons of Rome were not a generic inculcation of the rightness of empire but specific, such as the importance of good organisation, including building infrastructure: placing roads, forts, and towns at the centre of imperial strategy.[25]

## The practical and psychological effects of new building

Undertaking large infrastructure projects in new colonies was as much a part of British imperial strategy as soldiers and violence. Each project facilitated a specific practical action: making roads, bridges and harbours enabled the strategic deployment of violence; making permanent stone-built forts secured the peace; and making towns enabled settlement and established the spatial framework of British civil society. The psychological impact of this new built environment was also profound: an invasive spatial–material experience that was not just unsettling but intentionally disruptive for the Scottish Gaels living in the Highlands. Large, newly built objects rearranged their world, dissecting, blocking, and passing over the spaces and places they knew. New building materials and technologies were also introduced: local stone was quarried and cut for the first time; unfamiliar building components such as sash windows, cast-iron grates, and brass hinges were brought in from the Lowlands. These new things were also often constructed by non-Native migrant craftsmen who brought new skills such as surveying, engineering, masonry, and house carpentry, and unskilled labourers (soldiers working on military roads, Lowland masons building Ullapool, Irish 'navvies' on the Caledonian Canal). Gaels would not cross the new military roads; they were excluded from the new forts that dominated the Great Glen and they refused to settle in the new planned towns. In the wider imperial context, Barbara Bush describes these unsettling impositions as the 'material impact of colonisation', a visual and spatial strategy for the exercise of power.[26]

Moreover, new buildings and structures represented the worldview of their builders. Bush defines this aspect of imperialism as 'symbolic empire': the assertion of power beyond its physical impact as another important part of the toolkit of imperialism.[27] Here, the iconography of Rome can be immediately identified. Philip Ayres puts the case that, reaching far beyond politics, the idea of Rome defined the culture and cultural practices of the eighteenth-century British elite, casting all things in the light of Ancient Rome including the material world they built around themselves: objects and buildings made to represent their ideas and values.[28] For example, while nominally the head of clan Campbell, whose ancestral seat is Inveraray Castle in Argyll in the west Highlands, the second Duke of Argyll was born at Ham House in London and later lived in Surrey. He was a Whig politician and Field Marshall in the British Army who led the British forces against the Jacobites in the 1715 rebellion. As described by Ayres, the second Duke's tomb in Westminster Abbey 'gives classical expression to a life that was undoubtedly largely classical in its inspiration'.[29] Carved in marble, the Duke sits on his sarcophagus dressed in Roman armour, to his right is the figure of Pallas bearing a shield inscribed 'CN POMPEIVS', comparing the Hanoverian Duke to the Roman general Pompey who defended Rome against Caesar.[30]

Classicism, the design language of Rome, was, therefore, the universal design language of the eighteenth-century British elite. However, within that overarching framework, classicism could be used to represent more specific ideas, values, and qualities. When it came to building bridges, forts, and towns in the Scottish Highlands it follows that the British government not only looked to the strategic model of Rome, it also imitated Roman architectural forms and decoration. In the context of the Scottish Highlands, a new classically designed structure was not just a reflection of contemporary tastes but a specific representation of the self-image of the British government and its actors as New Roman imperialists. While the general message of a new fort is clear to all, lacking the classical education of the British elite, the nuanced meanings of Roman-inspired form and decoration would have been largely lost on the ordinary Gael. As such, much of this was internal, self-referential messaging intended to puff the pride of the imperialist and to make the colonist feel at home in a new strange land within a built environment that spoke their language. Barbara Bush argues that this self-fashioning was another part of the strategy of power, the link between colonialism and positive identity formation in the imagination of the rulers.[31]

A final point: to understand the complexities of cultural imperialism in the round, while not the focus of this chapter, the impact of Highland infrastructure projects should be considered alongside the new spatio-material experiences of the Highland elite in London and elsewhere in the south and overseas. The other side of imperial strategy was the assimilation of the Highland elite, the *fine*, into British elite society and culture.[32] Highland chiefs turned British aristocrats often became absentee landowners, leaving the Highlands to live among the English where – experiencing more pleasure than fear – they also had to navigate a new and unfamiliar material world: the *beau monde* of metropolitan London's squares, pleasure gardens, theatres, and taverns; or the assembly rooms of Bath and Cheltenham.[33] Highland aristocrats and the middle or *tacksman* class also found new roles, new experiences, serving the British government in North America, the Indian Subcontinent, and, later, Australasia and South Africa.[34] This process of assimilation fundamentally disconnected Highland aristocrats from the Highlands culturally as well as geographically, encouraging them to think as Britons rather than Gaels, in some cases putting Britain before Gaeldom in decision-making about their land and people (see Lord Macleod and the sale of his lands at Ullapool discussed below).

## The Tay Bridge at Aberfeldy

Built in 1733 in the wake of the first and second Jacobite Rebellions of 1715 and 1719, the Tay Bridge at Aberfeldy is the foremost monument to the British government's conquest of the Highlands: that is, phase one of forcible integration (Figure 2.1). It is a remarkable structure with profound practical and psychological significance. Practically, spanning the River Tay, the bridge was the centrepiece of the government's military road building programme in the Highlands overseen by Commander in Chief in Scotland, Lt General George Wade. Roads and bridges enabled troops and, importantly, field guns to move deep into the interior of the Highlands. Psychologically, spanning the river with five arches, the Tay Bridge was a large and visually striking, alien object imposed upon the Highland landscape as a symbol of the British presence. The bridge introduced unfamiliar technology and materials into the region. At a cost of £4,095, it was constructed of dressed stone worked by masons brought from England. The stone piers and cutwaters are supported by 1200 iron-shod oak pilings

**Figure 2.1** The Tay Bridge, Aberfeldy, Perthshire. Author's photograph

driven into the river bed: oak, iron, and the skills to work them all brought from the south. Designed by the leading (Lowland) Scottish architect William Adam, it is also a highly decorative Classical monument. The central arch bears the insignia of George II over a pair of crossed swords. The sides are decorated with stone cannon and tablets bearing Latin inscriptions. The parapets are topped with four stone obelisks that dominate the skyline. The hubristic Latin inscription, translated below, on one tablet is an elegy to Wade and his domination of the Highland landscape, including a direct comparison to Roman road-building in Britain:

> Admire this military road stretching on this
> side 250 miles beyond the limits of the
> Roman one, mocking moors and bogs, opened
> up through rocks and over mountains, and, as
> you see, crossing the indignant Tay. This
> difficult work G. Wade, Commander-in-Chief of
> the Forces in Scotland, accomplished by his own
> skill and ten years labour of his soldiers in the
> year of the Christian Era, 1733. Behold how
> much avail the Royal auspices of George 2nd.[35]

The Tay Bridge is a node in a network. Wade's masterplan was to create a network of forts and roads across the Highlands based on the Roman imperial 'limes' system.[36] The limes system was the Roman imperial strategy whereby territorial expansion and border security was facilitated by a network of roads and forts. As Edward Gibbon wrote of Roman roads in *The History of the Decline and Fall of the Roman Empire* (1776–89), 'Their primary object was to facilitate the march of the legions, nor was any country considered completely subdued till it had been rendered, in all its parts, pervious to the arms and authority of the conqueror'.[37] Serving from 1724–39, Wade oversaw the construction of four roads covering some 250 miles: Inverness to Fort William, Inverness to Dunkeld, Fort Augustus to Dalwhinnie over the mountainous Corrieyairich Pass, and Dalnarchardoch to Crieff via Tummel Bridge. Road-building took place from May to October: Wade's roads were metalled; that is, constructed of stone with gravel laid over.[38] All work, including forty stone-arched bridges, was undertaken by regular soldiers, working as labourers, and military surveyors (connecting to the wider empire, many of the British military surveyors who started their careers in the Highlands went on to work throughout the expanding overseas empire, including Canada, Florida, and Bengal).[39]

The Tay Bridge connected the Lowlands with the northern Highlands via the military road from Crieff to Dalnarchardock where it joined the main north–south road from Perth to the Great Glen, Fort August, and Inverness. It also guards the entrance to Glenlyon and the old drover's road to the west. It is hugely significant that Wade's roads were the first metalled roads in the Highlands and that, like Roman roads, they mostly follow straight lines, because of their immediate impact on the Highland landscape and, consequently, on the Highland people who refused to use or cross these new and alien, linear stone-spaces.[40] A new road enabled the movement of British troops – new people – into the Highlands while, through fear, restricted the movement of the Highland Gaels. For most of the eighteenth century, the only other large stone-built structure in the area of the Tay Bridge was the inn at Weem (Figure 2.2). First built by Wade as a site office for works at the Tay Bridge and beyond, this large, neat and regular building was one of many government-owned inns or King's Houses in the Highlands built at regular intervals along the military roads.[41] These provided accommodation for officers plus stabling for horses and a camp ground for the infantry. As reported by English traveller Henry Skrine in the 1790s, King's Houses were 'built originally at a great expence by government, which still allows annually a considerable sum for their repair and maintenance'.[42] The same system was employed in Canada where, after the Seven Years War, the British government built inns or 'mile houses' along the roads being laid to connect the port towns and coastal settlements of the Maritime provinces. This was another Roman idea.

**Figure 2.2** The Weem Inn, Weem, Aberfeldy, Perthshire. Author's photograph.

Roman roads featured state-owned inns or *mansion* for travelling officers every twenty miles. An exclusive space only accessible to officers and other members of the travelling elite, such as landowners and circuit judges, the accommodation and social space inside a Kings House was simple but nonetheless observed the design tastes of British polite society, providing a refuge in rooms that were, if basic, reassuringly familiar. The main parlour at the Weem Inn, for example, is a large, plain, open space with timber floorboards and wall panelling, punctuated by timber posts that support the ceiling on exposed cast-iron brackets (using the same materials technology as the pilings of the Tay Bridge). However, the fireplace is framed by a white marble neo-classical mantlepiece decorated with a Roman sarcophagus motif that projected politeness and civility to a select audience of colonial actors. It is a standard, prefabricated unit that would have been selected and brought up from a Lowland centre such as Edinburgh, flat-packed in sections before being installed by one of the Lowland masons working on the inn.

In 1910, the Scottish historian Thomas Wallace wrote, 'Nothing contributed more to the peace and prosperity of the Highlands than the roads that were constructed by General Wade and his successors'.[43] Wade's roads were made to enable the immediate military conquest of the Highlands, but they also began the longer term process of assimilation. State-sponsored road, bridge, and harbour building programmes continued under the auspices of the army until the 1760s and, later, under the Commissioners for Highland Roads and Bridges, 1803–28, which constructed a further 892 miles of road in the north of Scotland, taking flat, low-lying routes along the coast, glens, lochs, and rivers that, unlike Wade's roads, carried coach and cart traffic and connected towns and harbours.[44] From its triumphal beginnings with the Tay Bridge at Aberfeldy, the long-term strategy of road building by successive Westminster governments had, by the mid-nineteenth century, successfully brought the Highlands within what Jo Guldi terms the British 'infrastructure state'.[45]

## Fort George

Fort George represents phase two in the process of forcible integration: securing the peace. The crown jewel of the Highland limes system of roads and forts initiated by General Wade, Fort George is an immense, monumental, fortified site eleven miles north-east of Inverness on the southern shore of the Moray Firth (Figure 2.3). Commissioned and designed in the immediate aftermath of the 1745–46 Jacobite Rebellion, but taking over twenty years to complete, Fort George is not a single building but an enclosed military site that incorporates a range of buildings (stores, stables, barracks, chapel) and open spaces (parade grounds, supply yards, and connecting streets) behind a star-shaped perimeter of earth-filled ramparts. The accommodation buildings alone housed a governor's residence, officers' lodgings, and barracks for an artillery attachment and 1600 infantry troops.[46]

Like all the infrastructure projects considered here, Fort George had two purposes: practical and psychological. Practically its purpose was to control the navigation from the North Sea to Inverness, Loch Ness and the interior of the Highlands. The envisioned adversary was not so much the Jacobite Highlanders, but the French Navy. The guns on the ramparts of Fort George are trained across the water, waiting for French ships laden with arms and troops. In the event of a future uprising, Fort George would block supply lines and prevent foreign states accessing the interior with support for the Highlanders. This fits with a wider picture of European conflict and colonial expansion with other European powers using the same strategy against the British government elsewhere. A direct comparison can be drawn between Fort George and the Fortress of Louisbourg. The French built the Fortress of Louisbourg on the northern coast of Cape Breton at Ile Royale from c. 1716–44 – what would become the British colony of Nova Scotia. Its purpose was to guard the entrance to the Gulf of St. Lawrence,

Figure 2.3 Fort George, Ardersier, Inverness (Historic Environment Scotland).

and so access to the Great Lakes and the North American interior, from incursions by the British Navy.

Taken as a set with Fort William and Fort August, Fort George also fits within a deeper history of English, Scottish, and British military engagement in the Highlands that predates the 1745–46 Jacobite Rebellion. A chain of forts along the Great Glen was first conceived by Oliver Cromwell in the 1650s. Fort William at the western end of the Great Glen was first Cromwell's Fort Inverlochy: a quickly made wooden stockade, a frontier fort rebuilt in more permanent stone under William of Orange in the 1690s and renamed Fort William. At the eastern end of the glen, Cromwell also rebuilt Inverness castle. This became the first Fort George in 1727 after the first two Jacobite rebellions when it was rebuilt again by order of General Wade. Fort August, the mid-point of the chain, was also a response to the first two rebellions, built under Wade 1729 to 1742 and, an indirect Roman reference, named after Prince William Augustus, third son of George II (before he became (in)famous as 'Butcher Cumberland' for his persecution of Jacobites during and after the 1745 rebellion).

By the later eighteenth century, with the Highlands secured and government attention turning to settlement, the Highland forts became part of a wider imperial strategy. Fort George was used as a base for raising and training Highland regiments for services overseas where they were stationed in similar forts with similar names built for similar reasons throughout the British Atlantic and wider global empire. For instance, Fort George at the mouth of the Niagara River on Lake Ontario was built in the 1790s to defend the British against feared Indigenous American uprisings supported by the American Federal government.[47]

The psychological significance of Fort George is, however, perhaps greater than its practical. Completed decades after the '45, Fort George never fired a cannon and so could perhaps be considered an expensive white elephant in terms of government expenditure. However, like Edward I's string of castles put up along the coast from Chester to Anglesey following the earlier English conquest of Wales in the late-thirteenth century, building permanent stone fortifications was a slow process undertaken not to win the war, but to dominate the peace that follows. Unlike a timber stockade built quickly during the fighting, a stone-built fort was a permanent marker put down in the landscape by the conqueror. It is both highly visible from a distance and physically obstructive close up. An act of material imperialism, the construction of high walls, enclosing spaces that are both excluding and the source of promised violence, was a clear message to the Scottish Gaels living in that place that a new and unmovable authority has arrived and has no intention of leaving: that the Highlands is now their dominion, their place.[48] Like Edward I's castles at Caernarfon and Conwy, the sheer scale, stone mass, and evident permanence, the materiality, of Fort George was intended to crush the idea of future rebellion – and by this measure it was a complete success.

Fort George was designed by Colonel William Skinner, the King's Engineer for North Britain, and its construction contracted to the prominent British (Lowland Scottish) architects John, Robert, and James Adam (the sons of William Adam who designed the Tay Bridge). Skinner's design followed contemporary European (French) standards in fortification design.[49] The plan comprises a grid of streets, squares, and buildings framed within symmetrical, star-shaped perimeter walls. Not all British imperial forts follow this ideal in their design. While the symmetrical, star-shaped fort was the model for European military engineering since the late Renaissance, in practice many British forts of the global eighteenth century put strategic advantage, firing lines, and the dictats of climate and topography above the symbolism of pure geometry. A perfect star is surprisingly rare. Not so with Fort George. No doubt aided by the selection of a level site, Fort George is, above all, a symbol.

Moreover, while Skinner followed European design standards, the neo-classical design of the buildings within Fort George can, in the specific context of the mid-to-late eighteenth-century Highlands, be read as more than another example of the universality of classical culture at that time; more specifically representing the idea of the British state as the new Rome. Indeed, highlighting the pervasiveness of Roman history in British military culture, army surveyors working in the Highlands, well-read in Tacitus and his account of the Roman campaigns in the Highlands described in the *Agricola*, are known to have carried out archaeological surveys of Roman forts in their spare time.[50] Taking the long view of imperialist architecture and inner colonialism in the British Isles, the Roman iconography of Fort George and the Tay Bridge, again, bear comparison with Edward I's Welsh castles and the imperial-purple stone and Roman Eagle statue that dress the walls at Caernarfon.

Fort George was also an important symbolic space for the British soldiers who lived within its walls. For a British soldier garrisoned at Fort George in the later eighteenth century, the Highlands was still a potentially hostile territory: a strange land populated with strange, alien people with unfamiliar voices and customs. Even if never under attack, behind its deep ditches and high ramparts, protected by cannon, Fort George felt like a place of safety. Moreover, through the neo-classical design of its internal spaces, it felt like a familiar, British place. Dominated by the pedimented, neo-classical block of the governor's residence and officer's lodgings, the main square – in practice a parade ground – conveys a sense of urban civility more commonly associated with a polite square in London, Bath, or Edinburgh. Beyond the Highlands, this fits within a wider military building strategy with similar polite urban spaces connected to officer's lodgings at large-scale naval sites such as the Royal William Yard, Devonport, and Deptford Dockyard on the Thames (Figure 2.4). Retreating further from the outside world to the interior spaces at Fort George, British officers were abstracted entirely from the Highland locale into what was a facsimile of the sociable spaces of the south: once seated in the officers' mess, claret, silverware, and servants recreated the experience of polite dining found anywhere in Georgian Britain (Plate 3). This was not a unique quality of military sites and their officers' lodgings; rather, what is remarkable is that the British government thought it important to create these familiar facsimile domestic worlds within their military sites. As with the parlour of the Weem Inn and innumerable other interior spaces built by the British

**Figure 2.4** Governor's Residence and Officer's Lodgings, Fort George. Author's photograph.

around the world, consistent interior design extended a British 'horizon of meaning' throughout the empire.[51]

## Ullapool, Wester Ross

As noted by the Commissioners of Highland Roads and Bridges in their final report of 1823, 'the Highlands were at peace but in civilisation these remote mountain districts were at least 50 years behind the Lowlands and all parts of England'.[52] The planned town of Ullapool represents phase three of forcible integration: the 'civilising missions' launched in the decades after the 1745 Jacobite Rebellion to assimilate the Highlands once and for all into British society and culture at a time when there was an 'impatience with alternative ways of life'.[53] By aligning colonialism, capitalism, and culture, the British government sought to bring the peripheries of nation and empire under control.

As discussed by David Armitage, as put forth by the classical humanists of the sixteenth century, the English case for Anglo-Scottish union rested on the idea of 'the superiority of civility over barbarism and the necessity for civilised polities to carry their civility to those they thought barbarous'.[54] Moving forward in time, the implicit imperial bias in this idea was, in terms of eighteenth-century geopolitics, that British (read English and Lowland Scottish) society was essentially civilised and Gaelic society in the Highlands to the north was essentially savage and wild.[55] Civilising meant the cultural assimilation of Gaelic society in terms of its beliefs, values, customs, and rituals: to make them British. This worldview, bound in imperial perceptions of self as fundamentally superior – modern and civilised versus primitive and savage – provided the rationale for the superior people to impose change on the inferior people.[56] Indeed, the perceived barbarous and savage nature of Highland Gaels was often compared to that of Indigenous Americans (their homes described as wigwams).

Ullapool, on the north shore of Lochbroom in the region of Wester Ross in the northwest Highlands, was the first planned village established by the British Fisheries Society. Incorporated by Act of Parliament in July 1786, The British Fisheries Society for Extending the Fisheries and Improving the Sea Coasts of the Kingdom, was a quasi-governmental joint-stock company based in London. The Society was chaired by the fifth Duke of Argyll, grandson of the second Duke whose Roman-styled tomb lies in Westminster Abbey. Like his grandfather, the fifth Duke was a Field Marshall in the British Army and fought against a Highland Jacobite army (1745 Jacobite Rebellion), but he had a wider interest in the state of the Highlands and also chaired the Highland Society of London. Within the wider British project of Highland assimilation, the specific aim of the Society was to make new towns in the Highlands. As A. J. Youngson puts it, to the eighteenth-century mind creating new towns was 'the focus *par excellence* of civilising influences'.[57] In line with later eighteenth-century thinking, a new town would be a centre for industry that would be the catalyst for a capital economy based on the exchange of skills and products and, by this process, would suppress Highland culture and bring about a change in cultural practices from those considered barbarous (Scottish Gaelic) to those considered civil (British).[58] Accordingly, as peace became permanent, the later eighteenth-century Highlands experienced a new town building boom (towns in concept, often villages in practice; that is, small-scale settlements). T. C. Smout estimated in 1970 that some 150 planned villages were established across Scotland between 1750 and 1800.[59] Robert Naismith later put this figure nearer to 200.[60] The most recent study, by Douglas Lockhart, has put the total closer to 500.[61] The British Fisheries Society, however, only established four towns: Ullapool (1788), Tobermory on the Isle of Mull (1789), Stein on the Isle of Skye (1790), and Pulteneytown in Caithness (1807). Yet its public profile and status as a national, government-backed scheme meant it set the agenda for the hundreds of individual towns and village founded by private landowners in the later eighteenth and early nineteenth centuries. Overseen by a Board of Directors in London and managed on site by Lowland or English managers, the British Fisheries Society's mandate was to:

> employ the Capital Stock of the Company in purchasing Ground for the building of Free Towns, Villages, and Stations ... In the Highlands and Islands of Scotland, as the most effectual means of improving the Fisheries, Agriculture, Manufactures and other useful branches of industry there, and of employment for the Inhabitants at home.[62]

The Society's civilising mission was predicated on the belief that new towns would: attract both Lowlanders and Highland Gaels; generate wealth by capitalising on the Highlands natural resources in the form of the herring fishery; and promote civil – and civic – modes of behaviour. Although government sponsored, the Society was established and operated in the manner of an incorporated colonial company, like the Royal African Company or the East India Company. Its civilising mission for the Highlands was also framed in colonial terms. In 1786, the political economist John Knox presented *A Discourse on the Expediency of Establishing Fishing Stations in the Highlands of Scotland* to the Highland Society of London. In this foundational text, Knox proposes establishing towns in the Highlands as a colonial venture in the Atlantic context:

> Let us colonise in America, by which we shall be enriched, was the language of the last century. Let us abandon that distant country, by which we have been impoverished, is the language of the present day ... [consider] the advantages that would arise to manufactures and commerce from the establishment of a thriving, populous colony in these extreme parts of our island.[63]

While sharing the same concern with personal profit as the founders of English and Scottish colonial companies since the sixteenth century, as a late eighteenth-century political economist, Knox was not just interested in commercial exploitation of a new territory but invested in the ideas of capital economics, believing that the creation of towns based on commerce and industry would be the engine of the civilising mission.

As a national body committed to a Highland-wide town building programme, the British Fisheries Society followed in the wake of the Commission for Annexed and Forfeited Estates. The Annexed Estates Commission was established immediately after the 1745 Jacobite Rebellion and, while concerned with commerce and industry as a civilising force, was closely connected to the British military. The Commission was primarily established to manage the confiscated estates of Jacobite rebels; however, like the directors of the British Fisheries Society, its commissioners saw their wider mission as 'civilizing and improving the highlands of Scotland'.[64]

As noted by T. C. Smout, 'The Commissioners of the Forfeited Estates were obsessed by the thought that the Highlanders needed steadying and civilising: they were also gentleman well versed by their classical education in the civil and military habits of the Romans.'[65] Accordingly, after the Roman model, one of the civilising missions trialled was the establishment of colonial settlements or *coloniae* in the Highlands for veterans of the Seven Years War in Canada: *coloniae* were towns established by the Romans in conquered territory and settled with veteran soldiers.[66] The British government employed the same strategy in Canada with *coloniae* for Seven Years War veterans also established at sites such as Pictou in Nova Scotia.[67] Optimistically, the Commissioners reported in 1764 that 'the scheme for settling soldiers had succeeded' with the establishment of towns (villages) such as Fochabers, Callander, and Kinloch Rannoch.[68]

As peace became permanent, rebel estates were returned and the Commission was closed in 1774. One of the many projects in development at this time was for a new town at Ullapool on Lochbroom: a survey had been carried out and town plan produced as early as 1757 by military surveyor Peter May (Figure 2.5).[69] Reflecting the fluidity between British government bodies and their staff, this scheme was taken on by the British Fisheries Society for their first project twelve years later in 1788 when a new town plan was produced by another Annexed Estates surveyor, David Aitken, while May went on to work at Fort George. Here, two asides concerning Ullapool are worth mentioning as they highlight the complex geographies of British colonialism and the mobilities of its actors. First, in 1773, a year before the Commission was closed and five years before the establishment of the British Fisheries Society's new town at Ullapool, 200 Scottish Gaels sailed from Lochbroom for Canada aboard the *Hector*, settling at the veteran's *coloniae* at Pictou, Nova Scotia. Second, in 1788, in order to complete the paperwork for the sale of lands at Ullapool, the secretary to the Society had to travel from London to the English spa town of Bath to obtain the signature of Highland chief turned absentee landowner, Lord Macleod.

Ullapool was laid out and built under the direction of the Society's agent Robert Melvill. Mevill, a fishing merchant from Dunbar near Edinburgh, was appointed by the Society to oversee construction and to manage the town and its fishing business. Melvill arrived at Ullapool by ship in June 1788 bringing the people, skills, equipment, and materials needed to make a town from the Lothians (the Lowland region around Edinburgh):

> Eight thousand bricks and tiles, nineteen hundred and sixty seven pieces of fir timber being the roofing frames … twenty cartloads of lime, thirty barrels of oatmeal, ten barrels of barley, six cartloads of household furniture, two pairs

Figure 2.5 Ullapool, Lochbroom, Wester Ross (Historic Environment Scotland).

of cart wheels, one cart and a plough ... five builders, two joiners, a Slater, a blacksmith, two labourers, a heckler, a netmaker, a fisherman, a cooper and a fishcurer.[70]

Melvill reported to the Society that he was 'well pleased with the country and everything around us I hope to soon see a flourishing colony'.[71] Melvill's vision for the village was clear:

> If a town is intended in process of time to be built it should be done on a regular plan and a system of neatness and cleanness adopted, it should be at a convenient distance from the beach or where the fish is dressed and cured, if too near the people would apt to carry the fish to clean and dress them at the town which would occasion it to be dirty as the other villages in the north.[72]

Accordingly, Ullapool was laid out in 1789 to the simple grid plan designed by Aitken. Melvill had faith that this 'regular plan' would impose order on the Highland Gaels and prevent them from reverting to their barbarism.[73] Although, as shown in a sketch plan of the town as executed that year, Melvill himself comprised the regularity of the grid by building along the shore and, in so doing, breaking the parallel with the street above.[74] The plan for Ullapool fits with what Robert Home identifies as the 'British model of colonial town planning', including: 'a policy of deliberate urbanisation', the 'town planned and laid out in advance of settlement'; and, 'wide streets laid out in geometric, usually gridiron form'.[75] However, the plan does not include any public squares which Home also specifies. Focused instead around a set of waterfront industrial buildings, Ullapool's basic grid represents what Spiro Kostof terms the 'practical model' of town planning, 'factual, functional, cool, not in the least magical'.[76] By contrast, May's earlier Annexed Estates plan for Ullapool had followed that body's standard planning model of a grid with a central public square that provided a civic space overseen by a church and courthouse. This is more in line with Home's model of the typical British colonial town and was a typical eighteenth-century interpretation of Roman colonial town planning, whereby Roman colonial planners deployed an 'urban kit' of a grid with a central public square surrounded by civic buildings, as can be seen across the Highlands and European colonies throughout the Atlantic world from James Wadsworth's 1748 plan for New Haven, Connecticut, to the Spanish colonial capital of Santo Domingo in the present-day Dominican Republic, laid out in the sixteenth century.[77]

Following Ullapool, the British Fisheries Society used the same waterfront-industry focused grid-plan a year later at Tobermory but then, later, included town squares in its plans for Stein and Pulteneytown. This change in planning model suggests a shift in the balance of the Society's thinking from faith in the capital economy to something more civic as the engine to drive their particular civilising mission. This shift in planning policy coincided with Sir William Pulteney replacing the fifth Duke of Argyll as chair of the Society and suggests a growing distance from Knox and his influence at the Society's foundation. Pulteney, a Lowland Scot, had no personal connection to the Highlands but was deeply involved in urban planning: he owned the Bathwick estate at Bath and in the 1790s was closely involved with its development as Bath's second New Town, working with architects including Thomas Baldwin, Robert Adam, and Thomas Telford.[78]

New towns were intended to forcibly introduce a new way of life through the imposition of the grid, straight streets, and neat and regular stone-buildings. If the intention was to move the Highlands and its people from barbarism to civility, to assimilate Gaeldom into British society and culture – to make the same – difference also mattered as a power strategy.[79] May's 1757 plan for Ullapool reveals the sharp contrast between the formality of the proposed grid plan and the informal clusters or *clachan* of so-called 'black houses' that comprised the existing communities of Ullapool, Blairdu, and Kannchrine. These traditional settlements were destroyed to clear the way for the new grid. As Annette Smith writes of the Annexed Estates urban schemes, 'the grandeur of this vision becomes awe-inspiring ... a vision for a truly authoritarian society'.[80] The Scottish Gaels living in a place remade by others were, as Haldane describes, 'bewildered participants in a game where all the rules were changed'.[81] However, imposed order and the British idea of urban civility were also resisted. The Society's 1790 report on Ullapool criticises the Gaels' resistance to change as they ignored the grid and the Society's detailed and extensive building regulations and proceeded to build 'huts' 'scattered over the ground'; Melvill was instructed to remove them until 'the streets and lots marked out by Aitken could be properly restored'.[82] His subsequent attempts to impose order in Ullapool, to restore the grid, were met with further resistance, including rioting during which he was pulled from his horse and beaten.[83]

## Conclusion

Ultimately, Ullapool was not a great success as a fishing town. Like Wade's roads that did not prevent the 1745 Rebellion, or Fort George that never fired a cannon, it can be argued that the British Fisheries Society's urban experiments were failures: expensive white elephants. However, when viewed as interconnected outcomes of a single long-term and coherent strategy for the colonisation and assimilation of the Scottish Highlands – the making of North Britain – these government infrastructure projects were a singular success. Viewed in the context of similar infrastructure projects undertaken throughout an expanding overseas empire, the imperialist intentions behind British government strategy in the Highlands, the imperial self-image of the State and its actors, and the impact of both on Scottish Gaeldom, is most clearly understood when seen in the light of imperial Rome. Like the Romans, making roads, building forts, and establishing towns represent three phases of a forcible integration-by-infrastructure strategy undertaken by the British state in the Scottish Highlands over the course of the eighteenth century. Roads enabled military conquest. Forts, built after conquest, secured the peace. Towns then followed as part of the civilising mission to assimilate the Highlands into British society and culture.

## Notes

1. Linda Colley, *Britons: Forging the Nation 1707–1837* (New Haven: Yale University Press, 2009).
2. Colley, *Britons*, 119.
3. Silke Stroh, *Gaelic Scotland in the Colonial Imagination: Anglophone Writing from 1600 to 1900* (Evanston: Northwestern University Press, 2016), 36.
4. Stroh, *Gaelic Scotland in the Colonial Imagination*, 33.
5. Michael Hechter, *Internal Colonialism: The Celtic Fringe in British National Development, 1536–1966* (London: Routledge and Kegan Paul, 1975), 30.
6. Hechter, *Internal Colonialism*, 30.
7. J. G. A. Pocock, *The Discovery of Islands: Essays in British History* (Cambridge: Cambridge University Press, 2005), 136.
8. Pocock, *Discovery of Islands*, 145.
9. Colley, *Britons*.
10. Jane Ohlmeyer, 'AHR Forum: Seventeenth-Century Ireland and the New British and Atlantic Histories', *The American Historical Review* 104, no. 2 (1999): 447.
11. Ohlmeyer, 'AHR Forum: Seventeenth-Century Ireland', 457.
12. See Bernard Bailyn, *Atlantic History* (Cambridge, MA: Harvard University Press, 2019); *Atlantic History: Concept and Contours* (Cambridge, MA: Harvard University Press, 2005); *Soundings in Atlantic History: Latent Structures and Intellectual Currents, 1500–1830*, eds Bernard Bailyn and Patricia L. Denault (Cambridge, MA: Harvard University Press, 2009); *The Oxford Handbook of the Atlantic World: 1450–1850*, eds Nicholas Canny and Philip Morgan (Oxford: Oxford University Press, 2011); Nicholas P. Canny, *Kingdom and Colony: Ireland in the Atlantic World, 1560–1800* (Baltimore: Johns Hopkins University Press, 1988); *Atlantic History: A Critical Appraisal*, eds Jack P. Greene and Philip D. Morgan (Oxford: Oxford University Press, 2008); Jack P. Greene, *Creating the British Atlantic: Essays on Transplantation, Adaptation, and Continuity* (Charlottesville: University of Virginia Press, 2013); *The British Atlantic World, 1500–1800*, eds David Armitage and Michael J. Braddick (Basingstoke: Palgrave Macmillan, 2002).

13 Simon Gunn, *History and Cultural Theory* (Harlow: Pearson Longman, 2006), 175.
14 David Armitage and Michael J. Braddick, 'Introduction', in Armitage and Braddick, *The British Atlantic World, 1500–1800*, 5.
15 Stroh, *Gaelic Scotland*.
16 Kathleen Wilson, *A New Imperial History: Culture, Identity, and Modernity in Britain and the Empire, 1660–1840* (Cambridge: Cambridge University Press, 2004); Gunn, *Cultural Theory*; Barbara Bush, *Imperialism and Postcolonialism* (Harlow: Pearson Longman, 2006); Vivek Chibber, *Postcolonial Theory and the Specter of Capital* (London: Verso Books, 2013).
17 John Clive and Bernard Bailyn, 'England's Cultural Provinces: Scotland and America', *The William and Mary Quarterly*, 11.2 (1954): 207.
18 Stroh, *Gaelic Scotland*, 58.
19 Stroh, *Gaelic Scotland*, 35.
20 Stroh, *Gaelic Scotland*, 42.
21 Philip Freeman, 'British Imperialism and the Roman Empire', in *Roman Imperialism: Post Colonial Perspectives*, eds Nicholas J. Cooper and Jane Webster (Leicester: University of Leicester, 1996), 25.
22 David Armitage, *The Ideological Origins of the British Empire* (Cambridge: Cambridge University Press, 2000), 29–30.
23 Armitage, *Ideological Origins*, 129–30.
24 Freeman, 'British Imperialism and the Roman Empire', 20–1.
25 Freeman, 'British Imperialism and the Roman Empire', 26.
26 Bush, *Imperialism and Postcolonialism*, 59.
27 Bush, *Imperialism and Postcolonialism*, 46, 123.
28 Philip Ayres, *Classical Culture and the Idea of Rome in Eighteenth-Century England* (Cambridge: Cambridge University Press, 1997), 64.
29 Ayres, *Classical Culture*, 65.
30 Ayres, *Classical Culture*, 67.
31 Bush, *Imperialism and Postcolonialism*, 121.
32 Colley, *Britons*, 127.
33 Hannah Greig, *The Beau Monde: Fashionable Society in Georgian London* (Oxford: Oxford University Press, 2013); Bush, *Imperialism and Postcolonialism*, 123.
34 Andrew MacKillop, *'More Fruitful than the Soil': Army, Empire and the Scottish Highlands, 1715–1815* (East Lothian: Tuckwell Press, 2000).
35 Bruce Walker and Graham Ritchie, *Exploring Scotland's Heritage: Fife and Tayside* (Edinburgh: Royal Commission on the Ancient and Historic Monuments of Scotland, 1987), 46.
36 Bush, *Imperialism and Postcolonialism*, 116.
37 Edward Gibbon, *The History of the Decline and Fall of the Roman Empire. By Edward Gibbon, Esq; Volume the First* (Dublin: William Hallhead, 1776), 72–3.
38 A. R. B. Haldane, *New Ways Through the Glens* (Edinburgh: Thomas Nelson and Sons, 1962), 4.

39 Richard Hingley, 'Projecting Empire: The Mapping of Roman Britain', *Journal of Social Archaeology* 6, no. 3 (2006): 341.
40 M. C. Bishop, *The Secret History of the Roman Roads of Britain* (Barnsley: Pen & Sword, 2015).
41 Daniel Maudlin, 'Inns and Elite Mobility in Late Georgian Britain', *Past & Present* 247, no. 1 (2020): 37–76.
42 Henry Skrine, *Three Successive Tours in the North of England, and Great Part of Scotland* (London: W. Bulmer and Co., 1795), 145.
43 Thomas Wallace, 'Military Roads and Fortifications in the Highlands, with Bridges and Milestones', *Proceedings of the Society of Antiquaries of Scotland* 45 (1911): 318–33.
44 Haldane, *New Ways*, 250.
45 Jo Guldi, *Roads to Power: Britain Invents the Infrastructure State* (Cambridge, MA: Harvard University Press, 2012).
46 Gordon Ewart and Dennis Gallagher, 'The Fortifications of Fort George, Ardersier, near Inverness: Archaeological Investigations 1990–2005', *Post-Medieval Archaeology* 44, no. 1 (2010): 105–34.
47 Emily Mann, 'To Build and Fortify: Defensive Architecture in the Early Atlantic Colonies', in *Building the British Atlantic World: Spaces, Places, and Material Culture, 1600–1850*, eds Daniel Maudlin and Bernard L. Herman (Chapel Hill: University of North Carolina Press, 2016), 31–52.
48 Bush, *Imperialism and Postcolonialism*, 144.
49 Carolyn J. Anderson, 'Constructing the military landscape: The Board of Ordnance maps and plans of Scotland, 1689–1815' (PhD thesis, University of Edinburgh, 2010), 122.
50 Richard Hingley, 'Projecting Empire: The Mapping of Roman Britain', *Journal of Social Archaeology* 6, no. 3 (2006): 340.
51 Daniel Maudlin and Bernard L. Herman, 'Introduction', in Maudlin and Hernan, *Building the British Atlantic World: Spaces, Places, and Material Culture*, 6.
52 Haldane, *New Ways*, 29.
53 Stroh, *Gaelic Scotland*, 35.
54 Armitage, *Ideological Origins*, 51–2.
55 C. G. Caffentzis, 'Civilizing the Highlands: Hume, Money and the Annexing Act', *Historical Reflections* 31, no. 1 (2005): 182.
56 Stroh, *Gaelic Scotland*, 37.
57 A. J. Youngson, *After the Forty-Five: Economic Impact on the Scottish Highlands* (Edinburgh: Edinburgh University Press, 1973), 37.
58 Hechter, *Internal Colonialism*, 161.
59 T. C. Smout, 'The Landowner and the Planned Village in Scotland, 1730–1830', in *Scotland in the Age of Improvement: Essays in Scottish History in the Eighteenth Century*, eds Nicholas T. Phillipson and Rosalind Mitchison (Edinburgh: Edinburgh University Press, 1970), 75.
60 Robert J. Naismith, *The Buildings of the Scottish Countryside* (London: Victor Gollancz, 1985), 38.

61 Douglas Lockhart, 'Planned Villages in North East Scotland, 1750–1860', in *The New Town Phenomenon*, ed. John Frew (St Andrews: St Andrews University Press, 2000), 25–40.
62 National Records of Scotland (NRO)/ GD9/1/10.
63 John Knox, *A Discourse on the Expediency of Establishing Fishing Stations: Or Small Towns, in the Highlands of Scotland and the Hebride Islands* (London: J. Walter, 1786).
64 'Abstracts of the Act for Annexing Certain Forfeited Estates to the Crown Unalienably', *Scots Magazine*, April, 1752, 161.
65 Smout, 'Planned Villages', 90.
66 Annette M. Smith, *Jacobite Estates of the Forty-Five* (Edinburgh: J. Donald, 1982), 143.
67 Daniel Maudlin, 'Architecture and Identity on the Edge of Empire: The Early Domestic Architecture of Scottish Settlers in Nova Scotia, Canada, 1800–1850', *Architectural History* 50 (2007): 95–123.
68 Smith, *Estates of the Forty-Five*, 148.
69 NRS/RHP3400, 'A survey and design for a village at Ullapool', 1757.
70 NRS/GD9/4/63.
71 NRS/GD9/4/68.
72 NRS/GD9/3/37.
73 NRS/GD9/3/616.
74 NRS/GD9/3/617.
75 Robert Home, *Of Planting and Planning: The Making of British Colonial Sites* (London: Routledge, 2nd edn 2013), 10.
76 Spiro Kostof, *The City Shaped: Urban Patterns and Meanings Through History* (London: Thames and Hudson, 1991), 15.
77 Edward Bispham, 'Coloniam Deducere: How Roman Was Roman Colonization during the Middle Republic?', in *Greek and Roman Colonization: Origins, Ideologies and Interactions*, eds Guy Jolyon Bradley and John-Paul Wilson (Swansea: Classical Press of Wales, 2006), 74, 78.
78 Daniel Maudlin, 'Robert Mylne, Thomas Telford and the Architecture of Improvement: The Planned Villages of the British Fisheries Society, 1786–1817', *Urban History* 34, no. 3 (2007): 453–80.
79 Wilson, *New Imperial History*, 4.
80 Smith, *Estates of the Forty-Five*, 143.
81 Haldane, *New Ways*, 19.
82 Edinburgh, SRO/GD9/3/583.
83 Bush, *Imperialism and Postcolonialism*, 52.

# 3

# 'Housing the Poorest Poor': the Irish other in nineteenth-century Liverpool

## John Belchem

Ireland, often considered as both the first and last colony of the British empire, fits uneasily into conventional notions of colonial experience. Its geographical proximity (rather than exotic distance) and its formal integration within the United Kingdom, following the Act of Union (1801), seemingly place it apart from far-flung imperial territories and settlements. While historians deliberate and disagree over Ireland's precise 'colonial' status, there is broad consensus on two interconnected aspects of the ambiguous relationship between the metropole and its adjacent island. Ireland served as a laboratory for social, administrative, and constitutional policies subsequently adopted elsewhere in the empire, while the nationalist response in Ireland provided inspiration for independence movements in other colonies.[1] When applied to nineteenth-century Liverpool, the inner empire perspective adopted in this volume sheds light on similar but inverse developments of the Irish relationship. The flood of Irish migrants into Liverpool compelled the local authorities into new and experimental forms of social intervention, justified in the face of laissez-faire ideology and ratepayer parsimony by moral panic about the Irish and their 'contaminating' presence. Although stigmatised as the internal 'other', the migrants – an increasing presence – were by no means passive victims of crude prejudice and denigratory stereotyping. They were soon to formulate their own versions of Irishness, an ethno-confessional affiliation which served at first protective and defensive functions against disadvantage, disability, and discrimination, but then became increasingly assertive, allowing them to gain municipal representation and take the lead themselves in pioneering housing reform. Secure in their ethnic enclave, the Irish in Liverpool secured a form of nationalist home rule in the north end of the city, 'a piece cut off from the old sod itself'.

Following the Act of Union, the number of Irish arrivals in Liverpool expanded exponentially as free trade, implemented in phases, took full (and devastating) effect in the 1820s. Unable to compete, Irish domestic industries went into rapid decline: Ireland became a country exporting food and cheap labour. Transport developments facilitated the mass migration outflow – what would now be described as free movement within a single market. With the introduction of steam navigation in the 1820s, fares fell sharply for the passage across the Irish Sea and, if desired, for subsequent trans-shipment on the new 'Atlantic ferry'. Well ahead of the famine influx, the 1841 census already recorded 49,639 Irish-born in Liverpool, some 17.3 per cent of the population, seemingly immovably located at the bottom of the local occupational and social hierarchy.[2]

The Irish arrived during a turbulent but formative period of adaptation and expansion, as Liverpool sought new routes and markets together with a much-needed change in image and external perception following abolition of the infamous slave trade in 1807. With unashamed commercial pride, Georgian Liverpool had established itself as the 'slaving capital of the world', oblivious to external criticism. Having cut itself off from the mainstream of changing British ideology, Liverpool was soon faced with what Seymour Drescher has described as 'a threat not just to its economic base but to its cultural identity'.[3] As abolitionists claimed the high ground, materialist 'slaving' Liverpool stood condemned for barbarism, philistinism, and lack of civilised culture. After abolition, moral and social distancing (in the original sense of the term) developed apace. Reassessment of the past privileged those who had opposed the trade against the odds, most notably William Roscoe and his circle of merchant-scholars. Reviled at the time, the Roscoe circle were rehabilitated as role models for 'Liverpolis', the foundation figures of Liverpool's postabolitionist pre-eminence in the civilised culture of commerce, formative years in establishing the superiority of Liverpool gentlemen over Manchester men.[4]

Cultural rebranding was accompanied by rapid and successful economic realignment with the opening of lucrative new markets and trade to Africa and elsewhere across the oceans. Several of the new markets dealt with products produced by ongoing (and still legal) slave labour, but there was a distinct change in mood and character, symbolised by an increased cosmopolitan presence. With the opening up of new markets, ethnic diversity became increasingly apparent and welcome: significant numbers of Kru (from West Africa), Lascar (from the Indian sub-continent), Chinese, and other sea-faring communities within and beyond the 'black Atlantic', were drawn to the port and its open waterfront culture, often more than temporarily. Entranced by such developments, historians of the port have tended to focus on exotic (not always financially secure) transoceanic trade.[5] As it was, Liverpool's prosperity as global seaport was underwritten by its near hegemony in the movement of goods and people within and around the 'inland' Irish Sea, Liverpool's 'private celtic empire'.[6]

The arrival of unprecedented numbers of Irish on cheap passenger vessels from the 1820s challenged the smooth progress of Liverpool's postabolition realignment, exposing division between the cultured elite of Liverpolitans keen to promote grandiose schemes of civic adornment (such as the magnificent but costly St George's Hall) and social reformers anxious to deploy municipal resources in much-needed sanitary and public health intervention. As the Irish influx intensified, reformers called for urgent action to reverse Liverpool's growing and unenviable reputation as 'the black spot on the Mersey'. Night asylums, established in the early nineteenth century to provide temporary refuge for the 'houseless poor' (shipwrecked, stranded, castaway, robbed, sick, or destitute sailors who lacked any claim on the parish or call upon local charities) were rapidly adapted to take poor Irish arrivals in Liverpool off the streets, 'affording shelter to the most destitute and wretched of the human species'.[7] A much lauded innovation, Liverpool was the first to appoint a Medical Officer of Health, Dr Duncan, but his advocacy of heavy expenditure on sanitary works (which he believed the corporation could well afford with its vast income from dock dues) was accompanied less by materialist understanding of the poverty at the bottom of the local residential and social hierarchy with its vast casual labour market, than by 'racist' condemnation of the Irish famine influx into Liverpool.

Public health officials and social investigators had no hesitation in applying an ethnic label to the worst areas of the city, the 'squalid Liverpool' running along the low-lying westernmost strip from the Dingle to Sandhills, home to a population 'more dense than is to be found in any city of the civilised world'. The Irish tended to congregate around 'core-streets' in the city's two major working-class areas, close to the docks and the casual labour markets: the 'instant slum' of the north end with its purpose-built court housing, and the failed middle-class suburb of the south end, hastily 'made down' into overcrowded and cellared street housing (Figure 3.1). Over time, there was to be substantial concentration in the north end, extending out from the two pre-famine 'clusters', the eastern half of Exchange and Vauxhall Wards, and behind the docks in Scotland Ward. By contrast, in the south end, where there were original 'clusters' between Park Lane and the docks, and between the Custom House and Derby Square, there was less coherence and increased fragmentation, accentuated by a growing Ulster Protestant presence. In the statistical terms of historical demography, these were not Irish ghettos. Outside the 'scale trap' of core streets such as Lace Street, Crosbie Street, and Marybone ('as Irish as any part of Dublin'),[8] the index of segregation was not significantly high. The persistence rate was remarkably low (no more than 9–18 per cent, Colin Pooley has calculated, remained at the same address from one census to the next) as the Irish, lacking attachment to particular jobs or dwellings,

Figure 3.1 2 Court, Mount View, Liverpool, early twentieth century (c.1913). This image is part of a series of slum photographs taken by Richard Brown. On one of the doors on the distant wall it is just possible to discern a slogan proclaiming the allegiance of the court: 'God Bless the Pope'. Courtesy of Liverpool Central Library and Archives.

favoured frequent short-distance movements within familiar territory. Overall, the size of Liverpool Irish households was smaller than the average Liverpool household as they were often headed by a single parent and had fewer servants, but living conditions tended to be much worse because of high levels of multiple occupancy.[9]

'It is doubtful whether a town like Liverpool, which can be reached at a trifling expense by the most destitute of the Irish poor, will ever be as healthy as towns less accessible to that poverty-stricken people', Thomas Baines rued in his *History of the Commerce and Town of Liverpool*.[10] In a series of reports and publications in the early 1840s, ahead of the famine influx, Dr Duncan castigated the Irish 'who inhabit the filthiest and worst-ventilated courts and cellars, who congregate the most numerously in dirty lodging-houses, who are the least cleanly in their habits, and the most apathetic about everything that befalls them'.[11] The critical factor was not material or environmental circumstance, but 'racial' character.

> It may be said that this is merely the result of their greater poverty, which deprives them of a proper supply of the necessaries of life, and compels them

to select the most unhealthy (because the cheapest) localities as their places of residence. To a great extent this is true; but at the same time there appears to be, among the lowest class of Irish, such an innate indifference to filth, such a low standard of comfort, and such a *gregariousness*, as lead them, even when not driven by necessity, into the unhealthy localities where they are found to congregate; and which they render still more unhealthy by their recklessness and their peculiar habits.[12]

Unsuited to urban living, the 'low' Irish – a symbolic term with topographical and cultural connotations – were a contaminating presence responsible for Liverpool's notoriously high mortality rate and moral degeneration:

> By their example and intercourse with others they are rapidly lowering the standard of comfort among their English neighbours, communicating their own vicious and apathetic habits, and fast extinguishing all sense of moral dignity, independence and self-respect ... I am persuaded that so long as the native inhabitants are exposed to the inroads of numerous hordes of uneducated Irish, spreading physical and moral contamination around them, it will be in vain to expect that any sanitary code can cause fever to disappear from Liverpool.[13]

In the metaphoric logic of the diseased social body, the Irish in Liverpool embodied 'all the pathologies of violence, unreason and contagion that so obsessed the early Victorians'.[14] When the humanitarian crisis of the potato famine in the 1840s dramatically intensified the inflow, drastic interventionist social engineering became the order of the day. In the face of laissez-faire sentiment and ratepayer retrenchment, the expense was justified through ethnic denigration of the Irish 'other', a 'contaminating' presence within the unreformed and unprotected 'social body'. Such fears of the residuum were more than sufficient to counter ratepayer parsimony, ensuring much-needed expenditure on sanitary and public health schemes at a time when municipal funds were otherwise directed towards grandiose architectural projects of Liverpolitan civic pride. Duncan was an influential force in promoting the Liverpool Sanitary Act 1846 to establish a pioneer public health service with powers to enter and inspect cellars and lodging-houses, as well as to clean and drain the exterior environment in what he described as 'the most unhealthy town in England'. Duncan, however, was not sanguine of ready improvement 'so long as the influx of destitute Irish is allowed to continue unchecked'.[15]

As trans-shipment port and central hub of the famine Irish diaspora, Liverpool, 'the nearest place that wasn't Ireland', had to cope disproportionately with its casualties. Well over 90 per cent of Irish emigrants to the United States in the 1840s travelled via Liverpool, but many did not make it across the Atlantic. Whether by ill fortune (having been fleeced by the notorious waterfront 'sharpers'), ill health, or design, they remained in Liverpool.[16] Whatever their circumstances or original intention, they were categorised as 'the residuum of the Irish – that is, those cases who had not "wing" enough, when they came from Ireland to carry them across the Atlantic'.[17] Technically internal migrants exercising the right of free movement within a single market and united kingdom, the Irish who remained in Liverpool, whether by design or misfortune, were judged harshly, stigmatised, and treated as the local underclass, the internal other. 'Only fitted for the ruder form of labour', they were labelled as 'the dregs' by Father Nugent, an Irish-Liverpudlian himself, a kind of underclass, unable, unwilling, or unsuited to take advantage of opportunities elsewhere in Britain or the new world.[18] It was 'Irishness' of this order – immobile, inadequate, and irresponsible – that purportedly set Liverpool and its notorious social problems apart.

In the worst of the famine years, 'black' 1847, some 300,000 Irish arrived in Liverpool. Rushton, the stipendiary magistrate, calculated that within twelve hours of disembarkation, they were to be 'found in one of three classes – paupers, vagrants, or thieves'.[19] As migrants flooded in and typhus spread, 'lazaretto politics' were the order of the day to contain 'Irish fever'. Described by Duncan as a 'City of the Plague', Liverpool became in the words of the Registrar General's third quarterly report for 1847, 'the hospital and cemetery of Ireland'.[20] Commandeered by the Select Vestry, warehouses near the docks were crammed to bursting with fever victims; four old prison hulks were requisitioned as floating hospitals in the Mersey; and the sick were to be excluded from wealthy districts. Every step was taken to prevent the spread of fever beyond the 'low Irish', reinforcing the pattern of residential 'social distancing': at one point, no less than 88 per cent of sick persons under the care of the health authorities were Irish. The greatest incidence of death from fever, diarrhoea, and dysentery occurred in Scotland, Vauxhall, and Exchange in the north end and Great George in the south end, wards with large Irish-born populations – Frank Neal has calculated the number of such Irish deaths as at least 5,500 in 1847. In Lace Street alone there were some 472 deaths, one third of all the inhabitants. Ten Catholic 'martyr' priests fell victim to the 'Irish fever' while tending to their sick flock, as did a similar number of doctors and the Revd John Johns, the Unitarian domestic missionary.[21] Noting the cost of Irish in-migration in terms of mounting public expenditure on the poor law, police, and public health, the *Morning Chronicle* was prompted to observe: 'The town of Liverpool feels, through the sensitive medium of the pocket, that it has to pay a large price for the privilege of being the greatest port of the west, and that its advantages in being the outlet to America are nearly counterbalanced by the disadvantages in being the inlet from Ireland.'[22]

As Medical Officer of Health, Duncan sought ever greater powers and expenditure to tackle the town's notorious public health problems. There was an economic imperative here: the 'unhealthy' Irish presence put at risk more profitable and lucrative forms of migration, threatening Liverpool's pre-eminence as the human and commercial *entrepôt* linking the old world and the new. Integral to realignment following abolition of the slave trade, the passage of free migrants across the oceans contributed much to the seaport's economic growth. Migrants were valued as a form of outward 'cargo', as it were, balancing inbound commodity trades from the Americas and the colonies. Achieved through continued investment in an ever more impressive dock system, pre-eminence was readily apparent by the mid-nineteenth century: in 1851 Liverpool sent 455 ships to New York carrying 159,480 passengers, while Le Havre sent 124 ships and 31,859 passengers, and Bremen 132 ships and 19,431 passengers. Railway development was another important factor with feeder services from the industrial areas of Britain and further afield: the rail link between Hull and Liverpool provided a convenient short route for Scandinavians and north Germans wishing to cross to America.[23]

While crucial to the economic model of Liverpool shipping (and to the prosperity of the many agents, lodging-house keepers, chandlers, and other dealers servicing the needs of migrants and other passengers ahead of embarkation), the pattern of trade was not without risk and adverse domestic consequences. Gateway to the empire and the new world, Victorian Liverpool was what historical geographers term a 'diaspora space', a contact zone between different ethnic groups with differing needs and intentions as transients, sojourners, or settlers – and, as Duncan rued, with differing standards of personal hygiene. For those awaiting embarkation, the cheapest emigrant lodging houses were located in Liverpool's notorious 'sailortown', an urban strip of bars, brothels, street markets, and other services adjacent to the docks and the 'low Irish'.[24] The Health Committee noted that 'the worst description of these houses were those kept by low Irishmen, in courts and narrow streets, and they were chiefly frequented by migratory Irish people, vagrants, and others'.[25] Overwhelmed by the famine influx, the authorities were unable to implement the new bye-law clauses of the Liverpool Sanitary Act (1846) until August 1848, only to encounter a characteristic local difficulty: 'Fully nine-tenths of the Keepers are Irish, and about 29 per cent are unable to write. Experience has shown that few of them can be depended on for carrying out the Bye-laws, unless closely watched.'[26]

Moral panic about the Irish was to persist, reinforced in the 1860s amidst the commercial distress of the cotton famine and the subsequent onset first of typhus then of cholera. Drawing a convenient distinction between typhoid and typhus, the *Report of the Sub-Committee on the causes of the excessive mortality of the Town* refused to accord blame to the local authorities. Whatever the criticisms, sanitary reform had proved sufficient to reduce deaths from typhoid to a minimum: no such intervention, however, could contain typhus, the Irish fever. Trench, Duncan's successor as Medical Officer of Health, suggested that 'nationality' accounted for 'those personal habits and that indigence which I believe has more to do with typhus than mere external physical causes ... there are streets so open and so free from glaring physical defects of construction, that I could not include them in my presentment to the Grand Jury, and yet such streets, because of their being inhabited by poor Irish, are the foci of typhus'. Shearer, the Medical Officer to the Toxteth Board of Guardians, was more emphatic: the Irish were 'of naturally improvident and filthy habits ... We have a vast work to do to break this large section of the population off from their native ideas of health and cleanliness, the rustic *hygiene*, in short'.[27] Similar factors were also held accountable for the spread of cholera in 1866. Originally restricted to German and other emigrant ships (a public health hazard of a global port city like Liverpool), cholera took hold on land in Bispham Street, 'inhabited by the lowest of the Irish population, and situated in the worst part of what may be justly described as the chief fever district of the parish'. To Trench's horror, relatives of the first victim refused to allow the immediate removal and burial of the body, and insisted on holding a wake – 'one of those shameful carousals which, to the disgrace of the enlightened progress and advanced civilization of the nineteenth century, still linger, as dregs of ancient manners, among the funereal customs of the Irish peasantry'. Before the month was out, forty-eight persons living within a radius of 150 yards of the wake had died of cholera.[28]

In seeking to tackle the notorious problems of public health, Liverpool introduced pioneer legislation, beginning with the Liverpool Building Act of 1842 and the Liverpool Sanitary Act (noted above) to improve light, ventilation, and (rudimentary) sanitation in the worst of the lodging houses, courts, and cellars. However, such proud Liverpool 'firsts' had adverse (albeit unintended) consequences. In the absence of any provision for those displaced (some 25,000 between 1844 and 1851), overcrowding was exacerbated in adjacent areas, given the need to remain close to casual labour markets and informal networks of collective mutuality. In another pioneer exercise, Liverpool went a step further in the 1860s, deviating again from the hegemonic ideology of laissez-faire, to provide municipally built houses. Once again, however, there was no provision to rehouse those displaced by the St Martin's Cottages scheme, opened in 1869.[29] While welcoming Liverpool's innovative record in public health and urban improvement, the *Daily Post* published a series of supplements calling for urgent action to tackle the disastrous consequences of displacement caused by slum clearance and commercial, warehouse, and railway expansion. Averse to relocating to the better air of the outskirts, labourers, the *Post* rued, crowded into 'contiguous streets' in close proximity with 'the numerous indigent who sponge on the employed' and 'the congenial vultures of society – the thieves, vagabonds, roughs and prostitutes':

> Hence, it is that there are found herding and congregating together in many streets the three sections of the lower orders of society – the labourer, the mendicant, the rogue, and hence it is that the improvements and opening out of some districts have really brought these sections into close relationship, to the manifest physical injury of all and to the demoralisation of the labourer.[30]

Although rehousing clauses were incorporated into subsequent national legislation on slum clearance, notably the Artisans' and Labourers' Dwellings Improvement Act (1875), displacement continued apace, aggravating the housing crisis of the 1880s.[31] As in 'Outcast London', the slum clearance schemes in 'Irish' Liverpool, implemented by the local Insanitary Property and Artisans' Dwelling Committee, appointed in 1882, were tantamount to eviction. The time lapse between clearance and construction was long, and on completion, the level of rent – generally far beyond the 'affordable rent' of three shillings (15p) per week acknowledged by Alderman Forwood, the 'Tory democrat' who chaired the Committee – way above the means of most of those displaced.[32] These 'improvement' schemes were premised on the notion of 'levelling up': once the worst houses had been demolished, better tenants would move into the newly erected model dwellings, the displaced poor occupying the houses they had vacated. In Liverpool there was no such upward trajectory, as the impact of slum clearance, accentuated by railway clearances and the northward expansion of the docks, brought new slums into existence. At the Commission of inquiry into unemployment in 1894, H. E. Williams, an expert witness on rents, reported on the deterioration of housing between Great Homer Street and Scotland Road vacated by respectable inhabitants 'filtering-up' to be replaced by what he described as 'very bad indeed, bad class of tenants … the low Irish from the bottom parts of the city, court houses and cellars, etc … this particular place has become a city of chip merchants, donkey owners, pigeon breeders and all kinds of ruffians of all shades. In some streets, doors, stairs, and floors, become the spoil of the chip merchants, lead piping and iron removed to marine store dealers, and we all ask where are the police!!'[33]

By this time, however, the allegedly 'feckless' Irish of the north end, by no means passive victims of crude prejudice and denigratory stereotyping, were proving themselves adept at laying claim to urban space. Over the years, the Irish in Liverpool had formulated their own versions of

Irishness, an ethno-confessional affiliation (Irish and Catholic became synonymous) which served at first protective and defensive functions against disadvantage, disability, and discrimination, but then became increasingly assertive, leading to a form of home rule in Irish Liverpool, not excluding the 'poorest poor'. Some 150,000–200,000 strong by the late nineteenth century, Irish Liverpool is perhaps best approached through comparison with large migrant communities overseas, enclaves within which 'ethnic' culture was not only retained but rewarded.[34] In Irish Liverpool, however, there were no specific dietary, dress or linguistic requirements, the traditional consumer products of enclave economies.[35] 'Irishness' flourished without a specific language other than the local '*Patois*', a precursor of the distinctive scouse accent. Without designated ethnic badge products (other than specially imported shamrock for St Patrick's Day), 'Irishness' was marketed as a cultural and political project in itself. There was no place for such English misrepresentations as the 'stage Irishman', but there was a lucrative trade in 'authentic' images of Ireland and its people, depicted in dioramas, waxworks, lantern shows, and music-hall 'spectacles' with casts of up to a hundred, the more sentimental the better ('I love old Ireland still' and 'The boat that brought me over' were particular concert favourites).[36] For cultural and literary theorists, diaspora is posited as valorised space, a creative 'in-between' without secure *roots*, the point of departure for existential transnational *routes* crossing geographical, chronological, and imaginative boundaries.[37] Possibly the case at individual artistic level, this was not how diaspora was experienced by the bulk of migrants in Irish Liverpool. As they adjusted to new surroundings, they displayed little relish for any 'interstitial' space or creative indeterminacy other than the delights of the vast entertainment sector in Liverpool, landfall of American popular culture. Although often articulated in the latest fashionable idiom such as blackface minstrelsy, simple nostalgia infused their literature, balladry, and popular entertainment a packaged construction of memory of the old homeland, the heritage handed down to the second generation with mythic intensity.

Forged in competitive contrast with Protestant and established forms of philanthropy and welfare, Liverpool-Irish charitable and political endeavour proudly reached down to 'the lowest depth'.[38] This was very different from the approach of the wealthy Unitarian elite who, being excluded from municipal power, stood forward to apply business acumen, scientific rationality, and trained professionalism to Protestant philanthropic provision in Liverpool. 'There was an evil worse than suffering, worse even than death, and that was demoralisation', William Rathbone averred, adding that in a large town like Liverpool 'the danger was not in giving too little, but in giving too much, and thereby bringing about the very evil of mendicancy'.[39] Having curbed the growth of indiscriminate charitable provision, the 'deformation of the gift', the Central Relief Society pioneered the practice of 'scientific charity'.[40] While lacking an equivalent wealthy donor base, the Catholics continued with traditional 'alms-giving', convinced of its superior welfare and spiritual benefits. Protestant charity, the *Catholic Institute Magazine* critically observed, 'proceeds with a fixity of system, a calm calculation of practical results, a rigid economy of good works, which utterly destroy to Catholic eyes all that in Charity is most beautiful and most holy'.[41] Catholic charities relied on 'the magic of the poor man's penny', building up resources from below to help those at the very bottom, 'the thousands of homeless, moneyless, raimentless, foodless creatures that call the Catholic Church their mother in Liverpool'.[42] 'I want the poor people with me', Father Nugent, charitable entrepreneur and champion of the poor on the streets proclaimed: 'I want the very poorest of the poor, in order that I may throw some ray of comfort and consolation across the path of their troubled lives.'[43] As the Protestant investigators into Squalid Liverpool acknowledged, the Catholic priest was 'the parson, the policeman, the doctor, the nurse, the relieving officer, the nuisance inspector, the School Board inspector all in one. He knows every den of fever and filth in his parish, and he never ceases fighting the impossible in trying to mend matters.'[44]

Backed by the support of local priests and charities, Irish nationalist politicians in the north end embraced the 'ancient Catholic virtue of Holy Poverty', the proud hallmark of being genuinely Irish. Soon under the control of Irish nationalist councillors, the north end of the city came to be regarded, in A. M Sullivan's words, as 'a piece cut off from the old sod itself'.[45] Aided by some enthusiastic electioneering by a local priest, Laurence Connolly secured victory in Scotland Ward in 1875, the first of the forty-eight Irish Nationalists (INP) to sit on the council between 1875 and 1922. Over the years, the INP was carried forward by a radicalising dynamic, driven as much by progressive change in the composition of its council members as by mounting frustration at the Liberals' failure to deliver home rule. On retirement from the council, members from established middle-class professions and occupations (doctors, lawyers, and rich businessmen like Connolly) tended to be replaced by those with a more popular style: butchers, shopkeepers, penny-a-week insurance collectors, undertakers, and others who attended to the daily needs of the Liverpool-Irish. When redistribution in the 1880s opened up the possibility of gaining one of the new Liverpool parliamentary seats, 'Dandy' Pat Byrne put himself forward as the local man made good. Having started work as a dock labourer, Byrne was a real 'rags to riches' story, having acquired a string of public houses, a remarkable wardrobe, a fortune estimated at

£40,000, a seat on the city council (where he championed the Irish poor), and parliamentary ambitions.[46] It took the personal intervention of Parnell to force him to withdraw his candidacy in favour of a carpetbag outsider, T. P. O'Connor, a national figure with the celebrity required to represent the Irish beyond the constituency, throughout the length and breadth of Britain.[47]

'Tay Pay' held the seat for over four decades, for the most part continuing to see his first priority as representing the Irish in Britain. However, his constituents were not neglected: his electoral committee, often meeting in the Morning Star, 'Dandy' Pat Byrne's most famous pub, operated as a political 'machine' ensuring the continued success of the INP at municipal level. Offering a form of what has been called 'Nat-Labism', a pragmatic blend of ethnic, confessional, and class interests, the INP reached into parts beyond conventional 'Lib-Labism' elsewhere, seeking to ameliorate working and living conditions for the 'poor Irish'.[48] Forthright in its independence from British political parties and unequivocal in commitment to denominational education, extensive social reform for 'the poorest poor' and full-blown Irish nationalism, the INP under Austin Harford was the hegemonic political force in Edwardian Irish Liverpool, leaving little space or need for class, confessional, or Gaelic alternatives, such as the Labour Party, the Catholic Federation, or Sinn Fein.[49]

Beginning in 1898, Harford led the campaign for 'betterment of the district'. It started in a seemingly negative and internecine manner, calling for an end to demolition and the replacement of INP councillors, venal politicians in league with 'the big bugs and moneyed snobs of the gilded chamber … making a bit out of insanitary property, the tramways, or anything else that offered'. Viewed by the Harford brothers, the clearances undertaken by the Insanitary Property Committee constituted a coordinated attack on the economic, religious, and political coherence of the Irish enclave (and hence of the future of the INP) in the north end, 'beggaring our churches and schools and scattering the people to other districts, where the associations of an alien religion are bound to do incalculable harm'. Dwellings were replaced by 'warehouses, public-houses and mills for the capitalist, the brewer and the speculator', along with the relocation of mortuaries, refuse 'destructors', tanneries, and stables, noxious health hazards unwelcome elsewhere in town: this 'unhousing of the labouring classes' was undermining the customer base of traders and shopkeepers (and Catholic churches). Demolition was driven by crude political advantage, 'confined almost entirely to those districts in which there is what some consider an inconvenient superfluity of a certain class of voters'. The Tories, it seemed, 'want to wring the Scotland Division from the Nationalist representation, and the most feasible means of achieving that end appears to be the eviction of the Irish voters through the destruction of "insanitary property"'. Determined to prevent such an outcome, Harford had the temerity to challenge the great 'Tay Pay' himself at the general election of 1900 (until John Redmond, leader of the Irish Parliamentary Party, prevailed upon him to withdraw):

> Could anyone tell him what Mr O'Connor had done for the division? The demolition of insanitary property had gone on, but the people had not been re-housed. They were now in a position that unless they were careful in a short time their stronghold would be taken by the Tory party.[50]

Somewhat chastened, O'Connor hastily befriended Harford to adopt the 'Nat-Lab' position on housing and social reform. Looking back, he acknowledged the lesson he had learnt in Liverpool-style gerrymandering: 'Their opponents had endeavoured to transform a Nationalist stronghold into a Tory stronghold by the demolition of property, and he was convinced that even the ablest leaders of Tammany in New York could learn something from the Tory wire-pullers of Liverpool.'[51]

Harford continued to oppose 'wholesale demolitions', encouraging the hapless tenants of Whitley Street in 1902 to take direct action to defend the roof over their heads: they were eventually evicted by being 'smoked out'.[52] Increasingly, however, he concentrated his efforts (with the support of other INP councillors such as Flynn and O'Shea) on making 'the Re-housing of the Labouring Classes a practical question', by insisting that each presentment to the Council should be accompanied by 'a scheme for the rehousing of the persons who will be dispossessed by the demolition of the insanitary houses'. Soon after his motion was accepted (after initial opposition and defeat), he was elected to the new Housing Committee which replaced the Insanitary Property Committee.[53] Its most energetic member, Harford quickly developed expertise in the provision of housing for the 'poorest poor', while safeguarding the political interests of the INP by opposing any attempt to 'utilise the Housing Committee as a political weapon for the destruction of the Catholic and Irish vote in the centre of the city'. He refused to endorse plans to rehouse those dispossessed in the Scotland and Exchange Divisions 'not in the demolition areas and in the vicinity of their work, but four or five miles away on the extreme boundary of the city'.[54] Furthermore, he sought an alternative to 'workhouse-like' tenement blocks, previously advocated by Forwood in his pioneer (and short-lived) proposals in the 1880s for affordable municipal housing close to work. Speaking on return from a housing conference in Liege (one of several such European engagements), Harford noted that 'no city in Europe had gone so far as Liverpool in the practical direction of "housing the poorest poor"', but, he insisted, 'more comprehensive operations of housing the people generally must be taken up, with the block tenement system altogether discarded in favour of single houses'.[55] The much-praised 'self-contained' flats and cottages of the Bevington Street scheme apart, however, municipal provision remained predominantly tenement in form, but with design modifications to ensure a single defensible space (Figures 3.2–3.4). Liverpool pioneered new look blocks designed 'as far away from the tenement appearance as possible', with individual front doors opening onto a balcony.[56] While applauded at European congresses, as in Vienna in 1910, municipal housing in Liverpool still fell short of Harford's ideal:

> We are convinced that all housing schemes ought to contain ordinary clothes-washing conveniences, such as boiler with hot and cold water supply, baths, in at least a proportionate number to the population of each area or block of dwellings, more playgrounds with gymnasia for children, the cultivation of plants and flowers among the people, the planting of trees wherever possible, the opening of reading rooms and libraries, and lectures and exhibitions from time to time in the reading rooms on hygiene and domestic economy (including cooking).[57]

Harford's commitment to wholesale housing reform – his determination to make 'slumdom' a word of the past in Liverpool[58] – gained much approval in the Catholic and nationalist community. His election as deputy chairman of the Housing Committee in 1907 was hailed in the local Catholic press as 'An Irish Victory', Harford being, as T. P. O'Connor observed, 'Liverpool by birth and training, but Irish by race'. At a special banquet in Harford's honour, John Redmond, the Irish leader, praised the work he had done already in connection with 'the great question of the housing of the working classes ... probably the greatest of their social problems, the problem that lay at the root of the temperance question, and the question of public health, and at the root of almost all those questions which concerned the social well-being and the happiness of the people'.[59] By shifting the emphasis from slum-dwellers to the slums themselves, Harford and the INP provided a timely counterweight to the anti-Irish moralism which still prevailed in liberal and professional quarters. Although much reduced, the death rate continued to tell against Liverpool in league tables of civic health. Echoing his predecessors, Dr Hope, the Medical Officer of Health, persisted in blaming drink, dirty habits, and incompetent domestic budgeting, failings which placed the Irish in Liverpool below the 'national minimum' standards of Edwardian citizenship and civic responsibility.[60]

'Bright homes and healthy people were the things they were striving after', Harford informed a keen-to-learn visiting delegation from Keighley in 1913: 'The cost of one Dreadnought would clear away all the slums of Liverpool and convert it almost into a garden city.'[61] On the eve of the First

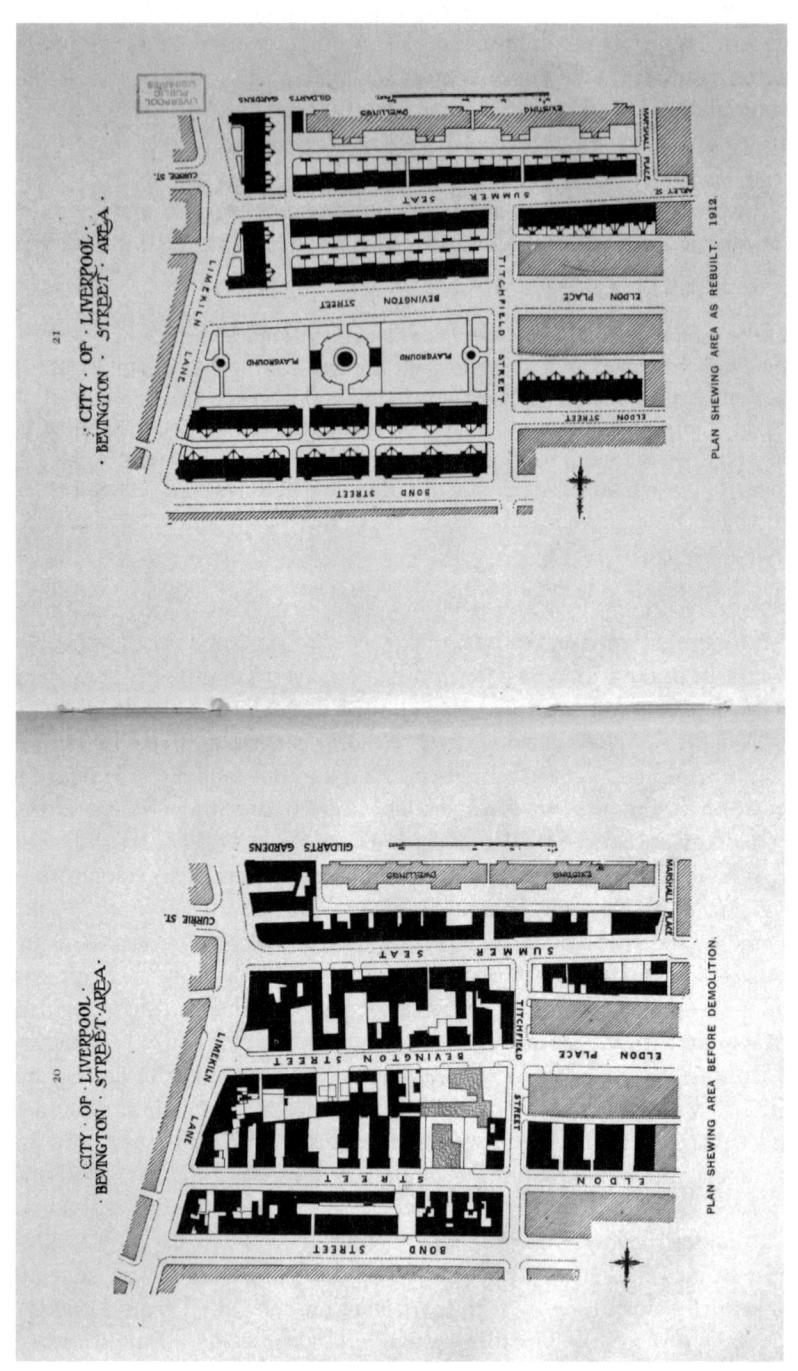

**Figure 3.2** Before and after plans of the pioneering Bevington Street scheme, promoted by Harford and Irish nationalist councillors, with its 'self-contained' cottages and flats and open spaces. Courtesy of Liverpool Central Library and Archives.

**Figure 3.3** Early photograph of the pioneering Bevington Street scheme, view from Titchfield Street (c.1912). Courtesy of Liverpool Central Library and Archives.

World War, Harford and the INP could take pride in their record on the Housing Committee: of the 22,000 insanitary court houses noted in the 1860s, only 2,771 remained and these were scheduled to disappear along with 5,646 others 'which though less objectionable, are of an antiquated, undesirable and unhealthy type'; having belatedly acknowledged the need to provide rehousing in the 1890s, the Corporation in 1914 was responsible for 2,721 dwellings and 10,223 inhabitants. None but the dispossessed were allowed to become Council tenants. In areas where the Housing Committee had been active, there was a remarkable improvement in the death rate 'whilst those breaches of the law which may be traced to overcrowding and bad environment have considerably decreased'. All in all, the improvement in health, crime, and rental receipts was 'a striking testimony to the moral character of the tenants'.[62]

Local socialists, however, were unimpressed. Unable to break the electoral hold of the INP in the north end, they criticised the nationalists for 'their one great scheme of "Re-housing the Poorest of the Poor"' conducted at the expense of a campaign against poverty itself.[63] Socialists were incredulous of the self-enclosed horizons, the 'mental and physical

A VIEW OF SELF-CONTAINED COTTAGES IN BEVINGTON STREET.
Looking from Titchfield Street.
(This street was formerly only 28 feet wide, and is now 60 feet wide).

**Figure 3.4** Early photograph of the pioneering Bevington Street scheme, view from Limekiln Lane (c.1912). The new buildings facing Limekiln Lane were in tenement form but with design modifications (individual front doors opening on to balconies) to ensure single defensible space. Courtesy of Liverpool Central Library and Archives.

starvation', of 'Irish slummies' whose lives (even when rehoused) extended no further than 'the sad blot called Paddy's Market'. A correspondent to the *Liverpool Forward* described his impressions of 'A Day in the Slums': 'what appalled me most was not the open ashpits, not the endless gin shops, not the beautiful and costly Roman Catholic churches, not the stuffed and broken windows, not the stinking refuse in the gutters, but the grave content amongst a people who are living their lives without knowing what life is'.[64] The Catholic press, by contrast, applauded the faith and mutuality which held the community together: 'Next to the splendid faith of the Irish poor, which keeps them from falling into the terrible depths of degradation and despair attained by so many of their neighbours of other nationalities, it is grand to witness their sympathy and generosity to each other.'[65] With the establishment of the Catholic School for Mothers to lessen the infant mortality rate (one-third of the children born in Liverpool were Catholic but only one-quarter of the children reaching school age were Catholic), Archbishop Whiteside was confident 'the Church in Liverpool would go ahead fast'.[66] To the alarm of Protestants, Whiteside repeatedly praised his co-religionists for their fecundity when 'race suicide' was otherwise advancing rapidly in England, 'due, it is to be feared, in the main to the terrible sin of criminal sterility'.[67] As public health duly improved, the social problem was redefined: the cause for concern was no longer the death rate, but the high birth (and survival) rate among the Liverpool Irish. As family size went into decline among the rest of the population, Protestant Liverpool began to fear being swamped by Catholics.

By the early twentieth century, the 'low Irish' had adjusted in various ways to urban living, although militant cultural nationalists, advocates of Sinn Fein, believed much remained to be done through 'a non-political and non-sectarian Irish society of social workers in Liverpool to improve the conditions of slum life'.[68] As conditions began to improve in the north end, the Catholic press sought to deflect attention away from the proverbial binge-drinking and violent disorder of Scotland Road, 'unrivalled in this town and surpassed in few, if any others, for poverty, vice and crime'.[69] In a series which brought new meaning to the sobriquet 'Black Spot on the Mersey', the *Liverpool Catholic Herald* drew attention to the 'no-go' cosmopolitan area around Mill Street and Beaufort Street in Toxteth, characterised by 'lodging-houses for negro, lascar and other foreign seamen, mulatto children, drunken men and women, and street fights. These streets are not considered desirable beats by the police, many of whom have come to grief in the perambulations therein.'[70]

By the First World War, Liverpool, once notorious for the worst slums in Europe, had become the 'Mecca for housing experts', a transformation due, the *Liverpool Catholic Herald* noted with justifiable pride, 'to Irish Catholics who stirred up public opinion, made an end of the municipal creation of new slums more congested and more appalling than the old ones, and set on foot, and are still successfully carrying on, a scheme of municipal housing which has attracted the favourable attention of the leading authorities in Europe and America.'[71] The poor Irish of the north end should be considered as pioneers in Liverpool's distinctive housing history, a pattern which still prevails: in recent decades alternative forms of collective housing provision have undergone twists and turns, successes and failures, from the days of SNAP (Shelter Neighbourhood Action Project) and the 'Co-op spring' of the 1970s through to the 2015 Turner Prize for Assemble and the Granby Four Streets.[72]

Throughout the troubled interwar period, the Liverpool-Irish came under renewed pressure and scrutiny in consequence of an adverse conjuncture of 'second wave' migration, economic depression, and political realignments. Categorised in biological and cultural terms by eugenicists, they were to encounter 'racial' prejudice, but even so they fared considerably better than some other British subjects in 'cosmopolitan' Liverpool. The new arrivals from the Irish Free State, like the long-settled inhabitants of T. P. O'Connor's north end fiefdom, took their place (albeit often lowly) in the 'white' majority, above the discrimination and institutional racism deployed against 'coloured' British subjects of otherwise similar legal status.[73] The adverse economic climate notwithstanding, the Catholic church persisted with its prestige project, 'The Cathedral in our Time'. Hailed by Sir John Summerson as 'the supreme attempt to embrace Rome, Byzantium, the Romanesque and the Renaissance in one triumphal and triumphant synthesis',[74] Lutyens's design matched the extravagant ambition of the new archbishop. The doyen of the 'Kerry gang' of priests in the archdiocese, 'Dickie' Downey (1928–52) was a revered (and typically non-ecumenical) Irish-Liverpudlian, born in Kilkenny but brought up and educated in Liverpool where he attended St Edward's College junior seminary. By dwarfing the tower of the Anglican cathedral (and all but outstripping St Peter's in Rome) the proposed edifice was of immense symbolic importance, attesting to the Catholic contribution to Liverpool – to be surrounded by high-quality modern apartment blocks, the final eradication of 'slumdom' (Plate 4). As in the earlier construction of the parochial infrastructure of worship, education, and welfare, the burden of finance fell upon hard-pressed ordinary Catholics, now enjoined not only to donate but also to purchase a range of special products such as Cathedral tea and Cathedral cigarettes. Only the crypt was built before funds ran out. It was not until the early 1960s that construction work began on Gibberd's radically different design, to be christened on completion with characteristic scouse wit as 'Paddy's wigwam'.

## Notes

1 Kevin Kenny, 'Ireland and the British Empire', in *Ireland and the British Empire*, ed. Kevin Kenny (Oxford: Oxford University Press, 2004), 7–25.
2 R. Lawton and C. G. Pooley, *The Social Geography of Nineteenth-century Merseyside* (Liverpool: University of Liverpool Press, 1973).
3 Seymour Drescher, 'The Slaving Capital of the World: Liverpool and National Opinion in the Age of Abolition', *Slavery and Abolition*: 9 (1988): 128–43.
4 John Belchem, '"Liverpool's story is the world's glory"' in *Merseypride: Essays in Liverpool Exceptionalism*, ed. John Belchem (Liverpool: Liverpool University Press, 2nd edn, 2006), 3–30.

5 John Belchem and Donald MacRaild, 'Cosmopolitan Liverpool' in *Liverpool 800: Culture, Character and History*, ed. John Belchem (Liverpool: Liverpool University Press), 311–92.
6 See the interesting portrayal of 'Liverpool and the Celtic Sea' in Robert Scally, *The End of Hidden Ireland: Rebellion, Famine and Emigration* (New York: Oxford University Press USA, 1995), 184–217.
7 *Description of the Liverpool Night Asylum for the Houseless Poor* (Liverpool, 1839).
8 *Catholic Times*, 4 November 1887.
9 J. D. Papworth, 'The Irish in Liverpool 1835–71: segregation and dispersal' (PhD thesis, University of Liverpool, 1982); C. G. Pooley, 'The Residential Segregation of Migrant Communities in mid-Victorian Liverpool', *Transactions of the Institute of British Geographers*, ii (1977): 364–82; Richard Dennis, *English Industrial Cities of the Nineteenth Century* (Cambridge: Cambridge University Press, 1984), 39–41.
10 Thomas Baines, *The History of the Commerce and Town of Liverpool* (London, 1852), 677–8.
11 W. H. Duncan 'On the Sanitary State of Liverpool', 31 August 1840, in *Local Reports on the Sanitary Condition of the Labouring Population of England* (London, 1842), 293.
12 W. H. Duncan *Physical Causes of the High Mortality in Liverpool*, Liverpool, 1843, quoted in G. Kearns and P. Laxton, 'Ethnic Groups as Public Health Hazards: the Famine Irish in Liverpool and Lazaretto Politics', in *The Politics of the Healthy Life: An International Perspective. History of Medicine, Health, and Disease Series,* ed. E. Rodriguez-Ocana (Sheffield: European Association for the History of Medicine and Health Publications, 2002), 18–20.
13 Duncan, 'On the Sanitary State', 293–4.
14 Scally, *Hidden Ireland*, 206.
15 Kearns and Laxton, 'Ethnic Groups as Public Health Hazards', 18–20.
16 John Belchem, *Irish, Catholic and Scouse: The History of the Liverpool-Irish, 1800–1939* (Liverpool: Liverpool University Press, 2007), 4–5.
17 *Liverpool Catholic Herald*, 27 January 1905.
18 Parliamentary Papers (PP) 1870(259)VIII: Select Committee on Prisons and Prison Ministers Acts 1870, q. 4148.
19 Quoted in Canon Bennett, *Father Nugent of Liverpool* (Liverpool: Liverpool Catholic Children's Protection Society, 1949), 38.
20 Kearns and Laxton, 'Ethnic Groups as Public Health Hazards', 14.
21 See Frank Neal, *Black '47: Britain and the Famine Irish* (Basingstoke: Macmillan, 1998).
22 'Labour and the Poor: Letter 1: The burdens upon towns – Irish pauperism', *Morning Chronicle*, 20 May 1850.
23 G. Read, 'Liverpool – The Flood-gate of the Old World: A Study in Ethnic Attitudes', *Journal of American Ethnic History* 13 (1993): 31–47.
24 Graeme Milne, 'Maritime Liverpool' in Belchem, *Liverpool 800*, 300–8.

25 Liverpool Record Office 352.4NUI: Report to the Health Committee of the Town Council ... sanitary operations in the Nuisance Department, 1 January 1847–31, March 1851.
26 Liverpool Record Office 352.4HEA: Report to the Health Committee of the Borough of Liverpool, on the Health of the Town during the years 1847–1850.
27 Liverpool Record Office 614.147 HEA: Mortality Sub-Committee, 9–46, 95–117.
28 PP 1867–8 (4072) XXXVII, *Report of the Cholera Epidemic of 1866 in England*, 229–32.
29 Bertie Dockerill, 'Liverpool Corporation and the Origins of Municipal Social Housing, 1842–1890', *Transactions of the Historic Society of Lancashire and Cheshire*, 165 (2016): 39–56.
30 *Daily Post*, supplements, 24 August and 2 September 1864.
31 Gareth Stedman Jones, *Outcast London: A Study in the Relationship between Classes in Victorian London* (Harmondsworth: Verso, 1976, revised edn 2013).
32 P. J. Waller, *Democracy and Sectarianism: A Political and Social History of Liverpool 1868–1939* (Liverpool: Liverpool University Press, 1981), 87–8.
33 *Full Report of the Commission of Inquiry into the Subject of the Unemployed in the City of Liverpool* (Liverpool, 1894), 101–2.
34 For a critical introduction to the 'enclave-economy hypothesis' of Alejandro Portes and colleagues, see J. M. Sanders and V. Nee, 'Limits of Ethnic Solidarity in the Enclave Economy', *American Sociological Review*, 52 (1987): 745–67.
35 See Donna Gabaccia, *We Are What We Eat: Ethnic Food and the Making of Americans* (Cambridge, MA: Harvard University Press, 1998, revised edn 2000); Hasia Diner, *Hungering for America: Italian, Irish and Jewish Foodways in the Age of Migration* (Cambridge, MA: Harvard University Press, 2001).
36 *Liverpool Catholic Herald*, 6 October 1899.
37 For a useful introduction to the works of Homi Bhabha, Avtar Brah, and other theorists, see John McCleod, *Beginning Postcolonialism* (Manchester: Manchester University Press, 2000). See also, Paul Gilroy, *The Black Atlantic: Modernity and Double Consciousness* (Harmondsworth: Verso, 1993).
38 See Belchem, *Irish, Catholic and Scouse*.
39 *Daily Post*, 5 December 1866.
40 W. Grisewood, *The Poor of Liverpool and What is to be Done for them* (Liverpool, 1899).
41 'Liverpool Catholic Charities: No. 1', *Catholic Institute Magazine*, January 1856.
42 'Church-Going in Liverpool', *Catholic Institute Magazine*, November 1855.
43 *Catholic Times*, 29 October 1886.
44 *Squalid Liverpool. By a Special Commission* (Liverpool, 1883), 38.
45 *Nationalist*, 6 December 1884.
46 For biographical details of Byrne and all other Irish National Party councillors in Liverpool, see the appendix in B. O'Connell, 'The Irish Nationalist Party in Liverpool, 1873–1922' (unpublished MA thesis, University of Liverpool, 1971).
47 See L. W. Brady, *T P O'Connor and the Liverpool Irish* (London: Royal Historical Society, 1983).

48 The term 'Nat-Labism' was coined by Sam Davies in '"A Stormy political Career": P. J. Kelly and Irish Nationalist and Labour Politics in Liverpool, 1891–1936', *Transactions of the Historical Society of Lancashire and Cheshire*, 148 (1999): 156.
49 Belchem, *Irish, Catholic and Scouse*.
50 *Liverpool Catholic Herald*, 27 January 1899–28 September 1900; 5 May 1899 dates the beginning of the campaign to October 1898. Unfortunately, the holdings at the British Library do not start until 1899.
51 *Liverpool Catholic Herald*, 1 July 1904.
52 *Liverpool Catholic Herald*, 8 and 15 August 1902.
53 *Liverpool Catholic Herald*, 12 October 1900.
54 *Liverpool Catholic Herald*, 5 October 1907.
55 A. B. Forwood, *The Dwellings of the Industrious Classes in the Diocese of Liverpool and how to improve them* (Liverpool, 1883).
56 S. D. Adshead and P. Abercrombie (eds), *Liverpool Town Planning and Housing Exhibition and Conference, 1914* (Liverpool, 1914), 118–28.
57 *Liverpool Catholic Herald*, 22 October 1910.
58 *Liverpool Catholic Herald*, 1 March 1913.
59 *Liverpool Catholic Herald*, 30 November–7 December 1907.
60 Matthew Vickers, 'Civic image and civic patriotism in Liverpool 1880–1914' (unpublished DPhil thesis, University of Oxford, 2000). Hope incurred the wrath of labour leaders when he attributed a rise in infant mortality to the general transport strike of 1911, see 'How Poor Children Died' and 'Truth about the strike', *Liverpool Weekly Mercury* 21 and 28 October 1911.
61 *Liverpool Catholic Herald*, 1 March 1913.
62 *Liverpool Catholic Herald*, 1 August 1914.
63 'Why Liverpool is Unhealthy', *Liverpool Forward*, 30 May 1913.
64 'A Day in the Slums', *Liverpool Forward*, 1 June 1912.
65 *Liverpool Catholic Herald*, 7 February 1902.
66 *Liverpool Catholic Herald*, 23 May 1914.
67 *Liverpool Catholic Herald*, 22 February 1913.
68 *The Liverpool Irishman, or Annals of the Irish Colony in Liverpool* (Liverpool, 1909), 6.
69 J. Allden Owles, *Recollections of Medical Missionary Work* (Glasgow, 1909), 43.
70 'Black Spot on the Mersey', *Liverpool Catholic Herald*, 10 January–14 February 1902.
71 *Liverpool Catholic Herald*, 17 May 1913 and 11 April 1914.
72 Matthew Thompson, *Reconstructing Public Housing: Liverpool's hidden history of collective alternatives* (Liverpool: Liverpool University Press, 2020).
73 Belchem, *Irish, Catholic and Scouse*.
74 Quoted in Joseph Sharples, *Liverpool: Pevsner Architectural Guides* (New Haven and London; Yale University Press, 2004), 84.

# 4

# Architecture of the state in Ireland: the colonial question, 1800–1922

*Richard J. Butler*

The political interpretation of nineteenth-century Irish public architecture was a problem that interested writers of the time.[1] For the Rev. James Hall, visiting from Essex in 1807, Dublin's many new public buildings were inseparable from the broader political settlement of the years after the Rebellion of 1798 and the Act of Union that followed two years later: 'as it was in France in the days of Louis XIV and … now in Dublin,' he thought, 'there is a curious contrast between the grandeur of the national buildings and public monuments, and the poverty of the great body of the people'.[2] Thirty years later, when many new courthouses were under construction in provincial towns – fuelled by loans from the British state – the *Waterford Mirror* took a different line, cautioning against greed and the poor use of public money: there would soon be, they feared, 'a court-house in every village and every townland'. 'Our county will then present a novel scene, unlike whatever before existed, when temples of justice are as numerous as churches and chapels.'[3] William Thackeray, in his *Irish sketch-book* of 1842, used the public gallery of Irish courtrooms as a valuable listening posts for understanding the country and its people. He thought Cork's county gaol was 'as fine and as glancing as a palace', but, he added, 'so neat, spacious, and comfortable, that we can only pray to see every cottager in the country as cleanly, well lodged, and well fed, as the convicts are'.[4]

Following in their wake, this chapter attempts to suggest answers to some difficult questions: to what extent was the new architecture of the British state in nineteenth-century Ireland 'Irish', and in what ways was it 'British', 'colonial', or even 'imperial'? What did these new buildings represent, how were they interpreted, and what has been their legacy? This chapter thus adds a built environment angle to the longstanding debate within Irish historical and literary studies concerning Ireland's 'colonial' or 'semi-colonial' status in the years between the Act of Union in 1800 and the establishment of the Irish Free State in 1922. It is necessarily selective in its case studies, shining a light on particular aspects of architectural production and questions of legacy, and on certain types of public buildings.

It is divided into three sections: first, it presents an overview of existing writings on the 'colonial question' within Irish studies and the related but problematic issue of 'Irishness' within Irish architectural history. Second, it suggests a new framework for understanding the 'architecture of the state', with all its myriad complexities and shifting boundaries, by focusing on production, funding, and agency. Third, it reflects on the troubled legacy of so many of these buildings during the revolutionary years from 1916 to 1923. From travel writers in the early 1800s to conservation and heritage campaigners today, Irish public architecture has always been a focal point for the accumulation of a palimpsest of interpretations, representations, and meanings. The 'colonial question' reveals important interplays between British political and cultural hegemony, the idea of the 'inner empire' or the 'empire at home', and the fundamental hybridity of Irish architectural production.

Ireland's relationship with Britain during the long nineteenth century was a deeply troubled one. 'Legislative independence' of the late eighteenth century ended in a spectacular rebellion, the invasion of French forces, and the forced marriage of the Act of Union.[5] In terms of architecture, there were many continuities between the eighteenth and the nineteenth centuries, but while many of the great public buildings of Georgian Ireland were concentrated in Dublin or in nearby stately homes, the nineteenth century saw a new architectural richness pervade the most distant provincial towns.[6] New streets, squares, and axial vistas appeared framing courthouses, prisons, what were termed 'lunatic asylums', workhouses, Church of Ireland churches, police barracks, and 'model' schools. These buildings formed the backdrop to endemic social and political unrest, centring on issues of political status (rebellion), land (agrarian unrest and secret societies), and religion (sectarian rioting and resistance to demands for payment of tithe), among many others. Architecture, of course, played a role in almost every aspect of these events: the 'Rockite' rebels of the early 1820s crowded new extensions to the county gaols in Cork, Limerick, and Tralee.[7] Over 130 new workhouses opened their doors only a few years before the catastrophe of the Great Famine – an event that completely overwhelmed institutions not designed for such profound destitution.[8] Political radicals of the Fenian and Land War movements of the late nineteenth century were tried in courthouses such as in Dublin's Green Street, and sentenced to imprisonment in jails such as Kilmainham.[9] In 1916 and the messy years that followed, another generation of rebels found themselves raiding police barracks for weapons, commandeering workhouses for military purposes, or, when caught, perched in the dock or incarcerated in prison cells.[10] Ireland 'under the Union' – a phrase not without meaning in its own right – with its MPs in Westminster, was governed in a manner that had aspects of both 'home' and 'empire'; it was, for example, the only part of the empire apart from India to have a Viceroy, and its day-to-day management was entrusted to the position of the Chief Secretary for Ireland.[11]

## The 'colonial question'

The 'colonial question' within Irish studies has provoked rich debate far beyond the temporal confines of the long nineteenth century. It is, for example, a point of contention within medieval, Elizabethan, and early modern studies.[12] Throughout, Ireland rarely fits neatly into any classic definitions of 'colony' or 'imperialism', both terms complicated by centuries of complex migration patterns and the geographical proximity of Ireland to the metropole. For the nineteenth century, much of the current debate rests on the differences between a *de jure* and a *de facto* colonial state: few scholars would argue that it fitted neatly into the former, but most agree that it had many characteristics of the latter.[13] Legally, the country was represented by MPs in Westminster and was, at least in part, governed by British civil servants in Whitehall. Similarly, the established Protestant church, at least until the latter half of the nineteenth century, was a united entity encompassing England and Ireland. Landed elites, engineers, scientists, administrators, and military officers moved freely between the two islands – indeed some had permanent bases in both. In many legal and administrative respects, Ireland was governed as a 'home' territory, not as a 'colony', and historians of contemporary India or of British territories in West Africa would see little in common with governmental structures in Ireland.[14]

However, in many important respects Ireland was treated – from the moment of the Act of Union onwards – as an entirely different country demanding policies in areas such as general administration, policing, military activity, and social issues that were not seen as appropriate for the metropole.[15] Comparative studies of policing, prison reform, the poor law, and the treatment of mental health have revealed these fault-lines in great detail.[16] The British state's response to the Great Famine of 1845–52 is often taken as instructive in this regard, coupled with the unanswerable but provocative question of whether such a catastrophe would have been permitted to occur in the Home Counties.[17] In terms of religion, Ireland was, similar to many British colonies, a mission field, and the nineteenth century witnessed what historians refer to as the 'second reformation' of Protestant missionary activity.[18] Beyond social or religious questions, Irish people were seen by many British elites as a separate – and inferior – race, in need of the 'civilising' force of British culture.[19] In an incisive essay,

David Fitzpatrick analyses the question of 'Ireland and the Empire' and concludes that the Irish administration 'remained distinctively colonial in both form and function', and that Ireland was 'exceptional' and 'akin to a colony' within the United Kingdom.[20] His view is supported by Patrick Joyce, among others, for whom state administration in nineteenth-century Ireland was 'semi-colonial'.[21] By way of contrast, K. Theodore Hoppen is much more sceptical about using the term 'colonialism': the term, he argues, has become 'so capaciously vague as to lose much in the way of analytical bite'.[22] Yet his analysis of how British elites considered Irish problems makes a strong case for the applicability of a 'colonial' framework with early paternalistic attempts to 'consolidate' the two kingdoms into one rational, distinctly Anglo-Saxon state, giving way later in the nineteenth century to an acceptance of fundamental and unreconcilable difference, and eventually of disengagement.[23]

In parallel with the work of political and social historians, the 'colonial question' has also been considered by historians of Irish architecture. Their approaches have mostly focused on an essentially Victorian debate centring on questions of national identity, architectural style, and what – if anything – was distinctively 'Irish' about Irish architecture. Within a poststructuralist paradigm, the intellectual foundations and implicit assumptions of these questions now seem rather uneasy. Replying to Nikolaus Pevsner's influential lecture series and later book *The Englishness of English Art* (1955), Edward McParland's essay 'The Englishness of Irish Architecture?' (1974) demonstrates the extent to which English architects gained commissions in Georgian Ireland. Focusing on patronage more than on architectural style, McParland notes that after the Act of Union, there was a more balanced flow in architects moving in both directions between the two islands and several Irish architects such as Richard Morrison (1767–1849) developed extraordinarily successful careers at home.[24] McParland's discussion of public architecture focuses more on the great architecture of eighteenth-century Dublin than on what came later in provincial towns. For Alistair Rowan, questions of style are more to the fore in his essay 'The Irishness of Irish Architecture' (1997). With a chronological range that extends from the prehistoric to the early twentieth century, he identifies what can be seen as a 'colonial' character in the new public architecture of the years after the Act of Union: the 'symbolic implications of the Church of Ireland's new buildings', he argues, was that 'the [Protestant] ascendancy was still in power'. The many new courthouses built by these elites, often in the Greek Revival style that was popular in the early nineteenth century throughout much of Europe, were 'monumental and repressive', 'international in style', and 'totally foreign in their point of reference'. Rowan here enmeshes architecture and politics: the adopted architectural style was a foreign imposition, but so too by implication were its patrons, with, as he argues, an overarching focus on commissioning new buildings to 'reinforce the rule of law'.[25]

Similar viewpoints have emerged from other historians in recent years. Ciarán Ó Murchadha, writing about the neo-classical courthouse in Ennis, Co. Clare, built during the Famine years, links 'the language of public architecture', as he terms it, with the Protestant politics of a county that had seen the surprise election of the nationalist Daniel O'Connell in the late 1820s and the coming of Catholic Emancipation. He argues that the 'splendour of the new courthouse ... was intended at once to reassure the Protestant gentry of the permanence and invincibility of imperial authority, and overawe the nationalists disaffected with the futility of attempting to challenge it'.[26] More recently, Alex Bremner, Kathleen James-Chakraborty, and others have made valuable contributions to this debate.[27] Furthermore, several contributors to the *Art and Architecture of Ireland: Architecture, 1600–2000* volume (2014) tackle the question of public architecture, including John Montague, who sees the funding of many Church of Ireland churches built after 1800 as 'politically motivated', with the dual aims of 'appeas[ing] those in the established Church who had lost status following the Act of Union', and 'restat[ing] a claim on the physical landscape in compensation for the loss of political power'.[28] Barry Crosbie, in a recent essay, notes the 'British architectural styles and symbolism of the colonial administration' visible in Irish public buildings such as courthouses but also banks and theatres.[29] Margaret Kelleher and Katie Barclay have investigated how British imperialism manifested itself in the drama (and architecture) of the Irish courtroom and prison in major new studies on nineteenth-century Irish history.[30] For Barclay, Irish courthouses – almost universally neo-classical in style – 'embodied the masculine virtues valued during the era, self-control, truthfulness, responsibility, whilst acknowledging the law's role in producing rights and justice'. 'Such messages', she continues, 'tied courthouses, and the practice of law, into the wider Enlightenment project of nation and Empire-building'.[31] The 'rule of law' that these courthouses represented was culturally contingent on concepts of Anglo-Saxon cultural and intellectual superiority – and the right of Ascendancy elites to rule Ireland.

## Processes of production

The 'architecture of the state' poses definitional challenges for historians of nineteenth-century Ireland; what can be termed 'state' or 'public' architecture is open to various interpretations. As an entity, the 'state', in its various forms, underwent radical change throughout this period, and especially in the first few decades after the Act of Union. In Ciaran O'Neill's words, 'Ireland moved from a very light-touch libertarian state with alarming rapidity. By the 1840s it had a totalising, pervasive, state infrastructure with arguably as extensive an information network as any other contemporary society.'[32] Here, following O'Neill and others, I interpret the 'state' as the hegemonic entity of British political and administrative government, operating through Westminster and the civil services in Whitehall and, to a lesser extent, Dublin Castle; this may also be termed simply 'central government'.[33] One helpful way to navigate the broader question of the architecture produced by the state is to consider processes of production, funding, and agency. This allows for a division into three broad categories: first, the architecture that grew out of the state's central functions and represents perhaps the most unequivocal examples of state power: army barracks, fortifications and signal towers (Figure 4.1), and major public works such as piers and navigations.[34] Second, buildings planned and funded by new entities established directly by the increasingly proactive nineteenth-century state, such as lunatic asylums (via centralised commissioners established in 1817) and workhouses (Figure 4.2) (via the yet more centralised British 'Poor Law Commissioners' and their Irish assistants from 1838).[35] Third, and perhaps most interesting, was the architecture that was the result of the state working with existing political and administrative bodies – especially Irish local government in the form of the 'grand jury' system (to be considered shortly).[36] Of these three broad divisions, the last is the most rewarding in terms of how it exposes the complexities of the hybrid 'semi-colonial' experience of nineteenth-century Ireland, and as such it is the primary focus here. It was, for example, the state's collaboration with the Irish grand juries – the principal organ of Irish local government – that produced the rich network of courthouses and prisons that many later generations saw as the main legacy of the 'British state' in Ireland, however much this perspective overlooked the quite distinct agendas of the local elites who planned these buildings. By contrast, the purpose, meaning and indeed legacy of military barracks, coastal and river fortifications, and even asylums and workhouses is more straightforward and uncontested: these were designed for the protection of the state itself, or for implementing top-down decisions concerning 'solutions' to Irish social and economic problems.

Grand juries were responsible for the great courthouses and prisons of nineteenth-century Ireland, but their building depended to a large extent on generous loans from the British state. The British state and the Irish grand juries maintained what can only be described as a reluctant friendship, born for the most part out of pragmatism and necessity, with grand

**Figure 4.1** The *tête de pont* (or bridgehead) fortifications at Shannonbridge, Co. Offaly, built c. 1815. Military fortifications along the crossings of the River Shannon mark some of the clearest examples of an architecture that represented the hegemonic power of the British imperial state in nineteenth-century Ireland (photograph by author, 2014).

juries from the early eighteenth century onwards drawing much of their bureaucratic legitimacy from the British imperial state and its judicial system in Ireland. They had dual administrative and judicial functions in Irish counties: they were sworn in at the biannual assizes to indict accused persons and send them forward for trial; they were also asked to approve of 'presentments' (funded by local taxes) to pay for the upkeep of local roads, services such as infirmaries, and new public buildings. Their roles and responsibilities were set out in various Irish (and later British) acts of parliament.[37] Though grand juries formed the essential core of nineteenth-century Irish local government, they were temporary bodies dissolved at the end of each assizes. Their composition varied somewhat but almost always included the principal landholders – and therefore taxpayers – in each county.[38] As Hoppen has pithily remarked, the governing of Ireland 'under the Union' was 'subcontracted to a collection of local Protestant notables'.[39] Furthermore, grand juries in Ireland held much greater power than their namesakes in contemporary Britain or elsewhere.[40] As the complexity and scale of their work increased from the early nineteenth century onwards, they began to employ some permanent staff to manage their affairs, such as

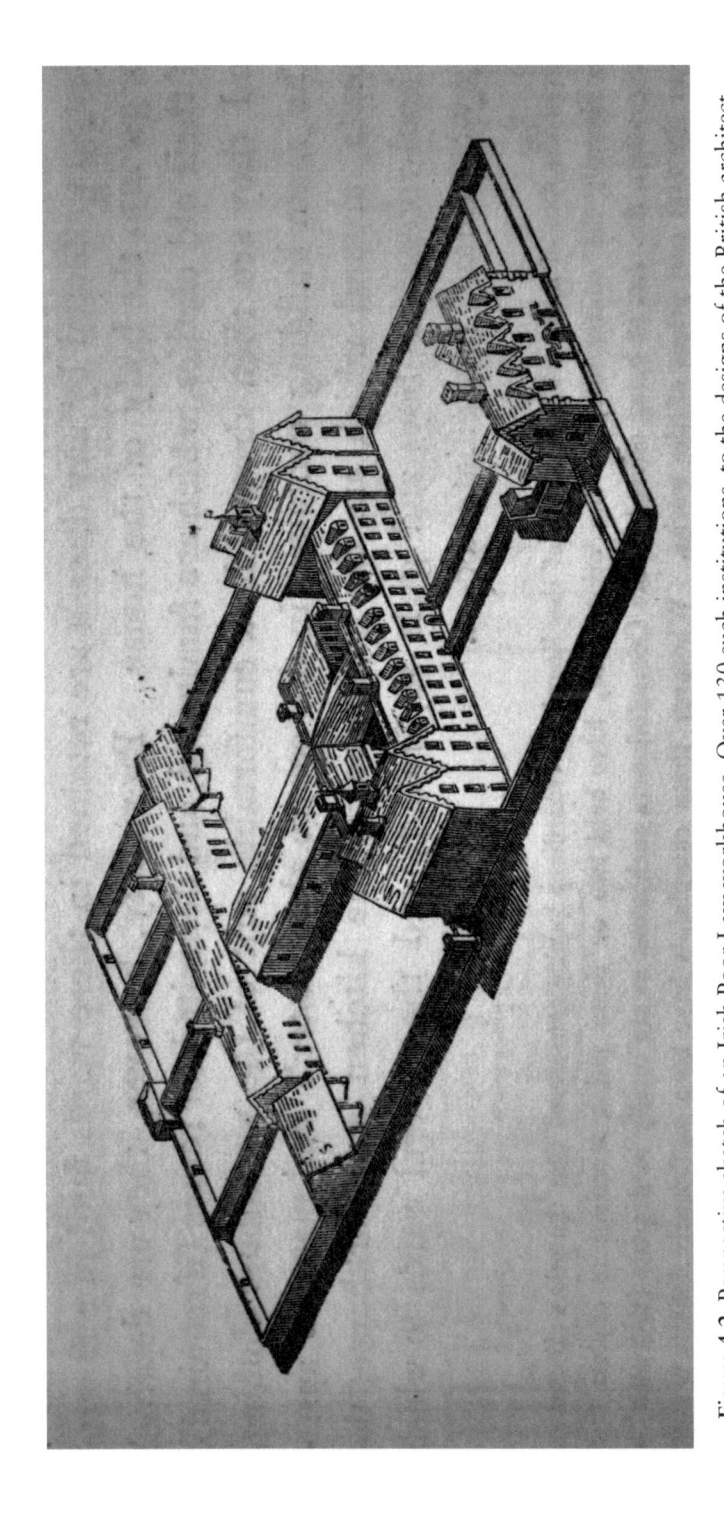

**Figure 4.2** Perspective sketch of an Irish Poor Law workhouse. Over 130 such institutions, to the designs of the British architect George Wilkinson, were built in Ireland around 1840, marking the beginning of a new top-down British experiment in 'solving' Irish social problems. From Samuel Carter Hall and Anna Maria Fielding ('Mr. & Mrs. S. C. Hall'), *Ireland: its scenery, character, &c.* (3 vols, London, 1841–43), vol. 3, p. 345.

treasurers, county surveyors, and clerks.[41] The twenty-three or so men who gathered twice each year shared a great deal in terms of social class, political inclination, and kinship.[42] As a form of local government, they represented, by and large, the 'New English' colonisers of the seventeenth century. They were a highly politicised and divisive stratum of government and were often accused of incompetence or jobbery by nationalist politicians such as Daniel O'Connell.[43]

## Courthouses

The British state – through political figures such as Robert Peel, Irish Chief Secretary between 1812 and 1818 – sought to limit 'old corruption' among Irish grand juries. However, it also created, through its new public-works loans schemes, vast opportunities for extraordinary profligacy in architectural production.[44] The first to benefit was the new Four Courts in Dublin – undoubtedly, today, Ireland's greatest courthouse – where construction had been slowly proceeding since the 1770s to the designs of the architects Thomas Cooley and later James Gandon. After 1800, the project benefited from almost £20,000 in loans, which allowed construction to proceed more rapidly, and the building was completed by around 1805.[45] For grand juries outside of the metropolis, the repair of damaged buildings in some assize towns after the 1798 rebellion and the high agricultural prices – the result of provisioning needs for the Napoleonic wars – fuelled a new confidence in replacing older, modest court or market buildings in towns such as Armagh, Dundalk, and Derry (Figure 4.3).[46] But the boom years of building new courthouses only began properly after 1817 with the passing of the Irish Public Works Loan Act.[47] This was part of a broader, imperial response to the economic hardship brought about by the end of hostilities and the sudden collapse in agricultural prices – felt keenly in Ireland.[48] Of the £1,750,000 promised by the state to alleviate unemployment, £250,000 was allocated to Ireland.[49] Further emergency legislation – relating only to Ireland – in the years that followed made it easier for grand juries to obtain loans, for any kind of public work, with relatively little oversight or scrutiny.[50] In the House of Lords the prime minister, Lord Liverpool, made it clear that though he found the general principle of these measures 'objectionable', the severity of poverty and unemployment in Ireland created 'special circumstances'.[51] Tracing the distribution of loans in both jurisdictions shows the diverging paths followed by Britain and Ireland at this time. Very few new courthouses in Britain benefited from these loans; by comparison, almost every new Irish courthouse was backed by significant central government funding. Between 1817 and 1832, the total number of loans for new Irish courthouses was

Figure 4.3 Dundalk courthouse, by John Bowden and Edward Parke, built 1813–21. The County Louth grand jurors, who commissioned this landmark public building, insisted that it rigorously adhered to every detail of Stewart and Revett's *Antiquities of Athens* (1762).

twenty-seven; in Britain the number was just two, with funds instead directed largely to collieries and canal companies.[52]

The effects of this surge of funding were soon evident in most Irish provincial towns. In 1828, the *Freeman's Journal* condemned what they saw as 'the caprice of grand juries', adding 'it has frequently happened that grand juries have decided that new courthouses ... were requisite, and the old ... sessions' houses should be pulled down, which, if altered or enlarged, would have perfectly answered the purpose ... at great expense and taxation to the people'.[53] Yet, as the state depended on these bodies to implement social reforms, act as magistrates, and play key roles in the yeomanry and the police, the channelling of so much government money into the funding of new courthouses was seen as regrettable but unavoidable.[54] Grand jurors, of course, had their own agendas, and used government loans to copy what were seen as the most sophisticated courthouse designs from neighbouring counties, and also to provide extensive space for meeting and socialising – especially in the 'grand jury room', the nucleus of local administration. Individual grand jurors also sought, occasionally, to shift the location of the assizes itself, to benefit – architecturally and economically – their home towns.[55] By the late 1820s, competition and jealously marked grand jurors' decisions about whether to commit to the costly replacement of what were often relatively new courthouses. The state's agendas of alleviating unemployment and reinforcing its hegemonic power via the rule of law were overshadowed by more local forces of consumption, family prestige, and inter-county rivalry. These rivalries can also be read, of course, as competing performative displays of loyalty to the imperial state through grander and grander public architecture. These forces were only further strengthened by the comments of visiting assize judges, who were best placed to compare – and at times condemn – grand jurors' courthouses as they travelled around the country twice yearly.[56] The effects of this were picked up by James Bicheno, visiting Ireland in 1829, who thought the Irish landed elite 'spoilt by indulgence'. 'The Government,' he argued, 'has always been ready to help them on every emergency, and they have never been taught to rely upon themselves. Incredible sums have been expended.'[57]

These dynamics played out in the building of some of provincial Ireland's most impressive courthouses in the towns of Tralee, Carlow, and Monaghan. More than a reaction to any recent agrarian or nationalist unrest, or any kind of coordinated strategy from the British state, these new courthouses grew out of grand jurors' architectural and aesthetic appreciation of a new courthouse design for Tralee, Co. Kerry, by the gifted Irish architect William Vitruvius Morrison (1794–1838). His chief innovation had been to refashion the courtroom as a semi-circular space with surrounding corridors, providing ample space for circulation and meeting spaces. In exterior appearance, Morrison allowed the shape of the courtrooms to dictate the exterior appearance of the building, bulging out on either side of the central portico, placing the entire composition on a high podium (Figure 4.4). The antecedents for this design are beyond the scope of this chapter, but the effects that it had on Irish grand jurors were quite striking.[58] Seen as the latest, most fashionable, and most advanced plan for an Irish courthouse, it was quickly adopted by leading grand jurors in several counties; central government loans fuelled this wave of building. Henry Westenra, third baron Rossmore, and MP for Monaghan, sensed this competitive spirit and wished to bring Morrison – who was at the time engaged in private work for Westenra at his country estate – to the attention of the Monaghan grand jurors.[59] By the mid-1820s Monaghan was the only county among its neighbours not to have invested in a new courthouse since the Act of Union. Westenra informed a Dublin Castle official that the Kerry grand jurors had recently adopted this 'far preferable' design, and in neighbouring Cork, the design 'has been so much approved of ... that a very great anxiety prevails there (as I have been this day informed) to substitute the Kerry plan in the place of a courthouse they built 12 years ago at an expense of nearly £20,000'.[60]

Figure 4.4 Tralee courthouse, Co. Kerry, by William Vitruvius Morrison, built 1830–33. Morrison's elegant and creative design was a favourite among Irish grand jurors in the late 1820s who rushed to secure funding for replacing their principal administrative building. Photograph taken c. 1900. Reproduced courtesy of the National Library of Ireland (Lawrence Collection, ref. L_ CAB_07558).

Westenra's plans were in turn derailed by a bitter political split between more liberal and conservative Protestants on the Monaghan grand jury, and in the end, they sourced an alternative design from an architect with fewer links to their MP. However, the grand jurors of the southern counties of Kerry and Carlow adopted Morrison's design – with generous government loans to help – and new courthouses were built in these counties between 1830 and 1834.[61] Both are remarkably similar in design. Once more, it was embarrassment and jealousy rather than any kind of imperial agenda or response to unrest that pushed the Carlow jurors to commit to a new courthouse, and in particular the caustic remarks of a visiting assize judge in 1827:

> [I] could not but express [my] astonishment at the state of the [old] county court-house. Upon looking round [I] could see no accommodation for the public, for the bar, for juries or for the judge. There was no evidence of cleanliness in its condition, nor of taste in its structure. It was altogether unsuitable for all or any of the purposes to which a court-house should be devoted [and] was, in a word, everything that was odious and was a reproach to the county.[62]

As Ireland's most impressive provincial courthouses, Morrison's work in Tralee and Carlow must be seen in the context of these complex local forces, which outweighed, it can be argued, more national or imperial agendas, even if never escaping them entirely. Furthermore, in each of these counties, new showpiece assize courthouses appeared alongside much larger numbers of new quarter-sessions courthouses in smaller towns; almost all were funded by government loans.[63] This new architecture of the state represented the interwoven agency of local elites and the imperial state.[64] While Rowan sees these buildings as the legacy of grand jurors who 'voted funds to reinforce the rule of law' – and thus of representing and performing loyalty to the state itself – they are also the legacy of more local narratives of competition and consumption.[65]

## Prisons

The building of Ireland's new county gaols and bridewells was similarly entwined in competing local, national, and imperial agendas – and the boom in construction began somewhat earlier than in the case of courthouses owing to a surprisingly interventionist policy from central government.[66] The Irish Prisons Act of 1810 allowed grand juries to obtain loans for the building of prisons – provided that government had first approved of the proposed design, location, and contract.[67] It followed an inquiry the year before into the mismanagement of Dublin's prisons and a series of scandals in provincial cities involving grand jury corruption, poorly built prisons, or the selection of unsuitable and unhealthy sites.[68] As prisons – especially the larger county gaols in assize towns – became more architecturally complicated, grand jurors drew down huge amounts of government funding to build new and often very distinguished prisons. After 1810, most counties obtained loans of between £6,000 and £10,000 to replace old prisons, but some obtained much more. The Cork city grand jurors borrowed £40,427 for a new gaol built between 1819 to 1825; in Derry the jurors obtained £29,537 to extend a small prison built only thirty years previously; and in Meath the sum of £22,200 was used to employ the architect John Hargrave to design a new gaol in Trim, now admired by architectural historians for its dramatic tiered entrance and rusticated façade (Plate 5).[69] As with courthouses, local feelings of jealousy and competition played a role in grand jurors' deliberations concerning new prisons, but – unlike courthouses – there were also much more clearly formulated agendas from the state itself and from Irish civil society concerning penal reform. The maintenance of law and order was undoubtedly a factor in these debates, but so too were less acknowledged issues such as humanitarianism, charity, 'rational' punishment, and Benthamite utilitarianism.

The great wave of Irish prison building after 1810 owed as much to enthusiastic grand jury borrowing as it did to the lobbying work of the state's Inspector General of Prisons, greatly expanded in the early 1820s, and a long-forgotten Irish charity, the Association for the Improvement of Prisons and of Prison Discipline (AIPPD), founded in 1818.[70] Both sought in their annual reports to expose abuses within prisons and to encourage grand jurors to abandon older unsuitable buildings, combining a belief in 'rational' punishment and a genuine humanitarianism with a desire to create a more efficient national prison system. As noted above, travelling assize judges had powerful opportunities to embarrass jurors into committing to new building work, and they often read aloud the most recent criticisms from the inspectors and the AIPPD. While the inspectors' powers were routed in laws and bureaucratic process, the AIPPD were able to employ social pressure from a civil society perspective. Formed of an alliance of evangelical Anglicans and middle-class Quakers, they had influential connections in Dublin banking circles, maintained a close relationship with their namesakes in London, the Society for the Improvement of Prison Discipline (SIPD), as well as celebrity reformers such as Elizabeth Fry.[71] The combination of these actors and the availability of generous loans meant that almost every Irish prison was replaced – at least once – between the Act of Union and the Great Famine. Around 1830, the state prison inspectors, James Palmer (c. 1780–1850) and Benjamin Blake Woodward (c. 1767–1841), boasted that they had overseen the building of almost 100 new Irish prisons over the course of ten years, both county gaols and smaller bridewells.[72] Such levels of building were unprecedented in Irish history.

In most counties the availability of such generous government loans and the efforts of the inspectors and the AIPPD played a much larger role in instigating new building than changes in the local levels of crime or violence. We can see this in the counties of Armagh and Louth, where grand jurors had delayed expanding their gaols until well into the 1830s. The condition of Armagh's small old gaol was a continual source of frustration to the AIPPD. In 1821, they commented that 'the defects in the original plan present formidable obstacles' to the efficient management of the gaol but hoped that the grand jurors would take seriously the issues of ventilation, heating, religious service, education, and the care of female prisoners.[73] Despite soaring crime rates in the mid-1830s and a series of plans put forward by the inspectors and various architects, the parsimonious grand jurors could not be convinced to build an extension; the gaol had just twenty-seven cells – not much more than a provincial bridewell.[74] By the time various practical issues involving the gaol's restricted urban site had been resolved, crime rates were falling, the AIPPD had faded from its early prominence, and the jurors explained to the inspectors that any extension would be too great a burden on the county's cess-payers.[75] The decision to expand the gaol was instead forced by two assize judges in the mid-1840s, who commented:

> When attending your county on a former occasion, I had reason to complain of the state of your jail [, which] was in a lamentable state, it being utterly impossible to procure accommodation for the safety – the moral safety – of those persons deposited in it for trial, or those undergoing their punishment. I am, however, happy to understand that, since then, you have granted a presentment amounting to five thousand pounds for its improvement .... [There] has been a vast improvement in modern times [which] has had the effect of making jails rather a school for teaching morality and religion, than as formerly, a school for demoralising the habits, and teaching vice.[76]

Their interventions finally encouraged jurors to employ the architect William Murray to build a sixty-one-cell wing to the rear of the gaol between 1846 and 1849, an addition that almost tripled the total number of cells. A similar dynamic can be seen in neighbouring County Louth, where John Neville designed an entirely new gaol in Dundalk, built between 1849 and 1854.[77] For over twenty years the inspectors had lobbied without success to convince the grand jurors to improve their old and rather cramped gaol.[78] When they eventually committed to the project, however, crime rates were declining in the county.[79] Neville's design, which cost £14,500, provided for 126 cells in two radial blocks behind a rather menacing façade (Figure 4.5) that hides the circuitous efforts over so many years of the government inspectors to convince the local grand jurors to take seriously the issue of penal reform in their county. Yet the effect was nonetheless an impressive essay in Italianate classicism – praised at the time and ever since – and included a fanciful belvedere inspection tower that faced onto a green surrounded by a cast-iron railing of fasces.[80]

The extent to which Ireland's nineteenth-century courthouses and prisons can be seen as an architecture with a 'colonial' or 'imperial' legacy is complicated by the complex range of forces that acted upon grand juries, who owned and used these buildings. The state's involvement was primarily financial, by way of loans, and – in the case of prisons – in legislation designed to make gaols rational and more humane spaces than they had been in the eighteenth century. The state's inspectors and assize judges communicated these ideas to individual grand jurors. For the short-lived AIPPD, a powerful sense of charity and duty pervaded their many interventions into local debates – however sceptically we might now regard their patrician tone and earnestness. In the interactions between the state and local government in the building of Irish prisons and courthouses, we should not

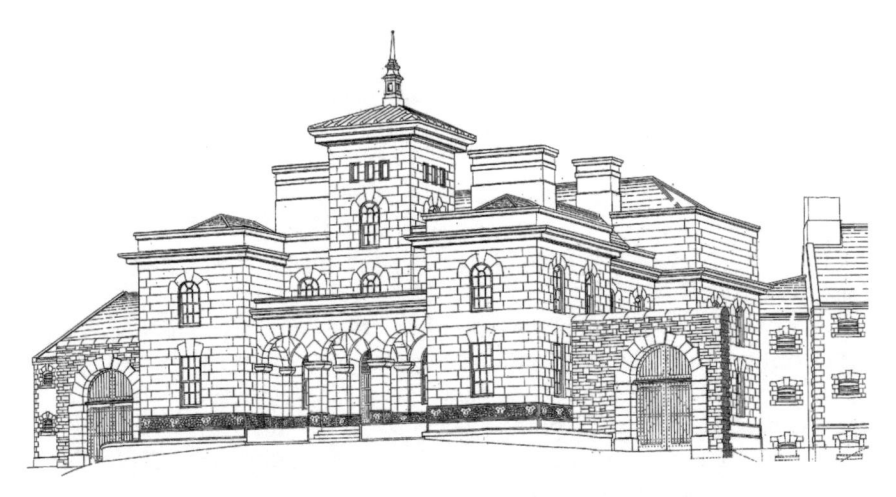

**Figure 4.5** Dundalk county gaol, by John Neville, built 1849–54. Neville's careful use of massing and rustication gave his Italianate façade a uniquely severe and repressive character, but the Louth grand jurors took many years to commit funding to the new building. From the *Civil Engineer and Architect's Journal* (April 1853), p. 121.

overstate the extent to which these were 'colonial' or 'imperial' buildings – at the risk of neglecting so many overlapping local and national agendas.

## Questions of legacy

Later generations forged their own interpretations of what and who these buildings represented. It was, of course, inevitable that the architecture of the state would be instrumentalised in later political unrest and rebellion, and in particular the legacy of the incarceration and execution of political prisoners in institutions such as Dublin's Kilmainham gaol is now well chronicled – most famously in the immediate aftermath of the 1916 Easter Rising.[81] Of the long history of these buildings, the revolutionary years from 1916 to 1923 stand out arguably as the most important in terms of shaping and reshaping their political meanings. Many IRA volunteers, on inheriting this architectural legacy, left no doubt about what and who these courthouses and prisons represented when they burned so many of them during the War of Independence (1919–21) and the Civil War (1922–23). Complex earlier meanings – of competitive local elites, public works loans, or the lobbying of charitable organisations – were collapsed into more top-down and two-dimensional ideas of imperial power: what made courthouses and prisons such rewarding targets for rebels was that they represented, in an uncomplicated manner, the imperial British state – and thereby, in a time of conflict, the enemy. The destruction of the revolutionary years created a new year-zero for many of these buildings, colouring all subsequent interpretations of their legacy. Even today, when the histories of many of these buildings are written (particularly for a public history of tourist audience), what happened during a few short years in the 1910s and 1920s is often given far more prominence than their long nineteenth-century history, which is generally reduced to a simple statement of their date of construction.[82]

Courthouses and prisons were, of course, only some of the many types of buildings that were attacked during the revolutionary years. The country estates of the Irish Protestant landed class, the 'Big Houses', were regular targets, with 275 burned between 1920 and 1923 – seventy-six during the War of Independence and almost 200 in the Civil War.[83] Similarly, the occupation and partial destruction of the Four Courts in Dublin (Figure 4.6) is a very widely studied episode in the Civil War with the resultant loss of centuries of historic documents in the fire at the adjacent Public Record Office.[84] James S. Donnelly and others have studied the burning of Cork City and provincial towns in County Cork during the War of Independence, and others have looked at the quite spectacular destruction of so much railway infrastructure – especially masonry viaducts – by rebel groups.[85] As in any conflict, rebels and soldiers alike commandeered, looted, burned, and destroyed public buildings. For Jason Knirck, the destruction of public architecture in Ireland during the revolutionary years represented legible sequences of contested claims of ownership and possession over the judicial and political power that these buildings embodied: attacks on these buildings were meant as attacks on the colonial or imperial state.[86] So clear was the association between the architectural entity of the Irish courthouse and the hegemonic presence of the British state – by the time of the Civil War – that Kevin O'Higgins, a minister in the Free State Government, reassured the Dáil (the Irish Parliament) that 'Let there not be that prejudiced criticism about British Courts. ... These are not British Courts. There are no British Courts in Ireland at present. There are no Courts in this country at the moment that are not Irish Courts.'[87]

Provincial courthouses and prisons were also targeted during the revolutionary years.[88] Similar to the fate of Big Houses, the Civil War was a more dangerous time for public architecture than the War of Independence, with anti-Treaty IRA rebels engaging in much destruction in provincial towns especially during 1922. A brief look at two of these – Wexford and Tullamore, Co. Offaly – shows how this generation understood their nineteenth-century inheritance. Wexford's assize courthouse had a long and contentious political history: it had been built in the immediate aftermath

Figure 4.6 The Four Courts, Dublin, on fire, 30 June 1922. Occupied by anti-Treaty IRA rebels in April 1922 and shelled by the Free State army two months later, the retreat of the rebels was marked by explosions that destroyed much of one of Dublin's greatest Georgian buildings and the adjacent Public Record Office. Reproduced courtesy of the National Library of Ireland (W. D. Hogan Collection, ref. HOG57).

of the 1798 Rebellion, it was located at the end of a bridge that had played host to gruesome scenes of sectarian fighting and rebel executions.[89] The grand jurors, keen to display their Protestant credentials, commissioned two portrait medallions for the courthouse's main façade, of George III – the then monarch – and William III – the hero of the 'Orange' faction.[90] It is unclear, of course, if the IRA groups who torched the courthouse knew of this legacy, and both portraits had been painted over in the shifting political sands of the 1860s.[91] Early in the morning of 18 June 1921, the courthouse was almost completely destroyed by fire, and in later years it was demolished and a new courthouse built elsewhere.[92] The site is now an unlovely surface-level car park, its nineteenth-century legacy entirely vanished. In Tullamore the assize courthouse and the adjacent county gaol survive much more intact, but both were targeted during the revolutionary years. Here the nineteenth-century background was one of local celebration at the construction of these buildings in the 1820s and 1830s: a prominent local family, the Burys, had lobbied for many decades to move the location of the assizes from the village of Philipstown (now Daingean) to Tullamore. When they eventually succeeded, they organised a public festival to mark the economic prosperity that these large institutions would bring.[93] By 1919 this legacy had faded into insignificance when British forces occupied both the courthouse and gaol, staying for the duration of the War of Independence. During the Civil War, anti-Treaty IRA rebels briefly took their place; but as they were displaced by the Free State army in July 1922, they torched both buildings, reducing them to empty shells.[94] An unsympathetic report in the *Freeman's Journal* condemned the destruction, saying the courthouse was 'one of the best buildings of its kind in Ireland' and that there was 'much indignation amongst the townspeople at the destruction of valuable public property'.[95] The courthouse was later rebuilt (shorn of the British coat-of-arms from the top of its pediment), but the gaol was mostly demolished to make way for a factory, leaving only its main façade.[96] Its gaunt ruin (Figure 4.7) was a powerful political symbol in postcolonial Ireland. This was made all the clearer by a posed

**Figure 4.7** Tullamore county gaol, Co. Offaly, in ruins, c. 1930s. Surpassing even the most romantic nineteenth-century Gothick ruin, the gaol was burned by anti-Treaty IRA forces in 1922 and later mostly demolished. Its erasure from the urban landscape of Tullamore signified to people at the time the retreat not solely of the anti-Treaty rebels but more substantially of the British imperial presence in Ireland. Courtesy Offaly County Library Offaly (ref. OCA/P50/14).

**Figure 4.8** Men hoisting an Irish tricolour atop the ruins of Tullamore gaol, 1937. This posed photograph captured a historic moment in the history of the town as the nineteenth-century prison gave way to a factory. From Michael Byrne, 'The county courthouse at Tullamore and the making of a county town', *Journal of the Offaly Historical and Archaeological Society*, 1 (2003), pp. 108–25, at p. 123. Courtesy Michael Byrne and Offaly County Library (original now held at Offaly County Library).

photograph (Figure 4.8) of men hoisting the Irish tricolour on top of its rubble in the 1930s.[97]

Many other types of public buildings were targeted, perceived by rebels to represent either the British imperial state in 1919–21 or the Free State government after 1922. These included police and military barracks, and occasionally Church of Ireland churches. Royal Irish Constabulary police barracks in Ballinamuck, Co. Longford and Ballytrain, Co. Monaghan were just two among many that IRA rebels sacked.[98] In Limerick, a very extensive early nineteenth-century military barracks was destroyed by anti-Treaty forces as they retreated from that city in the summer of 1922.[99] Protestant churches generally escaped destruction in these years but one exception was St Catherine's Church, Ahascragh, Co. Galway, which was destroyed by arson in July 1922. It was 'the work of demons' according to the local Catholic priest, who organised the passing of a resolution expressing sympathy and friendly relations with their neighbours. The church was later rebuilt, but the culprits were never publicly identified.[100]

The trail of destruction in the 1910s and 1920s forwarded a new definition of which buildings represented the 'architecture of the state' and which did not. Nonetheless, many courthouses, prisons, workhouses, and the great majority of Protestant churches escaped untouched, and where damage did occur repair and reconstruction proceeded quite quickly in the late 1920s.[101] Many settled into rather unremarkable postcolonial uses, including as council offices, schools, or were cleared for new housing or hospitals.[102] The revolutionary years overshadowed the long nineteenth-century history of many of these buildings, including – as this chapter has attempted to resuscitate – some of the agendas of the local elites who oversaw their planning and construction. This spurt of activity was concentrated heavily in the first half of the nineteenth century, in the aftermath of rebellion and the Act of Union and fuelled by generous loans from the British state. This chapter has focused on certain kinds of public buildings that grew out of interactions between the state and local elites, producing a kind of hybrid architecture that represented the uneasy détente between these entities. Yet much more work remains to be done into these buildings and other types of architecture – especially Church of Ireland churches – to understand more fully how they were understood at different times and by different people.[103] Much as Ireland's colonial or imperial status in its long nineteenth-century history is a matter of ongoing debate, the architecture that resulted from this political status is also ripe for further analysis.

## Notes

1 I am grateful to Conor Lucey, Ciaran O'Neill, and Jay Roszman for reading earlier drafts of this chapter and for their extremely helpful comments and suggestions.
2 James Hall, *A Tour Through Ireland*, 2 vols (London, 1813), 1: 43.
3 *Waterford Mirror*, 17 July 1835.
4 William Thackeray, *The Irish Sketch-book 1842* (Dublin: 1st edn 1843, repub. 1990), 77–83.
5 Douglas Kanter, 'The Foxite Whigs, Irish Legislative Independence and the Act of Union, 1785–1806', *Irish Historical Studies* 36, no. 143 (2009): 332–48.
6 See Conor Lucey's Chapter 5 in this volume; Lindsay Proudfoot, *Property Ownership and Urban and Village Improvement in Provincial Ireland, ca. 1700–1845* (London: Historical Geography Research Series 33, 1997); David Dickson, *Old World Colony: Cork and South Munster, 1630–1830* (Cork: Tower Books, 2005), 411–36.
7 James S. Donnelly, Jr, *Captain Rock: The Irish Agrarian Rebellion of 1821–1824* (Madison: University of Wisconsin Press, 2009), 290–336; Richard J. Butler, 'Cork's Courthouses, the Landed Elite and the Rockite Rebellion: Architectural Responses to Agrarian Violence, 1820–27', in *Crime, Violence and the Irish in the Nineteenth Century*, eds Kyle Hughes and Don MacRaild (Liverpool: Liverpool University Press, 2017), 87–111.

8 John O'Connor, *The Workhouses of Ireland: The Fate of Ireland's Poor* (Dublin: Anvil Books, 1995), 120–54.
9 Richard A. Keogh, '"Why, it's like a '98 trial": The Irish Judiciary and the Fenian Trials, 1865–1866', in Hughes and MacReild, *Crime, Violence and the Irish in the Nineteenth Century*, 131–48; Niamh O'Sullivan, *Every Dark Hour: A History of Kilmainham Jail* (Dublin: Liberties Press, 2007).
10 *Atlas of the Irish Revolution*, eds John Crowley, Donal Ó Drisceoil, and Mike Murphy (Cork: Cork University Press, 2017), 346.
11 *The Irish Lord Lieutenancy, c. 1541–1922*, eds Peter Gray and Olwen Purdue (Dublin: University College Dublin Press, 2012).
12 Brendan Smith, *Colonisation and Conquest in Medieval Ireland: The English in Louth, 1170–1330 (Cambridge Studies in Medieval Life and Thought: Fourth Series, Series Number 42)* (Cambridge: Cambridge University Press, 1999); Nicholas Canny, *Making Ireland British, 1580–1650* (Oxford; Oxford University Press, 2001); *Ireland and the British Empire*, ed. Kevin Kenny (Oxford: Oxford University Press, 2004); Jane Ohlmeyer, *Making Ireland English: the Irish Aristocracy in the Seventeenth Century* (New Haven; Yale University Press, 2012).
13 David Fitzpatrick hints at this dichotomy in 'Ireland and the Empire', in *The Oxford History of the British Empire, vol. 3: The Nineteenth Century*, ed. A. Porter (Oxford: Oxford University Press, 1999), 494–521.
14 Scott B. Cook, *Imperial Affinities: Nineteenth-Century Analogies and Exchanges between India and Ireland* (New Delhi: SAGE Publications, 1993), 7–38.
15 Virginia Crossman, 'Colonial Perspectives on Local Government in Nineteenth-century Ireland', in *Was Ireland a Colony? Economics, Politics and Culture in Nineteenth-Century Ireland*, eds Terrence McDonough and Terry Eagleton (Dublin: Irish Academic Press, 2005), 102–16.
16 Stanley Palmer, *Police and Protest in England and Ireland, 1780–1850* (Cambridge: Cambridge University Press, 1988); *Asylums, Mental Health Care and the Irish, 1800–2010*, ed. Pauline M. Prior (Dublin: Irish Academic Press, 2017); Richard J. Butler, 'Rethinking the Origins of the British Prisons Act of 1835: Ireland and the Development of Central-Government Prison Inspection, 1820–35', *The Historical Journal* 59, no. 3 (2016): 721–46.
17 James S. Donnelly, Jr, *The Great Irish Potato Famine* (Stroud: The History Press, 2001), 11–36, 229–45.
18 Irene Whelan, *The Bible War in Ireland: The 'Second Reformation' and the Polarization of Protestant-Catholic Relations, 1800–1840* (Dublin: The Lilliput Press, 2012); G. A. Bremner, *Imperial Gothic: Religious Architecture and High Anglican Culture in the British Empire, C. 1840–1870* (New Haven: Yale University Press, 2013), 350–63.
19 Richard McMahon, *The Races of Europe: Construction of National Identities in the Social Sciences, 1839–1939* (London: Palgrave Macmillan, 2016), 247–86.
20 Fitzpatrick, 'Ireland and the Empire', 495–6.

21 Patrick Joyce, *The Rule of Freedom: Liberalism and the Modern City* (London: Verso Books, 2003), 35–56; *The State of Freedom: A Social History of the British State Since 1800* (Cambridge: Cambridge University Press, 2013), 44–5.
22 K. T. Hoppen, *Governing Hibernia: British Politicians and Ireland, 1800–1921* (Oxford: Oxford University Press, 2016), 1–3, 53–4.
23 Alvin Jackson, 'Ireland, the Union, and the Empire, 1800–1960', in Kenny, *Ireland and the British Empire*, 123–35; Joe Cleary, 'Amongst Empires: A Short History of Ireland and Empire Studies in International Context', *Éire-Ireland* 42, no. 1–2 (2007): 11–57; Stephen Howe, 'Questioning the (Bad) Question: "Was Ireland a Colony?"', *Irish Historical Studies* 36, no. 142 (2008): 138–52; Barry Crosbie, 'Ireland and the Empire in the Nineteenth Century', in *The Cambridge History Of Ireland: Volume III, 1730–1880*, ed. James Kelly (Cambridge: Cambridge University Press, 2018), 617–36.
24 Edward McParland, 'The Englishness of Irish Architecture?', *Cambridge Review* 95, no. 2220 (3 May 1974): 112–16.
25 Alistair Rowan, 'The Irishness of Irish Architecture', *Architectural History* 40 (1997): 17–18.
26 Ciarán Ó Murchadha, *Sable Wings over the Land: Ennis, County Clare, and its Wider Community during the Great Famine* (Ennis: Clare Local Studies Project (CLASP Press), 1998), 240.
27 Bremner, *Imperial Gothic*, 350–63, 431–36; *India in Art in Ireland*, ed. Kathleen James-Chakraborty (London: Routledge, 2016).
28 John Montague, 'Church of Ireland Churches in the Nineteenth Century', in *Art And Architecture Of Ireland: Volume IV: Architecture 1600–2000*, ed. Rolf Loeber (New Haven: Yale University Press, 2014), 305.
29 Crosbie, 'Ireland and the Empire in the Nineteenth Century', 624.
30 Margaret Kelleher, *The Maamtrasna Murders: Language, Life and Death in Nineteenth-Century Ireland* (Dublin: University College Dublin Press, 2018).
31 Katie Barclay, *Men on Trial: Performing Emotion, Embodiment and Identity in Ireland, 1800–45* (Manchester: Manchester University Press, 2019), 84.
32 Ciaran O'Neill, 'Bourgeois Ireland, or, on the Benefits of Keeping One's Hands Clean', in Kelly, *Cambridge History Of Ireland: Volume III, 1730–1880*, 525.
33 Virginia Crossman, 'The Growth of the State in the Nineteenth Century', in Kelly, *Cambridge History Of Ireland: Volume III, 1730–1880*, 542–66.
34 For an overview and key readings, see Loeber, *Art and Architecture of Ireland: Volume IV: Architecture 1600–2000*. See also some recent work: Adrian J. Kirwan, 'R. K. Edgeworth and Optical Telegraphy in Ireland, c. 1790–1805', *Proceedings of the Royal Irish Academy*, 117C (2017): 209–35; Judith Hill, 'Architecture in the Aftermath of Union: Building the Viceregal Chapel in Dublin Castle, 1801–15', *Architectural History*, 60 (2017): 182–217; Evan Wilson, 'The Naval Defence of Ireland during the French Revolutionary and Napoleonic Wars', *Historical Research* 92, no. 257 (2019): 568–84.
35 Lunatic Asylums (Ireland) Act, 1820 (1 Geo. IV, c. 98); Poor Relief (Ireland) Act, 1838 (1 & 2 Vict., c. 56); O'Connor, *Workhouses of Ireland*, 68–76;

Loeber, *Art and Architecture of Ireland: Volume IV: Architecture 1600–2000*, 200–2, 212–14.

36 Anglican churches also fit into this category, see Loeber, *Art and Architecture of Ireland: Volume IV: Architecture 1600–2000*, 304–8; Bremner, *Imperial Gothic*, 350–63.
37 See for example 'An Act to Prevent the illegal raising of Money by Grand Juries and the misapplying of Money legally raised, etc.', 1705 (4 Anne, c. 6); Grand Jury (Ireland) Act, 1836 (6 & 7 Will. IV, c. 116).
38 P. J. Meghen, 'The Administrative Work of the Grand Jury', *Administration: Journal of the Institute of Public Administration of Ireland*, 6:3 (Autumn 1958): 247–64; Virginia Crossman, *Local Government in Nineteenth-Century Ireland* (Belfast: The Institute of Irish Studies, 1994), 33–41.
39 Hoppen, *Governing Hibernia*, 3; Brendán Mac Suibhne, *The End of Outrage: Post-Famine Adjustment in Rural Ireland* (Oxford: Oxford University Press, 2017), 64.
40 Niamh Howlin, *Juries in Ireland: Laypersons and Law in the Long Nineteenth Century* (Dublin: Four Courts Press, 2017).
41 Brendan O'Donoghue, *The Irish County Surveyors, 1834–1944* (Dublin: Four Courts Press, 2007), 3–25.
42 David M. Nolan, 'The County Cork Grand Jury, 1836–1899' (MA diss., University College Cork, 1974); David Broderick, *Local Government in Nineteenth-century County Dublin: The Grand Jury* (Dublin: Four Courts Press, 2007), 14.
43 Speeches by George Dawson and Daniel O'Connell in *Hansard* 1 (3rd ser.), 9 Dec. 1830, cols 909–32; Broderick, *Local Government in Nineteenth-century County Dublin*, 10.
44 Douglas Kanter, 'Robert Peel and the Waning of the "influence of the Crown" in Ireland, 1812–1818"', *New Hibernia Review* 5, no. 2 (2001): 54–71.
45 Edward McParland, *James Gandon: Vitruvius Hibernicus* (London: The Book Service Ltd, 1985), 144–65; *Returns of all sums of money ... in aid of public works in Ireland, since the union*, H.C. 1839 (540), xliv, 12.
46 Armagh (built 1807–10); Derry (built 1813–17); Dundalk (built 1813–21), *Dictionary of Irish Architects*, www.dia.ie. Accessed 29 June 2023.
47 Public Works Loan Act, 1817 (57 Geo. III, c. 34); A. R. G. Griffiths, 'The Irish Board of Works in the Famine Years', *The Historical Journal* 13, no. 4 (Dec. 1970): 634–52; Frederick O'Dwyer, 'Building Empires: Architecture, Politics and the Board of Works, 1760–1860', *Irish Architectural and Decorative Studies*, 5 (2002): 108–75.
48 L. M. Cullen, *An Economic History of Ireland since 1660* (London: Harper Collins, 1972), 100–20.
49 Ruth Heard, 'Public Works in Ireland, 1800–1831' (MA diss., Trinity College Dublin, 1977).
50 Public Works Loan (Ireland) Act, 1818 (58 Geo. III, c. 88); Employment of the Poor (Ireland) Act, 1822 (3 Geo. IV, c. 34).

51 *Hansard* 7 (2nd ser.), 23 May 1822, col. 727; M. W. Flinn, 'The Poor Employment Act of 1817', *Economic History Review* 14, no. 1 (1961): 82–92.

52 *Account (since the union) of all sums of money ... for public works ... for England and Scotland*, H.C. 1847 (718), liv, pp. 160–1. The majority of these loans were for terms of five to ten years, repayable with 5 per cent interest, and most loans were paid off in full.

53 *Freeman's Journal*, 23 April 1828.

54 Gearóid Ó Tuathaigh, *Ireland before the Famine, 1798–1848* (Dublin: Gill and Macmillan, 1990, 2nd edn 2007), 29–41, 80–93; Shane Kilcommins, Ian O'Donnell, Eoin O'Sullivan, and Barry Vaughn, *Crime, Punishment and the Search for Order in Ireland* (Dublin: Institute of Public Administration, 2004), 1–37; Hoppen, *Governing Hibernia*, 51–3.

55 Donal A. Murphy, *The Two Tipperarys: The National and Local Politics ... of the Unique 1838 Division into Two Ridings: No. 1 (Regional Studies in Political & Administrative History* (Nenagh; Relay, 1994); Michael Byrne, *Legal Offaly: The County Courthouse at Tullamore and the Legal Profession in County Offaly from the 1820s to the Present Day* (Tullamore: Esker Press, 2008).

56 Neal Garnham, *The Courts, Crime and the Criminal Law in Ireland, 1692–1760* (Dublin: Irish Academic Press, 1996), 71–86, 104–8, 119–32.

57 James Ebenezer Bicheno, *Ireland and its economy, being the result of observations made in ... the autumn of 1829* (London, 1830), 137.

58 *The Architecture of Richard Morrison (1767–1849) & William Vitruvius Morrison (1794–1838)*, ed. Ann Martha Rowan (Dublin: Irish Architectural Archive, 1989), 10; Edward McParland, 'The public work of architects in Ireland during the neo-classical period' (PhD thesis, Cambridge University, 1975), 246–7.

59 Rowan, *Morrison*, 149–53.

60 Henry Westenra to William Gregory, 25 July 1827 (National Archives of Ireland, CSORP 1827/1453). D. R. Fisher, *The History of Parliament: The House of Commons, 1820–1832*, 7 vols (Cambridge: Cambridge University, 2009), 7: 696–700.

61 *Returns of all sums of money ... in aid of public works in Ireland, since the union*, p. 13; *Second report of the commissioners on public works, Ireland*, H.C. 1834 (240), 12.

62 *Finn's Leinster Journal*, 11 April 1827 (the judge was the lord chief justice, Charles Kendal Bushe).

63 *Returns of all sums of money ... in aid of public works in Ireland, since the union*, 12–13; Butler, 'Cork's courthouses', 96–8.

64 Barclay, *Men on Trial*, 59–91.

65 Rowan, 'Irishness of Irish Architecture', 18.

66 Butler, 'Rethinking the Origins of the British Prisons Act'.

67 Prisons (Ireland) Act, 1810 (50 Geo. III, c. 103).

68 Forster Archer, 'Report of the state of gaols of Ireland for the year 1802', f. 3 (Houses of the Oireachtas Library, Dublin, MS.7H28); *Inspector general's report on ... the prisons in Ireland for ... 1807*, H.C. 1808 (239), ix, pp. 5,

16–17; *Report from the commissioners appointed to inquire into ... the state prisons and other gaols in Ireland*, H.C. 1809 (265), vii; *Hansard* 15 (1st ser.), February 19, 1810, col. 468; anon., 'Prison abuses in Ireland', *The Examiner*, 14 October 1810.
69 *Returns of all sums of money ... in aid of public works in Ireland, since the union*, 6–9.
70 Anon., *A statement of the objects of the association for the improvement of prisons and of prison discipline in Ireland* (Dublin, 1819); Anon., *First report of the association for the improvement of prisons and of prison discipline in Ireland, for 1819* (Dublin, 1820), 5–6; Prisons (Ireland) Act, 1821 (1 & 2 Geo. IV, c. 57); Prisons (Ireland) Act, 1822 (3 Geo. IV, c. 64); Oliver MacDonagh, *The Inspector General: Sir Jeremiah Fitzpatrick and the Politics of Social Reform, 1783–1802* (London: Croom Helm Ltd, 1981), 319–26; Butler, 'Rethinking the Origins of the British Prisons Act', 730–44.
71 Robin Evans, *The Fabrication of Virtue: English Prison Architecture, 1750–1840* (Cambridge: Cambridge University Press, 1982), 239–41.
72 *Ninth report ... on ... the prisons of Ireland, 1831*, H.C. 1830–31 (172), iv, 7–9, 11–13.
73 Anon., *Third report of the association for the improvement of prisons, and of prison discipline in Ireland, for 1821* (Dublin, 1822), 24–6.
74 *Prisons of Ireland: report of inspectors general, 1825*, H.C. 1825 (493), xxii, 26; *Fifth report ... on ... the prisons of Ireland, 1827*, H.C. 1826–27 (471), xi, 7, 26–7; *Sixteenth report ... on ... the prisons of Ireland, 1838*, H.C. 1837–38 (186), xxix, 8, 24–5; drawings by William Murray, 1837 (Irish Architectural Archive, RIAI Murray Collection, Acc. 92/46.20–22).
75 *Twenty-first report ... on ... the prisons of Ireland, 1843*, H.C. 1843 (462), xxvii, 3, 28–9.
76 *Armagh Guardian*, 4 March 1845 (the judges were Philip Crampton and Robert Torrens).
77 John Neville, 'Dundalk County Prison', *Civil Engineer and Architect's Journal* 16, no. 229 (April 1853): 121.
78 *Prisons of Ireland: report of inspectors general, 1825*, H.C. 1825 (493), xxii, 51; *Seventh report ... on ... the prisons of Ireland, 1829*, H.C. 1829 (10), xii, 40; *Sixteenth report ... on ... the prisons of Ireland, 1838*, H.C. 1837–38 (186), xxix, p. 31; *Nineteenth report ... on ... the prisons of Ireland, 1841*, H.C. 1841 (299), xi, 36.
79 *Tables showing the number of criminal offenders committed for trial ... in Ireland ... in the year 1845*, H.C. 1846 (696), xxv, 9 (and subsequent annual reports); *Twenty-fifth report ... on ... the prisons of Ireland, 1847*, H.C. 1847 (805), xxix, 54.
80 *Dublin Builder*, 5:87, 1 August 1863, 121; Thomas Lacy, *Sights and Scenes of our Fatherland* (London, 1863), 223–4; Christine Casey and Alistair Rowan, *The Buildings of Ireland: North Leinster: the Counties of Longford, Louth, Meath and Westmeath* (London: Penguin, 1993), 247.

81 Pat Cooke, *A History of Kilmainham Gaol, 1796–1924* (Dublin: Office of Public Works, Ireland, 1998); Fearghal McGarry, *The Rising: Easter 1916* (Oxford: Oxford University Press, 2010), 254–6.
82 Pat Cooke, 'Kilmainham Gaol: Confronting Change', *Irish Arts Review*, 23 (2002): 42–5; Richard J. Butler, 'The Afterlives of Galway Jail, "Difficult" Heritage, and the Maamtrasna Murders: Representations of an Irish Urban Space, 1882–2018', *Irish Historical Studies* 44, no. 166 (Nov. 2020): 295–325.
83 Terence Dooley, *The Decline of the Big House in Ireland* (Dublin: Wolfhound Press, 2001); Terence Dooley, *Burning the Big House: The Story of the Irish Country House in a Time of War and Revolution* (New Haven: Yale University Press, 2022).
84 Ronan Keane, 'A Mass of Crumbling Ruins: The Destruction of the Four Courts in June 1922', in *The Four Courts: 200 Years: Essays to Commemorate the Bicentenary of the Four Courts*, ed. Caroline Costello (Dublin: Incorporated Council of Law Reporting for Ireland, 1996), 159–68; Yvonne Whelan, *Reinventing Modern Dublin: Streetscape, Iconography and the Politics of Identity* (Dublin: University College Dublin Press, 2003).
85 James S. Donnelly, Jr, "Unofficial' British Reprisals and IRA Provocations, 1919–20: The Cases of Three Cork Towns', *Éire-Ireland* 45, nos 1–2 (2010): 152–97; 'Railways: Campaign of Destruction', in *Atlas of the Irish Revolution*, 688–90.
86 Jason Knirck, *Afterimage of the Revolution: Cumann na nGaedheal and Irish Politics, 1922–1932* (Madison: University of Wisconsin Press, 2004), 63–8.
87 Dáil debates, 29 September 1922.
88 An exception is Gemma Clark, *Everyday Violence in the Irish Civil War* (Cambridge: Cambridge University Press, 2014), 62–70.
89 James Glassford, *Notes of Three Tours in Ireland in 1824 and 1826* (Bristol, 1832), 127; Rowan, *Morrison*, 172–3; Jarlath Glynn, *Wexford: Then & Now* (Dublin: Pitkin Publishing, 2013), 60–1, 88–9.
90 Lacy, *Sights and Scenes*, 408
91 *Dublin Builder*, 4: 61, 1 July, 1862, 172. [Author Query on date raised]
92 *Irish Examiner*, 22 June 1921.
93 Printed notice concerning Tullamore's new gaol, 13 September 1826 (Westmeath County Library, Howard Bury Papers, P1/28); Michael Byrne, 'The County Courthouse at Tullamore and the Making of a County Town', *Journal of the Offaly Historical and Archaeological Society*, 1 (2003): 108–25.
94 Byrne, 'The County Courthouse at Tullamore', 121–3.
95 *Freeman's Journal*, 2 July 1922.
96 *Irish Builder*, 67:15, 8 August 1925, 650; *Offaly Independent*, 25 September 1937.
97 Photographs taken during demolition, c. 1930s (Offaly County Library, P50/14, acc. nos 434–5); *Midland Tribune*, 25 September 1937. I am grateful to Michael Byrne for these references.
98 *Atlas of the Irish Revolution*, 596, 621
99 *Atlas of the Irish Revolution*, 706–7.

100 *Irish Independent*, 25 July 1922; *Connacht Tribune*, 21 October 1922; *Atlas of the Irish Revolution*, 779.
101 Christine Casey, *The Buildings of Ireland: Dublin* (New Haven: Yale University Press, 2005), 96–8, 145–6.
102 Butler, 'The Afterlives of Galway Jail'.
103 Bremner, *Imperial Gothic*, 350–63.

# 5

# Studied indifference: eighteenth-century Irish architecture in modern British architectural histories[1]

*Conor Lucey*

In response to new political jurisdictions and academic discourses, postwar historians of eighteenth-century British architecture, led by Rudolf Wittkower, Sir John Summerson, David Watkin, and others, abandoned the broad strokes of late nineteenth-century narratives in favour of an increasingly Anglocentric position and its associated, and inevitable, centre–periphery thesis.[2] But a history of British architectural innovation in the Georgian era with England as the sole fulcrum is undeniably problematic, not least when considering the complex evolution of Palladianism and neo-classicism, the twin poles of the classical paradigm at the heart of British and Irish design for the period. Given that the formal qualities of Palladianism have long been associated with the Whig political hegemony and its attendant project of cultural improvement – a position only recently challenged by Barbara Arciszewska, Elizabeth McKellar, Dana Arnold, and others – the singular lack of a representative public building in that style in London has long been an obstacle for historians of architecture in Great Britain.[3] This position is aggravated by the existence of superlative examples of Palladian civic architecture at the supposed margins, not least the much-lauded Parliament House in Dublin (1728–39), designed by the enigmatic Sir Edward Lovett Pearce (Plate 6 and Figure 5.1).[4]

This chapter takes the form of a selective review of the interpretation and reception of eighteenth-century Irish architecture in modern British architectural histories. It argues that the minimising of Irish buildings in the British historiography expresses a misplaced confidence in the superiority of English design in the story of the supposed 'national' character of Palladianism – an historical position, characterised by David Watkin as 'the worship of England', that continues to be reinforced in both academic and populist contexts.[5] While historians of Georgian Britain have customarily acclaimed the Irish Parliament House as a 'strikingly original'[6] design and a 'sophisticated synthesis of Classical and Palladian sources',[7] the following analysis demonstrates how its significance as (arguably) the acme of representative public architecture in the early eighteenth-century Anglophone

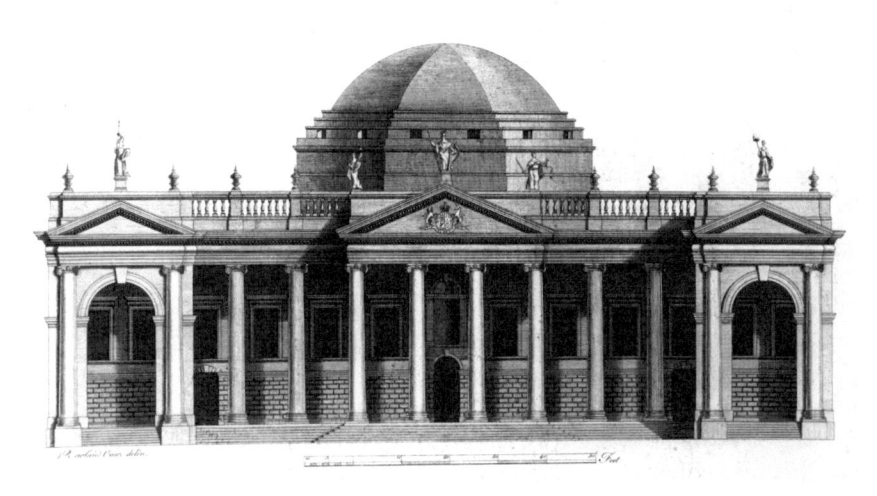

**Figure 5.1** Bernard Scalé after Rowland Omer, 'The Geometrical Elevation of the Parliament House Dublin', engraving, 1767. Courtesy of the Irish Architectural Archive.

world has been downplayed: commissioned by the wrong parliament, designed by the wrong architect, and situated in the wrong city on the wrong island, it upsets established hierarchical narratives that insist on the authority of England (and the primacy of English archetypes) for the dissemination of architectural modernity in the British empire. Taking its cue from modern scholarship on the forging of British national and imperial identities, and reflecting on Ireland's contested place within that history, this chapter proposes that a new synthesis of British and Irish architectural histories offers opportunities to dismantle artificial partitions, bringing 'traditionally separate spheres of scholarship and understanding into genuine dialogue'.[8]

Although the history of Pearce's design is well rehearsed in Irish history, a brief précis is likely necessary for many readers of the present volume. Of critical importance at the outset is an understanding of both the sovereignty of the Dublin parliament and its subordinate relationship to Westminster, reflecting Ireland's complex political identity as an 'unruly palimpsest' forged from 'an untidy jumble [of] "kingdom", "colony", "dependency", and, faintly, "nation"'.[9] Given the intricate and longstanding social, cultural, and political relationship between England and Ireland, the building has generally been regarded as a sign of the growing confidence of the ruling Protestant Ascendancy class during the unsettled years of the 1720s, when the passing of the Declaratory Act (by which the Irish House of Lords lost its appellate jurisdiction), economic recession, and the introduction of debased coinage encouraged a 'feeling of self-assertion'.[10] It has also been understood to embody what David Hayton has termed 'Irish Whiggism', committed to 'the preservation of the powers of parliament and the liberties of the subject; the rejection of administrative corruption; concern for the prosperity of Ireland; and fear of the revival of Catholic power'.[11] This 'patriotic' ideology was central to its role in government throughout the eighteenth century: although not wholly autonomous as a legislative body, the Irish Parliament was instrumental in voting taxes and introducing heads of bills. As a consequence, opinions and interpretations of the building in iconographical terms are varied in Irish scholarship. Conceived under the imprimatur of William Conolly (1662–1729), the renowned Speaker of the House of Commons who boasted impeccable 'patriot' credentials, Patrick Walsh has recently described Pearce's design as both 'a statement in stone' of the 'early Georgian Irish political, cultural and ideological nation, in all its complexities and contradictions', and as an expression of the 'economic patriotism' characteristic of its parliamentary elite.[12] On the other hand, given its 'modest legislative output, constitutional subordination to the Castle and to the Irish and British privy councils, and its management by a handful of faction leaders', David Dickson has characterised the building as 'an exaggerated political statement'.[13] Importantly, for our purposes, the Parliament House was not understood then or now to be the 'Epitome of the Kingdom' in the same manner intended for Castletown House, county Kildare (built 1722–29), the grand country pile of Speaker Conolly;[14] Pearce's recommendation of locally sourced materials for the building specification of the Parliament House, for example, being understood less in terms of patriotic motivation, as at Castletown, and more in terms of his 'shrewd' lobbying for this high-profile commission.[15]

The subsequent architectural history of the Parliament House during the course of the eighteenth century need not detain us, but some political context is necessary to shed light on the building's reception in modern British scholarship. Economic and legislative gains serving the patriot interest, following the reform of the Navigation Acts in 1779 and the repeal of the Declaratory Act in 1782, were quickly dashed following the violent Rebellion of 1798, an uprising organised by the Society of United Irishmen, a republican group influenced by the ideas of the American and French revolutions who sought 'an equal representation of all the people in parliament'. This invigorated concern for a union of the two island kingdoms, since recognised as an 'increasingly integrative tendency of British political thinking on Ireland after 1750'.[16] In the wake of the

Acts of Union in 1800, which marked the formal creation of the United Kingdom of Great Britain and Ireland, the Parliament House in Dublin was effectively redundant, and was subsequently repurposed in 1804–08 as the headquarters for the Bank of Ireland (established by royal charter in 1783).

In formalist terms, as we shall see, the building has received unanimous praise from historians and critics on both sides of the Irish Sea. Conceived in response to the richness of the British classical canon at the beginning of the eighteenth century, it has long been celebrated for its academic rigour (with a nod to Palladio and Vitruvius) and the visual clarity of its composition. Hailed as exemplary of both the Anglo-Palladian style and an incipient European antiquarianism, Pearce's grandly scaled portico and colonnade, reflecting his discerning architectural connoisseurship, invariably drew on ancient and modern sources but achieved a 'dramatic and monumental effect' that was bold and innovative for its date (Figure 5.2).[17] The general consensus is that the building embodies 'a rare moment in Irish, indeed in European, architecture',[18] and its architect enjoys a reputation as 'one of the pioneers of European neo-classicism'.[19]

Figure 5.2 Sir Edward Lovett Pearce, colonnade of Parliament House, Dublin, 1729–39. Photograph by Louis Haugh.

## Palladianism on the peripheries

For readers unfamiliar with the architectural history of Ireland, it is important to recognise how the Anglocentrism of British architectural history generally, and its pernicious influence on the reception of Irish architecture particularly, is reinforced in modern, accessible texts aimed at the general reader. A typical example of this propensity is Robert Tavernor's *Palladio and Palladianism* (1991), part of the popular 'World of Art Series' published by Thames and Hudson, which includes substantial sections on Andrea Palladio's theory, practice, and legacy, the seventeenth and eighteenth-century iterations of Palladianism in Great Britain (principally England), and Anglo-Palladianism in America, but not a single reference either to Ireland or to an Irish building.[20] But such sins of omission were not always the rule. Early surveys from the British perspective, such as Banister Fletcher's *A History of Architecture on the Comparative Method* (1896), and Reginald Blomfield's two-volume *A History of Renaissance Architecture in England, 1500–1800* (1897), understood Irish eighteenth-century architecture properly as an expression of English sensibilities. So, while Fletcher devotes a discrete chapter to Irish architecture of the early Christian and mediaeval periods, its 'Renaissance' architecture is 'included with English architecture of that period'.[21] Indeed, while the Parliament House is curiously ignored in both surveys, Blomfield asserts that Dublin's neo-classical Custom House (1781–91) 'ranks high in the record of the eighteenth century': in common with Newgate Prison and Somerset House in London, it symbolises 'the final effort of the eighteenth century tradition … the three are probably the finest public buildings erected in Great Britain since the time of Wren'.[22] The language is significant here: these are the finest eighteenth-century buildings 'in Great Britain', a reminder of Ireland's constituency within the United Kingdom at the time of publication.

A more holistic approach is advanced in A. E. Richardson's *Monumental Classic Architecture in Great Britain and Ireland* (1914), a book concerned with examining the 'academic aspect of Neo-Classic architecture'. The narrative begins in 1730, a year that represented, according to the author, 'the earliest date at which both architects and amateurs sought to interpret the true Classic spirit'; an orthodox classicism that emerged under the aegis of celebrated English architect Richard Boyle, Lord Burlington (who, it should be remembered, possessed titles in both the English and Irish peerages).[23] Richardson describes how the 'Roman Palladian phase of *English* architecture' represented a move towards 'the appreciation of monumental qualities',[24] and defines 'monumental architecture' as possessing 'an indescribable austerity and remoteness, a sense of reposeful dignity […] and simplicity of effect that impresses the mind at once with the greatness of the idea'. Significant, for our purposes, is the suggestion that the 'immutable idea' is embodied in a design 'irrespective of nationality or period'.[25] For Richardson, the 'first building of importance' to embody these qualities was Dublin's Parliament House.[26] In other words, Burlington's classical ideal was realised in Dublin; by implication, its location in Dublin rather than London was immaterial to his thesis. Formalist concerns clearly trumped national identities here, perhaps encouraged by the fact that the building no longer served its original purpose as a seat of government.

Here we must pause and introduce some further historical context. While the formal rejection of the Acts of Union was a perennial debate of the nineteenth century, the revolutionary period of the early twentieth century in Ireland inaugurated the series of events, notably the founding of the Irish Free State in 1922, that would ultimately result in independence from Britain. With the establishment of the Republic of Ireland in 1949, the nation's histories – both political and architectural – would soon take on a different complexion.

Although writing in the decades that witnessed Ireland's departure from the political jurisdiction of Westminster, Sir John Summerson's seminal *Architecture in Britain, 1530–1830* (1953) understood Irish Palladianism to be 'as intimately joined to the London school as if the Irish Sea were no greater an affair to negotiate than a couple of English counties'.[27] On the other hand, we witness in this text the beginning of the gradual diminishing of Irish buildings in the development of British architecture: as political boundaries were drawn between the islands – and indeed on the island of Ireland itself – so Irish architecture was awarded a subsidiary role in this narrative. While acknowledging that Ireland possesses 'two or three at least' of the 'finest monuments' in the Palladian style in the British Isles,[28] the chapter entitled 'The Palladian Movement' is almost exclusively devoted to the English country house and its evolution in the work of Burlington, William Kent, and Colen Campbell, the key exponents of the Anglo-Palladian school in England. Pearce, described by Summerson (in later, revised editions of the book) as 'one of the most interesting figures in the whole Palladian school', is confined to a later chapter that examines, in descending order, the role of books in the dissemination of the style, Palladianism in the provinces (namely Bath and Liverpool), the second generation of Palladian architects (including Isaac Ware, Sir Robert Taylor, and James Paine), the development of the villa typology, Palladianism in Scotland, and, finally, Palladianism in Ireland.[29] Some of the 'finest monuments' of Palladianism, in Summerson's own estimation, are thus relegated to a supplementary role in his account of its origination and maturation.

A more measured account of the significance of the Parliament House is presented by Dan Cruickshank in *A Guide to the Georgian Buildings of*

*Britain and Ireland* (1985), a book undertaken with the cooperation of the National Trust and the Irish Georgian Society (and no doubt the impetus for its more impartial approach). Cruickshank is unequivocal that early attempts at forming a public architecture in the Palladian idiom in Great Britain got off to 'a bad start'; by contrast, 'something remarkable had happened in Ireland'. Despite no attempt to account for the stimulus of such a 'remarkable' event, Cruickshank is clear that Pearce produced a building 'of supreme importance'. He continues:

> it is the only really major and successful building produced by the Palladian movement in its early phase. Of course, Pearce was not a Palladian in the Burlington mould but this building, with its gravity, its powerful and classically correct external detailing and, in particular, its mighty temple-like portico, is very much in the English Palladian manner – even if the bold recession of the portico within flanking colonnaded wings is more Vanbrughian than Burlingtonian.[30]

Despite being 'the only really major and successful building' of its type in these islands, the building is damned with faint praise: Pearce was 'of course' not a Palladian architect 'in the Burlington mould', and so its pedigree as the foremost civic monument of the age is undermined. Significant too is the reference to Sir John Vanbrugh, a key exponent of the baroque style in England, which acts to further diminish Pearce's exercise in Palladian classicism. For Cruickshank, no English public building of the period compares with its pioneering design and uniquely representative character, yet it is not considered a paradigm of British Palladianism.

Giles Worsley's *Classical Architecture in Britain: The Heroic Age* (1995), although evidently stimulated by the author's 'growing dissatisfaction with the conventional view of the period' (unambiguously a reference to Summerson's *Architecture in Britain*), nonetheless remains squarely on familiar terrain.[31] Acknowledging the Anglocentric nature of British architectural histories generally – with England as the 'dominant cultural influence' – Worsley arguably does little to complicate Summerson's line of argument. Describing Dublin's Parliament House as 'a sophisticated synthesis of Classical and Palladian sources which contemporary English architects would have found hard to match', and as 'a building which Burlington would have been proud to include in his projected rebuilding of Whitehall', the building is nonetheless confined to a chapter entitled 'Palladianism on the peripheries'.[32] Under Pearce, according to Worsley, 'Irish architecture had shone forth as being as advanced as anything in England and considerably more so than anything in Scotland or America'.[33] Paradoxically, Worsley is unwilling to consider the Irish Parliament House as a key building in a broader, far-reaching history that considers Palladianism as part of a wider British phenomenon *without* a single, dominant cultural centre.[34] Francis Dodsworth's account of the 'governmental connotations' of Palladian classicism reiterates this long-standing position: here it is William Kent, specifically for his Treasury Building at Whitehall (1733–36) – although its design postdates the construction of the Dublin building (noted here in passing only) – who is celebrated as the first architect, since Inigo Jones, to achieve an expression of antique *virtus*.[35]

This is arguably the crux of the historiographical problem. Style, as the material embodiment of national, political, and/or cultural identities, is an established trope in architectural histories: the Palladian style was long held to embody a key moment in the development of a specifically national taste in British architecture. With that in mind, it would appear that historians will not (or perhaps cannot?) entertain a history of such an emblematic architectural style and its reach in colonial and imperial terms if forced to acknowledge that one of its most iconic and representative public buildings, no matter how monumental, 'remarkable', or 'strikingly original', was erected on the peripheries. This is surely at the root of Frank Salmon's recent account of Kent's unrealised designs for a new parliament building for London (created 1733–40/1), which contains no reference to Pearce's building in Dublin or to the extensive Irish scholarship devoted to it (discussed below).[36] Describing how Kent's drawings 'go to the heart of what might be seen as a problem long latent in the history of British "Palladianism", namely the failure of the genre to produce significant public architecture', Salmon overlooks what we might call the 'Irish context' for these English designs.[37] Indeed, an Irish context would necessarily extend to the fact that Kent's 'concept of the barrel vault over an apsidal space ... from Palladio's restoration of the "Temple of the Sun and the Moon" in Rome', was the same source already cited and realised in Pearce's design for the House of Lords in Dublin, the foremost Pearcean interior to have survived the building's conversion to a bank in the early nineteenth century (Figure 5.3).[38] With reference to the corpus of designs prepared in answer to a 1732 report calling for new accommodation for the London parliament, Salmon characterises the response – including proposals from such luminaries as Burlington, Kent, and Nicholas Hawksmoor – as 'a sudden rush of enthusiasm in Lord Burlington's program to beget a national architecture for Britain'.[39] But the reason for this 'sudden rush' is not accounted for, and the fact that Dublin's Parliament House had opened for business a year earlier, in 1731, is not entertained as a possible factor in the impetus to 'beget a national architecture'.[40] Salmon examines William Kent's designs in splendid isolation – context would, of course, moderate the significance of Kent as the foremost authority in the Palladian idiom (the purpose of the

Figure 5.3 Sir Edward Lovett Pearce, House of Lords, Parliament House, Dublin, 1729–39. Photograph by David Davison. Photograph by David Davison.

exhibition and the accompanying publication from which Salmon's essay derives), and London as the locus of architectural innovation.

Salmon's oversight was inadvertently bolstered by a recent exhibition (2015/16) held at the Royal Institute of British Architects in London, entitled 'Palladian Design – the good, the bad and the unexpected'.[41] Focused predictably on English and Scottish architects, it ventured beyond Great Britain to include historic buildings in America, France, Germany, India, Indonesia, and Russia.[42] The Irish school of Palladianism, though Irish buildings were entirely omitted from its wide geographical sweep, was represented – if not formally acknowledged – by the display of Pearce's annotated edition of Andrea Palladio's *I quattro libri dell'architettura*[43] (Figure 5.4). (As Edward McParland has shown, Pearce was unique among his English and Irish peers for his empirically based yet discriminating appraisal of Palladio's villa typology.)[44] But here Pearce suffers the ignominy of being characterised as a 'distinguished amateur architect' in

*Eighteenth-century Irish architecture* 137

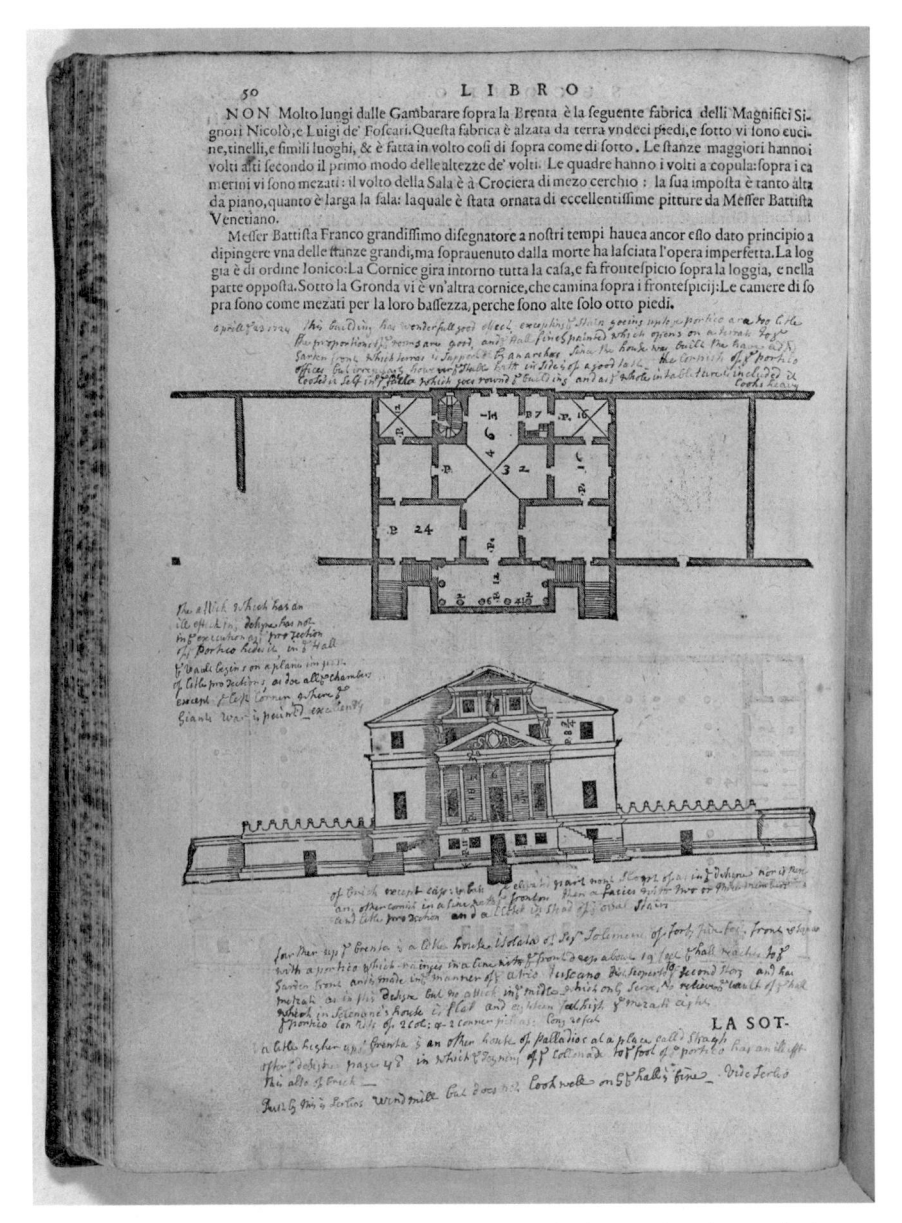

**Figure 5.4** Sir Edward Lovett Pearce's annotated edition of Andrea Palladio, *I quattro libri dell'architettura*, Venice, 1601. RIBA Collections.

the accompanying catalogue: while the modern architectural profession was certainly in its infancy in the eighteenth century, this is not a distinction bestowed upon Vanbrugh, Burlington, or Kent in the same publication, all of whom enjoyed a similar status.[45]

## The view from 'abroad'

In concert with the formal appraisal of Pearce's design as a paradigm of orthodox classicism, Irish architectural historians have done much to develop and complicate our understanding of the Parliament House and its semiological significance in cultural and political terms. At the outset, however, the literature on the 'Irishness', or indeed 'Englishness', of eighteenth-century Irish architecture, though still somewhat embryonic, requires attention. Alistair Rowan, addressing this issue in 1997, echoed Banister Fletcher in creating a distinction between an 'Irish' architecture with identifiably 'national' characteristics (largely confined to vernacular details of material, construction, and ornament) and the 'international Italianate and Palladian taste' that was introduced by the Protestant Ascendancy class in the late seventeenth century: in one fell swoop, according to Rowan, 'Irishness perforce goes underground'.[46] More typically, questions of 'national' character have been subsumed into increasingly complex readings and interpretations. Christine Casey has remarked how the building's 'scale and magnificence vividly evoke the confidence and sense of purpose' of its sitting members,[47] noting the 'remarkable' achievement of the Irish MPs 'to deliver a building of such scale and grandeur'.[48] And in his recent account of the city's 'meaning-laden urban terrain', Robin Usher describes Pearce's design as one that 'intentionally outshone Westminster and made the [British] government's local outpost – the Castle – appear dull and introverted'. The Parliament House, according to Usher, was a building 'always meant to be showy'.[49]

In these evaluations equating form with identity, Casey and Usher echo and amplify the scholarship of Edward McParland, the foremost historian of eighteenth-century civic architecture in Ireland, whose seminal *Public Architecture in Ireland, 1680–1760* (2001) squarely situates Irish Palladianism within its British contexts and remains the standard text.[50] Here, it is important to acknowledge that McParland and those who preceded him refuse to entertain the case for exceptionalism in Irish architectural design of the period.[51] So while Maurice Craig describes Pearce's work as being 'the earliest important public building in these islands to embody the full Burlingtonian ideals of correctness',[52] England was, in the more emphatic words of McParland, 'the school in which Irish taste [was] formed'.[53] Indeed, Irish scholarship generally insists on a British context for

Pearce's design. Although McParland is certain that the architect produced 'one of the finest buildings of the 1720s in Europe',[54] he is unequivocal that, 'The triumph of the Dublin Parliament House – the earliest major public building in the Burlingtonian style in the British Isles – is Pearce's; but that triumph would have been inconceivable without the inspiration of the Apollo of the Arts' (a popular contemporary reference to Burlington).[55] So, despite being 'pioneering as a public building in its neo-Palladianism',[56] in a style that was 'still radical in Britain',[57] and with no parallel in London in terms of magnitude and political iconography, it is 'inconceivable' without Burlington's influence.[58] Significantly, McParland is also the only author to have addressed the explicit bias in these English-authored architectural histories, noting as early as 1974, that 'no account of British architecture can be complete if it ignores Ireland'.[59] In his 'A bibliography of Irish architectural history', published in the journal *Irish Historical Studies* (1988), he notes that Albert Richardson's *Monumental Classic Architecture* (discussed above) and its 'integrated view' of British and Irish architecture was 'then original and still exceptional'; later, in the same publication, he describes Summerson's *Architecture in Britain* as being 'insular in contrast with Richardson's survey'.[60] (In these remarks, McParland is characteristically more diplomatic than Craig who complained of 'the deplorable ignorance of English writers about Irish buildings'.)[61]

Conversely, a different thread in the scholarship on Irish architecture is the persistent notion of Ireland's cultural provincialism: just as Irish architects were indebted to their English counterparts for inspiration, so their designs betray their origins on the fringes of metropolitan sophistication. In an essay of 1992, revisiting themes first aired in 1974, McParland introduces the idea that Pearce's architectural taste was not 'impeccably Burlingtonian', describing how the architect 'slips the leash' in projects of a more obviously baroque character, such as the obelisk at Stillorgan House, county Dublin for the 2nd Viscount Allen.[62] For McParland, this is evidence of a type of eclecticism characteristic of a culture of design that lay, 'beyond the reach of the style police in the real centre of influence, London'.[63] But as style recedes in significance as a rubric within modern architectural histories generally, so too does its corresponding and confusing taxonomies of Palladianism, neo-Palladianism, Anglo-Palladianism, neo-classicism, and 'new classicism'. On this issue, Barbara Arciszewska has recently characterised 'current definitions' of the Palladian style, focused on the national character of English Palladianism, as 'highly problematic',[64] although her illuminating account of British architectural theory, concentrated on classicism as 'a visual protocol of the Hanoverian regime and of the landed and commercial elites that supported it', falls short of a full appraisal of Irish architecture as a constituency of its English (or British) counterpart.[65]

Acknowledging that the Earl of Shaftesbury's aspirations for a noble public architecture were 'most eloquently (and unexpectedly) visualised at the time by the Parliament House in Dublin', discussion of that building is glossed only, and the unrealised designs of Burlington and Kent for London take precedence.[66]

### A national or imperial architecture?

From the foregoing, it is arguable that Ireland is the principal casualty of modern (and contemporary) histories of British classical architecture: Scotland, if only by default, retains a preeminent position based on the nationality of many of the foremost architects of the period, such as Colen Campbell, James Gibbs, and Robert Adam; while America, though it seceded from British rule in 1783, enjoys a new centrality in histories of Atlantic world architectures. If we accept that a parliament house was 'that project on which, all through the eighteenth century, focused the hopes of British architecture', is the Dublin building the elephant in the room?[67] Historians of eighteenth-century Irish architecture have long been mindful of its British contexts for obvious reasons, but buildings like the Parliament House – a seat of government in an authoritative antique style that loudly signalled classical ideals of civic virtue and a modern constitutional identity – confound postcolonial narratives.[68] Is a reversal of influence – from Dublin to London, from Pearce to Kent – palatable to those who understand classicism as a signifier of British culture and imperialism?[69]

Challenges to this entrenched position have been intermittent – Kerry Downes understood the 'imposing domed public buildings' of Dublin, including the Parliament House ('which was run from Westminster'), as 'more truly imperial emblems than all Nash's London terraces'[70] – and sustained opposition, somewhat predictably, has come from the small pool of Irish scholars already cited here. In the context of a conference entitled 'Parliamentary buildings and their use' held in 2000, where the respective institutions of Dublin, Edinburgh, and Westminster were compared and appraised, Edward McParland was emboldened to argue that 'rather than illustrating Pearce's debt to Burlington, it might be easier to suggest some dependence on William Kent's part on the Dublin Parliament House'.[71] Most recently, reflecting on the 'distinct parallels in the relationship of Dublin with London, and of Vienna, Dresden and Munich with the fringes of the Holy Roman Empire', Christine Casey described Pearce's building as 'a work of international significance in terms of typology, and the most significant public building in the new Palladian manner in Britain'.[72]

There was no such equivocation in the eighteenth century. The anonymous author of *Letters addressed to parliament, and to the public in general, on various improvements of the metropolis* (1787), reluctantly conceded that the Irish Parliament House was 'greatly superior to that of London',[73] and the Chevalier de la Tocnaye, visiting Ireland in 1796, was struck by the pronounced disparity between the accommodation provided for MPs at Dublin and those 'deputies or representatives of greater nations'.[74] Ireland's lead in state-sponsored design education also raised eyebrows. Describing the Dublin Society for improving husbandry, manufactures, and other useful arts, founded in 1731 (and renamed the Royal Dublin Society in 1820 when George IV became its patron), architect and polemicist John Gwynn decried how 'Ireland, Britain's younger Sister, seems to have got the start of her in the encouragement of all the useful and ornamental arts. [...] And should we not be displeased, as a Nation, to be ranked, by Foreigners, after one of our own Colonies?'[75]

Contemporary scholarship on British and American architecture, informed by theoretical paradigms forged in material culture studies, is keen to demonstrate shared vocabularies of design and making in both vernacular and academic contexts; classical orthodoxies are no longer seen as fixed and immutable. In a recent overview of the literature of eighteenth- and nineteenth-century British Atlantic histories, Daniel Maudlin understands transatlantic cultural production as 'an increasingly complex, multilayered exchange between Britain and America; not just an outward ripple, or a simple two-way process, but one axis of a network of inter-trading Atlantic hubs'.[76] And in the introduction to *Architecture and Urbanism in the British Empire* (2016), Alex Bremner describes the 'complex and as yet unresolved relationship between the historiography of "British" architecture on the one hand, and of "British colonial" architecture on the other'. He continues: 'Typically, these two subjects have been treated separately, both geographically and historically. But are they separate subjects, or can they be seen as integrated or even indivisible?'[77] If Ireland has been largely (and typically?) overlooked in these recent histories of 'multilayered exchange' between Britain and its colonies, it is clear that at least one axis of that exchange – namely, Ireland's debt to British architectural authority – is already well established in the literature.[78] This brings to mind Sean Connolly's suggestion that the 'key feature' of Ireland in the eighteenth century was its 'ambiguous status: too physically close and too similar to Great Britain to be treated as a colony, but too separate and too different to be a region of the metropolitan centre'.[79] David Hayton too has counselled against placing too much emphasis on 'the element of confrontation in Irish Protestant patriotism', and that men like William Conolly, instigator of the Parliament House project and lobbyist for Pearce as its architect, 'were aware of the advantages of working with Britain and its emerging global empire rather than engaging in futile flag-waving in pursuit of an unrealisable dream of self-sufficiency'.[80] And in a more specifically architectural context, Barbara Arciszewska has argued that 'The suggestion of a rigid association between specific architectural idiom [Palladianism], and just as specific political cause [Whiggism], though still commonly accepted', might benefit from reflecting on the 'polysemic nature of representation and inherently ideological character of all historical narratives'.[81] With this in mind, should the Parliament House properly be understood as a British building, anticipating the 'union of multiple identities' characteristic of the British state after 1800?[82] Does it lose its semantic power if simply understood as a monument to colonial patriotism? Will recognising the design's Britishness add a much-needed dimension to what has been characterised as a 'profound ambivalence' in Ireland's relationship to its Anglo-Irish cultural patrimony?[83] Can Dublin's Parliament House be both British *and* Irish?

Unlike the public buildings of the later eighteenth century, such as James Gandon's Custom House (1781–91), whose sculptural iconography speaks more directly to an imperial mindset, the political context and purpose of Dublin's Parliament House is undoubtedly more complex (Plate 7).[84] While the discourse on art in Georgian Ireland understood Irish art to be 'essentially English', adopting a language 'distinctly colonial' in tone, contemporary descriptions of Pearce's design often strongly emphasised its uniquely national associations.[85] In *A Fragment of the History of Patrick* (1753), a satirical pamphlet published by dramatist Henry Brooke, the role of the Parliament House in matters of governance was contrasted with that of Dublin Castle, seat of the British administration: the Parliament House was where 'most of Patrick's [Ireland's] business was transacted', being 'more peculiarly Patrick's house than any other'.[86] The authors of *Views of the most remarkable public buildings, monuments and other edifices in the city of Dublin* (1780), also recognised how Dublin had outshone London in housing its government, suggesting that 'Upon the whole, prejudice itself must acknowledge, that the British Empire (we might have added Europe herself) cannot boast of so spacious and stately a Senatorial-Hall' (Figure 5.5).[87] And Pearce's design would certainly have featured prominently in the never-realised *Vitruvius Hibernicus*, announced in 1754 by Dublin publisher and bookseller George Faulkner and intended as 'an original work of specifically Irish flavour'.[88] Indeed, Faulkner's proposal made much of the fact that his book would be 'in the same Size, Paper and Manner of Vitruvius Britannicus', and hoped that 'our Nobility and Gentry' would endorse 'this most Patriot and useful Work'.[89] This brings to mind Ian McBride's suggestion that while Irish national identity in the

Figure 5.5 Bernard Scalé after Rowland Omer, 'A Section of the House of Commons Dublin', engraving, 1767. Courtesy of the Irish Architectural Archive.

early modern period was essentially Anglocentric, the 'very existence of a parliament in Dublin inevitably stimulated the development of a separate corporate identity within the Irish elite'.[90]

That said, proposals for how a supposedly Irish architecture might be satisfactorily constituted within a British architectural history may be identified from the rich literature on national and imperial identities in the long eighteenth century, advancing 'three kingdoms' or 'four nations' approaches. From the early 1970s, historians such as J. G. A. Pocock and Hugh Kearney called for a more inclusive definition of British history: just as Pocock recognised Irish history to be 'to an inordinate degree the history of responses to England',[91] so Kearney argued that 'no single "national" interpretation [of the British Isles], whether English, Irish, Scottish or Welsh, can be treated as self-contained. A "Britannic" framework is an essential starting point for a fuller understanding of these so-called "national" pasts.'[92] Indeed, while Linda Colley formally omits Ireland from her compelling narrative of the forging of British national identity in the period 1707–1837, considering its condition (principally its majority Catholic population) too distinct from its cousins on the so-called 'Celtic fringe', she is nonetheless unequivocal that Anglo-Irish elites fully endorsed the 'common' view of 'dual nationalities' as a peculiar quality of an emerging British national consciousness.[93] This duality is arguably woven into the very fabric of the Parliament House itself: at the laying of the foundation stone on 3 February 1728/9, a speech glorifying the 'pile majestick' and its 'noble plan' wished for the continued glory of both 'Great Briton' and the author's 'Native Isle'.[94] The visual corollary of this rhetoric was equally unambiguous: personifications of Hibernia frequently accompanied Britannia (and Scotia) in imperialist propaganda throughout the course of the Georgian period, including Irish-born engraver John Dixon's *The Oracle* issued in 1774 (Figure 5.6).[95] More striking still is the characterisation of Dublin as 'the second City in the British Dominions'

**Figure 5.6** John Dixon, *The Oracle, Representing Britannia, Hibernia, Scotia and America*, mezzotint, 1774. Yale Center for British Art, Paul Mellon Fund, B2013.1.

in Pool and Cash's unabashed tribute to 'the public spirit that has lately begun to display itself in the nation'.[96]

This question of identity is indeed central to modern histories of the Protestant, Anglo-Irish ruling class in Ireland, the patrons of Pearce's innovative classical design. Colin Kidd's account of the intricate 'weave of Irish identities' in the seventeenth and eighteenth centuries – with its roots in discrete Old Irish (with roots in an ancient Gaelic ancestry), Old English (descendants of Anglo-Norman colonists), and New English (post-Reformation and post-Cromwellian settlers) constituencies – points to a Protestant Irish nation both 'protean and fabulous, but also opportunistic and self-serving'.[97] This is echoed in David Hayton's characterisation of Ascendancy identity in the early Georgian period as 'splintered or overlapping' but also 'unusually delicate'.[98] Something of this complexity is encapsulated in a pamphlet of 1751 composed by Nicholas Archdall (1690–1763), a member of the Irish Parliament for county Fermanagh and a staunch defender of Ireland's sovereignty in the face of the proposed union with Great Britain at mid-century:

> Great Britain may be consider'd as the Mother of many children, and all her Colonies settled in America, or elsewhere, as so many Daughters ... But Ireland should be looked upon rather as a Sister, whom England has taken under her protection, on condition she complies with the Economy of the Family.[99]

As we have seen, Irish architectural historians are adamant that Irish architects complied with the domestic economy: but in an attempt to appease the household, did the sister (Ireland) unwittingly offend the matriarch (England)? After all, it was Pearce, not Burlington – in Dublin, not London – who satisfied the Earl of Shaftesbury's call for a parliament house of Augustan magnificence.[100] Is it time for the lady of the house to forgive her errant sibling and welcome her back into the family bosom? If Irish buildings were to enjoy parity in histories of British architecture we might avoid the limits imposed by national allegiances, and move instead towards the recognition of Dublin's eighteenth-century architecture as an expression of the same 'visual idiom' and 'specific code of building' marshalled by English architects and patrons to serve a common British identity.[101] But for that to happen, historians of English architecture must concede the achievements on the sister island by acknowledging Dublin as one of the foremost centres of British architectural innovation, and its eighteenth-century buildings as paragons of a shared classical taste.[102]

## Notes

1 The argument herein was first presented at the biennial conference of the European Architectural History Network, held in Dublin in June 2016. I am grateful to Prof. Elizabeth McKellar for selecting my paper for her session entitled 'Constructing the "Georgian": Anglo-Palladianism, identity and colonialism, c.1700 to the present'. A second version was presented at the Institute of Irish Studies seminar series at Queen's University, Belfast on 30 April 2018, at the kind invitation of Prof. Peter Gray. For the present chapter, I am grateful to Prof. David Hayton and Dr Ivar McGrath for scholarly advice; and to Prof. Christine Casey, Dr Edward McParland, and Dr Richard Butler for insightful comments on various drafts.
2 Rudolf Wittkower, *Palladio and English Palladianism* (London: Thames and Hudson, 1974); Sir John Summerson, *Architecture in Britain, 1530–1830* (London: Penguin, 1953); David Watkin, *English Architecture: A Concise History* (London: Thames & Hudson, 1979).
3 Frank Salmon, 'Public commissions' in Susan Weber (ed.), *William Kent: designing Georgian Britain* (New Haven and London: Yale University Press, 2013), p. 315. For the challenge to the received view, see Barbara Arciszewska, 'Classicism: Constructing the Paradigm in Continental Europe and Britain', in *Articulating British Classicism: New Approaches to Eighteenth-Century Architecture*, eds Barbara Arciszewska and Elizabeth McKellar (Aldershot: Ashgate, 2004), 1–35; Dana Arnold, *The Georgian Country House: Architecture, Landscape and Society* (Stroud: Sutton Publishing, 1998), 5–15; Alexander Echlin and William Kelley, 'A 'Shaftesburian Agenda'? Lord Burlington, Lord Shaftesbury and the Intellectual Origins of English Palladianism', *Architectural History*, 59 (2016): 221–52.
4 Edward McParland, *Public Architecture in Ireland 1680–1760* (New Haven: Yale University Press, 2001), 177.
5 David Watkin, *The Rise of Architectural History* (London: Architectural Press, 1980), 95.
6 Summerson, *Architecture in Britain*, 351.
7 Giles Worsley, *Classical Architecture in Britain: The Heroic Age* (New Haven: Yale University Press, 1995), 166.
8 Alex Bremner, 'The Expansion Of England? Rethinking Scotland's Place in the Architectural History of the Wider British World', *Journal of Art Historiography*, 18 (2018): 17.
9 Thomas Bartlett, '"This famous island set in a Virginian sea": Ireland in the British Empire, 1690–1801', in *The Oxford History of the British Empire, Vol. 2: The Eighteenth Century*, ed. P. J. Marshall (Oxford: Oxford University Press, 1998), 255.
10 Maurice Craig, *Dublin 1660–1860: A Social and Architectural History* (London: Cresset Press, 1952), 124. For a more recent discussion, see L. M. Cullen, 'Swift's *Modest Proposal* (1729): Historical Context and Political Purpose', in *Ourselves Alone? Religion, Society and Politics in Eighteenth-*

*and Nineteenth-Century Ireland*, eds D. W. Hayton and Andrew R. Holmes (Dublin: Four Courts Press, 2016), 55–6.

11 D. W. Hayton, *Ruling Ireland 1685–1742* (Woodbridge: Boydell Press, 2004), 38.

12 Patrick Walsh, *The Making of the Irish Protestant Ascendancy: The Life of William Conolly, 1689–1729* (Woodbridge: Boydell Press, 2010), 3, 185. Walsh cites Maurice Craig, suggesting that the latter's characterisation of a 'colonial patriotism' be replaced with the 'more accurate' term 'economic patriotism', see Maurice Craig, *The Architecture of Ireland: From the Earliest Times to the Present* (London: Batsford, 1982), 182.

13 David Dickson, *New Foundations: Ireland 1660–1800* (Dublin: Irish Academic Press, 2000), 89.

14 Edward McParland, 'Eclecticism: The Provincial's Advantage', *Irish Arts Review Yearbook* (1991/1992): 210.

15 Edward McParland, 'Building the Parliament House in Dublin', in *Housing Parliament: Dublin, Edinburgh and Westminster*, eds Clyve Jones and Sean Kelsey (Edinburgh: Edinburgh University Press, 2002), 138. Robin Usher describes this move as 'an obvious sop to the patriots', see Robin Usher, *Protestant Dublin 1660–1760: Architecture and Iconography* (London: Palgrave Macmillan, 2012), 140.

16 James Kelly, 'The Origins of the Act of Union: An Examination of Unionist Opinion in Britain and Ireland, 1650–1800', *Irish Historical Studies* 25, no. 99 (1987): 237.

17 Casey, *Dublin*, 382.

18 McParland, *Public Architecture*, 195.

19 Howard Colvin, *A Biographical Dictionary of British architects, 1600–1840* (New Haven: Yale University Press, 3rd edn 1995), 745.

20 Robert Tavernor, *Palladio and Palladianism* (London: Thames and Hudson, 1991).

21 Sir Banister Fletcher, *A History of Architecture on the Comparative Method* (London: Athlone Press, 17th edn 1961), 527. The recently revised edition of this classic text remains on familiar territory. For his account of 'The Early Georgian Era', Stephen Brindle identifies Sir Christopher Wren, Lord Burlington, James Gibbs, and William Kent as the foremost designers of note. James Gandon's Custom House retains its preeminence in Irish architecture, being distinguished as one of two Irish buildings to make the list of 'key buildings' for the period under review, and indeed the only Irish building illustrated in the entire essay. Stephen Brindle, 'British Isles, 1500–1830', in *Sir Banister Fletcher's Global History of Architecture*, ed. Murray Fraser (London: Bloomsbury, 2019), 233–71.

22 Reginald Blomfield, *A History of Renaissance Architecture in England, 1500–1800*, 2 vols (London: George Bell and Sons, 1897), II: 268.

23 A. E. Richardson, *Monumental Classic Architecture in Great Britain and Ireland* (London: B. T. Batsford, 1914), xxv.

24 Richardson, *Monumental Classic Architecture in Great Britain and Ireland*, 5

25 Richardson, *Monumental Classic Architecture in Great Britain and Ireland*, 2.

26 Richardson, *Monumental Classic Architecture in Great Britain and Ireland*, 11.
27 Summerson, *Architecture in Britain*, 218.
28 Summerson, *Architecture in Britain*, 216.
29 Summerson, *Architecture in Britain*, 351.
30 Dan Cruickshank, *A Guide to the Georgian Buildings of Britain and Ireland* (London: Weidenfeld and Nicolson, 1985), 143–4.
31 Worsley, *Classical Architecture in Britain*, xi.
32 Worsley, *Classical Architecture in Britain*, 166.
33 Worsley, *Classical Architecture in Britain*, 273.
34 For a similar appraisal see the review of Worsley's book by Marlene Elizabeth Heck in *The Pennsylvania Magazine of History and Biography* 120, no. 3 (July 1996): 273–5.
35 Francis Dodsworth, '*Virtus* on Whitehall: The Politics of Palladianism in William Kent's Treasury Building, 1733–6', *Journal of Historical Sociology* 18, no. 4 (2005): 282–317. For a similarly marginal account of the building, see James Stevens Curl, *Georgian Architecture in the British Isles, 1714–1830* (1993; rev. edn Swindon: English Heritage, 2011), 57.
36 Salmon, 'Public Commissions'.
37 Salmon, 'Public Commissions', 315.
38 Salmon, 337. Summerson did in fact acknowledge that Pearce preceded Kent in this antique citation, although the later editions of his book omit this reference, see Summerson, *Architecture in Britain 1530–1830* (1953), 217.
39 Salmon, 'Public Commissions', 337.
40 Salmon follows the example of Fiske Kimball who, in two articles describing Kent's designs for a new parliament house in London, avoided any reference to the Dublin building. Fiske Kimball, 'William Kent's Designs for the Houses of Parliament, 1730–1740', *Journal of the Royal Institute of British Architects*, 3rd series, 39 (1932): 735–55, 800–7. Reference to Kent's 'ambitious' designs for a Parliament House in London are also devoid of Irish context in Joseph Rykwert, *The First Moderns: The Architects of the Eighteenth Century* (Cambridge MA: MIT Press, 1980), 173. Predictably, there is no reference to Ireland in Joseph Rykwert, *The Palladian Ideal* (New York: Rizzoli, 1999).
41 Charles Hind and Vickey Wilson, 'Palladian design: the good, the bad and the unexpected', held at the Royal Institute of British Architects (9 September 2015–9 January 2016).
42 For an insightful review of this exhibition, see David Hemsoll, *Journal of the Society of Architectural Historians* 75, no. 3 (2016): 377–9.
43 *Palladian Design: The Good, the Bad and the Unexpected*, ed. Marie Mak Bortensen (London: RIBA, 2015), 48–9.
44 McParland, *Public Architecture*, 180–1.
45 Bortensen, *Palladian Design*, 48. On the broader issue, see *The Role of the Amateur Architect*, ed. Giles Worsley (London: The Georgian Group, 1994).
46 Alistair Rowan, 'The Irishness of Irish Architecture', *Architectural History* 40 (1997): 13.
47 Christine Casey, *Dublin* (New Haven: Yale University Press, 2005), 380.

48 Casey, *Dublin*, 381.
49 Usher, *Protestant Dublin*, 140. Usher adds that just as the Castle's architectural shortcomings spoke of a 'complacent government', so the 'splendour' of the Irish Parliament 'signalled robust ability' and 'genuine competence'.
50 This book represents the culmination of his published research on the Parliament House from the 1970s onwards.
51 For Constantine Curran, Pearce's 'introduction of Palladio to Ireland' corresponded 'approximately with its revival in England in the hands of the Burlington group'. C. P. Curran, 'The Architecture of the Bank of Ireland, part I, 1727–1780', in *The Bank of Ireland 1783–1946*, ed. F. G. Hall (Dublin and Oxford: Hodges, Figgis, and Co. and Blackwell, 1949), 434.
52 Craig, *Dublin*, 124.
53 McParland, 'Eclecticism: The Provincial's Advantage', 210.
54 McParland, *Public Architecture*, 49.
55 Edward McParland, 'Edward Lovett Pearce and the Parliament House in Dublin', *The Burlington Magazine* 131, no. 1031 (1989): 99. This in some senses echoes Sir John Summerson's original assessment of Pearce's design: in the first edition of *Architecture in Britain*, Summerson had in fact argued that 'Pearce can hardly be the real designer of the building, for the stylistic evidence points in another direction. The two main interiors, the Lords' and the Common's chambers, are so close in style to Lord Burlington that one is almost bound to assume his participation in them.' Noting the Earl's titles in both the English and Irish peerages, Summerson was satisfied that Burlington's 'silent but effective influence … may be taken for granted'. Summerson, *Architecture in Britain*, 216–17. For the Irish response, see Maurice Craig, 'Burlington, Adam and Gandon', *Journal of the Warburg and Courtauld Institutes* 17, no. 3/4 (1954): 381–82; Maurice Craig, 'The Quest for Sir Edward Lovett Pearce', *Irish Arts Review Yearbook* 12 (1996): 27–34.
56 McParland, *Public Architecture*, 185.
57 McParland, 'Building the Parliament House in Dublin', 136.
58 McParland, 'Edward Lovett Pearce and the Parliament House in Dublin', 99.
59 Edward McParland, 'The Englishness of Irish Architecture?', *Cambridge Review* 95, no. 2220 (1974): 113. See also McParland, *Public Architecture*, 5.
60 Edward McParland, 'A Bibliography of Irish Architectural History', *Irish Historical Studies* 26, no. 102 (1988): 162–3. McParland had in fact made a similar point some years earlier, noting how A. E. Richardson 'showed, in the attention he paid to [James] Gandon, and to Ireland, a more just sense of proportion than that shown by many later British historians', see Edward McParland, *James Gandon: Vitruvius Hibernicus* (London: Zwemmer, 1985), xv. His review of Worsley's *Classical Architecture in Britain* is equally pointed and astute, finding the author's account of Irish Palladianism 'as traditional as Summerson's'. See *Irish Historical Studies* 30, no. 119 (1997): 494.
61 Craig, *Dublin*, 128.
62 McParland, 'Eclecticism: The Provincial's Advantage', 212.

63 McParland, *Public Architecture*, 203.
64 Barbara Arciszewska, *Classicism and Modernity: Architectural Thought in Eighteenth-Century Britain* (Warsaw: Wydawnictwo Neriton, 2010), 17.
65 Arciszewska, *Classicism and Modernity*, 31.
66 Arciszewska, *Classicism and Modernity*, 344.
67 Summerson, *Architecture in Britain*, 345.
68 On the embeddedness of power and identity in symbolic state buildings, see Lawrence J. Vale, *Architecture, Power, and National Identity* (New Haven: Yale University Press, 1992).
69 Dana Arnold, *Reading Architectural History* (London: Routledge, 2002), 98–100.
70 Kerry Downes, *The Georgian Cities of Britain* (Oxford: Phaidon Press, 1979), 61.
71 Edward McParland, 'Building the Parliament House in Dublin', 138.
72 Christine Casey, 'Art and Architecture in the Long Eighteenth Century', in *Cambridge History of Ireland, vol. 3, 1730–1880*, ed. James Kelly (Cambridge: Cambridge University Press, 2018), 407–8.
73 Anon., *Letters addressed to parliament, and to the public in general, on various improvements of the metropolis* (Dublin, 1787), 225.
74 Jacques-Louis de Bougrenet, Chevalier de La Tocnaye, *Promenade d'un Français dans l'Irlande* (Dublin, 1797), 16–17.
75 John Gwynn, *An essay on design* (London, 1749), 91–2. On Dublin's pre-eminence in this respect see Michael Snodin and John Styles, *Design and the Decorative Arts: Georgian Britain, 1714–1837* (London: V&A Publications, 2004), 77.
76 Daniel Maudlin, 'Introduction', in *The Materials of Exchange between Britain and North East America, 1750–1900*, eds Daniel Maudlin and Robin Peel (Farnham: Ashgate, 2013), 3.
77 G. A. Bremner, 'Introduction', in *Architecture and Urbanism in the British Empire* (Oxford: Oxford University Press, 2016), xii.
78 A notable exception, for an earlier period, is *'The Mirror of Great Britain': National Identity in Seventeenth-Century British Architecture*, ed. Olivia Horsfall-Turner (Reading: Spire Books, 2014).
79 S. J. Connolly, 'Eighteenth-Century Ireland: Colony or Ancien Regime', in *The Making Of Modern Irish History: Revisionism and the Revisionist Controversy*, eds D. G. Boyce and Alan O'Day (London: Routledge, 1996), 26.
80 D. W. Hayton, 'The Emergence of a Protestant Society, 1691–1730', in *Cambridge History of Ireland, vol. 2, 1550–1730*, ed. Jane Ohlmeyer (Cambridge: Cambridge University Press, 2018), 166–7.
81 Arciszewska, *Classicism and Modernity*, 56.
82 Laurence Brockliss and David Eastwood, 'Introduction: A Union of Multiple Identities', in *A Union of Multiple Identities: The British Isles, C1750–C1850*, eds Laurence Brockliss and David Eastwood (Manchester: Manchester University Press, 1997), 7.

83 Arciszewska and McKellar, *Articulating British Classicism*, xxiv.
84 Murray Fraser, 'Public Building and Colonial Policy in Dublin', *Architectural History* 28 (1995): 102–23.
85 Tom Dunne, 'Writers on Irish Art and Artists before Strickland', in *Art and Architecture of Ireland Vol. II: Painters and Painting 1600–1900*, ed. Nicola Figgis (Dublin: Royal Irish Academy, 2014), 127. The importance of employing local (Irish) 'hands' in the making of public architecture generally, and of a Parliament House specifically, was a view expressed throughout the period, see McParland, *Public Architecture*, 187.
86 Henry Brooke, *A Fragment of the History of Patrick* (London, 1753), 8. Cited in McParland, 'Building the Parliament House in Dublin', 140. See also Usher, *Protestant Dublin*, 142.
87 Robert Pool and John Cash, *Views of the most remarkable public buildings, monuments and other edifices in the city of Dublin* (Dublin, 1780), 29. This is in fact a direct quotation from an earlier text with a similar purpose: Walter Harris, *The history and antiquities of the city of Dublin* (Dublin, 1766), p. 412.
88 Christine Casey, 'Books and builders: a bibliographical approach to Irish 18th century architecture' (PhD thesis, University of Dublin, 1992), 25.
89 *Dublin Journal*, 17 August 1754.
90 Ian McBride, '"The common name of Irishman": Protestantism and Patriotism in Eighteenth-Century Ireland', in *Protestantism and National Identity: Britain and Ireland, c.1650–c.1850*, eds Tony Claydon and Ian McBride (Cambridge: Cambridge University Press, 1998), 236–7.
91 Originally published in 1974 as 'British History: A Plea for a New Subject', it is reprinted in J. G. A. Pocock, *The Discovery of Islands: Essays in British History* (Cambridge: Cambridge University Press, 2005), 37.
92 Hugh Kearney, *The British Isles: A History of Four Nations* (Cambridge: Cambridge University Press, 1989), 1.
93 Linda Colley, *Britons: Forging the Nation 1707–1837* (New Haven: Yale University Press. 1992), 373. On this point, see Michael Hechter, *Internal Colonialism: The Celtic Fringe in British National Development, 1536–1966* (London: Routledge, 1975), 109–10.
94 Henry Nelson, *The speech of the first stone laid in the Parliament-House to the Government*, 3 February 1728/9, cited in McParland, *Public Architecture*, 178.
95 Colley, *Britons*, 133–4.
96 Pool and Cash, *Views*, 6, 12.
97 Colin Kidd, *British Identities before Nationalism: Ethnicity and Nationhood in the Atlantic World, 1600–1800* (Cambridge: Cambridge University Press, 1999), 163.
98 D. W. Hayton, *The Anglo-Irish Experience, 1680–1730: Religion, Identity and Patriotism* (Woodbridge: Boydell and Brewer, 2012), 25.
99 Nicholas Archdall, *An alarum to the people of Great Britain and Ireland in answer to a late proposal for uniting these kingdoms shewing the fatal consequences of such an union* (Dublin, 1751), 5. On the significance of Archdall's

pamphlet in mid-century Ireland, see James Kelly, 'Public and Political Opinion in Ireland and the Idea of an Anglo-Irish Union, 1650–1800', in *Political Discourse in Seventeenth- and Eighteenth-Century Ireland*, eds D. G. Boyce, Robert Eccleshall, and Vincent Geoghegan (New York: Palgrave Macmillan, 2001), 123–4.
100 McParland, *Public Architecture*, 11.
101 Arciszewska, *Classicism and Modernity*, 144.
102 The more inclusive approach suggested by the title of Steven Brindle's recently published Architecture in Britain and Ireland, 1530–1830, is not reflected in the structure or content of his narrative. Organised into three parts, English architecture is unabashedly privileged in the book's structure and in page extent. For example, one single chapter, 'Early Georgian, 1714–1760', devoted to pertinent themes including 'Architecture and politics' and 'Stylistic labels and the Palladian manner', makes no reference to Irish architects or buildings, and is longer, in terms of page extent, than the standalone 'Architecture in Ireland, 1660–1760' chapter. Significantly, Brindle acknowledges the existence of an 'architecture in Britain' but argues that this 'does not necessarily amount to "British architecture", which is why Scotland and Ireland have their own chapters within this book'. Steven Brindle, Architecture in Britain and Ireland, 1530–1830 (New Haven and London, 2023), vii.

# Part II

Empire building in Britain

# 6

# An empire under construction: the view from inside East India House

*Emily Mann*

This chapter pieces back together a room in a building that no longer exists: the boardroom of the eighteenth-century headquarters of the English East India Company. The task of researching and reconstructing a long-lost space is common in the study of early imperial and colonial architectures – and can be questionable. How exactly might doing so add to knowledge and understanding of a history of extraction and oppression, and whose experiences and perspectives are recovered and prioritised in the process?[1] The story of the English East India Company, one of the most powerful and enduring corporations ever, is relatively well told, in large part through its own vast archive of minutes, accounts, and other documents now held by the British Library.[2] Yet, given the company's foundational role in Britain's overseas empire and lasting influence on the global economic and political order, it can seem to have left surprisingly little direct physical footprint anywhere in the world, and its built impositions and impacts remain less explored.[3] London, the company's centre of operations from its founding in 1600 to its handover to the British Crown in 1858, is no exception.

Of the immense East India Docks built in the early 1800s, only the entrance basin from the Thames remains (today a nature reserve in the shadow of the 'regenerated' Docklands), along with stranded stretches of perimeter wall and the roads that were established to connect the wharves to warehouses in the City.[4] A small proportion of those once extensive warehouses have been preserved as part of luxury developments, while between them and the docks, in working-class Poplar, a chapel and almshouse complex supported by the company from the seventeenth century survive in altered and fragmented form.[5] As for the company's headquarters in the heart of the City, East India House, in its place now rises the 'high-tech' home of Lloyd's insurance market, the inside-out design of which – pioneered by Richard Rogers post-Pompidou – 'split the city' as it emerged on London's skyline in the mid-1980s.[6] 'Hideous but exciting', commented a grocery assistant next door.[7] Exposing its service parts on the exterior for all to see, the steel, glass, and concrete edifice still exudes a futuristic confidence that, alongside the taller (and taller) towers that have surged around it since, suggests a deliberate disjuncture with and departure from the past.

Yet the past is persistent. Lloyd's, whose building in its prime spot has come to stand for the 'Big Bang' financial deregulation and computerisation with which its completion coincided in 1986, a pillar of a new age of capitalist imperialism and its architectures, has been forced to address its central involvement in the expansion and exploitation of Britain's earlier empire.[8] In June 2020, in the glare of the spotlight shone by Black Lives Matter on structural racism and its historical roots, Lloyd's issued an apology for the market's 'shameful' role in the transatlantic slave trade as insurer of ships and their cargoes – enslaved people and the goods they produced.[9] As with so many financial, commercial, and other institutions that make up the social and physical fabric of Britain, the East India Company, too (although no longer around to admit and address it), was deeply involved in the economy of slavery and the slave trade. The company had a role not just through the relationship between sugar and tea, and as suppliers to the slave trade through the import of, for example, cowrie shells from Asia for use as currency on the African coast, along with calicoes used to clothe the enslaved; it was even more directly involved through the forced labour and movement of Asians and Africans in the Indian Ocean region.[10]

The shared complicity of these two organisations dating from the seventeenth century, whose histories now overlap in the same space on London's Leadenhall Street, underlines both the depth and (through their transoceanic business concerns) extent of the city's and country's debt to a centuries-long history of 'accumulation by dispossession', to use David Harvey's phrase, and the still less acknowledged endurance of that process in new forms.[11] This chapter's small-scale contribution to recognising and understanding architecture's part in the process is to excavate the Leadenhall site, through a combination of textual and material evidence, with a particular layer in its sights – the East India Company's headquarters as rebuilt in 1726–29 – while keeping in view wider spatialities as well as the *longue durée* of company, country, and (in both senses) capital.[12]

## The long view

By the late 1720s, the East India Company had been based on the south side of Leadenhall Street for almost a century. On this well-inhabited 'great Thorough-fare' and 'Place of a great Trade', as John Strype praised it in his survey of the City in 1720, assorted buildings, cellars, and yards had steadily accumulated in both size and renown under the name of East India House, which gave a civic face to an already controversial corporation.[13]

The original company was founded by royal charter in 1600 as the Company of Merchants of London Trading into the East Indies, with a monopoly on English trade east of the Cape of Good Hope in southern Africa. The geographical terms of its founding charter did not stop the company diversifying its trade directly on the coast of West Africa, too, though it was forced to withdraw when King Charles II handed that monopoly to the Company of Royal Adventurers Trading to Africa in the 1660s (the Royal African Company, as it was reformed in 1672, located its headquarters a few doors away from East India House on Leadenhall Street).[14] By the end of the first decade of the eighteenth century, following a century of economic and political turbulence and the recent threat of a new rival firm, the now-merged United Company of Merchants of England Trading to the East Indies was busy buying up its previously rented property and adjoining premises in the City with a view to rebuilding the crumbling old house and creating new spaces to serve its globalising business operations: offices, committee rooms, sale halls, and warehouses for goods from textiles to tea.

In March 1726, the company directors approved the 'ground plat and front' presented by the merchant turned architect Theodore Jacobsen, a design that was to transform a tangled enclave with timber-framed frontage into a more orderly plan adorned with an extended Palladian-style stone façade. The work was carried out over three years under the general surveyorship of John James, whose contemporaneous position as joint clerk of works alongside Nicholas Hawksmoor at the Royal Hospital for Seamen in Greenwich, as well as surveyor to the fabric at St Paul's Cathedral and the Fifty New Churches, gives some indication of the perceived national importance of the corporate project.[15] With Jacobsen's original plans for the new East India House lost, little evidence remains for this incarnation of the company's headquarters, which was subsumed by an even larger remodelling in 1796–99 (completed by another architect to the country's royal and ruling elite, Henry Holland).[16] One of the few pieces of visual evidence for the Leadenhall Street elevation completed in 1729 is a wash drawing made by Samuel Wale in around 1760 (Figure 6.1), the view reversed by the experienced book illustrator ready for printed reproduction in *London and Its Environs Described* of 1761.[17] The six volumes in this series offered readers 'An Account of whatever is most remarkable for Grandeur, Elegance, Curiosity or Use', with 'useful cuts' engraved from 'original Drawings, taken on purpose for this Work', and the view of East India House proved useful indeed as the model for a handful of subsequent prints.[18]

The only substantively different view known to survive made an appearance at the Royal Academy exhibition of 1800, the selection committee for which showed an interest by accepting three views of the 'India House': one was by the company's surveyor Richard Jupp (who presented plans for

Figure 6.1 Samuel Wale, East India House, c. 1760, wash drawing, 7.6 × 15.2 cm, British Library.

the remodelling to the directors in 1796 and had designs of the front and pediment exhibited at the RA in 1798); the other two are identifiable as watercolours showing the 1729 and 1799 façades, the former (Figure 6.2), showing the building from the west, possibly drawn in retrospect to juxtapose with the latter's reveal of the just-completed new look as seen from the east.[19] One of the watercolours was marked for sale in the exhibition catalogue, and it appears that both were ultimately acquired by the company, then transferred (along with much of the corporate archive) via the government's India Office to the British Library.[20]

The scarcity of evidence for the 1729 building – despite the bounty of archival material for the company more generally – at least partly accounts for the low level of attention it has been given, yet its muted early reception has also contributed to a perception of its low interest ever since. A periodical piece on the 'Houses of the East India Company' in 1833 (the year in which the Charter Act removed the company's commercial functions in India and gave overall administrative authority to the government) illustrates the older and current façades (Figure 6.3), describing in some detail their elaborate emblematic schemes and saying nothing of the house erected in between.[21] Recent historians have tended to follow the consensus of older ones, moving swiftly past the demure Doric frontage by citing descriptions such as John Noorthouck's summary, in his 1773 *New History of London*, that 'the appearance of the building is nowise suited to the opulence of

Figure 6.2 *The House Occupied by the East India Company in Leadenhall Street, as Refaced in 1726*, chromolithograph by William Griggs after a watercolour by Thomas Malton, c. 1800.

the Company, whose servants exercise sovereign authority in their Indian territories and live there in princely state'.[22] That was not always or straightforwardly the conclusion, however, just as that 'authority' in India was not always or inevitably the case; other writers at earlier and later moments (as we will see) found the façade suitably 'stately' and 'magnificent'.[23] Besides, the expressions of disappointment are worth some reflection, making abundantly clear as they do the expected correlation between a building's appearance and the institution or inhabitants it was designed to house. Such accounts are thus more reliably read for the insights they offer into perceptions of and aspirations for the company at moments in time, than as objective and static evaluations of its home. A visitor entering the later building, following the company's demise, could not help but lament that 'any notion of Eastern magnificence which one might have previously entertained in connection with the mansion of the Company is rudely and effectually dispelled'.[24] Perhaps this merger, in minds, of building and occupier helps to explain the demolition of the headquarters in 1861, soon after the company was in effect dissolved.[25] While it stood, and even for several decades after, the descriptions in historical accounts, guidebooks, and the press (along with its representations at the RA) suggest, as John McAleer has pointed out, that the company was 'never far from the public gaze or historical imagination' in London, if not in Britain.[26]

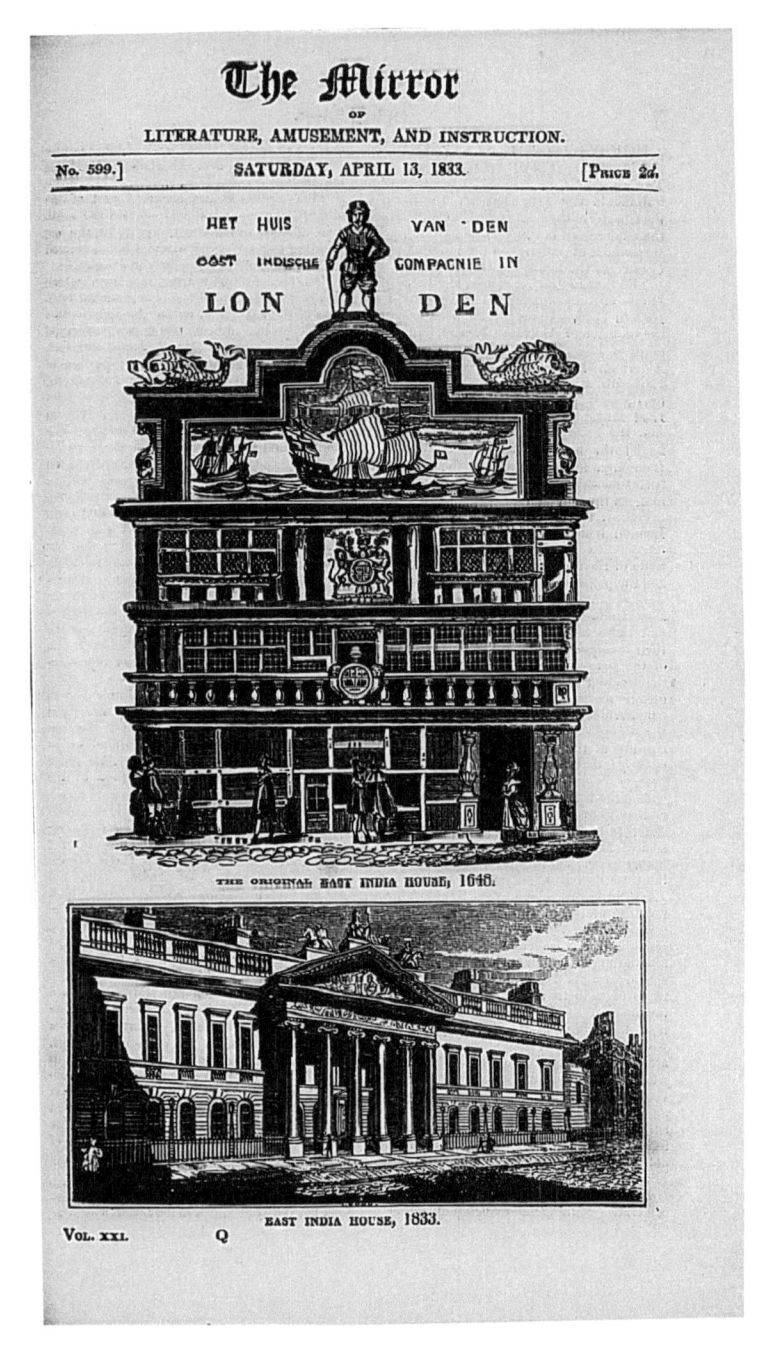

Figure 6.3 Old and new East India House illustrated in *The Mirror of Literature, Amusement and Instruction*, 13 April 1833.

The question of East India House's relation to the company's expanding (or diminishing) role in Asia, and to notions of and developments in the nation's empire more broadly, has been broached through detailed analysis of the earlier and later façades – the rhetorical sculptural scheme of the former shown to be manifestly maritime in theme, the latter more overtly imperial.[27] As for the building completed in 1729, it is the interior, rather than exterior, that has received the most sustained attention. Inside, as all early commentators agreed, the offices and storehouses – standing 'upon a great deal of Ground' – were 'admirably well contriv'd, and the publick Hall and the Committee Room scarce inferior to anything of the like Nature in the City'; it was by contrast that the 70-ft façade seemed 'very narrow' and not of 'an Appearance answerable to the Grandeur of the House within'.[28]

By far the most discussed feature of the original furnishing is the series of 'six pictures of the principal Forts & settlements belonging to the East India Company' which the antiquary George Vertue recorded as 'having lately been set up in their house in Leadenhall Street' in 1732, and which (as with the watercolour views of East India House) survive in the collections of the British Library – see, for example, the views of St Helena in the Atlantic Ocean (Figure 6.4), Bombay on the Arabian Sea (Plate 8), and Madras on the Bay of Bengal (Figure 6.5).[29] Previously studied principally from an art-historical perspective, these large canvases by George Lambert and Samuel Scott, and their display in the directors' court room alongside a very grand marble chimneypiece and relief by John Michael Rysbrack showing 'Britannia receiving the riches of the East' (Figure 6.6), have been persuasively positioned as a prototype for the artistic programme of the Foundling Hospital's slightly later court room (in a building also designed by Jacobsen, and with a chimneypiece marble relief also by Rysbrack, but here on the theme of charity).[30] As such, the paintings have been established as works of more historical than visual significance in the development of art and its public consumption in Britain. 'The history paintings donated to the Foundling Hospital were more complicated and allusive,' Douglas Fordham has argued, 'than the sea pieces commissioned by the EIC.'[31] However, Fordham's identification of a 'telling iconographic thread through the heart' of the two undertakings – addressing the public benefits of, or need to compensate for, making and spending money through global mercantile expansion (a thread manifested by the ropes and rigs of the ship that appears in both of Rysbrack's reliefs) – gives reason to investigate further the visual work of the earlier scheme within its own wider, interconnecting contexts beyond the purely art-historical or indeed economic. As Geoff Quilley has emphasised in his study of British art through the lens of the East India Company, which he purposefully began with East India House rather than the Foundling Hospital, the expansion of maritime

Figure 6.4 George Lambert and Samuel Scott, St Helena, c. 1731, oil on canvas, 78.5 × 117 cm, British Library.

commerce and its material culture is (and so historical study should be) inseparable from colonial and imperial dimensions.[32]

For Vertue, after all, these were not 'sea pictures', but 'pictures of the principal Forts & settlements belonging to the East India Company'. His single sentence recording the pictures' installation in the house in Leadenhall, in its shift from oil on canvas to stone fortresses overseas, to one of the nation's chief commercial streets, is usefully suggestive of the spatial reach and range invited in the minds (if not the bodies) of those who viewed both paintings and buildings. The conceptual movement inherent in the line dissolves boundaries between picture and place, art and architecture, metropole and colony, local and global. Moreover, the scheme in which the paintings had been 'set up' was presumably considered a success for the controversial company, if it was deemed to provide any kind of model for the controversial hospital. The similarity between the boardrooms is not coincidental – not merely because, as Brian Allen has noted, many of the founding governors of the Foundling Hospital were directors of the company.[33] Their boards shared a motivation for material display that helped to explain and legitimise their respective missions as reasoned and respectable in the light of the commercial and political concerns of the day.[34] In looking again at the 1729 building of East India House, the paintings produced shortly afterwards and the interior of which they were a part, this chapter aims to read them less from a single disciplinary perspective and more as their early viewers did, reuniting building, painting, and other furnishings in a composite visual and conceptual field, and as part of the integrated architectural setting of company, city, and colonial settlements. Taking the cue of eighteenth-century accounts, we start outside.

## The view from the street

Joseph Pote's *Foreigner's Guide* to London, first published in 1729 with the intention of giving the curious traveller ('Foreigner *and* Native') a 'regular Way to see what is most remarkable in this great City', noted the new facelift that had been given to the headquarters of the East India Company at the heart of the commercial centre.

> A very stately Building, all of Free-stone, just finished: This is one of the richest Magazines [storehouses] in the Kingdom. All the Offices, and the Hall for publick Sale are very noble and commodious, and the Goods in the Warehouses belonging to it (just before the Sale) are well worth seeing.[35]

With parallel text in English and French, Pote's *Guide* took its readers on a tour across the cities of Westminster and London and around their edges, setting off from St James's Palace and stretching as far as surrounding sights and towns; the final few pages provided a price list for passage by road and water. The 'regular Way' of seeing promoted by Pote was clearly a response to the difficulties even 'natives' faced in navigating and viewing the irregular urban sprawl that Daniel Defoe had recently declaimed – in his *Tour Thro' the Whole Island of Great Britain* (1724–27) – as 'this monstrous City', a 'great center' growing hastily out of shape and control.[36] The poet James Wright, describing rather more positively the 'Visionary Feast' of the 'Boundless Town' that awaited those who climbed to the top of the new St Paul's Cathedral, extolled how 'such a various and abundant store of pleasing Sights' made it difficult to know where to begin or indeed end.[37] The *Guide* directed travellers to East India House via the 'magnificent' building of the Royal Exchange ('it may be said there is no exchange in the Universe so fine as this'), the General Post Office (the 'very large' revenue-raising circulation point for letters to and from scattered parts of the globe), and Leadenhall Market ('having not its like in the World').[38] From East India House, the route continued to the Monument ('one of the boldest pieces of Architecture ever attempted [...] yielding a pleasant Prospect all over the City') and London Bridge, where the Thames river could be seen 'constantly Ebbing and Flowing' with the

'World's Treasure' and 'Tribute', as Wright summarised it.[39] In Defoe's eyes, the whole river from London Bridge to Blackwall (where East India Company ships were built and maintained) 'is one great Arsenal, nothing in the World can be like it'.[40]

The integration of the trading company's headquarters into a bilingual guide of what was 'most remarkable' about Britain's allegedly world-beating capital, and the recommendation of its offices and warehouses as well worth a visit, indicate that East India House in the eighteenth century was architecture and space experienced and understood in motion and interaction. It was on the circuit of people 'always in Motion and Activity', as Tom Brown described London's citizens in 1700 (Wright compared the 'Busy Traders' to swarming ants); and it was seen not just from the city streets (the 'so many *Veins*, wherein the People Circulate'), but from the building's own corridors and courtyards, as well as through its contents: the changing arrays of 'Goods' traded and transported over vast distances and geographies.[41] A straight vein linked the company's central organ in Strype's 'Place of a great Trade' with the ships that carried its lifeblood, a direct physical and economic connection that could be easily traced looking down from the Monument's viewing platform – or the dome of St Paul's, from where Wright admired how the masts of the vessels bringing the 'Riches of *both Indies*' gave the impression of a 'thick-set Wood of moving Trees'.[42] Visiting London later, in 1786, the German novelist Sophie von la Roche recorded attending 'the great tea auction' inside East India House, and from there travelling to the Customs House less than half a mile away on the Thames. 'It is impossible to describe the confusion of workmen and ships' hands there', she wrote, emphasising how such spectacles made the City rather than Westminster the centre of things: 'This portion of London shows far more clearly than St James's, that it is a great trading state, and that here is the residence of a mighty king.'[43]

As for the exterior of East India House, La Roche first gave the opinion that it was 'without much show [...] yet very effective' – although then echoed the books she may have consulted, by Noorthouck and others, in adding that it was 'not as fine as one might expect from the owners of dominions supplying sixteen million subjects and six million pounds sterling, and having a standing army of eighteen thousand men'.[44] By this point in the 1780s, the company's turn from 'mere traders' to a territorial force in India was at the forefront of public attention and the British government, concerned about the company's use of its intensifying power, had brought in legislation to assert more control.[45] In satirical prints commenting on the political debates in 1783–84, the Leadenhall Street front of East India House stands for the company that had got too big for its five bays: in one scene the building is being kicked like a football between rivals William Pitt

Figure 6.5 George Lambert and Samuel Scott, Fort St George, Madras, c. 1731, oil on canvas, 81 × 132 cm, British Library.

the Younger and Charles Fox (Figure 6.7); in another, entitled 'A Transfer of East India Stock', Fox carries it on his back like a strongbox, stealthily stowing it inside crown property.[46] The author of the later *Ambulator: or, A Pocket Companion in a Tour Round London* (1793) echoed earlier comments that the 'very confined' front did not 'vouch for the truth' of the company as a 'republic of commercial Sovereigns, who possessed extensive territories in distant regions of the globe'.[47] More recent historians have settled on the idea that the company's public image in the eighteenth century was 'consciously staid', determined by 'sturdy common sense'.[48] Certainly, the façade's balanced composition of classical giant pilasters in the sober and notionally strong Doric order, between a rusticated base and rooftop balustrade, was designed by Jacobsen to make a statement of fiscal order and legitimacy – announcing the company as a 'permanent fixture' in the nation's finances, as G. A. Bremner has put it – to all who visited or passed by.[49] 'In appearance, the architecture was solid and suitably reassuring,' McAleer has written, displaying 'values of common sense and stability, precisely the characteristics required to inspire confidence in shareholders subscribing to risky long-distance trading ventures.'[50]

Yet, to accept that the façade was 'solid and serviceable, but with no pretensions to beauty', as William Foster earlier put it, is to risk underestimating its modernity and fashionability when completed in 1729.[51] It would, after all, have compared closely to the aristocratic taste then being set by Lord Burlington in the West End – notably in the building closest to

Burlington's own mansion on his estate, Queensberry House, completed in 1723 and designed by Giacomo Leoni, who had recently produced the hugely successful first English translation of Palladio's *I Quattro Libri dell'Architettura*. The stylistic alignment had political advantages through the then close association of Burlington with the Whig prime minister Robert Walpole, closeness to whom was a 'deliberate strategy' by the company to secure its privileges, and whose Norfolk home of Houghton was at that time being completed in Palladian splendour (in pride of place a chimneypiece by Rysbrack, incorporating a Roman-inspired bust of Walpole and the inscription 'Senatus Britannici Princeps').[52] Referring to urban models, East India House followed the strict Palladian frontage of Queensberry (itself a revival of Inigo Jones's urban townhouse formula seen in Lincoln's Inn Fields), with the same arrangement of storeys, fenestration, and balustrade above, substituting the Doric order for the Composite.[53] Queensberry House had two extra bays, yet five (the number at East India House) were projected at the centre. Such a comparison – and of both new buildings to Jones's exemplars, in particular the five-bay river-front gallery then still standing at Somerset House – would have been best appreciated by a mobile viewer, crossing from Westminster to the City of London as Pote advised his travelling reader to do (Pote indeed picked out 'Queensborough', and Burlington's own house, among the very fine new buildings in Westminster).[54] As part of such a journey, East India House would have stood out for its façade entirely of stone, whereas the wall face of Queensberry House was of brick with stone dressings, leaving Leoni to complain that the ground storey was not given the smooth-faced masonry finish he had intended.

Rather than appearing 'comparatively unpretentious', as Allen has suggested ('relatively simple' and modest, in McAleer's words), the relatively extravagant new face of East India House made a particularly striking contrast with its neighbouring buildings on Leadenhall Street.[55] The Great Fire of 1666 had stopped on the east of the city at the top of Leadenhall, and so the building stock in this area was older, and therefore the visual impact of new buildings greater. As William Maitland noted in his 1739 *History of London*, Leadenhall Street was 'spacious, populous, and well inhabited; but the Houses escaping the great Fire Anno 1666, are not so sightly and uniform'.[56] Wale's view in *London and its Environs Described* (Figure 6.1) gives a flavour of the contrast – although the buildings on either side had undergone repairs – and underlines the need to compare East India House with surrounding buildings in space (as contemporary viewers would have done) as much as with its own formulations through time (as historians tend to do). East India House in fact set a trend in the City, heading a wave of major new civic and commercial buildings such as the Bank of England, opened in 1734 (for which Jacobsen submitted plans but lost out to George Sampson), and the Mansion House, the design competition for which was won by George Dance (the elder) in 1735.[57] As Daniel Abramson has concluded, Jacobsen's East India House, as one of the financial revolution's first purpose-built structures, 'attests to the City of London's capacity for advanced architectural patronage in the late 1720s and belies the common assumption that "the City contributed nothing to the art of the Stuarts and Georgians", as the eminent architectural historian John Summerson once wrote'.[58] It can indeed be seen to have initiated a phase of 'highly visible, assertive modernisation' in City building projects, which were aligned in the illustrations for *London and its Environs Described* with the most prestigious sites across the capital, including the Banqueting House, Somerset House, and the great houses and palaces of the West End.[59]

Wale's drawing also indicates that the façade was not quite so 'plain' and lacking in 'real ornament' as is typically assumed.[60] Beyond the pointed use of Doric in place of Composite, the arches above the three central windows on the ground floor – thus in easy view of passers-by – are shown to contain carvings. The detail is unclear, but suggestive of coats of arms. It can be assumed that this ornament provided at least some 'outward sign' of the business that operated within, corporate badges of identity endorsed by the overarching architectural language.[61] The hint in the later watercolour that the reliefs represented the old and new East India companies which were united in 1709 (whose arms featured sea lions and land lions respectively) adds a further possible layer of symbolic unity and strength in the harmonious design.[62] A fairly conventional ornament of that sort, in terms of subject, would help explain the apparent lack of comment drawn from contemporaries. The carver was likely John Boson, who worked for Hawksmoor and became one of a small group of craftsmen closely connected with the designs of William Kent (Burlington's protégé).[63] A 'man of great ingenuity' who 'undertook great works in his way for the prime people of quality', according to Vertue, Boson was a subscriber to Leoni's *Alberti* in 1726, and in 1733/4 took a long lease from Burlington on a plot in Savile Row (on his death in 1743, one of his executors was the painter of the company's settlements George Lambert).[64] Boson's bill for 'carvers work' at East India House (shared with his then partner John How) was £189 19s, an amount only exceeded for work he completed for the future king and Canterbury Cathedral.

The leading style and quality of craftsmanship ensured the stately and magnificent look on Leadenhall that Pote and others celebrated. James Ralph, in his 1734 *Critical Review of the Publick Buildings, Statues and Ornaments In, and about London* (which he dedicated to Burlington and directed towards a widening public for art and architecture), wished that the company directors had spent more than it seemed on their house, given its public role in communicating the 'majesty and wealth of the British nation' to foreigners especially, and his remark that the façade was 'unworthy [of] their figure in the trading world' is probably the original source for the subsequent criticisms.[65] Nevertheless, Ralph conceded that the 'fabrick indeed is built in taste' – by which he meant it followed the 'Burlingtonian classicism' that he aimed to popularise.[66] The problem was 'there is not enough of it': it (he) wanted a portico.[67] Ralph's *Review* provoked considerable debate, and the respondent in the *Grub Street Journal* countered that 'East India House, built under the direction of Mr James, is, for its magnitude, a well-considered structure', and that a portico on such a narrow street 'would have had an indifferent effect'.[68] He also dismissed Ralph's desire that this and other buildings were 'more costly', which 'proceeds from his being unacquainted with design and application of materials to the best advantage'.[69] Economy as well as taste underpinned the designs for rebuilding East India House in 1796. John Soane proposed retaining the Palladian front of the old building (with minor alterations) and constructing a corresponding wing, connecting the two with 'an appropriate portico'.[70] Writing later about his dispute with Jupp over the redesign, Soane remarked that his plan had a fairer claim than the building subsequently executed to 'public convenience, classical purity, and real magnificence [...] not only on a principle of just economy, but on the authority of one of the most esteemed works of the ancient masters'.[71] Proposed elevations by George Dance (the younger) and Henry Holland likewise retained the core of Jacobsen's building, though reclad with different designs, Holland's being very close to the final version.[72] The 1726 façade thus proved unusually durable in the way it adapted and grew. Perhaps, even, Ralph's sense that East India House looked unfinished was close to the mark and – like the Lloyd's building now in its place – it was designed for the possibility, if not express intention, of future change and expansion.[73]

That the façade of East India House left viewers wanting more seems precisely its point. Consider it alongside the five-guinea coins that were in production at the royal mint the same year as building work was completed in 1729. These coins – the highest possible denomination – were struck from gold provided to the mint by the East India Company; the corporate origin of the gold is indicated by the initials E. I. C. under the head of George II, the company having specially requested permission for this alteration where an elephant or elephant and castle representing the Royal African Company (sourcing its gold on what it called the 'Guinea coast') was more commonly found.[74] For both companies, the refining of raw material into splendid and covetable crafted product lent a respectable sheen to their very publicly contested trades – a 'shiny irreproachability', as

Helen Hills has written of the silver that was violently plundered through Spanish colonialism in South America and materially transformed so as to 'efface its own traumatic history'.[75] The gold that was shaped into the East India Company coins had been imported through Canton (Guangzhou), where the company's currency included large amounts of Spanish-looted silver, and in turn the gold coins could have purchased more such silver for export and further exchange on the Asian coast.[76] The lustre of the gold, as with the façade's bright white stone, glossed the tarnished trade. The company's acquisition of gold in Canton – about £12,000 of it apparently transformed into five-guinea coins – signalled the East India Company's strengthening stake and ambition in a sphere that was promotable as more immediately promising for the crucial metal, and so for trade in general, than the increasingly troubled and threatened monopoly on the West African coast. It must have gratified the company that the Queen was reported to have purchased a thousand pounds' worth of its five-guinea pieces.[77] Edge lettering on the coins, a feature designed to prevent them from being clipped and thus devalued, spelled out the motto 'DECUS ET TUTAMEN' ('An ornament and a safeguard'), conjuring in this case the purported dual advantages not just of the coin and the crown, but also the company. Coin and façade – the former possibly struck to celebrate the completion of the latter – had a crucial message to convey: that the company's business was low risk and likely lucrative.[78] The consolidation of gold on the one hand, and abstemiously yet calculatingly styled stone on the other, spoke in unison of a sound investment. To borrow from James Mayo on postmodernism, Palladianism was here 'as much a part of an economic force' as an architectural style.[79] Albeit in different materials and scales, coin and façade were representations of wealth well managed and securely stored.

Secure storage was another factor in Jacobsen's design for (as Pote called it) 'one of the richest Magazines in the Kingdom' which had become 'a common thorowfare to all sorts of people'.[80] An attempted robbery at the old East India House in 1711, which caused quite a stir and scandal (attracting the mirth of Jonathan Swift), revealed the porousness of the crumbling building and the need to strengthen its security.[81] The building had also come under physical attack by weavers in 1697, in a protracted dispute over textile imports that continued into the 1720s, and fire was a constant fear.[82] The rebuilding committee appointed in 1725 was instructed 'to view and examine the state of the buildings in and about the House, and what alterations are needful to be made for the better security of the House'.[83] The new façade may thus be read not as full frontage, but as frontispiece, a gatehouse to the large (and newly enlarged) complex that stretched behind. As the *Grub Street Journal* critic stressed, a portico would have 'made too great an encroachment on the parts within; which, I believe, are much better employed to other uses'.[84] The building, in his view, answered 'every purpose intended'.

In its self-conscious order, modernity, and economy, the fit-for-purpose façade of the new East India House might also be compared to a shift in the level of ornament carved on the ships built for the company's service – and it is perhaps no coincidence that the carver Boson had likely served his apprenticeship as a ship's carver and by the 1720s had his own yard at Greenwich, close to the Deptford shipyard that was then the busiest and most prosperous on the Thames, building thirty ships for the East India trade between 1715 and 1736.[85] The visual as well as physical proximity between street frontage and ship's stern is one that contemporaries may have been prone to conceive, as a later edition of Ralph's *Critical Review* described the Mansion House as having 'all the resemblance possible to a deep laden Indiaman, with her stern galleries and ginger bread work'.[86] The author of this and other additions to the 1783 edition was William Nicholson, who had served on East India Company ships in his youth and so may have been more prone than most to make such a connection. However, his disparagement of the architect, George Dance (the elder), as 'originally a shipwright' points to the employment as masons of Dance and his father, Giles, by the slave-trading South Sea Company (based a very short distance from Mansion House as well as East India House), and more broadly to an earlier fluidity between naval and civil architectures – 'to do him justice', Nicholson added, 'he appears never to have lost sight of his first profession'.[87] By the 1740s, the sterns of the East Indiamen built downriver at Deptford and Blackwall were plainer than the quite extravagant works of sculpture observed in the late seventeenth century.[88] They may have been less showy, but they were built to the highest specifications (particularly in relation to materials, and specifically the best English oak, which would make up almost the entire ship) and they were building, launching, and sailing for the east in steadily growing numbers.[89] Jean Sutton's investigations of the ships through the company's history found it true to generalise that they were 'the largest, most soundly constructed British merchantmen afloat'.[90] As on a successful East Indiaman, at East India House viewers were led to speculate about the riches safely stowed inside.

## The view from inside

The eastern door of the 1729 façade opened into a long corridor stretching inwards by more than 200 feet, leading on both sides into a series of rooms, staircases, and yards. A few doors down on the right were entrances to the sales room, committee rooms, and, with openings from both these, the director's court room. There is no known surviving image showing the court room before the late eighteenth-century remodelling, but textual accounts confirm that this and other principal rooms remained intact, with the furnishings wholly or largely unchanged.[91] Thomas Shepherd's watercolour of the court room from around 1820 (Plate 9) is therefore valuable evidence for the room completed in 1729, and accords with written descriptions. According to Charles Knight's *London* (1843), the room was 'said to be an exact cube of 30 feet' and 'splendidly ornamented by gilding and by large looking-glasses', along with the six pictures hanging from the cornice and the fine marble chimneypiece.[92]

It appears not to have been noted previously how this centrepiece of East India House, in its dimensions and decoration, imitated the 30-ft single-cube drawing room at Wilton House in Wiltshire, renowned for the Palladian-style rebuilding and interiors overseen by Inigo Jones (but also, perhaps not coincidentally, as a house comprised of accumulated alterations and additions that gave historical value).[93] Just as Jacobsen was drawing up his designs for the company, the soon-to-be heir of Wilton and ninth earl of Pembroke, Henry Herbert, was engaged with Roger Morris in the design of Marble Hill House for Henrietta Howard, mistress of King George II, which was completed the same year as East India House with a smaller, 24-ft cube 'Great Room' at its heart. Plans and elevations for Marble Hill were printed in volume three of *Vitruvius Britannicus*, Colen Campbell's 'manifesto of English Palladianism', in 1725, alongside plans and a section showing Campbell's own newly completed 40-ft square 'Great Hall' for Walpole at Houghton; Wilton had appeared in volume two in 1717.[94] In dialogue with such eminent models and contemporary parallels, and indeed surpassing Marble Hill's 'Great Room' in size (so that a row of smaller windows was inserted above the main three, as at Houghton, to provide more light from the internal courtyard), the court room of East India House aimed for an internal splendour that was the opposite of staid. In the words of an 1803 account, it was 'a most superb apartment'; the architrave, frieze, and cornice were 'in very good proportion', the ceiling was ornamented with 'shells combined with scrolls', and the walls with 'festoons in stucco'.[95] The 'opulence' of the court room expressed the fiscal and cultural capital of the company, and revealed its sense of high status and serious ambition – a display evidently judged more worthy than the exterior 'of the Company's Trade and Figure in the World'.[96]

As in Howard's Great Room (and throughout Houghton), the directors' court room boasted very large and impressive doors made of mahogany, almost certainly sourced from Jamaica or Central America and transported in the same ships that carried sugar and slaves.[97] The lifting of import taxes in 1721 made this highly desirable and still novel wood – 'both a consequence and an emblem of economic growth', as Adam Bowett has shown – relatively cheap in England through the 1720s but increasingly scarce by mid-century; the price was paid by the enslaved peoples used in its labour-intensive extraction, and the rapidly deforested environments in which the same peoples suffered immediate ecological consequences.[98] It is not clear whether the use of mahogany at East India House extended to staircases and floorboards as at Marble Hill, the exuberance of which depended even more heavily on the slave trade through its financing from South Sea Company shares.[99] The court room floor was covered 'quite to the walls' with an 'uncommonly fine Turkey carpet'.[100] The fitted carpet must have been purpose-made for the new space, probably in India with Persian influence ('Turkey carpet' was a generic term for a hand-knotted pile carpet, and could even be English-made).[101]

The East India Company had a history of commissions for carpets through its overseas settlements: through Surat, the prominent company member Robert Bell in 1630 ordered a 'very faire long Turkey carpitt' from Lahore, a centre of carpet production at the time, incorporating his initials and coat of arms along with those of the Girdlers' Company for which it was a gift; and a decade or so later, the company official William Fremlin ordered himself a carpet studded with his family's coat of arms in the border and at the centre (seventeen times in all).[102] Both the Bell and Fremlin carpets were intended as table coverings: fitted floor carpets on the scale of that made for the court room were a new feature in England in the early eighteenth century, and the company was at the forefront of setting the trend.[103] From the earlier examples, though, we can guess that the company's carpet was adorned with its arms, as was certainly the case of two Coromandel lacquer screens made purposely for the court room and shipped in 1730.[104] The whereabouts of these armorial screens, as with the carpet, are not known, but what must be very similar examples were made for John Eccleston, a company director from 1721 to 1735, for one of the string of Childs of Osterley Park who served as directors in the same period (as part of a large set of armorial furniture), and indeed for Howard at Marble Hill.[105] Made in China, but known as Coromandel screens because they were transhipped from the Indian coast, these screens were highly prized for the lustrous look of gold, silver, and red decoration inset in smooth black lacquer.[106] The made-to-order screens integrated family and corporate coats of arms into the borders of scenes of court life, nature, and, in some cases, the production of silk, rice, and other goods.

The kaleidoscopic effect of rich polished mahogany, huge plush carpet, and ornate lacquerware, set against the gilded architectural detailing, is not well conveyed by Shepherd's watercolour. The pattern of the carpet, presumably ornate, is barely hinted at (it might by then, after a century of use, have been well worn), and the screens are not shown. Nor do we see the marble chimneypiece with Rysbrack's relief, which one account describes as dominating the east wall; nor an array of finer details including the company's ballot box constructed of Amboyna wood from Southeast Asia, ebony from India, and mahogany, likely from the Caribbean though possibly an Asian equivalent, and an early shield dial clock with finials and door panel decorated with company ships in what was typically a Chinoiserie scene.[107] The clock was a type known for the punctuality of its eight-day mechanism and, at around a metre and a half tall, and half that wide, made a forceful statement of the company's control of time: time was money.[108] Its control of space was reinforced by the display of 'mathematical instruments' above the mirrors, which given the maritime concerns of the company were surely navigational tools.[109] Consider also the tea and other drinks consumed, the silver and china ware in which they were served, the ink and inkstands used in the daily transactions, and the fine silks shown off in the directors' cuffs, cravats, and other attire, and the 30-ft cube court room may be seen as a cornucopia of commodities that advertised what the company had to offer and was already shaping domestic and colonial taste, trade, and manufacture.

The muted surviving image of the court room has perhaps steered art-historical attention in its focus on the paintings by Lambert and Scott at the expense of the wider range of material objects that played both individual and interactive roles in the visual effects and meanings of the room in 1729. Mildred Archer, whose work on the company and British art has made a lasting impression on interpretations of East India House (if not the art) despite being itself a 'product of empire', was certainly wrong to assert that there was 'no sign' in the company's headquarters of 'Chinese and Indian export wares – the products in which it dealt'.[110] While establishing that the company's collection of (English-made) furniture, sculpture, and painting 'illuminates the British connexion [sic] with India', Archer echoed the historian J. R. Seeley's line about England seeming to have expanded its empire 'in a fit of absence of mind' by suggesting that the company 'created almost insensibly a "public image" of itself', and that this image 'bore scant relation to its everyday concerns'.[111] Approached from the perspective of their wider setting, the paintings – and the public image – can be seen in a different light.

A note in pencil beneath the painting in the top left of Shepherd's watercolour (Plate 9), 'St Helena', indicates that the view of this Atlantic island settlement (Figure 6.4) was hung to the left of the company chairman's throne on the west wall, with a view of the Cape of Good Hope to the right. Showing vital 'way stations' with secure anchorage for refuelling and revictualling, these opening scenes (Lambert painted scenery for

**Figure 6.6** Michael Rysbrack, marble relief from the chimneypiece made for the court room in East India House, c. 1729, showing 'Britannia receiving the riches of the East', Foreign, Commonwealth and Development Office.

the theatre) conjure the journey repeatedly made by a steadily growing number of company ships to and from Britain and Asia, with Africa pivotal in between. The two locations were like gateways through which the trade was accessed and goods extracted. Three other paintings show the English presidencies in India – Bombay (now Mumbai), Madras (Chennai), and Calcutta (Kolkata) – together the 'beating heart of the company's operations'.[112] Bombay (Plate 8), the centre of English trade on the west coast, was acquired from the Portuguese through the marriage of Charles II to Catherine of Braganza in 1662; Madras (Figure 6.5), a thriving entrepot on the eastern coast, was fortified from 1639 onwards; and Calcutta, in the north, was fortified with great speed and energy between 1698 and 1702, the company seizing on its importance as the hub of an extensive system of land and maritime exchange.[113] One further painting depicted the settlement of Tellicherry (Thalassery), located south of Bombay on the Malabar coast, which was fortified from the 1680s; this was an important port for pepper and cardamom, but also strategically close to rival Dutch strongholds in the Carnatic.[114] If Rysbrack's relief presented the east as 'a geographic blur', as John Crowley put it (albeit the figures presenting their produce to Britannia may be identified as India, Asia, and Africa), the paintings, as Quilley has

*The view from inside East India House* 175

**Figure 6.7** Thomas Rowlandson, *Billy Lackbeard and Charley Blackbeard Playing at Football*, 1784, hand-coloured etching, 26.3 × 37.3 cm, Royal Collection Trust.

made clear, in their 'appeal to criteria of topographical verisimilitude' (for Crowley, 'pretensions to authenticity'), provided 'a point of contact for the London office with the material actuality of its global business'.[115]

Each of the paintings centres on a well-fortified settlement surrounded by shipping – the buildings and landscape the work of Lambert, the shipping by Scott. Neither artist had been to India, so they relied on a combination of manuscript and printed sources (visible, perhaps, in the variation of viewpoint that resulted, though these shifts also lent an appropriate sense of motion) and their imaginations. Whereas Allen has stressed the historical importance of the paintings within the development of British landscape art (noting that the format employed by Lambert is essentially that of the country-house view 'applied to unfamiliar territory') and Quilley has discussed their place in British maritime art ('the bias is with water not land'), McAleer has drawn attention to the composite significance of the scenes, which 'emphasised the dependence of shipping and maritime trade on shore-based factories and ports'.[116] Considering further the way the images seem to lie uniquely between landscape and maritime traditions, in a genre of their own, we might see the art-historical equivocation (and the artistic entanglement that produced it) as reflective of the company's long-equivocal relationship with land at a time when its reliance on it, economically and politically, was increasingly certain; as McAleer recognises, forts and shipping were 'the twin concerns of the East India Company at this time'.[117] The perception of the company as a force on land as well as sea had been signalled by the new arms taken on by the United Company, as regally displayed above the chairman's throne: the old company's sea-lion supporters with a zodiac sphere crest and the motto 'Deo ducente nil nocet' ('When God leads, nothing can harm') were replaced by rampant lions with a further lion in the crest, a regal crown between its paws, and the motto 'Auspicio regis et senatus Angliae' ('By the authority of the sovereign and senate of England'), emblematic of the 'company-state' that Philip Stern has dissected.[118] In the year that the United Company was formed (1709), the directors wrote to the president of Bengal in Calcutta that 'we must not despise the day of small things' – implying, as Stern pointed out, 'their hope that larger things were soon to follow'.[119] They had long been committed to building, in their own words, 'foundations as must in time induce a great & famous superstructure', and it is this growing superstructure, underpinned by the architecture of forts and ships, that they commissioned Lambert and Scott to recreate in paint.[120]

The hybrid artistic form of the paintings was thus at the service of what Stern summarised as a 'particular form of hybrid and composite sovereignty over a system that was at its core urban, coastal, and maritime in its orientation and rooted in the Company's constitution as a corporate body politic'.[121] The urban cores of the presidency paintings have been overlooked in the historiographical emphases on country-house or estate views, maritime art, and ships and forts. Lambert and Scott probably also had in mind city views, and specifically how London (the post-Fire plans for which provided a model for the colonial towns) was seen from the Thames, in reality as well as in representation – not least by the travellers guided across the city by Pote. Company, city, and colonial spaces connected and converged for viewers inside East India House.

Between land and sea, London and Asia, is the space of the ship (as highlighted by Scott's busy foregrounds), the movable structure that mediated between distant 'belonging' and the boardroom, and the vital link between dispersed sites of capital accumulation and the dividends paid to shareholders. Michel Foucault described the ship as a 'floating piece of space, a place without a place, that exists by itself, that is closed in on itself', yet company ships, Bremner has insisted, were extensions of the spaces in and from which they uplifted and offloaded their cargoes.[122] There was no dichotomy between land and sea for the East India Company, or indeed for the English state that supported it, which maintained that sea was just as much territory to be claimed and controlled as was land.[123] The company was expected to arm and defend its chartered rights on ship and shore, and even to act in the nation's defence if required. Through its sea power, the company literally occupied the space between England and Asia.[124] The paintings' general implied viewpoint from the deck of a ship, and their arrangement on three walls of the court room as if the windows of a captain's cabin across the stern (alongside the navigational instruments and the maps and charts that were stored in a chest), gave directors and visitors an impression of being onboard and with the power of a far-seeing eye. The room, not just the paintings, was a representation of the company's role, and a vehicle for long-term thinking as well as long-distance trade.

### From inside out

If the cabin analogy is too fanciful, the implied mobility is not. The paintings not only put the company's enterprise 'on the map', as Archer suggested figuratively, but were a form of mapping that has a parallel to the map-cycles of sovereign rulers.[125] In this way, the paintings do more specific work than reminding the directors 'of the geographical sweep of the company's activities'.[126] They lend it logic and coherence. The neat circuit they create masks unevenness and the unknown across the actual distance of more than 7,000 miles. The views of settlements in India locate the company in strategically placed settlements in four principal regions – successive imprints that are roughly equally spaced along the vast coastline from the northwest to southwest to southeast to northeast – suggesting a comprehensive and secure stake in the subcontinental trade and points from which influence might be extended over the territory in between. The view of the Cape evokes the company's vast claim, through its charter, to jurisdiction of the eastern hemisphere beyond this point. Cape Town was not, in fact, one of the settlements belonging to the English company (a fact quietly acknowledged in the painting, seemingly based on a Dutch source, by the ships sailing under the Dutch flag), but its value in terms of shelter and resupply put it firmly in the company's sights. The view of St Helena extends the company's reach into the Atlantic world. The island was more than a crucial port of call; more even than 'the principal link in that chain which connects this country with her Indian possessions', as it was later described. For the company, it held the possibility for constructing a Barbadian-style colonial plantation at the crossroads of east and west. 'Such a plantation could produce goods of both hemispheres,' Stern explains, 'while serving as the lynchpin in a wider, interconnected transhemispheric commercial and political system.'[127] While the economy that was envisaged failed to emerge, by 1723 over half of the island's residents were enslaved.[128]

Having pieced together the wider visual field of the court room, we can see that the map formed by the paintings spread even further. The unfolded lacquer screens led the eye further towards the east, underlining the importance of India not just for business within the subcontinent, but as transit point for the then growing China trade; the joinery of the multiwood ballot box was a material manifestation of interconnections across the East Indies and possibly also the West. And to this mapwork – the 'dreamwork' of imperialism, to borrow from W. J. T. Mitchell's interpretation of landscape as process – must be added maps themselves. The three huge tables purpose-made for the boardroom seem designed for laying out charts, maps, and plans for inspection.[129] The company's collection presumably included Herman Moll's *Map of the East Indies* of around 1715, the first large-scale map of the region published in England, which he embellished with the company's arms and dedicated to its directors (Figure 6.8). Stretching from Persia to Papua New Guinea, the map also includes inset images of the kind of plans and prospects that provided information for Lambert and Scott (the plan of Fort St George and the City of Madras in the bottom left was previously published together with the prospect to which Lambert evidently referred). Along with scales by which the London-based viewer could measure the degrees and hours of time east of London (measuring against the company clock), Moll provided detailed information on the 'Settlements, Factories, and Territories' of the region and 'what belongs to England, Spain, France, Holland, Denmark, Portugal &c'. The European competition inscribed in the map was also deeply embedded in the paintings, for which a series of ten canvases that were displayed in the headquarters of the Dutch East India Company in Amsterdam from 1663 were likely a spur and influence: among the Dutch settlements depicted in bird's eye view was Cananor (Kannur), little more than ten miles from Tellicherry.[130] Crowley has pointed out that the iconography of Rysbrack's relief, too, was Dutch.[131] The strength of the Dutch East India Company was by this point vastly diminished – in 1729, it ceased being profitable – and other rival companies (for example, Danish and Austrian) were on the verge of collapse. The English company's embrace of material display, its coinage included, may be taken as a sign of new confidence in its international standing and future expansion, and the mapwork a manoeuvre into opening territory.

The display was also, however, a deflection of intense public and parliamentary scrutiny at home that made the company's future far from certain. Defoe, in his 1720 pamphlet *The Trade to India Critically and Calmly Considered* (written in support of domestic weavers), accused the company of draining the nation of specie in exchange for trifles and frippery, thus turning real into 'imaginary wealth'.[132] It was bleeding Britain to death economically, he wrote starkly, 'her bullions which is [*sic*] the life and

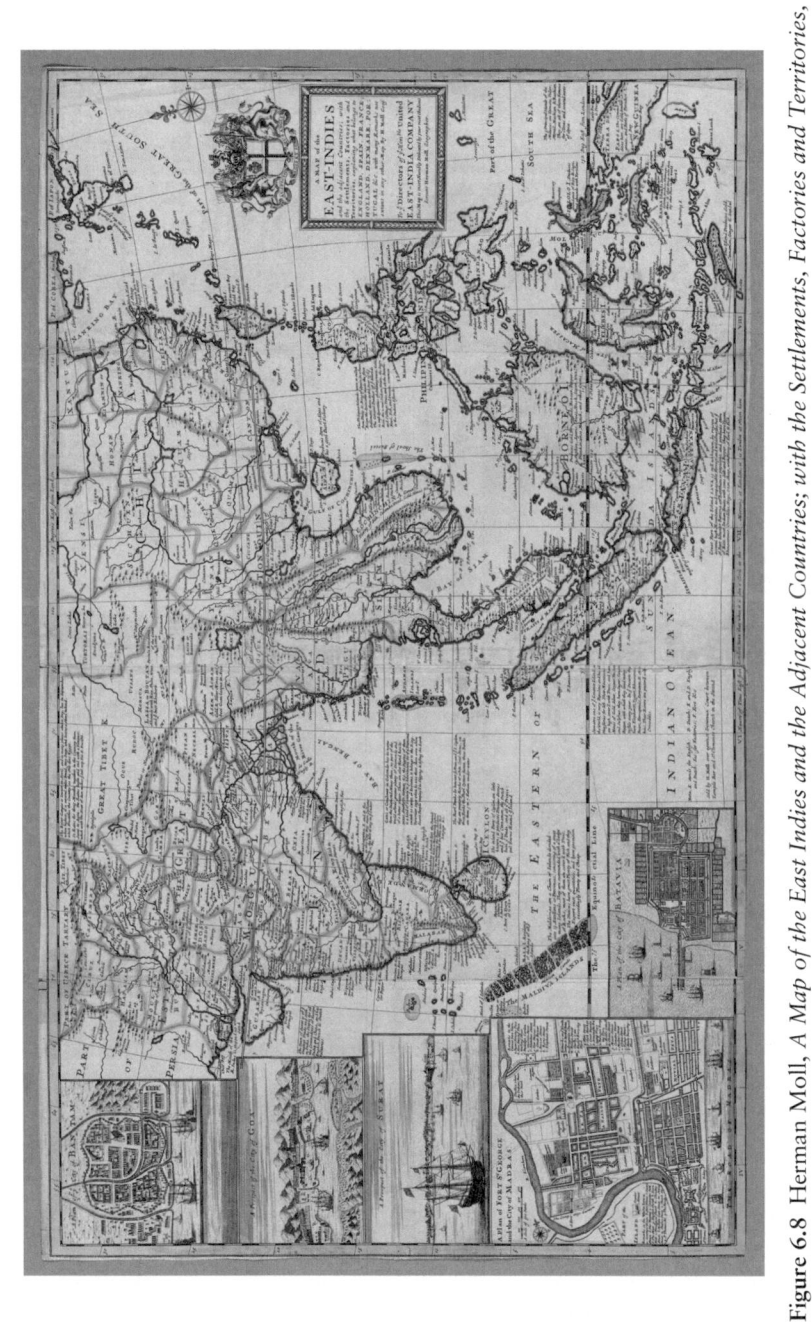

**Figure 6.8** Herman Moll, A Map of the East Indies and the Adjacent Countries; with the Settlements, Factories and Territories, explaining what belongs to England, Spain, France, Holland, Denmark, Portugal &c, c. 1715, 66 × 104 cm, Barry Lawrence Ruderman Map Collection, Stanford.

blood of her trade' flowing out to India like the blood of 'a body in a warm bath, with its veins open'd'.[133] Moreover, two pamphlets written as East India House was under transformation represent just the latest polemical publications in a decades-long dispute between those who supported the company's monopoly and those in favour of free trade. The author of *Some Considerations on the Nature and Importance of the East India Trade* (1728) asserted the trade's 'great Importance' to the nation and the 'vast Benefit the Public reaps' from the company, the company being necessary to build 'strong Forts and Magazines [...] an Expence that private Men can't possibly support'. Meanwhile, in *A Collection of Papers Relating to the East India Trade* (1730), the company was accused of keeping 'Forts abroad, at a great Expence to colour the Necessity of such Monopolies, and to oppress and rob the Natives there with security'. The publication of the *Collection of Papers* was no doubt timed in connection with the renewal of the East India Company's charter privileges the same year (which was passed by Parliament, but only for a further decade and a half), and the paintings of apparently well-fortified and frequented settlements – strikingly calm, reassuring scenes – served to counter claims that the forts, and thereby the company, were unnecessary to uphold the trade. Their hybrid form also appealed to minds (those in positions of political power) interested at once in land and maritime strength as the basis of an expanding empire, representing an inheritance – though by no means inevitable, in common with any country estate – with global reach.

Also in 1730, with England's Royal African Company similarly under attack and especially vulnerable, a series of prints showing off the forts under the company's control on the coast of West Africa was advertised as 'At this Time very proper for all Members of Parliament'. As I have shown elsewhere for the Royal African Company's propaganda, the East India Company's paintings – which were likewise widely disseminated in two series of prints, as well as copies on canvas – represented an intervention in the political-economic debate and revealed the significance of building in creating a corporate image of strength and creditability: very basically, in showing the company's worth to its critics, competitors, and clients (ultimately, the crown).[134] The East India Company's directors had previously made clear their view that buildings, as fixed assets and manifestations of history, 'backed its credit', and we can assume they counted their interiors, at least one so central as their court room, in the same way.[135]

As this chapter has shown by catching the company 'in the act of composing its powerful image', and history in the process of being made – to draw on Homi Bhabha's exploration of nation and narration – the remodelled and refurbished East India House was carefully calculated to give persuasive material reality (the opposite of trifles and frippery) to 'imaginary wealth'.[136] Though the company's meanings changed with time, its continued accumulation, and the eventual dispersal of its many 'small things' through government offices, museum collections, and even homes – the list of items auctioned off to the public before the building's demolition in 1861 was, according to the *Morning Post*, 'sufficient to furnish a moderately sized country town' – denote considerable success in its sales argument and self-fashioning as a national concern, though such efficiency was to work against it in the end.[137] The foreign secretary of the day can be seen walking through the court room's mahogany doors and seated against the backdrop of Rysbrack's relief, now a centrepiece of the council chamber in the recently rebranded Foreign, Commonwealth, and Development Office.[138] The company's arms preside over the British Library's Asian and African Studies Reading Room, while the tables and chairs lie protected in off-site storage. As for the 'yards and pieces of carpet without number', the 'thousands upon thousands of yards of wainscoting', and the 'superabundance' of 'every conceivable article of furniture' that went under the auctioneer's hammer over the course of several days, who knows where they may still be found. The physical legacy of the company in Britain's imperial history may seem strangely invisible, but it is just as strangely all around.

## Notes

1 Swati Chattopadhyay calls into question the scale and kind of spaces given attention, specifically in the study of the British empire in India, in *Small Spaces: Recasting the Architecture of Empire* (London: Bloomsbury, 2023). The East India Company's boardroom may not be 'small' in the senses that Chattopadhyay emphasises – overlooked, 'minor' spaces that open up stories of the marginalised – but the intention of my small-scale focus here is likewise not to be beholden to 'imperialist optics', rather to interrogate them to understand further empire's ideological and material infrastructure.
2 The company's history before the Battle of Plassey in 1757, commonly seen as a turning point from trade to territory, is less charted but the focus (as in this chapter) of increasing interest. See, in particular, Philip J. Stern, *The Company-State: Corporate Sovereignty and the Early Modern Foundations of the British Empire in India* (Oxford: Oxford University Press, 2011); Emily Erikson, *Between Monopoly and Free Trade: The English East India Company, 1600–1757* (Princeton: Princeton University Press, 2014); and Rupali Mishra, *A Business of State: Commerce, Politics, and the Birth of the East India Company* (Cambridge, MA: Harvard University Press, 2018).
3 Nick Robins notes the company's 'strange invisibility' in *The Corporation that Changed the World: How the East India Company Shaped the Modern*

*Multinational* (London: Pluto Press, 2nd edn 2012). As Robins discusses (11–12), the legacy in India is more tangible, though much company (as distinct from later imperial) architecture has been lost. The company's role as a collector and patron of art and architecture is nonetheless a growing area of concern (though with an emphasis on the period after 1757), notably in the work of John McAleer. For example, see John McAleer, *Picturing India: People, Places and the World of the East India Company* (London: British Library, 2017); Arthur MacGregor, *Company Curiosities: Nature, Culture and the East India Company* (London: Reaktion, 2018); and Geoff Quilley, *British Art and the East India Company* (Woodbridge, Suffolk: Boydell Press, 2020). The latter especially has informed my own study through its use of the company as a lens and a bridge between art history and imperial history, and in other ways as noted. On the company's material impact in Britain more generally (though again from 1757), see *The East India Company at Home, 1757–1857*, eds Margot Finn and Kate Smith (London: UCL Press, 2018).

4 *Poplar, Blackwall and Isle of Dogs*, Survey of London vols 43 and 44, ed. Hermione Hobhouse (London: London County Council, 1994), 585–92, british-history.ac.uk/survey-london/vols43-4/pp585-592. Accessed 1 April 2022. Robins suggests the docks are where the company's 'commercial supremacy was felt most tangibly'. *The Corporation that Changed the World*, 19–22.

5 On the development of the company's warehouses, see Margaret Makepeace, *The East India Company's London Workers: Management of the Warehouse Labourers, 1800–1858* (Woodbridge, Suffolk: Boydell Press, 2010), 17–39. On the buildings in Poplar, see Survey of London, *Poplar, Blackwall and Isle of Dogs*.

6 Bryan Appleyard, 'Lloyd's, the Decade of Controversy: Inside the Building that Split the City', *The Times*, 16 December 1988, 13.

7 'The Things They Say', *The Times*, 16 December 1988, 13.

8 Peter Conrad cast the Lloyd's building as one of 'Thatcher's Monuments' in a special issue of the *Observer* magazine, 23 April 1989. See also Florian Cord, 'Capital/Rebel City: London 2012 and the Struggle for Hegemony – Reflections on the Spatiality of Power', in *London Post-2010 in British Literature and Culture*, eds Oliver von Knebel Doeberitz and Ralf Schneider (Leiden: Brill, 2017), 39–56. I owe these references to Stephen Rosser, 'Rebuilding the City of London in the Age of Global Markets: A Study of Architectural Discourse' (PhD thesis, Birkbeck, 2022).

9 For the ongoing 'journey of research and reflection', see lloyds.com/about-lloyds/history/the-trans-atlantic-slave-trade, including Nicholas Draper's article on 'Lloyd's, Marine Insurance and Slavery'. Accessed 12 July 2023. On insurance's role in the growth of the trade, see Robin Pearson and David Richardson, 'Insuring the Transatlantic Slave Trade', *Journal of Economic History* 79, no. 2 (2019): 417–46.

10 See Michael D. Bennett, 'Slaves, Weavers, and the 'Peopling' of English East India Company Colonies, 1660–1730', in *Slavery and Bonded Labor in Asia*,

*1250–1900*, ed. Richard B. Allen (Leiden: Brill, 2021), 229–55. Alan Parkinson and Lynsie Chew's investigation into the relationship between the Royal African Company and East India Company suggests that the latter was given contracts to carry human cargo across the Atlantic. See Alan Parkinson and Lynsie Chew, 'Mercantilism, Globalisation, Unethical Practices, Corruption: A Case Study of the Relationship Between the English East India Company and the Monarchy in the Context of Collaborations in the Slave Trade and Other Commercial Activities in the Seventeenth Century', *Global Conference on Business and Finance Proceedings* 8, no. 1 (2013): 21–30 (26–8). When parliament passed the 1833 act abolishing slavery throughout British colonies, exceptions were made for the East India Company's possessions, St Helena (which had just passed to the crown) and Ceylon (Sri Lanka). See Andrea Major, *Slavery, Abolitionism and Empire in India, 1772–1843* (Liverpool: Liverpool University Press, 2012). On the cowrie shell market, see Jan Hogendorn and Marion Johnson, *The Shell Money of the Slave Trade* (Cambridge: Cambridge University Press, 1986), esp. 46, 56. I am grateful to Eleanor Stephenson for drawing my attention to the complex economics of the cowrie shell, and for continuing conversations about the extraction and investment of wealth by the East India Company and its employees. Stephenson has also uncovered that the East India Company purchased the Royal African Company's headquarters on Leadenhall Street in 1749 (see British Library, IOR/L/L/2/161), further connecting the companies, their spheres and their trade.

11 David Harvey, *The New Imperialism* (Oxford: Oxford University Press, 2003); also 'The "New" Imperialism: Accumulation by Dispossession', *Socialist Register* 40 (2004): 63–87.

12 This 'excavation' is inspired by the irony pointed out by the archaeologist Christopher Evans that '*Britannia* as a Roman province has commanded far more of the discipline's energies than has the archaeology of "Britain", the source of so many of the modern world's (system's) colonies', an omission 'all the more glaring in the context of London – the "mother" of colonies and seat of British Empire'. See '"Power on Silt": Towards an Archaeology of the East India Company', *Antiquity* 64 (1990): 643–61 (643). The omission is underlined by excavations in Leadenhall unearthing Roman mosaic.

13 John Strype, *A Survey of the Cities of London and Westminster* (London: Printed for A. Churchill et al., 1720), i, iv, 82. On the expansion of East India House, see William Foster, *The East India House: Its History and Associations* (London: Bodley Head, 1924), 46–52, 129–31. Foster's book on East India House was released just as the buildings that replaced it were being pulled down to make way for the first Lloyd's building on the site.

14 Margaret Makepeace, 'East India Company Trade in West Africa', Untold Lives blog, blogs.bl.uk/untoldlives/2016/01/east-india-company-trade-in-west-africa.html. Accessed 30 March 2022. See also the further reading by Makepeace.

15 For James's involvement, see Howard Colvin, *A Biographical Dictionary of British Architects, 1600–1840*, (New Haven: Yale University Press, 3rd edn 1995), 536–40; on Jacobsen, 533–5.

16 For Holland, see Colvin, *Biographical Dictionary*, 501–5; on the company's surveyor Richard Jupp, 566–7.
17 *London and Its Environs Described*, 6 vols (London: R. and J. Dodsley, 1761), II, between 262 and 263.
18 Several examples in the London Metropolitan Archives can be seen in the online London Picture Archive at londonpicturearchive.org.uk.
19 See the 1800 exhibition catalogue via chronicle250.com ('India House' entries on 35–36). The artist is in one case given as J. Malton, but both watercolours seem to be the work of Thomas Malton, who included an aquatint showing the new façade as seen from the west in his *Picturesque Tour through the Cities of London and Westminster, Illustrated with the Most Interesting Views* (London, 1792–1801). Malton hoped his printed *Tour* 'will not only convey to posterity a faithful representation of the Capital of the British Empire, at the close of the 18th century; but will also give a true idea of its RESOURCES, WEALTH, and MAGNIFICENCE' (iv). Chromolithographs of Malton's watercolours were published in William Griggs, George Birdwood, and William Foster, *Relics of the Honourable East India Company* (London: Bernard Quaritch, 1909).
20 Figure 6.2 shows the chromolithograph of Malton's view because the original watercolour could not be removed from its glass frame for digitisation by the British Library.
21 'Houses of the East India Company', *The Mirror of Literature, Amusement, and Instruction*, 13 April 1833, 225–7.
22 John Noorthouck, *A New History of London Including Westminster and Southwark* (London: R. Baldwin, 1773), 663. Cited in (among others) Foster, *The East India House*, 133; G. A. Bremner, 'The Metropolis: Imperial Buildings and Landscapes in Britain', in *Architecture and Urbanism in the British Empire*, ed. G. A. Bremner (Oxford: Oxford University Press, 2020), 125–58 (131); McAleer, *Picturing India*, 202. Half of Foster's chapter on 'The Rebuilding in 1726–29' is devoted to the previous building(s), 125–9.
23 Joseph Pote, *The Foreigner's Guide* (London, 1729), 82; Thomas Salmon, *Modern History*, 31 vols (London: Printed for Tho. Wotton, J. Shuckburgh, and T. Osborne, 1724–38), XVIII, 138; Henry Chamberlain, *A New and Compleat History and Survey of the Cities of London and Westminster* (London: Printed for J. Cooke, 1770), 544.
24 'The New Indian Council Sitting', *Illustrated London News*, 23 October 1858, 373.
25 The merger endures in, for example, the catalogue entry for Malton's watercolour in Tate's 2015 *Artist and Empire* exhibition catalogue (63), which says nothing about the image but uses it to explain the company, its building and displays.
26 John McAleer, 'Exhibiting the "Strangest of all Empires": The East India Company, East India House, and Britain's Asian Empire', in *The MacKenzie Moment and Imperial History*, eds Stephanie Barczewski and Martin Farr (London: Palgrave Macmillan, 2019), 27.

27 Elizabeth Allen, 'Visions of Empire: East India House and British Imperialism, 1661–1800', (MA dissertation, Courtauld Institute of Art, 2014). See also H. V. Bowen, 'East India House: The Domestic Architecture of Trade and Empire', in *Monsoon Traders: The Maritime World of the East India Company*, eds H. V. Bowen, John McAleer, and Robert J. Blyth (London: Scala, 2011), 95–9. On the broad point, see McAleer, *Picturing India*, 180, 198–201.
28 Salmon, *Modern History*, 138. Salmon was copied by the topographer going by the name of 'Don Manoel Gonzales', whose account (purportedly written in the early 1730s) was published in Thomas Osborne's *Collection of Voyages and Travels* (London, 1745, I, 117), and echoed by Samuel Richardson's updates to Daniel Defoe's *Tour thro' the Whole Island of Great Britain* in 1738.
29 George Vertue, 'Notebooks', *Walpole Society* 22 (1933–34): 37. The whole series can be viewed at artuk.org.
30 Douglas Fordham, *British Art and the Seven Years' War: Allegiance and Autonomy* (Philadelphia: University of Pennsylvania Press, 2010), 26–30; Brian Allen, 'The East India Company's Settlement Pictures: George Lambert and Samuel Scott', in *Under the Indian Sun: British Landscape Artists*, eds Pauline Rohatji and Pheroza Godrej (Bombay: Marg, 1995), 10. See also Brian Allen, 'From Plassey to Seringapatam: India and British History Painting', in *The Raj: India and the British 1600–1947*, ed. C. J. Bayly (London: National Portrait Gallery, 1990), 26–37.
31 Fordham, *British Art and the Seven Years' War*, 30. Quilley, in *British Art and the East India Company*, followed with 'the earlier pictorial cycle for the Court Room of East India House was much more prosaic, though no less forceful in asserting the symbiosis between global trade and national interest' (32). The founder of the Foundling Hospital, Thomas Coram, was a shipwright who made his money trading between Boston and London (29).
32 Quilley, *British Art and the East India Company*, 18, 48.
33 Allen, 'The East India Company's Settlement Pictures', 10. Quilley points out the further connection that both Scott and Lambert (the painters of the EIC settlements) were on the list of artist-governors of the hospital in 1746. See Quilley, *British Art and the East India Company*, 32.
34 Quilley notes that the 'idea of the public' implied by the two schemes 'was broadly the same, and in their formal aesthetic continuity, they offered two complementary facets of the popular politics of what might be termed "patriotic imperialism"'. Quilley, *British Art and the East India Company*, 33.
35 Pote, *Foreigner's Guide*, 20, 80.
36 Daniel Defoe, *Tour thro' the Whole Island of Great Britain*, 3 vols (London, 1724–27), II (1726), 94, 97.
37 [James Wright], *Phoenix Paulina: A Poem on the New Fabrick of St Paul's Cathedral* (London: Printed by G. J. for Arthur Collins, 1709), 11–12.
38 Pote, *Foreigner's Guide*, 72, 74, 80.
39 Pote, *Foreigner's Guide*, 82, 86. Wright, *Phoenix Paulina*, 17.
40 Defoe, *Tour*, II, 145.

41 [Tom] Brown, *Amusements Serious and Comical, Calculated for the Meridian of London* (Printed for John Nutt: London, 1700), 23. Wright, *Phoenix Paulina*, 14.
42 Wright, *Phoenix Paulina*, 17.
43 Clare Williams (trans. and ed.), *Sophie in London, 1786: Being the Diary of Sophie v. la Roche* (London: Jonathan Cape, 1933), 165.
44 Williams, *Sophie in London*, 165.
45 The India Act 1784 created the regulatory Board of Control.
46 For the latter, see britishmuseum.org/collection/object/P_1868–0808–5051. Accessed 13 July 2023. See also Richard Connors and Ben Gilding, '"Hereditary Guardians of the Nation": The House of Lords and the East India Company in the Age of the American Revolution', *Parliamentary History* 39 (2020): 159–60.
47 *Ambulator: or, A Pocket Companion in a Tour Round London* (London: Printed for J. Scatcherd, 1793), 13–14.
48 Allen, 'The East India Company's Settlement Pictures', 2, 5. In the latter case Allen cites Mildred Archer, 'The East India Company and British Art', *Apollo* 82 (1965): 401–2.
49 Bremner, 'The Metropolis', 131.
50 McAleer, *Picturing India*, 202. Here McAleer echoes Archer, 'The East India Company and British Art', 401–2.
51 Foster, *The East India House*, 132.
52 Dan Bogart, 'The East Indian Monopoly and the Transition from Limited Access in England, 1600–1813', in *Organizations, Civil Society, and the Roots of Development*, eds Naomi R. Lamoreaux and John J. Wallis (Chicago: University of Chicago and National Bureau of Economic Research, 2017), 36–7. On Houghton, see Elizabeth Angelicoussis, 'Walpole's Roman Legion: Antique Sculpture at Houghton Hall', *Apollo* 169, no. 562 (2009): 24–31. There was a close association between architects as well as patrons: for the work at Houghton Burlington recommended Colen Campbell, who was surveyor at Greenwich during the years that James was both clerk of works there and surveyor at East India House.
53 On Queensberry House, see *St James Westminster, Part 2*, Survey of London vols 31 and 32, ed. F. H. W. Sheppard (London: London County Council, 1963), 455–66, british-history.ac.uk/survey-london/vols31-2/pt2/pp455-466. Accessed 1 April 2022. See also Daniel M. Abramson, *Building the Bank of England: Money, Architecture, Society, 1694–1942* (New Haven: Yale University Press, 2006), 27.
54 Pote, *Foreigner's Guide*, 10. Malton later included a view of the extended Queensberry House (and East India House) in his *Picturesque Tour*.
55 Allen, 'The East India Company's Settlement Pictures', 16; McAleer, *Picturing India*, 202.
56 William Maitland, *The History of London from its Foundation by the Romans to the Present Time* (London: Printed by Samuel Richardson, 1739), 999.
57 A point Quilley also makes in *British Art and the East India Company*, 25.

58 Abramson, *Building the Bank of England*, 28.
59 Quotation from Quilley, *British Art and the East India Company*, 25.
60 Foster, *The East India House*, 132.
61 Perhaps missing this detail, vague as it is, Quilley suggested the façade was 'anonymised'. See Quilley, *British Art and the East India Company*, 27.
62 This hint was noted by George Birdwood, who had clearly studied the originals (and much other company material) up close. See Griggs, Birdwood, and Foster, *Relics*, vi.
63 Boson worked with John How at East India House. See *Dictionary of British and Irish Furniture Makers, 1500–1914*, eds Geoffrey Beard and Christopher Gilbert (Leeds: W. S. Maney, 1986), at bifmo.history.ac.uk/entry/boson-john-1720–43. Accessed 20 March 2022. See also James Ayres, *Art, Artisans and Apprentices: Apprentice Painters and Sculptors in the Early Modern British Tradition* (Oxford: Oxbow Books, 2014), 348.
64 Vertue, 'Notebooks', 116. After George Lambert, Boson was the second of the founding members of the 'Sublime Society of Beef Steaks', a patriotic artistic dining club that came together under the auspices of John Rich, manager of the Theatre Royal, Covent Garden, in 1735.
65 [James Ralph], *A Critical Review of the Publick Buildings, Statues and Ornaments In, and about London* (London: Printed by C. Ackers for J. Wilford and J. Clarke, 1734), 7.
66 Ralph, *Critical Review*, 7. According to Matthew Craske, the *Critical Review* was 'one of the most quoted, plagiarized and reprinted architectural texts of the mid-eighteenth century', and it thereby made a major contribution to architectural taste. See Matthew Craske, 'From Burlington Gate to Billingsgate: James Ralph's Attempt to Impose Burlingtonian Classicism as a Canon of Public Taste', in *Articulating British Classicism: New Approaches to Eighteenth Century Architecture*, eds Barbara Arciszewska and Elizabeth McKellar (London: Routledge, 2004), 98–9.
67 Ralph, *Critical Review*, 7.
68 *Grub Street Journal*, 18 July 1734.
69 *Grub Street Journal*, 11 July 1734.
70 Nicholas Brawer, 'The Anonymous Architect of the India House', *Georgian Group Journal* 7 (1997): 30.
71 Soane cited in Brawer, 'The Anonymous Architect', 30.
72 Brawer, 'The Anonymous Architect', 30–2.
73 Expansion soon happened, between the 1729 and 1799 remodellings. See Foster, *The East India House*, 136. In July 2023, the central Underwriting Room of the Lloyd's Building was temporarily closed for major refurbishment, though seemingly (judging by earlier reporting in the architectural press) not on the scale originally planned.
74 The company's request in November 1729 for the preparation of dies with the letters E. I. C. – 'to distinguish a large coinage of gold which they intend, "as hath been granted to the Royal African, the South Sea Company, and others"' – followed by the Treasury's approval and the issue of a royal warrant

to the master of the mint, is recorded in the *Calendar of Treasury Books and Papers, 1729–30* (London: HMSO, 1897), 153, 154–5, 159.

75  Helen Hills, 'Colonial Materiality: Silver's Alchemy of Trauma and Salvation', Medium Study, *MAVCOR Journal 5*, no. 1 (2021), doi: 10.22332/mav.ess.2021.6. The rebuilding and refurbishment of East India House, and the minting of the coin, came at a time of intense public and parliamentary scrutiny of the company's affairs and practices in the lead-up to its charter renewal in 1730, as discussed later in this chapter. The connection has also been made by Graham Birch, who has persuasively proposed that the coins could have been used as gifts, or rather bribes, in connection with the charter renewal. See Graham Birch, *The Metal in Britain's Coins: Where Did It Come From and How Did It Get Here?* (London: Spink Books, 2020), 65–7.

76  On the import of the gold through Canton, noted in the contemporary press, see Birch, *The Metal in Britain's Coins*, 64. As Birch notes (65), a major criticism of the company was its very large exports of silver. See K. N. Chaudhuri, 'Treasure and Trade Balances: The East India Company's Export Trade, 1660–1720', *Economic History Review* 21, no. 3 (1968): 480–502 (esp. 480, 493–5, 497–8). See also K. N. Chaudhuri, *The Trading World of Asia and the English East India Company: 1660–1760* (Cambridge: Cambridge University Press, 1978), 153–89. The master of the mint who oversaw production of the company's coins wrote, the same year, a tract concerning the relative values of gold and silver: John Conduitt, *Observations upon the Present State of Our Gold and Silver Coins, 1730* (London: Printed for T. Becket, 1774). On the use of silver in trade specifically at Canton, see H. B. Morse, 'The Provision of Funds for the East India Company's Trade at Canton during the Eighteenth Century', *Journal of the Royal Asiatic Society of Great Britain and Ireland* 2 (1922): 227–55 (esp. 228). For more recent work on the Canton trade, see Paul A. Van Dyke, *The Canton Trade: Life and Enterprise on the China Coast, 1700–1845* (Hong Kong: Hong Kong University Press, 2005). On the trust secured and growth under way by the mid-1730s, see especially 17–18.

77  The *Ipswich Journal*'s report of the Queen's purchase, and the possibility she didn't actually pay, is pointed out by Birch in *The Metal in Britain's Coins*, 67. The coins remain 'covetable', to quote one recent auction catalogue – 'one of the most sought-after issues, not just in British coinage, but in all European coinage as well', its appeal still tethered to Britain's emergence as a 'clear first-rate military and economic force' and the company's mark on its 'lustrous' surface: see coins.ha.com/itm/great-britain/great-britain-george-ii-gold-east-india-company-5-guineas-1729-ms63-ngc-/a/3085-30175.s?type=DA-DMC-NumistaWorldCoins-WorldCoins-3085-08052020. Accessed 13 July 2023. This particular example sold in August 2020 for USD $190,000.

78  Birch has suggested that the five-guinea coins, accompanied by small numbers of guinea and half-guinea coins, may have been minted to celebrate the completion of the new building: *The Metal in Britain's Coins*, 64–5.

79  James Mayo, 'Aesthetic Capital: The Commodification of Architectural Production', *Modulus* 22 (1991): 64–77.

80 Pote, *The Foreigner's Guide*, 80. Directors' minute cited in Foster, *The East India House*, 52.
81 Foster, *The East India House*, 49.
82 Jonathan P. Eacott, 'Making an Imperial Compromise: The Calico Acts, the Atlantic Colonies, and the Structure of the British Empire', *William and Mary Quarterly* 69, no. 4 (2012): 731–62. On fire-fighting measures, see Foster, *The East India House*, 62–7. On measures after the attacks, 71–2.
83 Cited in Foster, *The East India House*, 130.
84 'A Continuation of the Critical Review of the Publick Buildings, &c. Examined by Mr Hiram', *Grub Street Journal*, 18 July 1734.
85 Boson later worked on the decoration of the barge for the prince of Wales: see bifmo.history.ac.uk/entry/boson-john-1720-43. Accessed 20 March 2022. On Blackwall yard, see Survey of London, *Poplar, Blackwall and Isle of Dogs*, 553–65.
86 [James Ralph], *A Critical Review of the Public Buildings, Statues, and Ornaments, in and about London and Westminster* (London: J. Wallis, rev. edn 1783), 36–7.
87 On the Dances' work at South Sea House (worth over £700), see Colvin, *Biographical Dictionary*, 287. Quilley also makes the point that the line connects the Mansion House as a symbol of the City to the East India Company a short walk away. Quilley, *British Art and the East India Company*, 24–5.
88 Jean Sutton, *Lords of the East: The East India Company and Its Ships (1600–1874)* (London: Conway, 2000), 39. On Palladianism in ship decoration, see Andy Peters, *Ship Decoration, 1630–1780* (Barnsley, South Yorkshire: Seaforth, 2013); Peters notes (306, ebook) the navy's moves to curb elaborate decoration, and the negligible difference in decoration between navy and company ships given they were built alongside each other (and sometimes redirected to the other service).
89 In 1727, in fact, the East India Company's directors found that 'so many ships' were being built intended for the company's service that they considered how they could discourage the building of such ships: Survey of London, *Poplar, Blackwall and Isle of Dogs*, 553–65.
90 Sutton, *Lords of the East*, 37. Sutton notes how company and naval ships were built 'to the same high quality specifications and very nearly the same scantling' (45).
91 See, for example, *London*, ed. Charles Knight, 6 vols (London: Charles Knight and Co, 1841), V, 61; and 'Houses of the East India Company', 226. Also Foster, *The East India House*, 138, 140.
92 Knight, *London*, V, 61.
93 The extensive scholarship on the authorship of Wilton is summarised by John Martin Robinson in *Wilton House: The Art, Architecture and Interiors of One of Britain's Great Stately Homes* (London: Rizzoli, 2021), 66–7, 88–93.
94 Colen Campbell, *Vitruvius Britannicus*, 3 vols (London, 1715–25), III (1725), plates 93, 31, 34; II (1717), plates 61–4. T. P. Connor, 'The Making of

'Vitruvius Britannicus'", *Architectural History* 20 (1977): 14, 25. The influence of Campbell and his publication on the works at East India House was perhaps especially strong given his role as surveyor at Greenwich during James's time as both clerk there and surveyor for the company.
95 *European Magazine*, March 1803.
96 Defoe, *Tour* (1742), II, 105.
97 Adam Bowett, 'The English Mahogany Trade, 1700–1793' (PhD thesis, Brunel University, 1996); and 'Thomas Ripley and the Use of Early Mahogany', *Georgian Group Journal* 7 (1997): 140–5. As Bowett discusses, mahogany was also used as joinery wood during a similar period at the Admiralty Office, St George's Bloomsbury, Seaton Delaval and Cannons. Hannah Cusworth is undertaking doctoral research (2021–25) on the hidden history of mahogany at Marble Hill, Chiswick, and Kenwood, in collaboration with English Heritage and the University of Hull.
98 Naval Stores Act 1721. Bowett, 'The English Mahogany Trade'. Mahogany prices began to rise at the end of the 1720s, and the wood was an expensive extravagance by the 1760s. Jamaican mahogany, the most accessible, was reportedly 'almost all cut down' by 1748. See Jennifer L. Anderson, *Mahogany: The Costs of Luxury in Early America* (Cambridge, MA: Harvard University Press, 2012), 1.
99 On Marble Hill and slavery, see Laurence Brown's report for English Heritage, 'The Slavery Connections of Marble Hill House', June 2010.
100 *European Magazine*, March 1803, 168.
101 Oliver Impey, 'Eastern Trade and the Furnishing of the British Country House', *Studies in the History of Art* 25 (1989): 177–9.
102 On the Girdlers' carpet (still in the company's collections), see Griggs, Birdwood, and Foster, *Relics*, 73–4. The Fremlin carpet is now in the V&A. Daniel Walker, *Flowers Under Foot: Indian Carpets of the Mughal Era*, exhibition catalogue (New York: Metropolitan Museum of Art, 1997), 17–19, 48–57, 66–7.
103 John Wood, in his 'Essay Towards a Description of Bath' (1749), observed that 'as the new building advanced, carpets were introduced to cover the floors'; and Isaac Ware, in *A Description of Bath* (1756), wrote: 'the use of carpeting at this time has set aside the ornamenting of floors […] It is the custom […] to cover a room entirely; so that there is no necessity of any beauty or workmanship underneath'. Carpet manufacture and trade in Britain seem poorly documented. John Fowler and John Cornforth noted on the treatment of floors in *English Decoration in the 18th Century* (London: Barrie and Jenkins, 1974) that 'information about 18th-century carpets is very scanty' (213). See also Sophie Sarin, 'The Floorcloth and Other Floor Coverings in the London Domestic Interior, 1700–1800', *Journal of Design History* 18, no. 2 (2005): 136–8.
104 British Library, IOR G/12/30, 10 December 1730.
105 On the screen and other lacquerware made for the Childs at Osterley, see Yuthika Sharma and Pauline Davies, '"A jaghire without a crime": East India Company and the Indian Ocean Material World at Osterley 1700–1800', in Finn and Smith, *The East India Company at Home*, 88–107 (esp. 98–100).

The screens made for Child and Howard are eight-fold, that for Eccleston twelve-fold. Two six-fold screens were made for the owner of Cannons, the Duke of Chandos. Those made for the company were described as 'large', so probably twelve-fold.

106 W. de Kesel and Greet Dhont, *Coromandel Lacquer Screens* (Ghent: Snoeck-Ducaju and Zoon, 2002).
107 John Hardy, *India Office Furniture* (London: British Library, 1982), 18, 46–7. Griggs, Birdwood, and Foster, *Relics*, 57–8.
108 On 'company time' and its instability across space, see Mark R. F. Williams, 'Experiencing Time in the Early English East India Company', *Historical Journal* (2022): 1–22.
109 *European Magazine*, March 1803, 167.
110 Archer, 'The East India Company and British Art', 401. Quilley points out the 'air of post-imperial nostalgia' in the work of Archer and Foster before her – 'certainly not a critique of imperial power' (16).
111 Archer, 'The East India Company and British Art', 401, echoing J. R. Seeley in *The Expansion of England* (London: Macmillan & Co., 1883).
112 McAleer, *Picturing India*, 56.
113 See Stern, *The Company-State*, 182–4, and Philip Lawson, 'The Company's Expanding Universe: 1709–48', in *The East India Company: A History* (Abingdon: Routledge, 2013). A 'huge coup' for the company was the winning of an imperial firman from the Mughal emperor in 1717, granting it the right to trade in Bengal without payment of customs.
114 The description in the *European Magazine* in 1803 suggests a different arrangement of the paintings; the pencil note seems very deliberate, and the watercolour rendering above echoes the rough forms of the oil painting, likewise with the view of the Cape.
115 John E. Crowley, *Imperial Landscapes: Britain's Global Visual Culture* (New Haven: Yale University Press, 2011), 169; Quilley, *British Art and the East India Company*, 33. The figures are identified thus in, for example, 'Houses of the East India Company', 226.
116 Allen, 'The East India Company's Settlement Pictures', 11; Quilley, *British Art and the East India Company*, 32 (recall also Fordham's 'sea pictures'); McAleer, *Picturing India*, 53.
117 McAleer, *Picturing India*, 66.
118 Stern uses the later motto as a chapter heading, though mentions it only briefly at the end: *The Company-State*, 163.
119 Stern, *The Company-State*, 184.
120 Stern, *The Company-State*, 208.
121 Stern, *The Company-State*, 208. That the paintings support his argument is suggested by the use of the view of Bombay on the cover of his book, though neither it nor the series is discussed inside.
122 Michel Foucault (trans. Jay Miskowiec), 'Of Other Spaces', *Diacritics* 16, no. 1 (1986): 22–7. G. A. Bremner, 'Black Gold: Opium and the Architecture of Imperial Trade in Nineteenth-Century Asia', *Proceedings of the Society*

      of *Architectural Historians, Australia and New Zealand* 33 (2016): 66–74.
123 On the long influence of John Selden's *Mare Clausum* (1635), see Mark Somos, 'Selden's *Mare Clausum*: The Secularisation of International Law and the Rise of Soft Imperialism', *Journal of the History of International Law* 14, no. 2 (2012): 287–330 (esp. 288, on how it marked 'the birth of the legal foundations of modern imperialism').
124 Stern discusses it more conceptually in *The Company-State*, 13–14.
125 Suggested by Quilley, although he steps away from the idea. Quilley, *British Art and the East India Company*, 32–3.
126 McAleer, *Picturing India*, 191.
127 Stern, *The Company-State*, 22.
128 See Michael D. Bennett, 'Caribbean Plantation Economies as Colonial Models: The Case of the English East India Company and St Helena in the Late Seventeenth Century', *Atlantic Studies* (2022): 1–32.
129 *Landscape and Power*, ed. W. J. T. Mitchell (Chicago: University of Chicago Press, 2nd, edn 2002), 10.
130 Seven of the ten paintings, from the studio of Johannes Vingboons, survive in the collections of the Rijksmuseum.
131 Crowley, *Imperial Landscapes*, 19.
132 Defoe cited in Tillman W. Nechtman, *Nabobs: Empire and Identity in Eighteenth-Century Britain* (Cambridge: Cambridge University Press, 2010), 78.
133 Defoe cited in Nechtman, *Nabobs*, 78.
134 Emily Mann, '*Thirty different Drafts of Guinea*: A Printed Prospectus of Trade and Territory in West Africa', in *Court Country, City: British Art and Architecture, 1660–1735*, eds Mark Hallett, Nigel Llewellyn, and Martin Myrone (New Haven and London: Yale Center for British Art and Paul Mellon Centre for Studies in British Art, 2016), 411–32. The prints of the East India Company series were made by Elisha Kirkall (c. 1735) and Gerard Vandergucht (c. 1736).
135 Jonathan Eacott, *Selling Empire: India in the Making of Britain and America, 1600–1830* (Chapel Hill: University of North Carolina Press, 2016), 84.
136 *Nation and Narration*, ed. Homi K. Bhabha (London: Routledge, 1990), 3.
137 *Morning Post*, 5 April 1861.
138 On the transfer and retention of company ornaments as part of the new India Office, see G. A. Bremner, 'Nation and Empire in the Government Architecture of Mid-Victorian London: The Foreign and India Office Reconsidered', *Historical Journal* 48, no. 3 (2005), 734. In a report released in April 2024, a group of former senior diplomats and officials proposed significant reform to the Foreign Office, including ('perhaps') its 'colonial era' furnishings: 'The World in 2040: Renewing the UK's Approach to International Affairs', Hertford College, University of Oxford, and UCL Policy Lab, April 2024, p. 9.

Plate 1 'A Plott of the Cittie of London Derry' (c.1610), courtesy Archives Research Library, Trinity College Dublin.

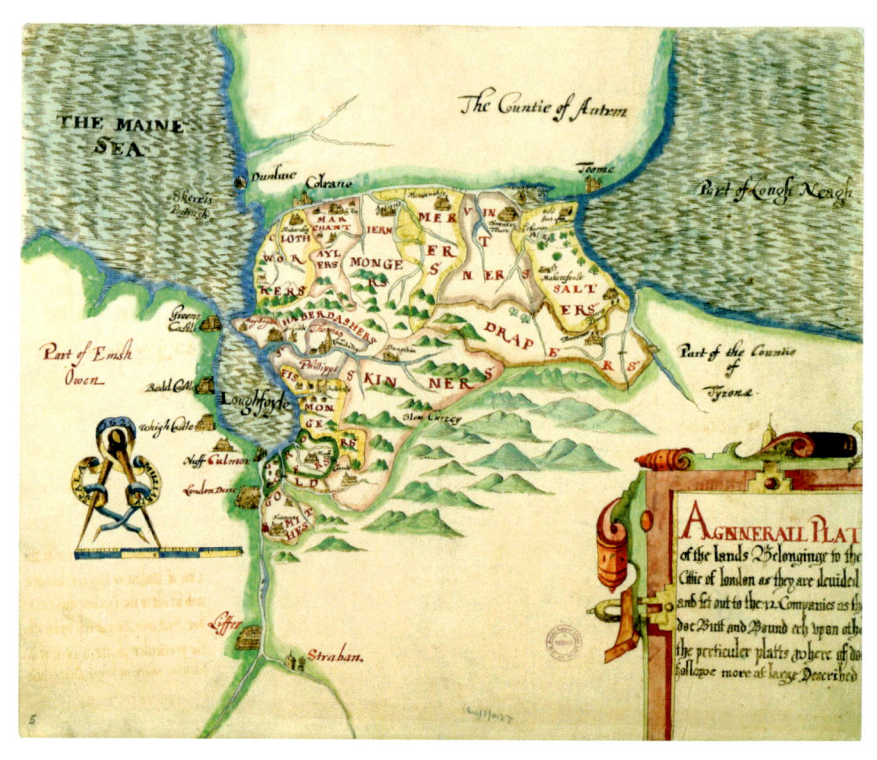

**Plate 2** 'A generall plat of the lands belonging to the Cittie of London …' from Thomas Stafford's *Pacata Hibernia, Ireland Appeased and Reduced; or, An Historie of the Late Warres of Ireland* (1633), courtesy of the Public Record Office of Northern Ireland (PRONI).

Plate 3  Interior, Officer's Mess, Fort George. Author's photograph.

**Plate 4** Located on the former workhouse site, the proposed Cathedral was an extravagant prestige project amidst the depression of the 1930s planned to symbolise the Catholic contribution to Liverpool, the very centre of a futuristic townscape with 'slumdom' eradicated. Courtesy of Liverpool Central Library and Archives.

**Plate 5** Trim gaol, Co. Meath, by John Hargrave, built 1828–34. After many years of inactivity, the state's prison inspectors convinced the County Meath grand jurors to commit to a new county gaol; the result was a powerful essay in the abstract propaganda of prison design (photograph by author, 2014).

**Plate 6** Sir Edward Lovett Pearce, façade of Parliament House (now Bank of Ireland), Dublin, 1729–39. Jacqueline O'Brien Collection, Irish Architectural Archive.

**Plate 7** Agostino Carlini, 'Friendly Union of Great Britain and Ireland with Neptune driving away Famine and Despair', pediment sculpture (detail), Custom House, Dublin, 1781–91. © OPW. Photograph by Con Brogan.

**Plate 8** George Lambert and Samuel Scott, Bombay, c. 1731, oil on canvas, 81 × 132cm, British Library.

**Plate 9** Thomas Hosmer Shepherd, directors' court room, East India House, c. 1820, watercolour, 15.9 × 22.2 cm, British Library.

**Plate 10** Lews Castle, Stornoway, Scotland (Michael Maclean, Flickr).

**Plate 11** Fredrick Marlett Bell-Smith, *The Heart of the Empire* (1909), Museum of Vancouver Collection (PA19).

**Plate 12** 'Australian Building' (1907), drawing of a concept proposed by Alfred Burr, as drawn by Charles William English. Collection National Library of Australia (NLA).

**Plate 13** Poster for the Empire Timber Exhibition (1920), by MacDonald Gill. Courtesy Caroline Walker.

**Plate 14** Ba Nyan, 'Timber Stacking' for the Empire Marketing Board. Courtesy of Manchester Art Gallery.

**Plate 15** Indian YMCA and adjacent Robert Adam terraces in Fitzroy Square. Photograph Mark Crinson, 2020.

**Plate 16** Ralph Tubbs and Stefan Buzas, design for the interior of the Dome of Discovery. Drawing by Stefan Buzas (1949?). Courtesy RIBA Collections.

# 7

# Foreign mud, home comforts: Taipans, opium, and the remitted wealth of Jardine, Matheson & Co. in Scotland

## G. A. Bremner

There has been much discussion in recent times about the property purchases of globe-trotting billionaires. Whether in London, New York, Sydney, or elsewhere, these purchases have attracted their fair share of negative press coverage. The focus has been not only on the way such property has been used to evade tax or buy citizenship rights (so-called Golden Visas), but also on concern over the legitimacy of the sources of wealth via which they were purchased. Issues of corruption, bribery, fraud, money laundering, drug dealing, and even state-sponsored murder haunt many of these properties and their owners, leading to pressure on government to tighten the regulations around their acquisition.[1] The publicity around this phenomenon is now such that public tours specifically highlighting these properties are available in cities such as London and Prague.[2] Indeed, so entrenched have money laundering practices become in London, especially concerning kleptocratic Russian oligarchs, that the city has now acquired the insalubrious moniker 'Londongrad'.[3]

But none of this is new. Controversy has dogged the nouveau riche and their habits of conspicuous consumption, certainly in Britain, at least since the seventeenth century. Not surprisingly, much of it was associated with imperial expansion. The first legion of such *arrivistes* were associated with the proceeds of slavery. Principal among them was the Beckford family of Fonthill fame, who owned vast chattel slave plantations in Jamaica. Various reports by English Heritage and the National Trust have since highlighted the connection between wealth generated from the transatlantic slave economy and country estate acquisition in all its gory detail.[4] Moreover, who can forget the infamous Nabob, that dubious figure – fêted and derided in equal measure – who, on his (sometime her) return from British India, wasted little time ploughing largely ill-gotten gains into acquiring estates, London townhouses, and other assets worthy of the aristocracy (which they aspired to emulate).[5] Rand Lords and Robber Barons, too, had gotten in on the act by the late nineteenth and early twentieth centuries.[6] Much later, and from a different era, one might point to the 'tarnished' money donated so freely to cultural institutions in Britain, such as museums and universities, by the likes of the Sacklers and Len Blavatnik, who are seen by some as attempting to 'wash' their reputations though large-scale philanthropy.[7]

Not all such wealth is intrinsically suspect, of course. But, even by the standards of the day, quite a lot was. Nevertheless, wealth that was acquired prudently, and with propriety, was often frowned upon by the traditional elite in Britain who, in their interminably snobbish fashion, considered 'new money' as somehow beneath their dignity, even though many would come to rely on it as the nineteenth century wore on. Again, a certain quantum of this wealth was generated from both formal and informal British imperial enterprise, and was openly recognised as such at the time. One group that has received comparatively scant attention in this regard are the so-called Taipans.[8] This group consisted mainly of British, including many Scottish, merchants who acquired spectacular fortunes through their business dealings in East Asia, primarily through what was known as the 'China Trade'. Part of the reason this line of business had a somewhat sullied reputation was its involvement in the notorious trade in opium, or 'foreign mud' as it was referred to by the Chinese. Included among the Taipans' ranks were the personnel of firms such as Jardine, Matheson & Co., Dent & Co., and Butterfield & Swire. Somewhat like their Indian cousins, the Nabobs, Taipans attracted some negative publicity. Perhaps most famously, James Matheson (1796–1878) was parodied by Benjamin Disraeli in his novel *Sybil; or, The Two Nations* (1845) as 'one McDruggy, fresh from Canton, with a million of opium in each pocket' (Figure 7.1).[9]

Very much like the Nabobs, however, the Taipan class often spent their wealth on acquiring vast estates and building large houses back in the United Kingdom, once they had essentially 'retired' from front-line duties in Canton, Macau, Hong Kong, Shanghai, or wherever they happened to be stationed. Early on, their careers were often relatively short. Such were the riches on offer that fortunes could be amassed in a matter of years. James Matheson was able to retire home at age 46, his business partner, William Jardine (1784–1843) (Figure 7.2), at 55, while Matheson's nephew, Alexander (1805–86), returned at 41.[10] By the time Jardine arrived back in Britain in 1839, shortly afterwards taking up a parliamentary seat, Jardine, Matheson & Co. had been in existence for only seven years. He had spent a total of around twenty years in the China Trade. He was followed not long after by his business partner, Matheson, who would also enter parliament. Both naturally lobbied on behalf of the Trade and the corporate interests of their class, even convincing Lord Palmerston, it has been suggested, to prosecute the First Opium War with China.[11]

In this respect Jardine and Matheson were sojourners, somewhat like their plantation and Nabob forebears. Like them, their wealth was used in

Figure 7.1 Portrait of James Matheson, by Henry Cousins (after James Lonsdale), 1837 (courtesy National Portrait Gallery, London, NPG D38310).

various ways to transform the British landscape on their return home. Their examples demonstrate how this particular trade – the China Trade, and its subsidiary enterprises – had a direct material affect in shaping modern Britain, adding not insubstantially to its accumulated wealth, and how this wealth was connected to the wider imperial economy. The peculiar and perhaps most important characteristic of this wealth, however, was its largely 'invisible' nature. Indeed, it may be described as invisible in a double sense: first, in the traditional economic sense in that members of the Jardine and Matheson families in Britain were benefiting from large amounts of remitted monies from East Asia; and second, that these funds were not pegged to any activity that drew specific attention to its sources.[12] To be sure, and as we shall see, the properties acquired by the Jardines and Mathesons were in themselves conspicuous, but little was included by way of obvious reference to the wealth that enabled their purchase. In looking at these material assets, it was, on the whole, difficult if not impossible to tell that they were connected to formal and informal British imperial designs half a world away, including the pernicious opium trade, unless the observer was in the know. Instead, the Jardines and Mathesons were far more focused on playing up their Scottish identity and ancestry. This is an important factor to bear in mind when thinking through how the idea of 'inner empire' was made manifest in the British Isles – the 'sin', so to speak, was not always inscribed on the perpetrator's face.

Figure 7.2 Portrait of William Jardine, by Thomas Goff Lupton (after George Chinnery), c. 1830s (courtesy National Portrait Gallery, London, NPG D36485).

## The Jardine, Matheson & Co. operation and 'free trade' imperialism

The advent of Jardine, Matheson & Co highlights in a broader sense the disproportionately high number of Scottish agency houses operating in the region following the abolition of the East India Company's (EIC) trade monopoly in the early 1830s, including the networks of Scottish patronage that sustained them.[13] Symptomatic of this phenomenon, Jardines would go on to establish substantial trading interests in tea and opium, among other commodities, quickly positioning itself at the centre of Britain's trading empire in Asia.[14] Indeed, the firm's *in situ* operations had a significant spatial impact, leading the way in both forming and re-forming the diffuse, circulatory, and transactional 'shape' of the modern British empire, and especially what has been termed the 'imperialism of free trade'.[15] This included port, warehouse, office, and manufacturing facilities in Britain,

India, China, Japan, and Australasia. The firm's centre of operations after 1844 was East Point, Hong Kong, with its vast array of such facilities sprawling around Causeway Bay (Figure 7.3).[16]

Given the amount of revenues generated via this trade, and the duties skimmed off it by the Exchequer, it naturally had profound political ramifications. Thus, the infrastructural circuits that tightly bound the Jardines business empire, along with the China Trade as a whole, had become increasingly indispensable to the maintenance and continued expansion of British commercial interests in the region by the 1830s. These interests amounted to an 'extrastatecraft' scenario in which the coalescence and exercise of these networks and their attendant infrastructures had become engines of power in their own right, exerting a gravitational political force that was irresistible.[17] These, it may be suggested, were the effects and consequences of free trade imperialism in action, whereby in order to protect key commercial assets (such as the opium monopoly and tea import duties), strategic intervention was required.[18] Thus, although not setting out to exercise 'imperial' dominion as such, in the immediate post-EIC trading environment, the China Trade had indeed become an 'empire' of sorts, with ever-growing political consequences. In a phrase, it had become 'too big to fail'.[19]

Figure 7.3 Jardine, Matheson & Co., headquarters, East Point, Hong Kong. Photograph by John Thomson, 1868/1871 (Wellcome Collection, London).

Therefore, before either Jardine or Matheson returned to Britain to live out the remainder of their lives, with fortunes in hand, they had already established a substantial architectural legacy along the South China coast and elsewhere. Both they and their successors resided at the foundations of a system that forced the mantra of 'free trade' economics when and where it suited, and one that, because of its centrality to British imperial revenue streams, could call upon 'state aid' in the form of military assistance to enforce its claims when needed. To be sure, the commercial structure of the China Trade followed its own internal logic, but became politically entwined when it drew within its orbit the informal imperial commitments of the British state, especially when it had achieved a certain scale. Despite the moral carping of Gladstone, and the fictional parody of China Trade Taipans by Disraeli, the strategic interests at stake were simply too significant, and British foreign policymakers knew it.[20]

## Returning home and the investment of foreign commercial earnings

Although there were many people involved in the frontline operations of Jardine, Matheson & Co. that one could point to in a study such as this, I will consider here only a handful of the earliest key protagonists. On the Matheson side we have James Matheson, co-founder of the company, and his nephew Alexander, who became managing partner following James's return to Scotland in 1842. These two men ploughed a considerable amount of their East Asian fortunes into acquiring property in their homeland of Scotland, as a result becoming two of the largest landowners in the United Kingdom. On the Jardine side, we have James's counterpart in William Jardine, and his nephew Robert, who eventually became head of the firm. Like the Mathesons, the two Jardines would also busy themselves acquiring Scottish estates on their return. Along with the Jardines we must also count the Keswicks, who came into the Jardine family (and therefore the business) via a succession of marriages through William's sister, Jean (to David Johnstone). The Scottish assets of the Keswick family would bear scrutiny in the same way as Matheson and Jardine, but, owing to the limitations of this format, I will not consider them here.

It should also be noted that both the Jardines and Mathesons had London residences, and were members of numerous gentlemen's clubs, primarily to exercise their political and financial interests and influence. All four were parliamentarians at various stages of their careers, so a London base was essential. There was also the London end of the operation, Matheson & Co., to consider. Founded in 1848 by James Matheson, this firm was established to handle financing and imports for both Jardine,

Matheson & Co. and Jardine, Skinner & Co. (Calcutta). It was headed by Hugh Matheson, another of James's nephews, who, by all reports, had refused to go to Hong Kong owing to his objection to the opium trade, preferring to play a role at arm's length in Britain instead.[21] James's London residence was on Cleveland Row, St James's, Westminster, while Jardine's was in Upper Belgrave Street, Belgravia – both very fashionable parts of the city.[22] In addition to these properties, Matheson owned great tracts of land in Australia where he had stationed kinsmen and other associates to manage it. These lands were used mainly for grazing sheep, again highlighting the global reach and imperial nature of these businessmen's affairs.

It is both interesting and important to observe in passing the familial connections that run through the firm from earliest times. As a clansman with a keen sense of loyalty, Matheson was inclined to support his kin (and associates thereof) when and where he could. Jardine did the same, although he was of lowland lineage. Keeping the business in-house, as it were, among relatives, was also a useful means of engendering trust, and was rather typical of the Scottish merchant diaspora at the time.[23] For instance, in a letter of 1841 concerning his purchase of land in New South Wales, Matheson talks of not only wanting to offer opportunities to emigrate for 'hard-working' tenants on his (and relatives') highland estates, 'whose clannish feelings will lead them ... to look to me for assistance in getting on in the world', but also to place relatives in key management positions.[24] Indeed, many of the agency house firms that established themselves in Canton, Macau, and later Hong Kong in the wake of the slow demise of the East India Company and its trading monopolies – indeed, a disproportionate amount – were headed by Scotsmen who operated in accordance with such inclinations.[25]

## The Mathesons

In this section I will trace specifically the investment activities of both the Mathesons and Jardines with respect to Scottish estate purchases, agricultural land 'improvement', and investment in great house building. The monetary figures shown here are given in pounds sterling (unless otherwise stated) at time of purchase, or works carried out, with approximate equivalent at 2020 prices (adjusted for inflation) provided in brackets.[26]

### *James Matheson of the Lews*

The first thing to note about James Matheson is that he was essentially a self-made man. According to the various accounts of his life, and those of his wider family, James rose from a comparatively 'obscure' position, owing his entire fortune to 'personal earnings and business industry'.[27] He was educated at the Royal Academy, Inverness, before transferring to the Royal High School, and later university, at Edinburgh. Although he studied arts and then medicine at Edinburgh, he did not take a degree, beginning a life of commerce instead, first at an agency house in London, before sailing east to join Mackintosh & Co. of Calcutta.[28] Here he would join the myriad other Scots and their firms operating in the country and China trades out of Calcutta, Canton, and Macau. After a number of failed and semi-successful ventures, James became a partner in the firm of Yrisarri & Co. at Macau. It was following the demise of Xavier Yrisarri in 1826 that Jardine brought Matheson into the firm of Magniac & Co., which they reconstituted as Jardine, Matheson & Co. in 1832. From this moment on, the meteoric rise of this firm to China Trade dominance is well known. Indeed, it still exists today as the Jardine Matheson Group, a global corporate behemoth maintaining a business portfolio with interests ranging from shipping, property, and financial services to retail and hotel management.

What we may reasonably glean from this is that the money ploughed by James Matheson back into his home country of Scotland came almost exclusively from his China Trade business and related enterprises. The wealth generated was considerable. His first large land purchase occurred in 1844, two years after his arrival back in Britain. This was for the entire island of Lewis, in north-west Scotland, comprising some 680 square miles, for £190,000 (£24.7m). In addition to this, he bought all the arrears owing on the estate for a further £1,417 (£184.2k), thus freeing his new tenants from debt.[29] Upon acquiring this land, he set about on a massive improvement campaign. This included, among other activities, the building of new farmhouses and offices across the estate, a number of drainage and reclamation schemes, a brickworks, a paraffin oil factory, a patent slip and quay, several shooting lodges and fish-curing houses, not to mention Lews Castle itself (Plate 10). In addition to this he erected many new schools for the island's population, and funded over 200 miles of properly surfaced road and bridge construction, prior to which had existed only forty-five miles of rough tracks and imperfectly formed roads.

In all, over a period of some thirty years, James Matheson spent in the order of £563,000 (£68.5m) on purchasing and improving the island, including taking leases on steamers to establish a regular transportation connection between Stornoway and the mainland. These improvements took the annual agricultural rental of the island from £9,800 (£1.3m) in 1844 to £13,300 (£1.63m) by 1880, with total annual income of nearly £20,000 (£2.4m).[30] Although he made some money from these rentals which were ploughed back into the estate, what is clear is that the entire venture was loss-making for Matheson. Indeed, by the standards of any previous era of Highland history, these improvements were considered 'fabulous'.[31] This did not seem to matter to him, however (as discussed below), and it is an undertaking that could only have been accomplished with substantial outside financial resources.

By most accounts James Matheson was a kind, generous, and scrupulously honest man. He gave great sums to charitable causes, both in Britain and China. Indeed, upon leaving the Asian scene for good, he was asked by his Parsi friend and long-time business associate, Jamsetjee Jejeebhoy (1783–1859), to drop by while passing through Bombay on his way back to Britain to attend a reception in his honour. On this occasion, 'surrounded by a numerous and brilliant gathering, composed of men of different lands, races, and religions', Matheson was presented with a service of plate valued at an astonishing £1,500 (£173k).[32] This was a mark of genuine respect for Matheson among his business associates, demonstrating the high regard with which they held both him and his services, especially the Parsi business community of Bombay.[33]

This tallies to some extent with Matheson's efforts to help tenants and crofters on his own lands in Scotland. There was of course an immediate benefit to his own estate in having fewer such tenants, and more productive and profitable ones at that, and in his lifetime Matheson's tenants never had security over their leases. In this regard, his 'clearance' of some of these tenants must be seen in the context of the broader Highland Clearances that took place in Scotland between about 1750 and 1860. However, unlike so many lairds in Scotland, Matheson, it seems, at least tried to treat his tenants with dignity. For instance, when it became clear to him that the island's growing population could not be sustained though self-sufficiency, he assisted over 2,000 people from the island to emigrate to Canada, paying for their passage, onward journeys, and considerable amounts of clothing and furniture. But his firm ideas on 'improvement', both economic and social, occasionally clashed with those of his largely uneducated tenants, who were more concerned with exercising what they saw as their ancient rights. Moreover, his efforts to educate them often met with stubborn resistance. This led to growing tensions between Matheson, his factor, and the island's crofters, coming to a head with the so-called Bernera Riot, where the management tactics of Matheson's factor Donald Munro (a loyal but imperious man) incited the crofters of Bernera to civil disobedience, ending in Munro's dismissal and lasting damage to Matheson's reputation as a fair and decent laird.

### Alexander Matheson of Lochalsh, Attadale, and Ardross

James Matheson's nephew, Alexander (1805–86), started life somewhat like his uncle. In 1825 his family was forced to forgo the last remnants of its heritable estates, at Attadale, leaving Alexander to find his own way in the world. After a time at the University of Edinburgh, and in the ways of Scottish clan association, James offered the young Alexander a position in the firm of Jardine, Matheson & Co., of which he became senior partner in 1842. Matheson was a particularly hard-headed businessman, who lobbied incessantly for the interests of his firm and that of the wider opium trade, both through his business associates in Britain, and when in London himself.[34] In 1839, for instance, he was sent back to London by James to promote the cause of compensation for opium traders after the seizure of over 20,000 chests of the drug by the then Imperial commissioner at Canton, Lin Zexu.[35] What became the First Opium War (1839–42) between Britain and China was in many respects orchestrated by William Jardine on advice provided to Lord Palmerston, then prime minister of the United Kingdom, which, through the subsequent 'unequal' Treaty of Nanking (1842), forced the Chinese Imperial authorities to pay compensation for the seized opium to the value of six million silver dollars.[36] The amount eventually paid to British firms, including Jardine, Matheson & Co., converted at £1,281,211 (£148m).[37]

Nor did Alexander share the moral outrage over the opium trade that had developed back in Britain. He is reported to have said of the whole affair: 'The cry against the drug trade in England is certainly very absurd, & I sincerely hope the saints will fail in their attempt to interfere with it.'[38] Also like his uncle, Alexander became an MP on his return to the United Kingdom, representing two different Scottish constituencies between 1847 and 1884, from which positions he was able to continue to lobby on behalf of China Trade interests.

Alexander's time in China, as well as his roles as a senior partner in Jardine, Matheson & Co. and its associated companies, accrued to him immense wealth. In an attempt to regain his ancestral lands and thus family pride, Matheson made his first large property purchase around 1839/40 on a return visit to Britain, acquiring the lands of Ardintoul and Letterfearn, to the south of Lochalsh, comprising 6,000 acres for £15,500 (£1.6m). Four years later he then obtained the lands of Inverinate, on the north side of Loch Duich, for £30,000 (£3.9m). Finally, in 1851, he was in a position to take back his ancestral possessions at Lochalsh, for which he paid £120,000 (£17.1m). Over the next ten years Alexander added the estates of Strathbran and Ledgowan, near Achnasheen, for £32,000 (£3.7m); Attadale, the other part of his ancestral lands, for £14,520 (£1.7m); and New Kelso and Strathcarron for £26,000 (£3.2m). In all, as described in the history of the Matheson family, he had acquired a 'magnificent stretch of Highland property, containing about 115,000 acres, at a total cost of £238,020 [£31.2m]'. The annual rents from these properties were £13,705 (£1.7m) by 1881.[39]

Like his uncle James, Alexander embarked on a campaign of improvements on his Wester Ross properties through the middle decades of the nineteenth century, spending a total of approx. £170,000 (£22m), including some £50,000 (£6m) on Duncraig Castle, his new family seat (Figure 7.4). If this were not enough, he was also accumulating property in the northeast of the county, in Easter Ross. Here he acquired the estate at Ardross, at over 60,000 acres, as well as those at Dalmore, Culcairn, and Delny and Balintraid, for a total outlay of £185,000 (£22.5m).[40] He made numerous improvements on these properties, too, amounting to some £230,000 (£28.5m), including the restoration of Ardross Castle. All of these purchases and improvements, since c. 1840, across the county of Ross, by Alexander Matheson alone, amounted to 220,000 acres (344 sq. miles) at an astonishing total cost of £773,020 (£94m). This does not include the properties he purchased around Inverness, which he spent a further £35,000 (£4.2m) improving.

Figure 7.4 Duncraig Castle, Scotland, from Mackenzie, *History of the Mathesons, with Genealogies of the Various Families* (1900).

By these calculations, it may be suggested that between them, James and Alexander Matheson spent in the order of approximately £180 million in today's money acquiring and improving land in Scotland following their lucrative sojourns in China as directors of Jardine, Matheson & Co. Combined, their total land holdings were in the order of 1,000 square miles, or around 3.5 per cent of Scotland's total landmass.

## The Jardines

Unlike the Mathesons, information regarding the property purchases of the Jardines – in this case, William and his nephew Robert – is harder to come by. We know of the names of some of the estates in Scotland acquired by them during and following their time in China, and even the addresses of their London townhouses, but exact acreages, or prices paid, are not complete. Here I will try to piece together some of this information.

### *William Jardine of Lanrick*

The life and times of William Jardine are reasonably well documented. Like his business partner James Matheson, he was born into relatively modest, middling circumstances on a tenant farm near Lochmaben, Dumfriesshire in 1784. Following an education in medicine at the University of Edinburgh, Jardine joined the East India Company as a ship's surgeon, before starting up as a 'free merchant' in Bombay in 1819. He had been lured by the wealth that Company employees could make via 'privileged tonnage', which allowed officers to partake in limited trade outside their normal employ. Later establishing himself in Canton, Jardine became a partner in the China agency house Magniac & Co. in 1826. It was through this association that he met Matheson, the two forming Jardine, Matheson & Co. following the dissolution of Magniac & Co. in June 1832.[41]

By all accounts, Jardine was a kind if shrewd businessman, with a particular facility for plain living, endurance, and even toughness. For this he acquired the sobriquet the 'iron-headed rat'. Like Matheson, on his departure from the Canton scene in 1839, he received an expensive piece of plate (silverware) from the Parsi merchants based there. The firm was widely known for its commercial integrity. Among the platitudes, which certainly appear genuine, was the remark that, in the estimate of the Parsi merchants, 'no man has more steadily, greatly, and successfully raised the commerce of his own country, and of the ports of India, particularly of Bombay, with China, than yourself'.[42] Indeed, the acknowledgements of the entire foreign merchant community were enthusiastic and voluble.

As mentioned, he returned home a very rich man, undoubtedly among the richest in the land. In this respect, like Matheson, Jardine was self-made, with the vast majority of his accumulated wealth coming directly from his China Trade interests.

We also know that shortly after arriving back in Britain Jardine purchased the estate of Lanrick, in Perthshire, with its 'castle' of antique heritage (Figure 7.5). According to the advertisement of sale, the estate, which was once part of the larger landholdings of the Haldanes of Gleneagles, was 1,910 acres in extent. Included in the sale were further farmlands at Wester Daldorn (377 acres), and Wester Deanstoun (130 acres).[43] Jardine reportedly paid £100,000 (£10.4) for the whole of these lands in 1840.[44] He had initially considered the estate of Castlemilk, near his birthplace in Dumfriesshire, but Lanrick proved a better buy. Castlemilk would later come into the family via his nephew Joseph Jardine (1822–61), who was also a partner in the firm. Little is known for certain about how William improved Lanrick. In any case, he would not enjoy it for long. Three years after purchasing the estate he died of bowel cancer at his Upper Belgrave Street property in London.

**Figure 7.5** Lanrick Castle, Perthshire, Scotland © Courtesy of HES (Scottish National Buildings Record).

Without heir, Lanrick passed to his nephew Andrew Jardine (1812–81), first son of his eldest brother David.[45] Little is known about Andrew, other than he was operating for the firm in China between 1832 and 1843. Following his return to Britain he became a partner of Matheson & Co. in London. What few accounts exist of Andrew's life and times tell us that he also purchased the Barony of Corrie (so-called 'lands of Corrie') in Annandale, Dumfriesshire, in 1853.[46] These lands apparently amounted to 9,838 acres, and can be added to the 2,821 acres he had acquired in Perthshire, including Lanrick.[47] As Andrew was also childless, upon his death his property reverted to his only surviving brother, Robert, who may be considered among the greatest of the Jardine Matheson Taipans.

### Robert Jardine of Castlemilk

After his education as Merchiston Castle school in Edinburgh, Robert made his way to London in 1843, entering the offices of Magniac, Smith & Co. But it was not long before he proceeded to China, taking up residence in Hong Kong for Jardine Matheson in 1849. In 1852 he was made a partner, going on to become head of both Jardine, Matheson & Co. (1865) and Matheson & Co., positions he would hold until 1882.[48] Upon his return to Britain in the 1860s, Robert entered the Commons as member for Ashburton (1865) in Devon, a seat previously held by his uncle, William. He later became member for Dumfries (1880) as a Liberal (later Unionist), a seat he held twice up to 1892.

While Robert had been busy sourcing teas for the firm's trade in Foochow (Fuzhou) in the 1850s, one of his other brothers, Joseph (1822–61), with the assistance of Andrew back in Scotland, purchased the estate of Castlemilk in Dumfriesshire.[49] Archive sources show that £87,667 (£9.6m) was remitted from Hong Kong to Scotland for this purpose.[50] However, shortly after realising this purchase, Joseph died, passing the estate to Robert. Indeed, Robert, upon his elevation to the peerage as a baronet in July 1885, was styled 'Sir Robert Jardine of Castlemilk'. The exact extent of property attached to Joseph's original purpose is not known, but, as one historian notes, it was over 8,000 acres.[51] Another has observed that Robert 'later added greatly to his territorial possessions'.[52] One example of this was his purchase of the lands of Breckonhill and Howcleuch, adjoining Castlemilk, for £13,050 (£1.68m) in 1858. This land amounted to 398 acres.[53] In addition to these properties, he acquired Lanrick in 1881 following his brother Andrew's death, as well as a London townhouse at 24 St James's Place. Today, the Castlemilk estate comprises some 25,986 acres, or nearly 41 square miles.[54] Robert's reported wealth at death was £1,114,489 (£138.5m).[55]

As with his uncles, brothers, and cousins, it would be fair to assume that the vast majority of Robert's wealth came from his China Trade dealings, including the smuggling of opium, which underpinned the trade in tea.

## The houses and memorials

Through their accumulated wealth, both the Jardines and Mathesons were able to erect, refurbish, and restore numerous properties throughout Scotland. Some of these were very large and conspicuous country houses. Among the more noteworthy are those already mentioned, including Lews Castle, on the Isle of Lewis (James Matheson); Duncraig Castle, Plockton, Ross-shire (Alexander Matheson); Lanrick Castle, Perthshire (William Jardine); and Castlemilk, Annandale, Dumfries and Galloway (Robert Jardine).

What seems clear about both the Jardines and Mathesons is that they were keen to identify as Scots, which, as discussed, extended to patronising their fellow countrymen, along with family members, into the China Trade business. Although they also owned and frequented London townhouses for political reasons, they acquired their Scottish properties at the earliest available opportunity, and spent long periods residing there. Gleaning the biographical accounts of these families, where they exist, tends to suggest that these key protagonists were determined to regain what were considered ancestral lands which had been given up due to misfortune. This appears to apply especially to the Mathesons, and in particular Alexander. For instance, it is observed in the genealogical history of the Matheson family, updated and extended in 1900, that:

> It must have been gratifying to themselves, as it certainly was to all good Highlanders, to see the estates of Lochalsh, Attadale, Ardross, and the Lewis, when they had to change hands from another set of Highland proprietors, coming into the possession of the representatives of the ancient stock who owned a large portion of the same lands many centuries ago [i.e., the Mathesons]. And the manner in which they have dealt with their new possessions, and with the inhabitants residing upon them, has, on the whole, been most creditable, and in consonance with the laudable and patriotic feelings and ambition which made them anxious to own the original heritage of their ancestors.[56]

Once reinstated as 'lairds', so to speak, these men wasted little time in displaying their wealth and authority through architecture, primarily in the form of grand stately houses, which had long been a tradition among the social elite in Britain.

What is perhaps interesting about these properties, considering their owners' strong identification with their homeland, is how they reflect a feeling for the romance and history of Scotland. Stylistically, they are designed in what became commonly referred to as the Scottish (or Scots/Scotch) Baronial, an approach among architects that became tremendously fashionable in the nineteenth century.[57] Even Lews Castle, which is more a species of Tudor Gothic, eschews the standard Palladianism of fifty years previous for a heavily castellated image that recalls rather more the seat of a medieval ruler than a modern corporate magnate. Both these medieval and 'Baronial' tendencies in Scottish great-house architecture were inspired not only by an increasing predilection for 'Gothick' forms in architecture, but also by the tide of enthusiasm that accompanied Walter Scott's 'Waverley' novels, especially those set in the Middle Ages, which romanticised Britain's chivalrous, 'medieval' past, including *Ivanhoe* (1819) and *The Abbot* (1820).

Lews Castle, designed by the Glasgow architect Charles Wilson, was erected between 1847 and c. 1855. It reportedly cost around £60,000 (£7.8m), but including outbuildings and landscaping was more in the order of £100,000 (£11m).[58] It was by far the largest, most conspicuous, and visually spectacular building on the island, unequivocally signalling the presence of a new social and economic order on Lewis, if not across Scotland as a whole. Although for many of the island's inhabitants the source of James's wealth remained a mystery, the house nevertheless embodied the economic power and reach of Scotland's (and Scots') involvement in the British imperial and wider global capitalist economy, demonstrating how the wealth generated by this activity had a very tangible impact on Scotland's ancient landscapes and way of life. In other words, in such a building we see how the sale of a pernicious narcotic nearly 6,000 miles away, and the millions in revenue this generated, including its role in the facilitation of the wider China Trade, transformed Scotland, altering it both physically and morally, however marginally.

At one level, such an event could be described as resulting from the proceeds of legitimate, 'legal' trade, and is therefore a private matter; at another, however, it can be interpreted as a form of wealth that was generated in large part (or at least most profitably) through the laundering of income garnered from the illegal smuggling of opium along the south China coast, and the role this cash (i.e., silver coinage) played in the purchase of tea and other goods which propped up the China Trade. Alongside this sits what may be perceived as the human cost in terms of the significant number of people in Imperial China, especially the southern regions, who regularly consumed opium – a number that some historians put in the tens of millions.[59] Although the sale and use of opium was hotly debated at the time – not all users were of course addicts, nor was opium illegal in Britain – a general view nevertheless emerged that the trade was at best morally suspect, and, in all good conscience, ought to be legalised (and therefore regulated) or outright banned.[60] The pressure (and propaganda) of the anti-opium lobby in Britain may have been exaggerated, but there were definitely social costs to heavy opium consumption in China, as many had reported. James Matheson was fully aware of this, even if he wished to downplay its significance.

Perhaps the most spectacular of the Matheson properties in this regard was Duncraig Castle, near Plockton, built by Alexander Matheson in 1866. Like Lews Castle, this building was a large and conspicuous pile, occupying a commanding position on the northern shoreline of the Lochalsh peninsula, overlooking Loch Carron. Built over three storeys, and containing more than eighty rooms, it was designed in a Neo-Jacobean-cum-Scots Baronial style by the noted Inverness-based architect, Alexander Ross, who, rather fortuitously, was married to the daughter of Matheson's factor on Harris.[61] Such a building, with its striking Scottish castle-like appearance, would certainly have satisfied Matheson's desire to see himself as a reconstituted laird of ancient lineage. As mentioned, it cost some £50,000, or around £6m in today's money, even though it would be safe to say that it would not be possible to erect such a building for that price now. Similarly, after buying Ardross estate from the Duke of Sutherland in 1845, Matheson proceeded in 1880 to rebuild the 'castle' substantially, essentially encapsulating the old house in a fabulous Scots Baronial carapace to designs by Ross.[62] These renovations cost something in the order of £7,000 (£860k)[63] (Figure 7.6).

What we know about Alexander Matheson is that he was an indefatigable advocate of the opium trade, and most enthusiastic about the profits it generated. For this reason, he was wary of the trade being legalised, and constantly lobbied the government in Westminster, and governors in Hong Kong, to resist calls to do so. Being a somewhat intemperate man, he was also a staunch detractor of what he wryly dismissed as the 'saintly' brigade of opium critics back in Britain.[64] It seems that, based on this evidence, he could hardly have cared less about the social ills caused by the pushing of huge quantities of opium into China by British, American, and other European merchants. Indeed, so enamoured was Matheson with this vital cash-crop, and the incredible wealth it brought him, that he had it represented on the plaster ceilings at Duncraig, in the form of poppies.[65] This is one of the very few instances where the true basis of China Trade wealth was represented in the fabric of a Jardine or Matheson property. In this respect, not only is Duncraig a prime example of what today would be described as conspicuous consumption, but also a rather dubious attempt at 'washing' Matheson's own reputation as someone who was, in part at least, nothing more than a grandiose drug dealer.

Figure 7.6 Ardross Castle, Ross and Cromarty, Scotland, © Crown Copyright: HES.

On the Jardine side we have Lanrick Castle, which, as mentioned, was purchased by William Jardine in 1840 on his return from China. The house was pre-existing, and included additions by the noted architect James Gillespie Graham. Although not built by Jardine, the 'castle' certainly had unmistakable Scottish charm, with its simple but distinct Scots Baronial-style architecture. One can readily imagine William being pleased with this purchase, recalling to mind as it did ancient Scottish ancestry. He no doubt had plans to rebuild and extend on a grander scale, but died in 1843 before anything could be done.

An example of what might have been achieved at Lanrick can be seen at Castlemilk (1864–73), where his nephew Robert (once the estate had passed to him) built a spectacular mansion in full-blown Scots Baronial style (Figure 7.7). Designed by David Bryce, who was among the premier practitioners of this style (and, indeed, one of Scotland's greatest architects of the nineteenth century), it cost £44,289 (£5.7m) to build.[66] But, as with Duncraig and Ardross, one could hardly build such an impressive structure for that money today. Alistair Rowan has observed how the estate's association with ancient feudal families such as the Bruces, Stewarts, and

Figure 7.7 Castlemilk estate house, Dumfriesshire, Scotland, © Crown Copyright: HES.

Maxwells would likely have inspired Jardine and Bryce to think along the grand and romantic lines they did.[67] This strategy would have keyed with the Jardines' desire to identify with and maintain their Scottish heritage. Indeed, being an MP and prominent local figure, Jardine built the house for display and public entertainment as much as anything else. Such a show, with its unmistakable Scottish allusions, enabled him to confirm to visitors not only the family's rootedness in (and thus commitment to) the locality, but also Robert's aspiration (now largely achieved) of placing his own name alongside those illustrious figures from the past as a worthy laird of Castlemilk. Again, knowing that the money to purchase the estate came directly from Hong Kong in the first place, it is relatively safe to assume that the cost of the new house was also met from accumulated China Trade sources, demonstrating once more how such remitted revenues left a very conspicuous trace on the Scottish landscape. In this respect, Castlemilk is indicative of what Miles Glendinning and Aonghus MacKechnie have called an architecture of imperial ebullience, embodying at once the global ambition and nationalist sentimentality of Scotland's 'second castle age'.[68]

Apart from the various properties, there were also memorials to both the Matheson and Jardine families. One such is the obelisk raised to William Jardine at St Mary's churchyard, Lochmaben, near to his birthplace. But the most impressive and interesting is the so-called Matheson Monument at Lairg burial ground in Sutherland. Erected in 1880, this was a classical, loggia-style structure in blue-grey marble, with Corinthian columns and a small central dome. It has been suggested that the columns, above entablature level, are capped with large poppy heads, as if referring to one of Matheson's principal sources of revenue.[69] As suggestive as this may be, they are actually flambeau urns (*pots à feu*), which were somewhat typical of this type of monumental architecture. More intriguing perhaps is the wreath of sculptured flowers hanging around the large white marble cross inside the loggia: are these poppies? Possibly, but it is difficult to tell for sure. If so, they would constitute another rare instance of the Jardines and Mathesons flaunting the sources of their wealth. However, given the moral indignation in Britain towards the opium trade in China, it would be odd to include so obvious a reference to this pernicious business.

## Conclusion

What the case of the China Trade firm Jardine, Matheson & Co., and its principal stakeholders, demonstrates is that substantial amounts of wealth generated via foreign business dealings were remitted back to Scotland, the home country of these stakeholders. These dealings involved the pernicious trade in opium, which, as the primary form of remittance on tea for a number of decades, contributed considerably to the balance sheets of the Jardine Matheson enterprise. It is therefore difficult, if not impossible, to disassociate opium and its attendant harms from the remitted wealth of both the Jardines and Mathesons in Scotland. Although these associations and concerns were not represented overtly to the properties discussed here, the insalubrious nature of the opium trade was an ongoing moral outrage in mid-nineteenth-century Britain. The social costs, even if exaggerated on occasion, were well known and understood. The trade must also be seen in the wider context of Britain's imperial interests in the region, along with its coercive and violent capabilities, which was furthered by the parliamentary activities of the key protagonists discussed here.

In this respect, what might be called the imperial regime of opium trafficking in China had a palpable, if indirect, impact on the modern Scottish landscape. These properties may therefore be seen in a similar light to those in England that have recently been interrogated for their links to transatlantic slavery.[70] In a similar way, these grand English country houses were the material outcome of remitted wealth, even if they rarely revealed those links in the fabric of their structures. These links and associations – looming in the background, oftentimes unspoken – may be considered the analytical 'counterpoint' in a Saidian reading of the people and spaces that comprised these buildings. As Said himself might have said, to 'hold and rule' such an estate, in Scotland, was to hold and rule a vast informal imperial enterprise in close, not to say 'inevitable', association with it.[71]

However, this is not to condemn either these protagonists or their properties from the moral standpoint of today, but rather to highlight the fact that, by bringing further evidence to bear, the connection exists, and that for a fuller and more nuanced appreciation of both the history of these properties, and that of Scotland (indeed Britain), such connections ought not be obscured or dismissed. As this chapter started out by suggesting, they are part of Britain's rather long history of providing opportunities for laundering money of dubious provenance on a massive scale, and are thus very much part of what might be called Britain's 'inner empire'.

### Acknowledgement

The author wishes to acknowledge the assistance of Geoffrey Stell in establishing which buildings to investigate for this study.

### Notes

1 See *Faulty Towers: Understanding the Impact of Overseas Corruption on the London Property Market* (London: Transparency International UK, 2017).
2 For example, see www.theguardian.com/uk-news/2016/mar/02/kleptocracy-tours-russia-ukraine-london. Accessed 15 January 2020; www.nytimes.com/2013/08/13/world/europe/on-the-crony-safari-a-tour-of-a-citys-corruption.html. Accessed 15 January 2020.
3 www.thetimes.co.uk/article/britain-has-become-addicted-to-dirty-money-h9lfl67r6. Accessed 3 February 2022.
4 For a classic short study of this phenomenon, see James Walvin, 'The Colonial Origins of English Wealth', *Journal of Caribbean History* 39, no. 1 (2005): 38–53. See also Stephanie Barczewski, *Country Houses and the British Empire, 1700–1930* (Manchester: Manchester University Press, 2014).
5 Tillman W. Nechtman, *Nabobs: Empire and Identity in Eighteenth-Century Britain* (Cambridge: Cambridge University Press, 2010).

6 J. Mordaunt Crook, *The Rise of the Nouveaux Riches: Style and Status in Victorian and Edwardian Architecture* (London: John Murray, 1999).
7 www.theguardian.com/education/2015/nov/03/oxford-university-accused-over-oligarch-len-blavatnik-75m-donation. Accessed 30 September 2021.
8 The standard study is Colin Crisswell, *The Taipans: Hong Kong's Merchant Princes* (Hong Kong: Oxford University Press, 1981).
9 B. Disraeli, *Sybil, or The Two Nations* (London, 1985 [first published 1845]), 74.
10 *Jardine, Matheson & Co., afterwards Jardine, Matheson & Co. Limited: An outline of the history of a China House for a hundred years 1832–1932*, ed. J. Steuart (Hong Kong, 1934), 22, 30.
11 J. Y. Wong, *Deadly Dreams: Opium and the Arrow War (1856–1860) in China* (Cambridge: Cambridge University Press, 1998), 311. Others have argued that this is exaggerated, however. See Glenn Melancon, 'Honor in Opium? The British Declaration of War on China, 1839–1840', *International History Review* 21, no. 4 (1999): 856.
12 For 'invisible' incomes related to imperial trade, see Matthew Simon, 'The Enterprise and Industrial Composition of New British Portfolio Foreign Investment, 1865–1914', *Journal of Development Studies* 3, no. 3 (1967): 280–92; Michael Edelstein, *Overseas Investment in the Age of High Imperialism: The United Kingdom, 1850–1914* (New York: Columbia University Press, 1982), 9–44.
13 This is part of a phenomenon that some historians have come to view as 'Scotland's empire'. For instance, see Tom Devine, *Scotland's Empire: The Origins of the Global Diaspora* (London: Penguin Books, 2012). The Scottish connection here is far from anomalous in the context of Asia, for the presence of Scots in the region was already considerable owing to their employment within the East India Company. See Andrew Mackillop, 'Locality, Nation, Empire', in *Scotland and the British Empire*, eds J. M. MacKenzie and T. M. Devine (Oxford: Oxford University Press, 2011), 54–83. See also Le Pichon, *China Trade and Empire*, 6; George McGilvary, 'Scottish Agency Houses in South-East Asia, c.1760-c.1813', in *The Scottish Experience in Asia, c.1700 to the Present: Settlers and Sojourners*, eds T. M. Devine and A. McCarthy (London: Palgrave Macmillan, 2016), 75–96; Susan Leiper, *Precious Cargo: Scots and the China Trade* (Edinburgh: National Museums of Scotland, 1997).
14 The nepotistic and Scots-centric structure of the Jardine, Matheson & Co. partnership can be found in J. K. Fairbank, *Trade and Diplomacy on the China Coast: The Opening of the Treaty Ports 1842–1854*, 2 vols (Cambridge, MA: Harvard University Press, 1953), I, 62; II, 56–7.
15 John Gallagher and Ronald Robinson, 'The Imperialism of Free Trade', *The Economic History Review* 6, no. 1 (1953): 1–15.
16 They had erected buildings there from 1841. G. A. Bremner, 'Tides that Bind: Waterborne Trade and the Infrastructure Networks of Jardine, Matheson & Co.', *Perspecta*, no. 52 (2019): 31–47.
17 It is worth noting here the connection between elected MPs in the House of Commons and East Indies commerce. As late as 1820, for instance, up to 100

MPs (out of 658) were holders of East India stock, causing no small conflict of interest, it might be suggested. See Bowen, *The Business of Empire*, 95–6. For the idea of 'extrastatecraft' see Keller Easterling, *Extrastatecraft: The Power of Infrastructure Space* (London: Verso, 2014).

18 John Darwin, *The Empire Project: The Rise and Fall of the British World-System* (Cambridge: Cambridge University Press, 2011), 36–41. For the way this impinged on the tea trade, see Alain Le Pichon, 'From Monopoly to Free Trade', *Journal of the Royal Asiatic Society Hong Kong Branch* 54 (2014):131–55.

19 Bernard Semmel, *The Rise of Free Trade Imperialism: Classical Political Economy, the Empire of Free Trade, and Imperialism, 1750–1850* (Cambridge: Cambridge University Press, 1970), 152–:4; Wong, *Deadly Dreams*, 425–9.

20 Wong, *Deadly Dreams*, 425–9.

21 Gregory Blue, 'Opium for China: The British Connection', in *Opium Regimes: China, Britain, and Japan, 1839–1952*, eds T. Brook and B. Tadashi Wakabayashi (Berkeley: University of California Press, 2000), 48 (n.14).

22 Richard J. Grace, *Opium and Empire: The Lives and Careers of William Jardine and James Matheson* (Montreal and Kingston: McGill-Queen's University Press, 2014), 289, 300.

23 The nepotistic and Scots-centric structure of the Jardine, Matheson & Co. partnership can be found in Fairbank, *Trade and Diplomacy*, I, 62; II, 56–7. The Scottish connection here is far from anomalous in the context of Asia, for the presence of Scots in the region was already considerable owing to their employment within the East India Company. See Andrew Mackillop, 'Locality, Nation, Empire', in MacKenzie and Devine, *Scotland and the British Empire*, 54–83. See also Le Pichon, *China Trade and Empire*, 6; George McGilvary, 'Scottish Agency Houses in South-East Asia, c.1760-c.1813', in Devine and McCarthy, *The Scottish Experience in Asia*, 75–96; Leiper, *Precious Cargo*.

24 Unpublished letter, J. Matheson to Messrs Edwards & Hunter, NSW (24 April 1841), Jardine Matheson Archive, Cambridge University Library (JMA), James Matheson Private Letter Book: C5/6, 139.

25 Le Pichon, *China Trade and Empire*, 6–7.

26 For this I used the Bank of England Inflation Calculator: www.bankofengland.co.uk/monetary-policy/inflation/inflation-calculator. Accessed 20 October 2021.

27 'Sir James Matheson of the Lews, Baronet', *The Celtic Magazine* 8, no. 83 (1882): 490; Alexander Mackenzie, *History of the Mathesons, with Genealogies of the Various Families* (Stirling: Ineas Mackay, 1900), 60.

28 Grace, *Opium and Empire*, 23–9.

29 'Sir James Matheson of the Lews, Baronet', 496.

30 'Sir James Matheson of the Lews, Baronet', 496, 500–1.

31 Mackenzie, *History of the Mathesons*, 143.

32 'Sir James Matheson of the Lews, Baronet', 492.

33 For this association and its mutual respect, see Jesse S. Palsetia, *Jamsetjee Jejeebhoy of Bombay: Partnership and Public Culture in Empire* (New Delhi: Oxford University Press, 2015), 31–2.

34 For lobbying of China merchants in Britain, see Wong, *Deadly Dreams*, 310–30.
35 Grace, *Opium and Empire*, 244.
36 For Jardine's role, see Wong, *Deadly Dreams*, 311.
37 *Hansard* 71, August 4, 1843, cc.240–42.
38 Matheson quotes in Richard J. Grace, 'Matheson, Sir Alexander, first baronet (1805–1886)', *Oxford Dictionary of National Biography*. www.oxforddnb.com/view/10.1093/ref:odnb/9780198614128.001.0001/odnb-9780198614128-e-40811. Accessed 22 September 2021.
39 Mackenzie, *History of the Mathesons*, 71–2.
40 Mackenzie, *History of the Mathesons*, 72–3.
41 For Jardine's background, see *Jardine, Matheson & Co.*, 1–16; Grace, *Opium and Empire*.
42 *Canton Register*, 29 January 1839, 23. For the extraordinary send-off that Jardine received from all the merchant community in Canton and Macau, see pages 22–4 of this newspaper.
43 *Liverpool Mercury*, 20 March 1840, 93.
44 *Memoranda Relating to the Family of Haldane of Gleneagles* (London: C. A. Macintosh, 1880), 26.
45 Last Will and Testament of William Jardine (1 September 1843), Edinburgh Sheriff Court Inventories: SC70/1/64, p. 215.
46 *Jardine, Matheson & Co.*, 53.
47 'Lanrick Castle' in *Ordnance Gazetteer of Scotland: A Survey of Scottish Topography, Statistical, Biographical and Historical*, ed. Francis H. Groome (Edinburgh: Thomas C. Jack, Grange Publishing Works, 1882–85).
48 *Jardine, Matheson & Co.*, 57; Richard J. Grace, 'Jardine, Sir Robert, first baronet (1825–1905), East India merchant and politician', *Oxford Dictionary of National Biography*. www-oxforddnb-com.ezproxy.is.ed.ac.uk/view/10.1093/ref:odnb/9780198614128.001.0001/odnb-9780198614128-e-34159. Accessed 30 September 2021.
49 'Letters on the Purchase of Castlemilk, 1855–1860', JMA: GBR/0012/MS JM/K13.
50 Unpublished letter, Andrew Jardine to Joseph Jardine (23 December 1859), JMA: GBR/0012/MS JM/K13.
51 Alistair Rowan, 'Castlemilk, Dumfriesshire – Part II', *Country Life*, 18 August 1977, 422.
52 *Jardine, Matheson & Co.*, 58.
53 *Glasgow Herald*, 27 August 1858, 6.
54 'Castlemilk Estates', www.whoownsscotland.org.uk/property.php?p=6400. Accessed 30 September 2021.
55 Grace, 'Jardine, Sir Robert'.
56 Mackenzie, *History of the Mathesons*, 60.
57 See Miles Glendenning and Aonghus MacKechnie, *Scotch Baronial: Architecture and National Identity in Scotland* (London: Bloomsbury, 2021).
58 'Lews Castle', *Gazetteer of Scotland*. www.scottish-places.info/features/featurefirst5266.html. Accessed 11 October 2021; 'Sir James Matheson of the Lews, Baronet', 501.

59 These figures are for the 1870s, and may be revised down a little for the 1830s and 1840s. See R. K. Newman, 'Opium Smoking in Late Imperial China: A Reconsideration', *Modern Asian Studies* 29, no. 4 (1995): 765–94 (esp. 783–4).
60 Grace, *Opium and Empire*, 208–9, 297; Wong, *Deadly Dreams*, 324, 413, 430–1.
61 'Alexander Ross', *Dictionary of Scottish Architects*, www.scottisharchitects.org.uk/architect_full.php?id=100284. Accessed 12 October 2021.
62 'Ardross Castle', Dictionary of Scottish Architects: www.scottisharchitects.org.uk/building_full.php?id=101395. Accessed 16 February 2022.
63 ardrosscastle.co.uk/pages/heritage.php. Accessed 16 February 2022.
64 Grace, 'Matheson, Sir Alexander'.
65 *New York Times*, 2 October 2008, www.nytimes.com/2008/10/05/realestate/keymagazine/105castle-t.html. Accessed 12 October 2021. See also image of ceiling in, 'Duncraig Castle', http://exceptthekylesandwesternisles.blogspot.com/2010/10/duncraig-castle.html. Accessed 12 October 2021.
66 Alistair Rowan, 'Castlemilk, Dumfriesshire – Part I', *Country Life*, 11 August 1977, 353.
67 Rowan, 'Castlemilk, Dumfriesshire', 351.
68 Glendinning and MacKechnie, *Scotch Baronial*, 164–201.
69 http://portal.historicenvironment.scot/designation/LB8019. Accessed 16 February 2022.
70 For instance, see *Slavery and the British Country House*, eds Madge Dresser and Andrew Hann (Swindon: English Heritage, 2016); 'Interim Report on the Connections between Colonialism and Properties now in the Care of the National Trust, Including Links with Historic Slavery', eds S-A Huxtable, C. Fowler, C. Kefalas, and E. Slocomb (Swindon: National Trust, 2020). For research by English Heritage, see: www.english-heritage.org.uk/learn/research/slavery/. Accessed 28 March 2023.
71 Edward Said, *Culture and Imperialism* (London: Verso, 1993), 95–116.

# 8

# Spaces of empire in Victorian and Edwardian London

*Richard Dennis*

Empire was everywhere and nowhere in late nineteenth- and early twentieth-century London. City directories bear witness to banks, restaurants, shops, theatres, hotels, blocks of flats, pubs, life assurance companies, and public institutions, all with 'Imperial' or 'Empire' in their titles, not to mention numerous streets named after explorers, battles, and colonies. Yet contemporaries constantly complained that London had no grand squares, impressive public buildings, avenues or vistas that bore comparison with lesser imperial cities: 'Why is it that London is deficient in all those public buildings which not only add to the splendour of continental capitals, but contribute so materially, at the same time, to the convenience and comfort of the public at large?'[1] Visitors from the empire were equally critical. Indian commentators observed 'a dull monotony of ugliness', 'no grandeur in the houses', and 'few handsome public buildings'.[2]

To Arthur Beavan, the author of *Imperial London* (1901), the Houses of Parliament might be splendid externally, but they were already inadequate accommodation for members of parliament: 'No other nation, great or small, houses its people's representatives so shabbily, and with so little attempt to provide the most ordinary conveniences for transacting an empire's affairs.'[3] There were numerous explanations for how this state of affairs had arisen. Britain's constitutional monarchy could not ride roughshod over individuals' property rights. Successive governments were not prepared to impose new taxes to pay for grandiose public works. The very success of London's economy meant that land values in the City and West End were far too high to permit extravagant buildings surrounded by extensive open spaces or at the end of wide boulevards from which their grandeur and authority might be appreciated. London itself lacked any directly elected, unified city government prior to the creation of the London County Council. Its predecessor, the Metropolitan Board of Works, had the authority to make certain forms of sanitary improvement – building a sewer network, carving new streets piecemeal to ease traffic congestion and facilitate slum clearance, and constructing Thames embankments – but it did not have the vision or the mandate to transform the city into a capital fit for empire.

This chapter treats architecture in its broadest sense, as the structures – economic, social, cultural, political – that accommodate daily life, and 'spaces' as defined by their occupancy and activity as much as their built form. Today we are all too aware of metropolitan spaces that bear no explicit markers of imperialism but owe their existence to profits generated by exploited or slave labour, or disregard for indigenous land rights in Britain's colonies. We are increasingly familiar with the long history of Black and Asian populations in London. However, although statues to fêted politicians and businessmen along with their homes juxtaposed with slums occupied by poor migrants may, with hindsight, seem to us to have been spaces of empire, my focus in this chapter is on communal or collective spaces where empire was practised, celebrated, and lived, rather than spaces whose imperial origins were suppressed or disregarded.

There was an ambiguity between being an 'imperial' and a 'global' city. To contemporaries, London was undoubtedly 'the world's capital', but that implied two overlapping empires – an empire of government and administration, focused on Westminster, Whitehall, and the royal palaces, and an empire of trade and finance, centred on the City. The latter embraced an 'informal empire' that included parts of Latin America, China, Turkey, and Egypt which, while not formally colonies, had strong economic links to Britain, reflected in a plethora of financial institutions with headquarters or agencies in the City. Nevertheless, trade with the empire, with or without these appendages, never constituted more than a modest proportion of Britain's total imports, exports, or movements of capital. Around 1910, when we might think that London's imperial role was at its zenith, only about 35 per cent of Britain's exports went to, and 25 per cent of imports came from, the empire. Viewing the period from the end of the Napoleonic wars to the First World War, London's trade was at first primarily with Europe, but from the 1870s, exports were increasingly directed to colonial possessions, latterly interpreted as an 'easier' market in the face of increasing competition from Germany and the United States.[4] Of course, London's docks were also a site of embarkation for colonists and soldiers travelling between the metropole and the periphery, numbers that swelled substantially as emigrants fled rural unemployment and urban degeneration at home, and both regular soldiers and volunteers fought colonial wars in Africa and Asia. Although the City and the docks therefore became increasingly imperial spaces by the late nineteenth century, they were still linked more strongly to the rest of the world than to the empire. It is hard to claim them as 'spaces of empire' as distinct from spaces of global business.

Londoners became more self-consciously 'imperial' the more the empire came under threat from pressures for more autonomy, from both self-governing colonies and opponents in Pan-African and Indian independence movements. Todd Kuchta argues that the 'rapid rise of suburbia and the slow but steady decline of empire' were 'intimately linked and mutually articulated historical trajectories'.[5] All suburbs, not just those with explicit imperial markers, or which accommodated employees in imperial businesses or returnees from colonial service, constituted imperial spaces. They were financed from the profits of investment in the colonies and trade in colonial commodities, but also followed inverse development cycles: when foreign investment peaked – in the early 1870s, late 1880s, and early 1890s – domestic building slumped; but when foreign investment was low, there were home building booms – in 1874–84 and 1898–1901. Jingoistic imperialism became more vocal the less assured the future of the empire. John MacKenzie suggests that the more anxiety there was about the capacity of the empire to survive and prosper, the more powerful the assertions of British cultural and moral superiority. This was true in the staging of successive international exhibitions, which shifted from combining both imperial and foreign crafts and manufactures to concentrating on colonial, and especially Indian, exhibits. More locally and intimately, imperial patriotism was evident in uniformed youth organisations, stained-glass windows in churches, and music-hall songs.[6] Empire was encountered in suburban London, especially among lower middle-class, predominantly Conservative- or Municipal Reform-voting Londoners, in these everyday, taken-for-granted ways.

Seeking to redefine how we should understand the relevance of empire to space and architecture in nineteenth- and early twentieth-century London, Felix Driver and David Gilbert noted how little attention had been paid to more everyday spaces of empire, such as commercial buildings and residential neighbourhoods.[7] They were also concerned that imperial space was conceived as fixed, a container for imperial functions, whether administration in Whitehall offices or organised regal, military, or civic processions. There had been little sense that the routines of bureaucracy or the processions themselves, or the crowds that observed them or occupied the same spaces to protest at the actions of imperial government, were as much part of the architecture as the buildings.[8]

Driver and Gilbert's emphasis on 'the relationships between different kinds of spaces – architectural, spectacular, representational, and lived' echoes Lefebvre's view of the production of space, connecting conceptual representations of space with perceived representational spaces and space as practised through occupancy and mobility.[9] Imperial space was produced less by architects and planners than by those who traversed and occupied it. To outsiders, London's imperialism was expressed in its busyness, its urgency, and its cosmopolitanism. Indian visitors were excited by the 'surging traffic' and 'this ocean of human life', including other Indians.[10]

The 1911 census tabulated the first detailed statistics on birthplaces of overseas-born London residents.[11] Just over 1 per cent of Londoners had been born in Ireland, just under 1 per cent in 'British Colonies or Dependencies', and nearly 4 per cent in other 'Foreign Countries', a figure inflated by large numbers of Jewish migrants fleeing from pogroms in the Russian empire. More than 20 per cent of residents in Stepney were 'foreign-born'. Even allowing for this pattern of refugee migration, London housed many more 'foreign-born' than 'empire-born'. Demographically as well as economically, London was more obviously a global than a purely imperial city.

Places where there were more than twice as many inhabitants from the empire than the London-wide average were mostly relatively affluent boroughs – Hampstead, Kensington, Westminster, Chelsea, Paddington, and Holborn. Farther out, the only areas where the empire-born were over-represented were Woolwich, associated with the Royal Arsenal, barracks, military schools, and hospitals, and, unique among districts outside the County of London, Ealing, which had a relatively large South Asian-born population. Note that the census enumerated those present on census day, including visitors on business or tourists, likely to be concentrated in central London, and omitted those 'normally resident' but absent on census day. Nor should we confuse birthplace with ethnicity. Most of those born in Asia or the Caribbean would have been the children of white colonial officials, while Black or Asian people born in London were excluded by birthplace from the counts of 'Caribbean', 'African', and 'Asian'.

The overall message is that the imperial presence was modest: 35,000 in a population of 4.5 million. However, the coarse scale of analysis (metropolitan boroughs ranged in population between 50,000 and more than 300,000) obscures some localised concentrations, discussed in more detail below.

## The ceremonial core

Contrary to assertions that London lacked imposing imperial spaces, improvements in Westminster throughout the nineteenth century enhanced the city's metropolitan profile. Charles Barry and Augustus Pugin rebuilt the Palace of Westminster (Houses of Parliament) in Gothic Revival style between 1840 and 1860, but most public buildings along Whitehall were erected in Classical or, later, Edwardian baroque styles, aligning British government with the glories of the Roman empire. Parliament Square was created in 1868 in conjunction with the building of the Metropolitan District Railway, and by the mid-1880s accommodated statues of four prominent Victorian prime ministers – Peel, Derby, Palmerston, and Disraeli. New government buildings lined the west side of Whitehall, including the New Treasury Offices, refashioned by Barry in the 1840s, and the Foreign, Colonial, India, and Home Offices, designed by Gilbert Scott, completed 1868–75, which began the process of removing King Street and widening Parliament Street.[12] Bazalgette's construction of the Victoria Embankment created a wide new boulevard and public gardens and afforded public access to new vistas of the Thames and its traffic.

To the north of Whitehall, Trafalgar Square was created between 1840 and 1844, again by Barry. Nelson's Column went up in the 1840s, though only completed with the addition of Landseer's four lions in 1867 and some imperial statuary of Generals Napier, Havelock, and Gordon. Trafalgar Square, however, was a somewhat ambiguous space of empire, as much used for anti-government and anti-imperial protests as to accommodate crowds watching royal processions. The square was designed to be looked at, and across – to Wilkins' National Gallery, itself opened in 1838 – but rarely used; hence, the installation of ornamental fountains to break up the space in which crowds might otherwise congregate. Following violent unemployment demonstrations in 1886–87, public meetings were banned from using the square, and when the ban was lifted five years later, restrictive regulations authorised government to choose which meetings to allow.[13]

Out of necessity, Trafalgar Square featured in the routes of Queen Victoria's Golden and Diamond Jubilee processions in 1887 and 1897. The latter was more obviously 'imperial', in both the length of the procession route – all the way from Buckingham Palace to St Paul's Cathedral, out along the Strand and Fleet Street, but looping back over London Bridge, Borough, St George's Circus, and Westminster Bridge – and its incorporation of troops from the colonies and ministers of the self-governing colonies. In 1887, *The Times* had recognised an imperial dimension, commenting that the procession represented 'the breadth and width of an unparalleled empire', but more of the visiting dignitaries had been European heads of state, Victoria's own extended family, rather than colonial representatives. The route in 1887, a brief circuit out from the palace via Piccadilly, Trafalgar Square, and the Embankment to Westminster Abbey, and even more quickly back through Horse Guards Parade and the Mall, was 'chosen to traverse London's widest streets to accommodate the greatest number of onlookers'. Yet it necessitated passing through the unimproved south end of Parliament Street, narrow and 'flanked by grimy and ignoble buildings … unworthy of its surroundings, and … practically incapable of decoration'.[14]

The widening of Parliament Street was at last completed in conjunction with the building of more government offices in 1908. The Queen's procession in 1897 had to negotiate not only this constriction but also the length of Strand and Fleet Street, an animated but hardly stately route, lined by a jumble of buildings of different vintages and styles, and still narrow where it paralleled Holywell Street. Jonathan Schneer, discussing the carefully orchestrated parade of the City Imperial Volunteers (CIV) returning from duty in the Boer War to a thanksgiving service in St Paul's, following the same route as the Queen three years earlier, notes how the crush of spectators caused frequent accidents and made it difficult for the CIV to pass by. Along Fleet Street, '[n]o longer surrounded by the architectural reminders of British imperialism and military success, the crowds grew unruly'. Schneer asks whether 'the lack of an imposing backdrop free[d] spectators from certain feelings of constraint'.[15]

By the time of the CIV homecoming, plans were already in hand for a grand processional way through the centre of London: the building of Kingsway and Aldwych, slicing north–south through the no-man's land separating City from West End, and eliminating disreputable neighbourhoods around Holywell Street and Clare Market. Kingsway was planned not by the imperial government but by the local state – the London County Council. The idea appealed 'to both reform-minded and imperial-minded' members of the council: it removed slums and improved road links between north and south London at the same time as providing a mile of frontages for Edwardian baroque blocks lining the 100-feet wide roadway. Kingsway was opened by Edward VII in 1905, but the buildings abutting the street took shape much more slowly and, in the face of opposition from private site-owners, failed to provide the unified façades which the LCC had planned.[16]

Meanwhile, as part of the memorialisation of Queen Victoria, Aston Webb upgraded the Mall from 'a fashionable promenade into a regal procession route'. One end was marked by the Victoria Memorial, unveiled in 1911, and a re-faced Buckingham Palace (1913); the other by Admiralty Arch (1912), a triumphal arch reminiscent of imperial Rome, connecting the Mall to Trafalgar Square.[17] Plans for the further 'imperialisation' of London were floated by *The Builder* in 1912 and, after the First World War but continuing Webb's vision of an imperial capital, in the London Society's *London of the Future* (1921). A processional way, extending from a reconstructed 'Imperial Palace' across the Thames to an 'Imperial Quarter', including an Imperial Parliament building, reflected aspirations for an empire reinvigorated as a colonial federation, but unsurprisingly proved too expensive, too autocratic, and contrary to alternative conceptions of London as the home city of a domesticated empire built on trade and mutuality of interest.[18]

## Empires of finance and trade

Looking west from the roof of the Royal Exchange, Niels Lund's *The Heart of the Empire* (1904) depicts Bank Junction with Mansion House to the south, the Bank of England to the north, the shops and offices of the Mappin & Webb building straight ahead, and St Paul's Cathedral looming above the scene, perhaps reflecting the doubtful alliance of God and Mammon that lay at the heart of British imperialism. John Belcher's neo-gothic Mappin & Webb building had been erected in 1870 on an acute-angled corner between Poultry and the then newly constructed Queen Victoria Street, which cut diagonally across the grain of existing City streets, thereby creating numerous angled intersections which lent themselves to the erection of symbolically progressive, 'flatiron' type buildings.[19] At street level, Canadian artist, Frederic Bell-Smith, reproduced Lund's mix of modernity and empire in his own version of *The Heart of the Empire* (1909) (Plate 11).[20] Bell-Smith depicted a busy scene of horse-drawn and motorised carts, cars and buses, news-vendor, fruit cart, passers-by of different classes, genders and ages, sailors on shore-leave, a contingent of marching soldiers, and, overseeing the scene, an equestrian statue of the Duke of Wellington in front of the Royal Exchange. The pediment of the Exchange, dating from 1844, depicts the figure of 'Commerce' flanked by City of London dignitaries, a variety of British, Turkish, Persian, and Armenian merchants and bankers, a cargo-manager and various other nationalities – Greek, Indian, Chinese, Levantine, and African, the latter kneeling while grasping a barrel, an image of subservience if not of slavery. This was a public proclamation of empire based on mutually beneficial trade but dependent on an assumed hierarchy of both race and class.[21]

Yet much of the City's involvement with empire was discreetly hidden away. The 1895 Post Office Directory listed 79 'Foreign and Colonial Bankers not carrying on business as London bankers', of which 20 included reference to Australia or New Zealand in their titles and as many again named other localities in the British empire, or places in Egypt and Latin America that were part of the 'informal empire'. Like 'London Bankers', they were concentrated along streets radiating from Bank Junction, including Threadneedle Street, Old Broad Street, and Cornhill, and on side streets such as Clement's Lane, but comparatively few fronted on Lombard Street, perhaps the most prestigious location for private and merchant banks (Figure 8.1). Few occupied particularly distinctive buildings. Some shared premises with other businesses, including other banks.

The Bank of New Zealand established a presence in London in 1862, initially with the Oriental Bank Corporation acting as its agents, but soon acquired its own office at 50, Old Broad Street. In 1877 the bank moved to

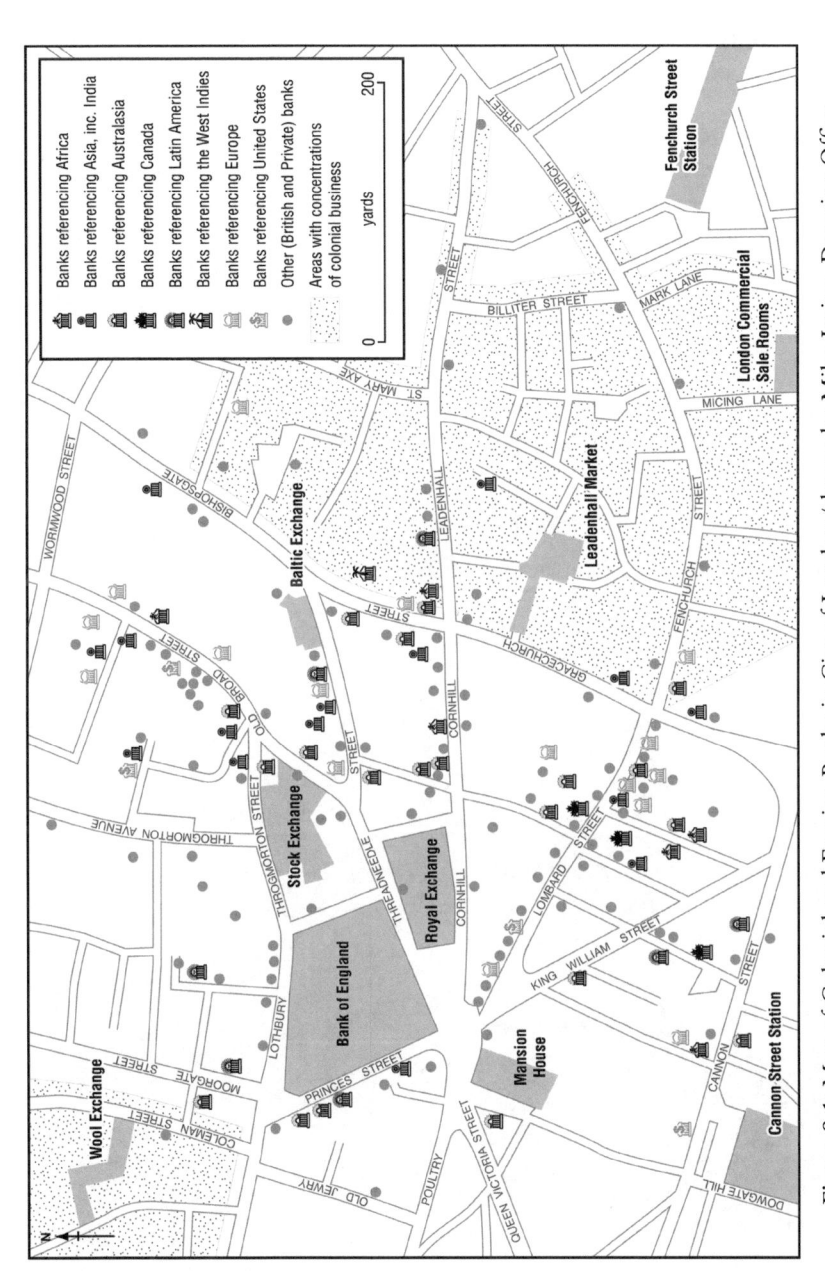

Figure 8.1 Map of Colonial and Foreign Banks in City of London (drawn by Miles Irving, Drawing Office, Department of Geography, University College London).

new premises on Queen Victoria Street, a handsome four-storey building on a triangular site adjacent to the Mansion House (Figure 8.2). However, the bank was neither the owner of the building nor responsible for appointing its architect, John Whichcord. He was commissioned by the National Safe Deposit Company to design high-security headquarters, anticipating countless clients eager to deposit their valuables in its underground vaults. The demand for its tiers of safes failing to materialise, the company was obliged to let not only the upper-floor office space, but also much of the ground floor. The Bank of New Zealand and its associated New Zealand Loan & Mercantile Agency Company took advantage of the opportunity to lease a prime site at a modest rent, remaining in occupancy for more than a hundred years. Whereas pre-completion engravings depicted the

**Figure 8.2** Photograph of Bank of New Zealand building, Queen Victoria Street, London (c. 1876), courtesy Bank of New Zealand Archives.

entrance to the National Safe Deposit Company's premises at the north (Bank Junction) corner of the building, subsequent images showed the Bank of New Zealand entrance at the north corner and the NSDCo's entrance on the less prestigious southwest corner, facing towards Blackfriars.[22]

Empire was more evident south of Leadenhall Street, where the headquarters of the East India Company were located prior to 1858. The London Commercial Sale Rooms, erected in 1811 on the east side of Mincing Lane dealt in 'all the choice products of earth, foreign and colonial', and were the site of tea auctions from the 1830s, when the East India Company's monopoly on the China tea trade was abolished. The façade featured a sculpture of Britannia, flanked by panels representing colonial produce, commerce, navigation, and science. Immediately across the street, four-storey offices and salerooms (including 'Colonial Refreshment Rooms'), erected in 1860, provided 200 individual offices and a top-floor exhibition space. A carving over the main entrance portrayed allegorical figures representing the West and East Indies around the shield of the Grocers' Company, itself surrounded by a wreath of 'Oriental vegetation' and shadowed by a palm tree.[23] Numerous similar, but often more specialised, buildings in the same area sustained colonial trade.

It was a short step from Mincing Lane to the Docks, for most Londoners an inaccessible space of bonded warehouses behind high walls and gates. Charles Booth described the workforce of dockers as almost exclusively British or Irish in origin,[24] but there were also sailors from overseas on shore leave, some of whom settled in Thameside communities, although their numbers, at least as enumerated in the census, were very small. In 1911, out of a population of over 442,000 in the metropolitan boroughs of Poplar and Stepney, which bordered the Thames, only 509 had been born in British Asia and 124 in British Africa. Booth's researchers, visiting Limehouse in 1897, showed more interest in 'Japs and Chinamen' than in Indian or African lascars. They interviewed 'an Indian, a Hindoo' and his wife, 'English or perhaps Irish', who lived in Jamaica Street. The man claimed to be a cook, employed in the City as curry maker, also at the 1895 Indian Exhibition at Earl's Court, but currently running an opium den patronised by 'Chinese & Lascars'. His wife commented that 'The Queen's Munshi Abdul Karim used to come here to smoke, so did many other Indians whose framed photos she showed to us.'[25] Confirming their longevity at the same address, the 1891 census recorded the couple, he born in Calcutta and his wife in Italy, with four lodgers, including one from Delhi. The census also identified a few sailors – from Cairo, Madras, Demerara (British Guiana), Bermuda, and Barbados – in or close to West India Dock Road, where the Strangers' Home for Asiatics, Africans, and South Sea Islanders (1857) functioned as lodging-house, employment agency, repatriation centre, and mission hall. Another institutional venture, the Ayahs' Home (in Mare Street, Hackney from 1900), accommodated Indian ayahs and Chinese amahs no longer required by white British families whom they had served as nannies.[26] The east London locations of the Ayahs' Home and of Booth's curry-maker contrast with the City, West End, and suburban localities where their erstwhile employers were based, again reflecting how London's imperial spaces mapped onto geographies of class.[27]

However, east London's imperialist sentiments mostly functioned without the presence of colonial subjects, expressed rather in street and house names, internal decorations, reading matter, and political allegiance of working-class and lower middle-class Londoners. Their primary space of empire was inside the home.

## Museumland

Many Londoners would have encountered the empire most explicitly in visits to new, or now publicly accessible, museums, and to international exhibitions. At the 1851 'Great Exhibition of the Works of Industry of All Nations', 53 per cent of exhibitors were from Britain and its colonies and dependencies. Imperial – and, especially, Indian – content increased in the 1862 International Exhibition. Meanwhile, the South Kensington Museum (later Victoria & Albert) opened in 1857, the same year that the British Museum became a properly public museum, including natural history and ethnographic exhibits that encompassed (but also went beyond) imperial possessions. However, the East India Company's own museum in Leadenhall Street, which had been extended as late as 1858 to accommodate Indian sculpture in a representation of 'a Mahometan musjid', was closed with the demise of the company and demolition of its building. Its collection mostly went into storage until re-emerging in 1874 as the Indian Section of the South Kensington Museum, housed in obscurity on the opposite side of Exhibition Road from the rest of the museum.[28] Here, it abutted the site of frequent temporary exhibitions, including the 1886 Colonial and Indian Exhibition, attended by 5.5 million people, which displayed every aspect of imperial arts, technology, economy, and society, including architecture. The Indian Empire was not only the largest exhibit, but the one visitors reached immediately after passing through the principal entrance on Exhibition Road. The Jaipur Gate led into a central avenue, and then through the Gwalior Gateway into the courtyard of an Indian palace, complete with Durbar Hall.[29]

The success of this exhibition stimulated plans to extend it into the following year – the Queen's Golden Jubilee – or even to make it permanent. In the event, the Imperial Institute opened in 1893, intended to 'represent the Arts, Manufactures, and Commerce of the Queen's Colonial and Indian Empire' and to be 'at once a Museum, an Exhibition, and the proper locality for the discussion of Colonial and Indian subjects'. Designed by Thomas Colcutt, the institute resembled some British buildings erected in India, but was imperial principally in its grandiosity and the height of its central tower – 287 feet. A foundation stone of Cape granite on a pedestal of Indian bricks seems to have been the principal material contribution the empire made to the structure of the building.[30]

The Imperial Institute proved less popular than the preceding South Kensington exhibitions, and less popular than a new round of increasingly populist spectacles, staged by the Hungarian impresario, Imre Karalfy, on exhibition grounds farther west, at Earl's Court. The Empire of India Exhibition (1895) featured an Empress Theatre, where 'India: A Grand Historical Spectacle' was presented, Imperial Court gardens, and an Indian City, but also a giant ferris wheel, twenty feet taller than Colcutt's tower. The Greater Britain Exhibition (1899) included a compound of thirty-five mud huts populated by 174 members of Zulu, Basuto, Mtabele, and Swazi tribes, who also participated in a theatrical extravaganza entitled 'Savage South Africa'.[31] The empire – and its architecture – had become a stage set for popular entertainment.

Among more refined cultural products of imperial trade, the Tate Gallery opened in 1897, housing the art collection of sugar refiner, Henry Tate, and the Horniman Museum (1901), situated in suburban south London, accommodated collections of arts and crafts, natural history, and musical instruments, accumulated on the back of the world's largest tea-trading company. Tate's sugar cubes and Horniman's tea would have been in the larders of many suburban homes.

## The suburbs

John Archer argues that European merchants and civil servants in the British and Dutch East Indies created the first suburbs, separate from the indigenous communities to which they attached themselves. By the late eighteenth century, suburbs analogous to today's 'gated communities' existed in Calcutta and Madras.[32] These in turn inspired suburbanisation in London, just at the time that anxieties about congestion, contagion, and physical and moral pollution were prompting moves to self-segregated neighbourhoods by City merchants and their families. Among early London suburbs, Nash's Regent's Park bears signs of oriental influence, including – in the case of Sussex Place – ten 'gourd-like cupolas' (Figure 8.3).[33] Mark Girouard

Figure 8.3 Photograph of Sussex Place, Regent's Park (photograph by author).

has likened a neighbouring early nineteenth-century development, the Eyre Estate in St John's Wood, to 'the garden quarters of Calcutta and other Anglo-Indian quarters'.[34]

In time, St John's Wood became part of an 'inner colonial perimeter', which extended through Bayswater – known by the 1860s as 'Asia Minor', Notting Hill – developed in part by Charles Henry Blake, a Bengal indigo planter and sugar dealer, and so-called 'Imperial Kensington'.[35] Westbourne Grove, Bayswater's principal shopping street, was nicknamed 'The Chowringhee of Bayswater' after a fashionable suburban street in Calcutta.[36] The development of Bayswater coincided with the accelerated return of East India Company officials after 1857–58, and the rise of a more mobile elite of colonial administrators, travelling to and fro between Britain and India. The suburb acquired a reputation as a home for returnees and a lodging-house district for British officials on furlough and Indian students and visitors to London.

Consider St Stephen's Road and Burlington Road in North Bayswater, where locally based builders erected long terraces of four- and five-storey terraced houses between 1859 and 1863.[37] Visiting in 1898–99, Charles Booth's colleagues noted 'grim, heavy looking but solidly built houses with bay windows ... pillared porches & balconies, fronts stuccoed & painted to first floor; some attempt at ornament on cornices & lintels'.[38] By then, almost all were divided into 'furnished apartments' or run as lodging houses. The 1891 census recorded 717 inhabitants living in 91 inhabited houses on the two roads of whom 62 (9 per cent) had been born in British India, Ceylon, and Burma (Figure 8.4). Some were the Indian-born children of British-born parents who had served with the East India Company, the Bengal Army, or the Indian Civil Service, so the proportion of the population connected to India was substantially higher than 9 per cent. Surveying a larger area north of Westbourne Grove, more than 4 per cent were South Asian-born, nearly 3 per cent were born in the British Caribbean or the white settler colonies, more than 3 per cent in Ireland, and almost 5 per cent 'foreign-born', mostly in continental Europe, but including migrants or visitors from South America, China, and Japan, often noted as 'British Subjects', indicating the extent of Britain's informal and commercial empire. Only 5 per cent of the Indian-born had names suggestive of South Asian ethnicity.[39] Among residents of mews cottages behind the street terraces, there were hardly any people born outside Great Britain. So, while Bayswater was identified with its Indian population, it was a home for returning colonists rather than the colonised, and was more broadly 'cosmopolitan' in its middle-class residents, but resolutely 'British' among its artisans and labouring classes.

The colonial imprint was also stamped on more distant London suburbs, where streets were developed by or in the grounds of houses formerly occupied by colonial merchants, officials, or military officers. In Enfield, on London's northern outskirts, Colonel J. R. Riddell, a former Indian Army officer, named his home 'Bycullah Park', commemorating a fashionable Bombay suburb. Following the extension of the Great Northern Railway to Enfield Chase in 1871, Riddell's fifty-four-acre Bycullah estate was subdivided and, by 1882, sixty villas for professional and business families had been erected with forty more under construction, all on lots of at least a quarter of an acre and with rental values of at least £70 per annum. Like colonial settlements in Indian and African cities, the estate had gates at each end of Bycullah Road and a gatekeeper's lodge.[40]

In Hampstead, John Teil, an East India merchant, commissioned the building of Kidderpore Hall in 1843, named after the district of Calcutta in which he owned tanneries. Fifty years later, the grounds were subdivided for large detached and semi-detached villas: today's Kidderpore Avenue and Kidderpore Gardens.[41] Kidderpore was also commemorated in the name of a house in Bedford Park, Croydon, occupied for eighteen years by

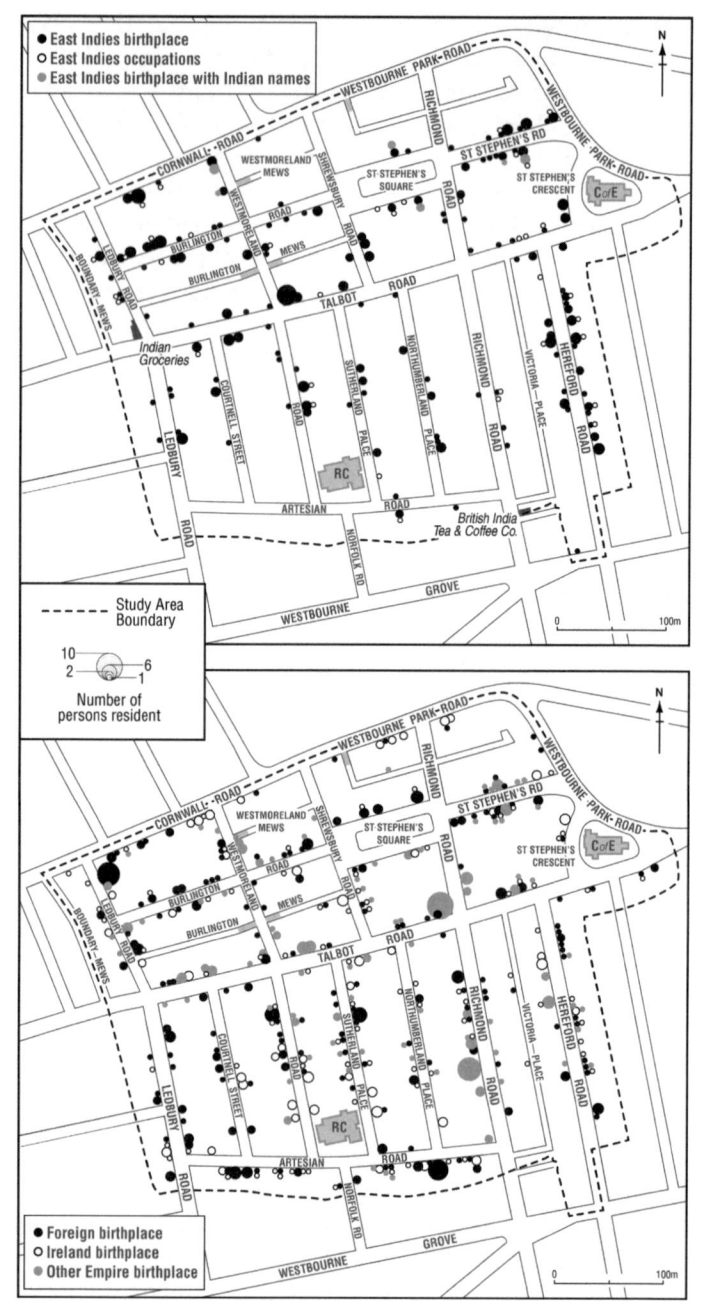

**Figure 8.4** Map of Colonial & Foreign-Born in North Bayswater, 1891 (drawn by Miles Irving, Drawing Office, Department of Geography, University College London).

the family of prominent Indian lawyer and nationalist politician, Womesh Chandra Bonnerjee. The house itself was typical of suburban villas, but it functioned as 'an oasis' for Indian students who congregated there on Sundays in what Rozina Visram calls 'a hybrid world' of Indian meals accompanied by Christian hymn-singing.[42]

Successive censuses recorded a sizeable Indian-born population in the west London suburb of Ealing. Along with Anglo-Indian officers and civil servants retiring to, or temporarily resident in, the area, served by local department stores that cultivated an 'empire-wide' trade, the Royal India Asylum for former officers and men of the East India Company relocated to Ealing in 1870.[43] The 1881 census enumerated 105 'lunatics' in the asylum, of whom nineteen were the wives, daughters, or widows of former officers or soldiers. The majority of soldiers and almost all soldiers' widows hailed from Ireland, and only one had been born in India. Among officers, civil servants, and their female relatives, nearly 20 per cent originated in India, and only one in Ireland, again indicating class differences in the colonial presence in Victorian London.[44]

Imperial references proliferated in street names in working-class and lower middle-class suburbs. Many streets can be dated from their names commemorating notable events, usually military engagements, or specific colonial administrators, army officers, or explorers. Other streets, named after cities or provinces in India or the settler-colonies, more broadly celebrated the expansion of empire (Figure 8.5). The Falcon Park estate in Battersea, developed by Alfred Heaver between 1879 and 1881, included Afghan, Cabul, Candahar, Khyber, and Nepaul Roads, variously commemorating places associated with the Second Afghan War (1878–80), thereby earning the estate the nickname of Battersea's 'North West Frontier'. West of Falcon Road, Musjid Road marked the first major action in the Afghan War, but other street names commemorated the Zulu War (1879): Tugela, Kambala, and Natal Roads and, briefly, Zulu Crescent. The houses were typical of the area, lacking any explicitly 'imperial' characteristics beyond some decorative features 'larded on to improve their rentability'. Most had double-height bay windows, a sign of respectability, but many housed more than one skilled working-class family. Most householders worked in building, manufacturing, and transport, whereas on other Heaver estates in Battersea and Clapham lower middle-class clerks and shopkeepers predominated. When new, houses in Musjid Road were 'let to respectable tenants at 12s 6d per week each'. Charles Booth labelled all the 'Afghan' streets 'fairly comfortable' with the exception of Musjid Road, which was 'Mixed. Some comfortable, others poor.'[45]

Patriotism was especially evident in the proliferation of Boer War names in the first decade of the twentieth century. Among street-names in London

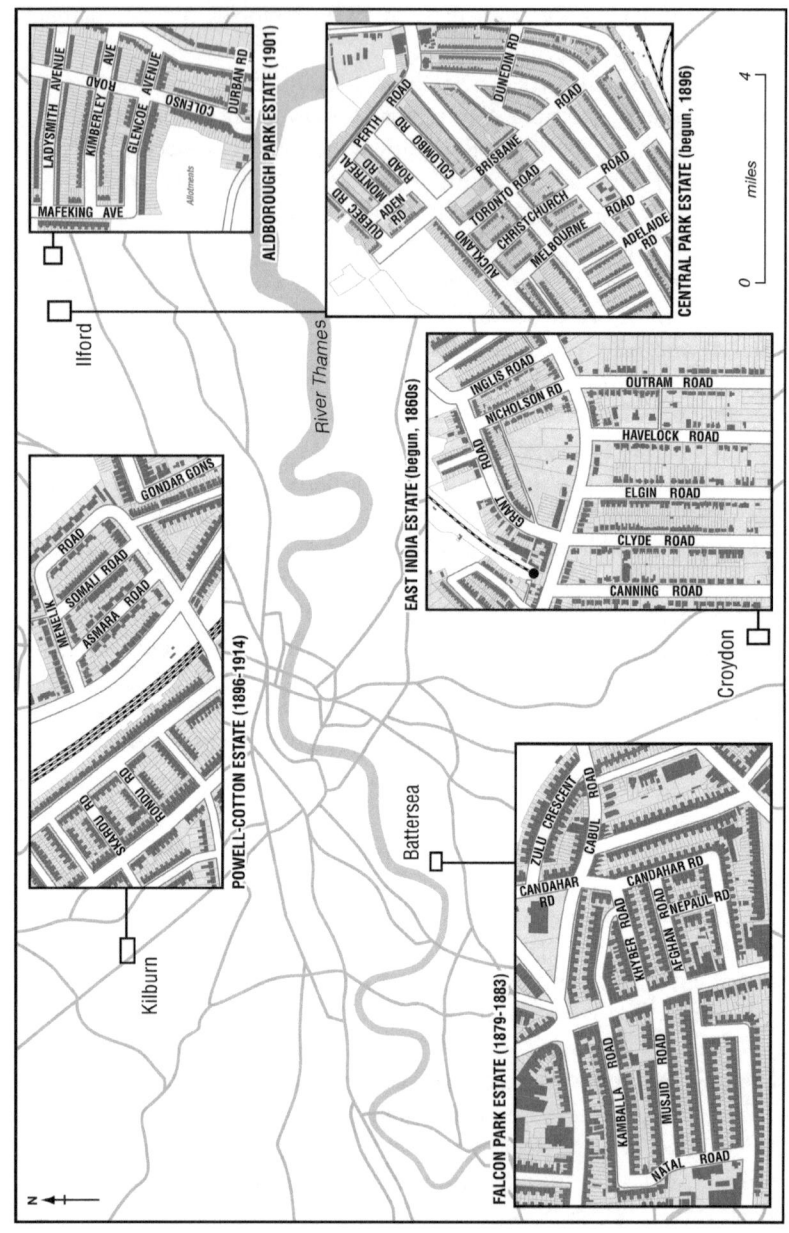

**Figure 8.5** Map of Imperial Street Names in Selected London Suburbs (drawn by Miles Irving, Drawing Office, Department of Geography, University College London).

suburbs in the 1911 census there were fourteen Kimberleys, nine Ladysmiths, nine Pretorias, seven Mafekings, five Natals, and four Durbans. Their spatial distribution is striking. Of these forty-eight streets, thirty-one lay in London's northeast quadrant, mostly in East and West Ham, Ilford, Leyton, Tottenham, and Edmonton. Leyton and Ilford also have numerous streets named after Australasian and Canadian cities, states, and provinces. Kuchta suggests that suburbia 'came to be seen as a breeding ground for bullheaded nationalism and downright jingoism'.[46] Charles Masterman, who was particularly critical of the cultural and physical degeneration he associated with suburbs as much as slums, thought that 'villadom' was devoted to 'the New Imperialism'.[47] Just as suburbs were sites of social reproduction for 'Victorian values' of thrift, temperance, and the importance of home and family, so they were sites for the reproduction of 'imperial values', nurturing future generations of patriots and colonists. Suburbs constituted markets for colonial products, their residents benefited from clerical and administrative jobs which sustained imperial government and trade, and many suburbanites had returned from time spent in the colonies, had relatives living overseas, or anticipated emigrating to self-governing parts of the empire. Their imperial consciousness, fuelled by newspapers such as the *Daily Mail* or through church missionary connections, was reinforced through streetscapes redolent with imperial names, and even through gardens planted with trees, shrubs, and flowers that had originated in distant climes.

Some garden practitioners thought that tropical plants should be confined to botanical gardens, such as Kew, or espoused a kind of 'horticultural nationalism' aligned to folk revivals in music, fashion, and cottage architecture. Others were happy to include exotics introduced as a consequence of British overseas trade, exploration, or colonisation. For many new suburbanites, the planting of exotic species was a deliberate way of distancing their gardens from the cottage gardens of the rural poor, material evidence of upward social and geographical mobility.[48] It is hard to discern a distinctly imperial horticulture as opposed to one that favoured foreign or exotic plants. Yet the cultivation and display of all kinds of exotics served to stimulate the suburban imagination of what life must be like for their cousins living in far-flung parts of the empire. The popularisation of imported plants, such as rhododendrons, itself signified the taken-for-grantedness of empire in British society. Garden architecture – Chinese or Moorish summerhouses or, to quote John Claudius Loudon, '[a] glazed mosque, pyramid, or pagoda, containing palms, &c.' – also invoked a domestication of colonial environments.[49]

Imperial associations were also evident in the rise of chain stores with branches on suburban high streets. A rival tea importer to Horniman, Thomas Lipton developed a trading empire of grocery stores through which he sold tea, packaged at prices affordable by working-class customers, made possible by running his own tea gardens in Ceylon, and bypassing the Mincing Lane tea auctions. Lipton employed Sinhalese servants at his home in Southgate, and advertised his tea using 'sandwich-men dressed up as Indians'.[50] By 1910, there were forty Lipton stores in central London and another twenty-four in suburban districts of the County of London. Lipton's letterhead depicted inner London warehouses and factories, provincial offices in Glasgow, Liverpool, and Dublin, and colonial offices in Colombo and Calcutta, arranged around its metropolitan headquarters (Figure 8.6). Lipton's was matched by Home & Colonial Stores, more than fifty of which were listed in the London Suburbs Directory for 1911. Incorporated in 1888, Home & Colonial brought the consciousness of empire into every suburban high street.

One colonial architectural form reinvented for home consumption was the bungalow. 'Bungalow' was, in a sense, a marketing ploy, much as blocks of tenements were rechristened as 'mansion flats' to appeal to the urban bourgeoisie. The word derived from 'bangalo', used to describe a house built in the Bengali style, originally a kind of thatched hut. British colonists in India modernised the form but retained the basic principle of a one-storey building with an overhanging thatched roof. 'Bungalow' became the standard term for such buildings by the 1820s. A house called 'The Bungalow' by its owner, Captain Bragg, formerly 'the Commander of the Ram Chunder East Indiaman', features in Thackeray's Christmas book, *Our Street* (1848); but the earliest real-life bungalow in the London area seems to have been Selhurst Lodge in Norwood (not far from the site of the re-erected Crystal Palace), occupied by retired army officer Captain Bamford between 1859 and 1861.[51]

Publicity celebrating life in hill stations or rural bungalows in India may have prompted a yearning for a world that had been lost in urbanising Britain. One consequence was the promotion of up-market bungalow communities in seaside, outer suburban, and riverside retreats in the 1870s and 1880s: on the North Kent coast; along the banks of the Thames in locations such as Weybridge and Maidenhead; and in an Arts & Crafts village, 'Bellaggio', on the Surrey/Sussex border, promoted as a 'Bungalow Club and Town', 'a Paradise', and a 'GARDEN of EDEN'.[52] Judging by the number of Bellaggio households 'headed' by housekeepers and gardeners in the 1891 census, most bungalow-owners must have had first homes elsewhere. Nevertheless, those present on census day included a lieutenant in the Royal Engineers, born in Dublin, a retired postmaster, born in British Guiana, and a doctor, born in Calcutta.

The earliest British bungalows often included colonial features, such as overhanging pitched roofs, verandahs, and balconies, and informal,

Figure 8.6 Lipton's Letterhead (1903) (private collection).

often asymmetrical, plans, contrasting with the formality and rigidity of Victorian terraced houses. Even if, in practice, most early bungalows included bedrooms in the roof space, the popular image was of buildings with all the rooms on one level, and therefore a different moral geography from typical multistorey townhouses. Numerous external doors and French windows made for permeable, less easily supervised boundaries between inside and outside, an ambiguity exploited by both Fred Horner, in his comedy 'The Bungalow' (1889), set in an artist's retreat beside the Thames in Putney, and George Gissing, in his novel *The Whirlpool* (1897).[53] In the latter, Cyrus Redgrave's bungalow in Wimbledon, not far south of Putney, is hidden by shrubbery in the grounds of his sister's house. Her husband was in India: '"She tried it, but couldn't stand the climate."' Hence, perhaps, her acceptance of her brother's affectation for a bungalow. Sibyl Carnaby, recently returned from touring the world, 'had a curiosity about the bungalow. Its exotic name affected her imagination.'[54]

In practice, bungalows intended for permanent residence were still rare, and those that appear in newspaper advertisements were – like Redgrave's – situated in the grounds of more substantial villas, or were designated bungalows by their occupiers to remind them of previous phases in their life spent overseas. An estate in Streatham, auctioned in 1879, comprised a 'very superior' family dwelling called 'The Shrubbery', but also a 'Cottage Residence known as The Bungalow, containing nine rooms'. Among other dwellings labelled 'The Bungalow' were examples in Kew, Acton, Hampstead, Finsbury Park, and the Arts and Crafts suburb of Bedford Park, Chiswick, the latter occupied by 'His Honour W. Ernst (late H.M. Colonial Judge)'.[55]

The verandah, a feature of many bungalows, had been advocated by Loudon in the 1830s in his design for a 'double-detached [i.e. semi-detached] suburban villa' in Porchester Terrace, Bayswater. Loudon argued that children and invalids could enjoy the health and recreational benefits of being outdoors without leaving the safety of the house. More generally, as in colonial settings, verandahs offered protection from the extremes of sun and rain. Highly ornamented verandahs with elaborate filigree ironwork were popular on Australian terraced housing during the nineteenth century, replicated in first-floor verandahs on Kensington (London) terraces around 1860, and in the advertising of East London building merchants, Young & Marten, at the turn of the century. However, it is hard to claim a direct colonial influence given earlier, if less fanciful, British verandahs on late Georgian and Regency seaside and spa terraces.[56]

## Imperial mansions

In 1868, architect T. Roger Smith had discussed the design of bungalows in India in a lecture at the Royal Institute of British Architects.[57] A few years later, Smith collaborated with another architect-lecturer with Indian experience, William H. White, in advocating purpose-built mansion flats.[58] White's father had been a doctor in the Bengal Medical Service. In the late 1860s, White practised in Paris, where he learnt about middle-class apartment life. Displaced by the Franco-Prussian War, he moved to Calcutta, where he worked in the Public Works Department of the Indian Government. He returned to London in 1873 as an examiner in architecture at the Royal Indian Engineering College, Egham.[59] White practised what he preached, residing long-term in Oxford and Cambridge Mansions, Marylebone, by which time he was secretary of the RIBA. Coincidentally, Oxford and Cambridge Mansions was the real block of flats in which Gissing situated Sibyl Carnaby in *The Whirlpool*![60]

There was nothing architecturally imperial – other than grandiosity – about mansion flats in late Victorian London, but many of their occupants had links with the colonies. Residents of Oxford and Cambridge Mansions in 1891 included two single women born in Jamaica, a banker's clerk whose wife had been born in the West Indies, a colonial broker's agent from Tasmania, an elderly widower born in Calcutta, another spinster from India, and a stock-exchange dealer born in India-Punjab. There were also children born in Cairo and Cape Colony. Similar colonial connections – often reinforced by military service – were evident in luxury flats in Kensington and Westminster.

For colonial servants on furlough, flats offered a convenient, low-maintenance base close to clubs, entertainment venues, and places of influence. For those returning permanently, they were equally attractive, whether as their only home for those unencumbered with small children, or a foothold in the West End for those also in possession of a country estate. Rich visitors from the empire could obtain serviced suites for the duration of their visit. Queen Anne's Mansions, overlooking St James's Park, regularly accommodated visiting dignitaries and returning colonial administrators: in May 1899, the retiring Chief Justice of Madras; in June 1902, Sir Henry Blake, at various times Governor of the Bahamas, Newfoundland, Jamaica, Hong Kong, and Ceylon; in April 1907, Sir Frederick Lugard, en route between appointments as High-Commissioner of Northern Nigeria Protectorate and Governor of Hong Kong; and in May 1908, the Maharajah of Kuch Behar, newly arrived from Calcutta.[61]

Queen Anne's Mansions was a short walk from the Houses of Parliament and close to Victoria Street. Newly laid out by improvement commissioners in the 1850s, by the 1890s Victoria Street was lined with blocks of 'chambers' (offices) and mansion flats, punctuated by luxury hotels and a proto-department store catering for colonial and military personnel. The opening of Westminster Palace Hotel, close to Westminster Abbey, coincided with the closure of East India House. Awaiting the completion of its own building on Whitehall, the newly constituted India Office leased a 140-room wing of the hotel for use by its staff until 1867.[62] More usually, the hotel accommodated colonial delegations and hosted conferences, meetings, and dinners of imperial and anti-imperial groups. In 1866, delegates from British North American provinces met there, preparing plans for Canadian confederation. In 1878, the Afghan Committee met to 'deplore the commencement of hostilities upon grounds which are not sufficiently justified by the information at present before the country'. In 1889, the Aborigine Protection Society gave a breakfast in honour of envoys from Matabeleland. In 1897, the United Empire Trade League hosted a luncheon for colonial premiers in London for the Diamond Jubilee. In 1909 a meeting was held to say farewell to Gandhi, who had been in London to represent the case of British Indians in Transvaal.[63]

Victoria Street housed numerous businesses and institutions that required easy access to parliament. Nine colonial and several more foreign government offices occupied premises on the street (Figure 8.7).[64] The same blocks of chambers also housed the offices of tea companies, Indian law agents, the East India Association, a variety of colonial railway companies, and countless engineers, surveyors, architects, and charitable societies, often associated with colonial causes.

Midway along the street were the premises of the Army and Navy Co-operative Society, and, on side streets to the south, administrative, warehouse, and manufacturing buildings supporting the society's extensive mail-order business. Members of the society, founded in 1871, included army and navy officers, privy councillors, peers, lords lieutenant, foreign and English ambassadors, and officers of the Royal Irish, Indian, and Colonial Constabularies. The store had depots in Bombay and Karachi and, by 1901, a branch in Calcutta. Until 1918, the store was officially members only, and its street frontage, devoid of plate-glass windows, suggested a private club rather than a department store. Here was a place where colonial officials could be equipped with whatever they needed to survive overseas, but also where products from the colonies were on sale to well-off Londoners.[65]

Among the residents of nearby mansion flats were members of parliament, civil servants, and those who lobbied them, retired army generals, and also wives and daughters with birthplaces in India or West Indies, but no male head of household present on census day. These were safe and

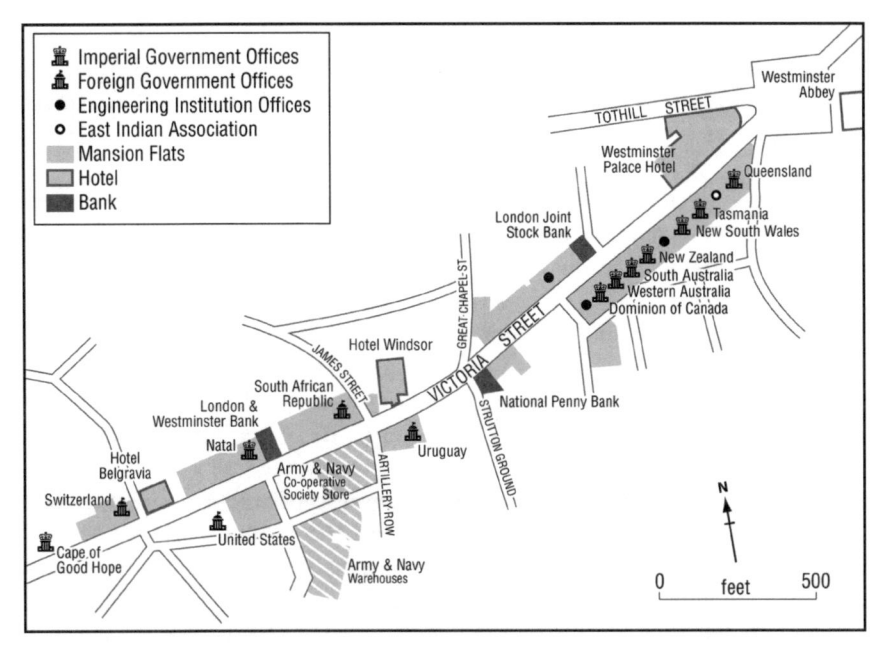

Figure 8.7 Map of Victoria Street, Westminster, c. 1895 (drawn by Miles Irving, Drawing Office, Department of Geography, University College London).

convenient places for family members to live while their husbands and fathers travelled on business.

## Conclusion

Almost every part of London could lay claim to be a 'space of empire', but few sites were particularly distinctive architecturally or recognisably 'imperial'. Exotic architecture was consigned to the theme parks of international exhibitions. There was more evidence of adaptation of colonial forms, as in the case of the bungalow or the verandah, and some parallels between the planning of suburbs in colonial settings and estate planning in London and other large cities where developers attempted forms of zoning and residential segregation. Yet the absence of town planning legislation in Britain prior to 1909 meant that these ideas were limited to the estates of large landowners, who had been implementing them for economic and social reasons throughout the nineteenth century, regardless of any imperial practice.

Central London was too much of a global city to have room for exclusively imperial spaces. The City and West End were kaleidoscopic in their diversity, synoptic in the interconnectedness of their different spaces, activities, and agencies. Colonial banks shared the area around the Bank of England with international merchant banks; in the West End, department stores such as Liberty's and, after 1909, Selfridge's, offered exotic fabrics and designs, but marketed themselves as cosmopolitan rather than imperial. By contrast, in the suburbs, space was sufficiently plentiful and cheap for accessible public venues, such as Kew Gardens, and for imperial residential and educational institutions.

Spaces are practised as much as made. Streets and squares became briefly imperial as imperial subjects and imperial celebrations occupied them or passed through them, sometimes accommodating temporary installations such as commemorative arches and exhibition buildings. The everyday practice of empire was mostly at a more private scale: how gardens were laid out, how homes were decorated, how connections with colonial cousins were memorialised in family photographs and treasured gifts.[66] The more empire itself was threatened, and the more the ties of empire depended on extended family links, strengthened by increasing emigration to settler colonies and modern communications, the more significant these private spaces became. Rather than searching for specific spaces, perhaps we should recognise that the spaces of empire were different and unique for every Londoner.

## Notes

1 J. H. Briggs, *Naval Administrations* (1897), 163. Quoted in M. H. Port, 'Government and the Metropolitan Image: Ministers, Parliament and the Concept of a Capital City, 1840–1915', *Art History* 22, no. 4 (1999): 567–92.
2 B. Malabari, *The Indian Eye on English Life* (1893), 46. Quoted in R. Visram, *Asians in Britain: 400 Years of History* (London: Pluto Press, 2002), 116; L. Baijnath, *England and India* (1893), 22–3. Quoted in A. Burton, 'Making a Spectacle of Empire: Indian Travellers in Fin-de-Siècle London', *History Workshop Journal* 42 (1996): 127–46.
3 A. H. Beavan, *Imperial London* (London: Dent, 1901), 111.
4 P. J. Cain, 'Economics and Empire: The Metropolitan Context', in *The Oxford History of the British Empire, Volume III: The Nineteenth Century*, ed. A. Porter (Oxford: Oxford University Press, 1999), 31–52.
5 T. Kuchta, *Semi-Detached Empire: Suburbia and the Colonization of Britain, 1880 to the Present* (Charlottesville: University of Virginia Press, 2010), 5.
6 J. M. MacKenzie, 'Empire and Metropolitan Cultures', in Porter, *Oxford History*, 270–93.
7 F. Driver and D. Gilbert, 'Heart of Empire? Landscape, Space and Performance in Imperial London', *Environment and Planning D: Society and Space* 16 (1998):

11–28; 'Imperial Cities: Overlapping Territories, Intertwined Histories', in *Imperial Cities: Landscape, Display and Identity*, eds F. Driver and D. Gilbert (Manchester: Manchester University Press, 1999), 1–17; D. Gilbert and F. Driver, 'Capital and Empire: Geographies of Imperial London', *GeoJournal* 51 (2000): 23–32.

8  They noted some commendable exceptions: R. Mace, *Trafalgar Square: Emblem of Empire* (London: Lawrence and Wishart, 1976); J. M. Jacobs, *Edge of Empire: Postcolonialism and the City* (London: Routledge, 1996); A. D. King, *Global Cities: Post-imperialism and the Internationalization of London* (London: Routledge, 1990).

9  H. Lefebvre, *The Production of Space*, trans. D. Nicholson-Smith (Oxford: Blackwell, 1991).

10  Burton, 'Making a Spectacle', 129.

11  Census of England and Wales 1911, Vol. IX, Birthplaces ... (London: HMSO, 1913).

12  M. H. Port, *Imperial London: Civil Government Building in London 1851–1915* (New Haven: Yale University Press, 1991).

13  Mace, *Trafalgar Square*.

14  *The Times*, 20 June 1887, 6. Quoted in T. Richards, 'The Image of Victoria in the Year of Jubilee', *Victorian Studies* 31 (1987): 8–32.

15  J. Schneer, *London 1900: The Imperial Metropolis* (New Haven: Yale University Press, 1999), 31–2.

16  Schneer, *London 1900*, 22. See also J. Winter, *London's Teeming Streets 1830–1914* (London: Routledge, 1993), 207–16; D. Schubert and A. Sutcliffe, 'The 'Haussmannization' of London?: The Planning and Construction of Kingsway-Aldwych, 1889–1935', *Planning Perspectives* 11, no. 2 (1996): 115–44.

17  T. Smith, "'A grand work of noble conception': The Victoria Memorial and Imperial London', in Driver and Gilbert, *Imperial Cities*, 21–39 (quotation on p. 27).

18  'Imperial London', *The Builder*, 5 January 1912, 11–13; T. R. Metcalf, *An Imperial Vision: Indian Architecture and Britain's Raj* (London: Faber and Faber, 1989), 179–80; D. Gilbert, 'London of the Future: The Metropolis Reimagined after the Great War', *Journal of British Studies* 43, no. 1 (2004): 91–119.

19  Jacobs, *Edge of Empire*, 38–69; I. S. Black, 'Rebuilding 'The Heart of the Empire': Bank Headquarters in the City of London, 1919–1939', *Art History* 22, no. 4 (1999): 593–618.

20  E. L. Ramsay, 'Modernity and Post-colonialism: *The Heart of the Empire (1909)* by F.M. Bell-Smith', *Labour/Le Travail* 52 (2003): 207–20.

21  P. Ward-Jackson, *Public Sculpture of the City of London* (Liverpool: Liverpool University Press, 2003), 318.

22  For the Bank of New Zealand, see BNZ Heritage, https://www.bnzheritage.co.nz/ and advertisements in *Daily News*, 13 February 1862; *Reynolds's Newspaper*, 7 December 1862, 7; *Standard*, 7 March 1877, 1. For the National

Safe Deposit Company, see *The Graphic*, 13 September 1873, 242, 256; *Morning Post*, 23 December 1875 and 26 October 1876; and NSDCo trade card advertised for sale at www.ebay.co.uk/itm/352773851979. Accessed 12 February2024.
23. For London Commercial Sale Rooms, see https://collage.cityoflondon.gov.uk/quick-search?q=London%20Commercial%20Sale%20Rooms&WINID=1582885077929. Accessed 12 February 2024. For Grocers' Company offices, see 'Offices and sale rooms in Mincing-Lane', *Illustrated London News*, 10 March 1860, 228–9.
24. Quoted in T. McCarthy, *The Great Dock Strike 1889* (London: Weidenfeld & Nicolson, 1988), 43.
25. Charles Booth Police Notebook, B346, 101, 119–29.
26. Visram, *Asians in Britain*, 51–60; *Illustrated London News*, 14 June 1856, 670.
27. Only a handful of ayahs were returned as such in 1881–1901 censuses, living in Islington, Paddington (3), and Hackney (2). Caroline Bressey cites examples of ayahs in Streatham, Gunnersbury, Selhurst, Paddington, and at the Ayahs' Home (then at 6 Jewry Street, Aldgate) advertising for employment: see C. Bressey, 'Four Women: Exploring Black Women's Writing in London, 1880–1920', in *Critical Perspectives on Colonialism: Writing the Empire from Below*, eds F. Paisley and K. Reid (London: Routledge, 2014), 179–98. See also Cook's contrast between 'the rich and cultured Orientals' in Bayswater and 'their poorer brethren' who 'live out in Poplar, Shadwell, or anywhere in the near vicinity of the East India Docks', in E. C. Cook, *Highways and Byways in London* (London: Macmillan, 1902), 295.
28. 'The New Museum at the East India House', *Illustrated London News*, 6 March 1858, 228–30; Metcalf, *Imperial Vision*, 142–9; *Survey of London: Volume 38, South Kensington Museums Area*, ed. F. H. W. Sheppard (London: LCC, 1975), 196–200.
29. *Illustrated London News*, 8 May, 10 July, 17 July, 1886. See also the map and descriptions in *Colonial and Indian Exhibition Official Catalogue* (London: William Clowes, 1886): https://archive.org/details/cihm_05255/page/n5/mode/2up. Accessed 12 February 2024.
30. Sheppard, *Survey of London 38*, 220–27; G. A. Bremner, "Some Imperial Institute': Architecture, Symbolism, and the Ideal of Empire in Late Victorian Britain, 1887–93', *Journal of the Society of Architectural Historians* 62, no. 1 (2003): 50–73.
31. 'India at Earl's Court', *The Graphic*, 8 June 1895, 9–10; 13 July 1895, 19; 'Greater Britain', *The Graphic*, 13 May 1899, 8. See also N. Kaabi-Linke and T. Kaabi-Linke, 'Digging for Redemption', *ArtAsiaPacific* 91 (2014): 123–8.
32. J. Archer, 'Colonial Suburbs in South Asia, 1700–1850, and the Spaces of Modernity', in *Visions of Suburbia*, ed. R. Silverstone (London: Routledge, 1997), 26–54.
33. E. Walford, 'The Regent's Park', in *Old and New London: Volume 5* (London, 1878), 262–86.
34. M. Girouard, *Cities and People* (New Haven: Yale University Press, 1985), 277–8.

35 E. D. Rappaport, *Shopping for Pleasure: Women in the Making of London's West End* (Princeton: Princeton University Press, 2000), 25; Kuchta, *Semi-Detached Empire*, 18–19; H. J. Dyos, 'The Speculative Builders and Developers of Victorian London', *Victorian Studies* 11 (1968): 646–7.
36 T. Kuchta, 'Bayswater', *Victorian Review* 39, no. 1 (2013): 30–5; E. Buettner, *Empire Families: Britons and Late Imperial India* (Oxford: Oxford University Press, 2004), 212–15. As well as drapers and Whiteley's department store, marketing colonial goods and appealing to colonial clients, smaller stores included two branches of the British-India Tea & Coffee Co. and, on nearby Talbot Road, Vale & Sons, who specialised in 'Indian Condiments': see advertisements in *Allen's Indian Mail and Official Gazette*.
37 City of Westminster Archives, Building leases, 0922/003/03 and 0922/006/02–03; Drainage plans, WDP1/2/1638/173–256.
38 Booth Police Notebook, B360, 13–15; see also B355, 231–5.
39 Including Gandhi, listed as 'visitor, barrister', staying in the house of a retired British army officer at 17, St Stephen's Square.
40 *A History of the County of Middlesex: Volume 5*, eds T. F. T. Baker and R. B. Pugh (London: VCH, 1976), 218–24; D. Pam, *A History of Enfield Volume Two – 1837 to 1914: A Victorian Suburb* (Enfield: Enfield Preservation Society, 1992), 22–6.
41 *A History of the County of Middlesex: Volume 9*, ed. C. R. Elrington (London: VCH, 1989), 73–5.
42 Visram, *Asians in Britain*, 82–84.
43 P. Hounsell, *The Ealing Book* (London: Historical Publications, 2005), 7, 62.
44 In addition to 1881 Census, see W. Ernst, 'Asylum Provision and the East India Company in the Nineteenth Century', *Medical History* 42 (1998): 476–502.
45 *Survey of London Volume 50: Battersea Part 2 Houses and Housing*, ed. C. Thom (New Haven: Yale University Press, 2013), 180–91; K. A. Bailey, 'The metamorphosis of Battersea, 1800–1914: a building history' (PhD thesis, The Open University, 1995), 266–73; *The Standard*, 16 October 1880, 8; Booth Police Notebook, B366, 185–7. Other strikingly named clusters of streets occur on the Powell-Cotton estate in West Hampstead (see Elrington, *Middlesex 9*, 47–51) and the East India estate in Addiscombe (see below, note 56).
46 Kuchta, *Semi-Detached Empire*, 28.
47 C. F. G. Masterman, *The Heart of the Empire* (London: Fisher Unwin, 1907), 14.
48 R. Preston, "Against this terrible invasion of foreigners we would protest", *Cabinet* 6 (Spring 2002): www.cabinetmagazine.org/issues/6/preston.php. Accessed 12 February 2024.
49 *Gardener's Magazine* 5 (1829): 266. Quoted in R. Preston, '"The scenery of the torrid zone": Imagined Travels and the Culture of Exotics in Nineteenth-Century British Gardens', in Driver and Gilbert, *Imperial Cities*, 194–211.
50 Visram, *Asians in Britain*, 44–5.
51 A. D. King, *The Bungalow: The Production of a Global Culture* (London: Routledge, 1984); M. A. Titmarsh (W. M. Thackeray), *Our Street* (London:

Chapman and Hall, 1848). Thackeray had been born in India and lived in Young Street, Kensington, almost certainly the inspiration for *Our Street*, although there is no mention of a bungalow there in *Survey of London Volume 42: Kensington Square to Earl's Court*, ed. H. Hobhouse (London: London County Council, 1986), 46–54. Reporting Bamford's role in two linked divorce cases, the *Croydon Chronicle* (1 February 1862, 4) disparagingly referred to his residence 'in a "bungalow", dignified by the name of Selhurst Lodge'. J. Coulter, *Norwood Past* (London: Historical Publications, 1996), 126, reproduces a photograph from 1867 which shows Selhurst Lodge as a single-storey cottage with a steeply pitched ridge roof and a wooden verandah, somewhat resembling a country railway station building.

52 See advertisements in *The Times*, 27 July 1887, 15; *Morning Post*, 17 May 1890, 8; *Standard*, 5 June 1890, 8.

53 A. D. King, 'Excavating the Multicultural Suburb: Hidden Histories of the Bungalow', in Silverstone, *Visions*, 55–85; G. Gissing, *The Whirlpool* (London: Lawrence and Bullen, 1897).

54 King, 'Excavating', 61; Gissing, *Whirlpool*, 183, 198.

55 *Standard*, 24 May 1879, 8; *Standard*, 26 November 1879, 8; *Acton Gazette*, 4 January 1890, 4; *London Daily News*, 17 April 1890, 8; *Barking, East Ham & Ilford Advertiser*, 3 May 1890, 4; *Sporting Life*, 8 February 1890, 8.

56 J. C. Loudon, *The Suburban Garden and Villa Companion* (London: Longman, 1838), 325, 680; S. Muthesius, *The English Terraced House* (New Haven: Yale University Press, 1982), 84, 174, 224–5; B. Turner, *The Australian Terrace House* (Sydney: Angus & Robertson, 1995). A mid-1860s terrace on Clyde Road, Addiscombe, named after the commander-in-chief of the British army in India during the Indian Mutiny, part of an estate on the site of the former East India Company Military Seminary, is still fronted by a continuous wooden verandah: *East India Estate Conservation Area Appraisal and Management Plan*, EIAMP_20140113.indd (croydon.gov.uk) (Croydon Council, 2014). Accessed 12 February 2024.

57 T. R. Smith, 'On Building for European Occupation in Tropical Climates, especially India', *Papers read at the Royal Institute of British Architects, Session 1867–68* (London: RIBA, 1868), 197–208.

58 T. R. Smith and W.H. White, 'Model Dwellings for the Rich', *Journal of the Society for Arts*, 31 March 1876, 456–66.

59 The same architect, Matthew Digby Wyatt, was responsible for converting Elm Grove, Ealing, into the Royal India Asylum, and Cooper's Hill, Egham into the Royal Indian Engineering College.

60 R. Dennis, 'Reconciling Geographies, Representing Modernities', in *Place, Culture and Identity*, eds I. S. Black and R. A. Butlin (Quebec: Les Presses de l'Université Laval, 2001), 17–43. Most of this chapter is a case study of Oxford and Cambridge Mansions.

61 R. Dennis, '"Babylonian Flats" in Victorian and Edwardian London', *London Journal* 33, no. 3 (2008): 233–47. The visitors listed were all reported in *The Times* 'Court Circular'.

62 British Library, *Untold lives blog,* https://blogs.bl.uk/untoldlives/2015/01/victorian-office-moves.html. Accesssed 12 February 2024.
63 *The Times*, 31 December 1866, 8; 23 November 1878, 5; 20 March 1889, 12; 12 June 1897, 18; 13 November 1909, 6.
64 Beavan, *Imperial London*, 101. See also *London Post Office Directory* (1895).
65 R. Dennis, *Cities in Modernity* (New York: Cambridge University Press, 2008), 57, 121–2.
66 In my own family, the carved elephant stool brought back from the Gold Coast by my grandfather, who served in the Royal Navy from 1897, then as a telegraph officer in Egypt and West Africa, and who named his retirement bungalow 'Takoradi'.

# 9

# Australia House: shaping Dominion status in the imperial capital, 1907–63

*Eileen Chanin*

Australia House was the first of London's so-called Dominion Houses, those High Commission buildings that housed offices for the governments of Britain's self-governing colonies, or 'Dominions', as they were known from 1907.[1] These buildings opened in central London from 1918. To federationists of the New Imperial era, who held hopes of uniting a Greater Britain, these prominent semi-public government buildings materially expressed the empire (much like the Greenwich Meridian confirmed London's central world position). More than the 'nerves of empire' (over 121,000 miles of submarine telegraph cable linking the Britannic world), these prominent buildings embodied the connectedness of a hoped-for 'imperial commonwealth' to London as 'the "heart" of the imperial organism'.[2] In the first quarter of the twentieth century, imperialists believed that the Dominions would be the key to maintaining British power. Thus, these 'Empire Houses' also became a key part of London's transformation when it was ascendant as a self-consciously financial, imperial, and regal capital. Architectural landmarks occupying prime sites, designed by eminent architects, and characterised by a high order of finish, they invested London with an imperial character, even long after the term 'British Dominions' applied in the process of decolonisation.

The Dominion houses reveal, as Alex Bremner has argued, how enmeshed were London-centric and Dominion conditions and experience.[3] Moreover, they highlight how the imperial relationship meant different things to different people. Apart from constitutionally being the governing centre, London's pull as the world's financial axis bore on changing relations. Significantly, so too did the push from the Dominions for national autonomy. Britain's semi-independent polities under the Crown that enjoyed the special position of the 'old Dominions', the white settler dominions of Canada, Australia, New Zealand, and South Africa, increasingly assumed greater responsibility and independence over their own affairs. They constructed their high commission buildings as the imperial project and decolonisation overlapped. As part of that change, these buildings opened to serve the interests of each

Dominion, and therefore exhibited autonomy more than imperial might. Praised in Britain when they opened for asserting the 'Imperial ideal', these important buildings also expressed the unravelling of Britain's empire in the evolution of Dominion status from 1907 onwards.

Australia House (1913–18) set the tone for those which followed it. These were Canada House, Trafalgar Square (1924), India House, Aldwych (1928–30), and South Africa House, Trafalgar Square (1931–33). New Zealand House came in two iterations, first on the Strand in 1916, and much later at Haymarket (1959–63). Planning for Australia House began shortly after the six separate Australian states federated as the Commonwealth of Australia in 1901, a time of high imperial fervour. India House and South Africa House were built in the period of devolution. Progress towards greater Dominion autonomy accelerated during that brief time, leading to the Statute of Westminster (1931) and eventual British Commonwealth of Nations.

By that time, the Dominion houses were among 'the sights of London'; today they are nationally protected historic buildings.[4] Given this it is remarkable that contextual discussion about these landmarks is scant, just as considering the relationship between architecture and empire has remained limited.[5] Their architectural history is somewhat critically neglected, much like the architecture of empire cries for attention.[6] Writing about them has been generally subsumed within biographical or political histories of the High Commissioners. Each High Commission issued commemorative descriptions of their particular building at their opening. All these are usually written from each country's perspective, with little consideration given to what can be read from each building.[7] Viewing these buildings as single objects obscures their collective importance. The ways in which growing nationalism contributed to their conception, construction, and use has generally been overlooked, as have the effects of inter-regional differences at play within each Dominion.[8]

John M. Mackenzie, historian of imperialism, urges embracing the multiplicity of histories that comprise the imperial past, as accounts have tended to take an essentially metropolitan approach.[9] He maintains that the material remains of empire should be considered, that architecture offers clues into many aspects of the history of empire, and has called on architectural historians to fill the gap in the literature on the architecture of empire.[10] Likewise, adopting the view that things made reveal the minds of the makers, historians of diplomatic architecture, Jane Loeffler and Ron Robin, have shown that chancery buildings can usefully highlight perspectives into a nation's political and cultural history.[11] By way of comparison, Iain Black describes how differentiated were the headquarters of the principal British clearing banks built in the City of London between

1919 and 1939. Like Mackenzie, he emphasises that in light of recent post-colonial literature, noting the particularities of time and space is essential in order to capture the complexities of imperial experience when considering key architectural projects.[12]

With this in mind, I will show how architecture reflects the changing dictates of time, place, economy, and client desires. Australia House embodied the interactions that occurred between local (Australian) and imperial (British) requirements and sentiments during its conception before the First World War. I will outline the background to the building's conception and construction, before considering its impact. Australia and Canada were the principal Dominions then; issues that concerned them similarly concerned New Zealand and South Africa.

## Australia House: context and process

Australia House was built in two stages. Background is needed to appreciate why, and also helps explain what was built. Official representation in London, for the transaction of affairs between the Commonwealth and Great Britain, became essential upon Australian federation. Australia's states were individually represented by Agents-General, usually seasoned politicians. Although largely immigration and commercial agents, they actively promoted trade, facilitated commerce, and focused on financial matters with Britain for each of their states. The Commonwealth government was autonomous in its internal affairs except for foreign relations, defence, and communications. Responsible government had brought with it responsibility for local defence and internal order and local control of the colonial military forces needed for this. This made it necessary, therefore, to express in London Australia's views on its defence, together with accessing capital markets to fund the infrastructure projects required for its nation-building initiatives. For example, a condition of Western Australia federating was the Commonwealth's construction of the Trans-Australian Railway (opened in 1917). Australia needed to redress the stereotypes that still bedevilled Anglo-Australian relations following the 1890s financial crisis, which underestimated the ability and integrity of Australian politicians and which blamed (what were regarded in Britain as) excessive wages paid to Australian labour for British investment capital losses.[13] Boosting and coordinating immigration more efficiently was vital. Promoting commercial and migration opportunities in their country was integral to each Dominion's expansion and economic progress. The speed of change wrought by increasingly faster communication and transport added to the necessity for a nodal point in London to serve Australia's national interests.

## Shaping Dominion status in the imperial capital, 1907–63   251

Commonwealth representation could help diminish apprehensions about Australia's remoteness, remove confusion generated in Britain by the different states promoting their interests, and dispel British ignorance about Australian conditions.

The maturing dominions of Canada and Australia could exploit the networking and marketing potential allowed by a prominent presence in London, the world's financial and mercantile fulcrum. Thrusting for self-achievement, these Dominions looked to benefit from being part of a worldwide interlinked 'Britannic' system. Both could benefit from the chain of 'Anglo-Saxon' power encircling the globe by Britain's control of the money market, its grip on the world's shipping, and its markets.[14] London was a backdrop to their strategies for prosperity, the essential stage on which to secure advantages sought from the imperial centre.

Viewed from Australia, the empire bore little resemblance to how it was viewed from London. With Australian federation, independently minded federation fathers, confident in their own government, were ready to discard the imperial embrace even if separatist character was at odds with British notions of sovereignty.[15] As Stuart Ward pointed out, Australia's regional needs, as it forged its own national defence and foreign interests, undermined the mutuality of the imperial ideal which was understood in different ways as imperial and local priorities diverged.[16]

Melbourne was the seat of the Commonwealth government from 1901 until 1927. It was a mega-city in which lived 41 per cent of Victoria's population of over 1.2 million people. Melbourne was envied globally for its wide streets (100-feet wide), magnificent government buildings, leafy suburbs, electric trams (from 1889), and the twelve-storey Australia Building, claimed to be the world's tallest (in 1889). Architecture enhanced Melbourne's rapid rise in the wake of the Victorian gold rush between 1851 and the late 1860s. In 1904, with plans for a London building under discussion in Melbourne, federal politicians saw architecture as an important political agent in itself. They envisaged erecting in London a building that would gain stature for Australia, one to visually communicate a clear identity for Australia globally and domestically. One to serve as a symbolic statement of the magnitude and importance of the world's newest state and its only continental nation. With federation still in its infancy, to architecturally symbolise Australia's global position would both advance the new federal government's national objectives abroad and strengthen a federal mindset in Australia. A building that expressed the new nation's position in the world would represent national unity (as the Trans-Australian Railway would do), and thus help resolve local tensions among the Commonwealth's six states.

John Taverner, the Agent-General of Victoria in London (1904–19), recommended that Australia's Commonwealth government should build on the Strand for the future High Commission (established in 1910) and the Agents-General of the Australian States with their staffs. A liberal federationist, Taverner spotted opportunity with the broadening work of government departments as modern business information increasingly became more essential to commercial life.[17] Demonstrating this growing hunger for business information were the commercial museums (information centres) springing up worldwide, such as the Imperial Institute, South Kensington (1887–93).[18] Built to promote trade and foster Greater Britain connections, it was intended to perpetuate in its halls and galleries a series of exhibitions displaying colonial resources from which Britain could extract wealth. Conceived as an Imperial Hub, the Institute was the first purpose-built structure erected in London that could permanently serve as a reminder of British possessions abroad and their importance to British commercial and economic interests. Under-resourced, it failed to live up to these ambitions. In 1902 the Institute was placed under the Board of Trade. The Board's Commercial Intelligence Branch opened a trade information centre in the City, which included Trade Enquiry Offices for the governments of Canada and Queensland. Both governments demonstrated how desires for trading self-sufficiency were increasingly becoming a part of the competitive commercial environment. (The Institute's management was transferred to the Colonial Office in 1907. The Institute was demolished in 1956–62.)

Taverner advocated the centralising of Australian government offices and interests in one building, suggesting that it be identified as the 'Australian Building'. Instructed to build markets for Victoria, Taverner was mindful of the benefits to be gained from establishing a recognisable presence. An example came from the way the Equitable Life Assurance Society of America led globally in employing architecture as a valuable public relations tool. The Equitable Buildings in Sydney (1895) and Melbourne (1896) were both landmarks that matched Australian expectations for advanced buildings.[19] Consequently, London architect Alfred Burr was engaged to draw the initial plans for Taverner's 'Australia Centre' concept. These were presented to Australia's Parliament and publicised in London in 1907 (Plate 12).[20] A forerunner for uniting government agencies appeared in the 1908 Franco-British Exhibition, Shepherd's Bush, with a 60,000 square foot Australian Pavilion. Here the Australian states exhibited jointly for the first time, sharing the cost of erecting the temporary structure. Above its entrance, electric lights blazed the name 'Australia' (Figure 9.1).

Resulting from Taverner's drive, the state of Victoria led the Dominions in erecting purpose-built premises to house their government offices in London. Victoria House (1907–09) was a six-storey building with a twenty-five-foot frontage on the Strand's eastern end and a depth of sixty-five feet facing what would become a new thoroughfare named Melbourne Place,

*Shaping Dominion status in the imperial capital, 1907–63* 253

**Figure 9.1** Australia Pavilion (Entrance), Franco-British Exhibition, London, 1908. Photographed by H. W. Mobsby. Courtesy John Oxley Library, State Library of Queensland.

running from Strand to Aldwych. Designed by Burr, with R. Norman Shaw as consulting architect, it stood 120 feet high; its steel frame (among London's earliest) excited Muirhead Bone who drew it as it was erected. The building elevated government offices for Dominion members beyond their previously unimpressive state (Figures 9.2–9.3). They largely existed in Victoria Street, within flats converted to offices, where they were criticised for being inconspicuous. Victoria House suggested to observers that the imperial ideal was at last finding expression in London architecture.[21]

Always viewed as part of the 'Australian Building' scheme, Victoria House was the precursor for this larger complete plan (which London's press publicised). Importantly, Victoria House was designed as a showcase and meeting place besides housing administrative offices for the Agent-General and his staff. The ground floor, with its windowfront onto the Strand, was an exhibition space which displayed Victoria's products. This was a prototype for government buildings in central London. Up to then, governments typically displayed their nation's wares at dedicated exhibitions (like the 1886 Colonial and Indian Exhibition that triggered

Figure 9.2 'Victoria House', New London Offices for the Government of Victoria (Australia), Strand, 1909. Courtesy State Library of New South Wales.

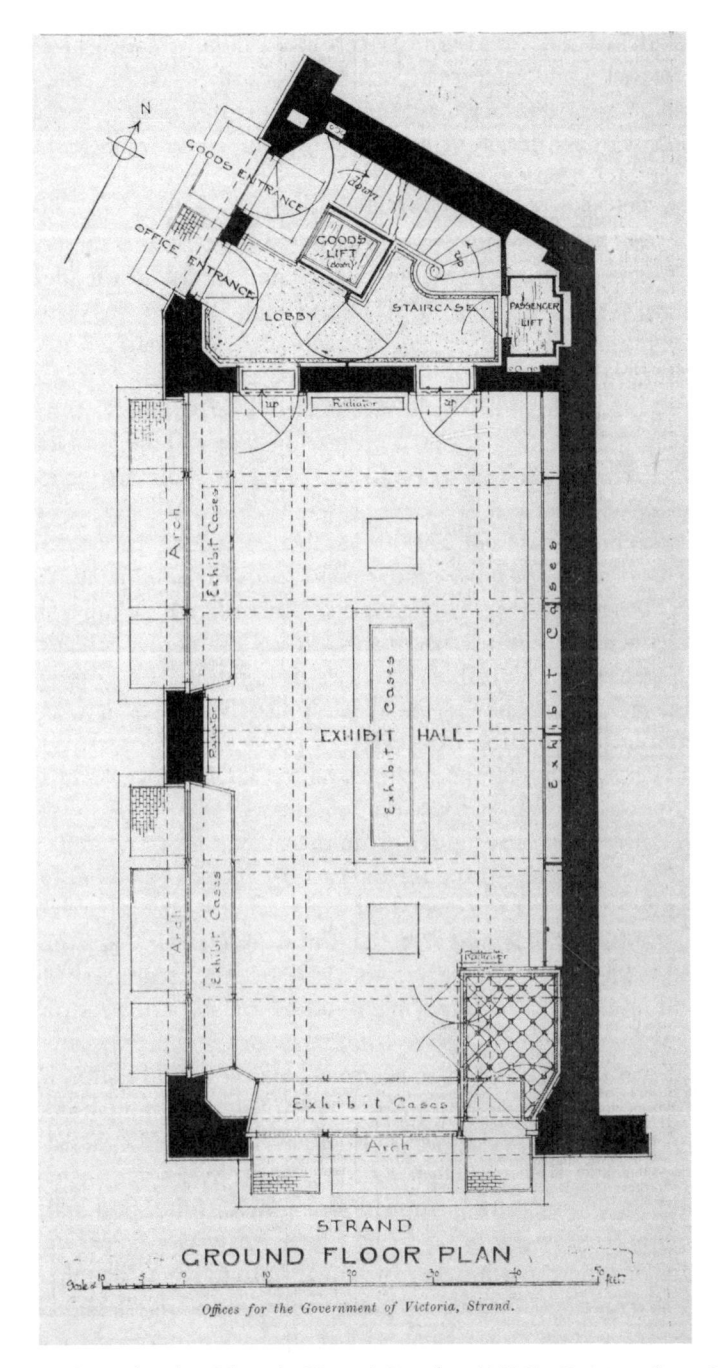

*Shaping Dominion status in the imperial capital, 1907–63* 255

**Figure 9.3** Floor plan for 'Victoria House', London (1909). Courtesy State Library of New South Wales.

the Imperial Institute), and which were now largely staged at exhibition grounds further afield, such as at Shepherd's Bush.

Victoria House was faced in Portland stone and roofed in green slate. The arches of its ground floor façade were detailed with blocked columns, every other block larger and square (a device seen in the entry arch of Melbourne's Equitable Building). The sixth floor held storerooms and could be used for additional displays. The fourth floor displayed mining exhibits. The fifth floor held reading rooms and served as a rendezvous for Victorian visitors to London. Marble and mahogany from Victoria were used throughout. Bronze fittings featured the Victorian crest, showing a demi-kangaroo, its paws holding an Imperial Crown. A gilded bronze figure representing Progress (by F. W. Pomeroy) surmounted a turret cupola roofed in copper. Victoria adopted protectionist trade policies. Doubling its trade with Britain in the four years to 1907, Victoria anticipated expanding trade relations further.

Costing approximately £16,000 (equivalent today to £1.257m), the building was in its purpose and finish, and by employing Australian materials, Phase 1 of the envisioned larger 'Australian Building'. This future centre was intended to house the offices of the Commonwealth and serve as the headquarters for Australian activities in London. The Commonwealth expected that the Australian states would house themselves in it, and invited New Zealand (a Dominion from 1907) to join them. Construction began in 1913. The war slowed and at times halted its progress. King George V officially opened Australia House on 3 August 1918.

Today, Australia House figures prominently on the Strand at its Aldwych corner. It rises on a free-standing trapezoidal block occupying an area of 24,326 square feet (a little over half an acre). Its façade stretches some 600 feet fronting the Strand (on the south and east), Aldwych (on the north), and Melbourne Place (at its western side, seamlessly adjoining Victoria House). It is an imposing building of six storeys fronted with Roman Doric columns and bronze-framed windows under a steep mansard. Styled in Beaux-Art manner, with monumental allegorical sculptural groups ornamenting its vast single east-facing bay entrance, it commands attention.

In terms of architectural expression, Australia House bypassed the neo-baroque manner typical of Edwardian buildings. Ever since ancient Greece and Rome, the classical style implied strength, security, and stability and thus was employed to express power. Classicism was a common architectural language widely used throughout the empire to strengthen the bonds of unity.[22] Buildings of the Edwardian baroque articulated the classical language of architecture in 'Grand Manner', with sculptural and decorative flourishes intended to evoke Britain's maritime domination of the globe, in what has been called the closest Britain ever came to formulating an expressly 'imperial' style in architecture.[23] Architects were urged to draw on the architecture of Britain's first empire to inspire the 'Third British Empire' of the twentieth century. Designing for London called for monumental treatment, proclaimed Stanley Adshead, Professor of Town Planning at London University, 'as understood by Vanbrugh, Wren, Poelaert, MacKim, and the rest'.[24]

Showy, stately style was what London needed to be made a capital city suitable for an imperial power. Edwardian majestic splendour was best expressed by the iconography of the Queen Victoria Memorial (unveiled in 1911, completed in 1924) as part of Aston Webb's upgrading of the Mall with funds coming from around the empire. The stately neo-classical Admiralty Arch at the Mall's eastern end was part of the axis that Webb established to give London the Processional Road it cried out for. Webb deployed formal classical style for this 'imperial vista' that linked Trafalgar Square to Buckingham Palace, the geographic and ritual centres of London. Elaborate outer gates to the Memorial represented the dominions of Australia and Canada. They encircled the Memorial at the empire's courtly centre to demonstrate the interdependency between the empire's core (the Crown) and its far-flung Dominions. Equally they indicated growing Dominion muscle: Australia and New Zealand contributed £40,000 of the £154,000 needed to build the Memorial.[25]

A more restrained classicism tempered Australia House, akin to that employed in Melbourne for the Commonwealth Offices Building (1911–13). John Smith Murdoch, Senior Assistant to the Australian Director-General of Public Works, and the Commonwealth's future Chief Architect (1923–29), designed the five-storey building. Its notable use of Victorian marble and timber and its reinforced concrete construction reflected Murdoch's predisposition to classical style and Beaux-Arts order with a ready adoption of new technology.

Murdoch knew the Westminster-based Aberdonian architect A. Marshall Mackenzie. With his Paris-trained son A. G. R. (Alick) Mackenzie, they were known for their sympathy with dignified Beaux-Arts architectural manner, an 'international style' that financial elites favoured and governments globally thought was ideally suitable for civic purposes. The Mackenzies designed the Beaux-Arts Classical Waldorf Hotel (1906–07) in London's Aldwych. It showed their sensitivity to context in designing with reference to immediate surroundings, which crucially met the London County Council's insistence that anything built nearby respected the Strand's two classical eighteenth-century churches of St Clement Danes and St Mary le Strand, and Somerset House. Having designed a scheme proposed for Canadian Government Offices in Aldwych (1907, but never built) (Figure 9.4), the Mackenzies were engaged to refine Burr's earlier plans and redesign Australia House.

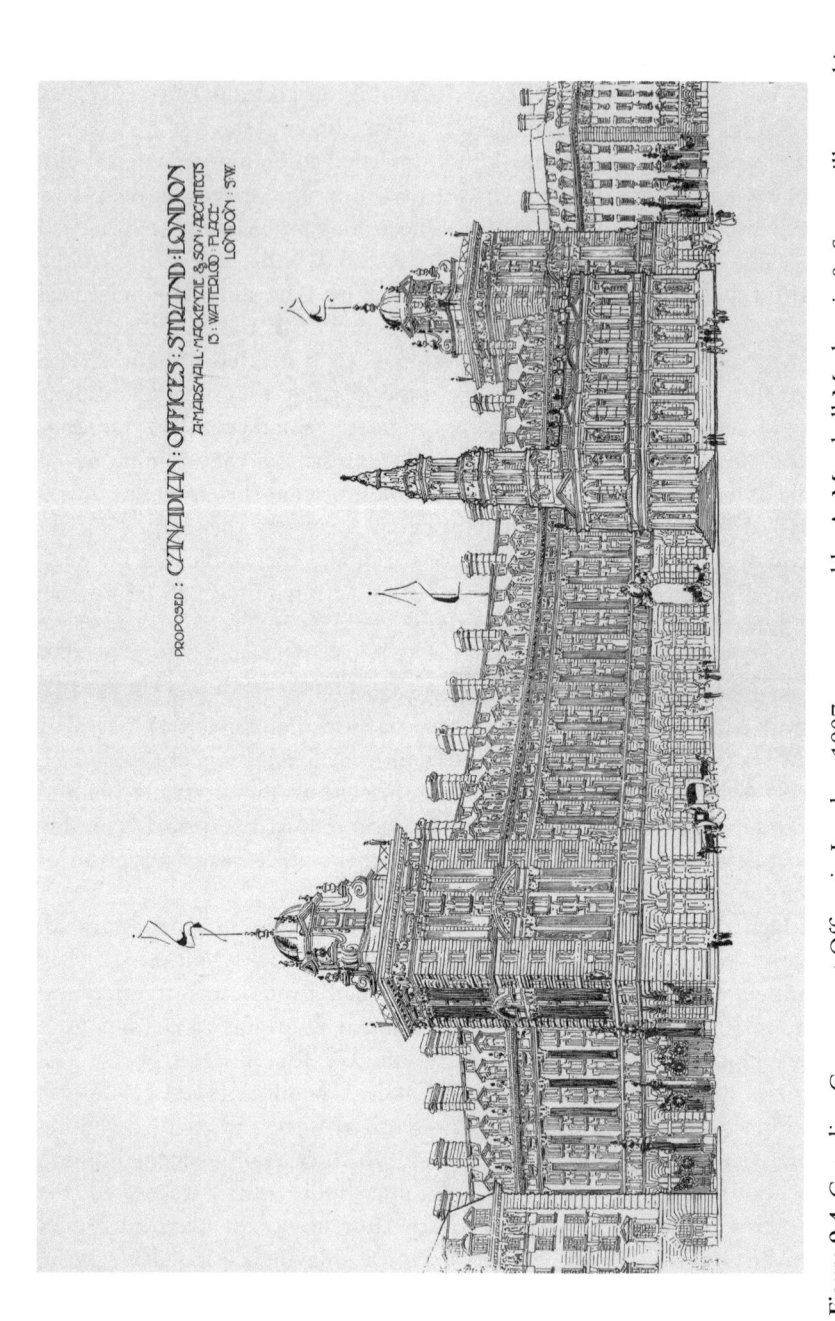

**Figure 9.4** Canadian Government Offices in London, 1907, as proposed by A. Marshall Mackenzie & Son, as illustrated in *The Builder*, 17 August 1907. Courtesy State Library of New South Wales.

A more unified composition resulted which emphasised the building's eastern entrance (Figure 9.5). Murdoch oversaw the Mackenzies and their associates, working with them in London in 1912–13, to ensure they met Australian specifications for an 'all Australian' building. Patriotic bodies and protectionist lobbyists in Australia demanded this. The Australian Natives' Association, at the forefront in their nationalist orientation, with the motto 'Advance Australia', and spokesmen at every level of the new national government (plus a branch in London from 1915), vigorously promoted achieving greater national self-sufficiency through developing local resources and manufacturing. They expected the building to showcase Australian resources, like the popular annual Australian Manufactures and Products Exhibition (which they initiated in Melbourne) promoted Australian-made products. Their boosterism matched the growing national sentiment that typified the times.[26]

Australia House was erected against the noise and rhetoric of patriots in Melbourne championing Victorian industries, of imperialists idealising about federating the empire with London as the imperial city, and about an empire bound together economically through imperial trade preference. It was a time of intense competition in the face of waning British pre-eminence when the rivalling Dominions wrestled with the imperial organisation of trade. Kinship ties were part of Dominion discourse, but Australia and Canada, both high-income countries with similar economies, pursuing protectionist trade polices to promote industrial development, and fixed on building their prosperity, grew disaffected with imperial trade relations.[27] British industry was heavily dependent on export markets, yet Australian agencies rankled at the disregard shown by complacent British manufacturers for Australian orders; requiring products better suited to particular Australian conditions, they urged that British manufacturers be more responsive to consumer demands. At the same time, Australia grew its primary resources and manufacturing capacity and foreign trade. Australia's economy revived from the 1890s depression by diversifying and building new markets for Australian wool in continental Europe. As in Canada, Australian manufacturing industries were on the rise with urban growth: in just four years to 1908, industrial production grew by 44 per cent.[28] Australian and Canadian trade grew faster with foreign markets beyond Britain when both Dominions became increasingly important markets for British traders.[29] At a time when Britain's trade with imperial and particularly Dominion markets grew faster than did its foreign trade, Australia's share of foreign trade outpaced its imperial trade and British trading connections.

Local (Australian) pressures and diverging interest (apparent in trade results) added to the independent architectural stance that Australia

Figure 9.5 Australia House, London, Strand Elevation (1918). Courtesy State Library of New South Wales.

House reflected. Similar contributing factors also influenced later Dominion houses. So too did the understandable pride which governments took in their nations' achievements. Canada's and Australia's progressiveness was evident in the urban development projects of their cities. In Australia, with possibly the highest per capita income in the world at that time, the more densely populated cities of Melbourne and Sydney embraced architectural modernity. The new capital city of Canberra was inaugurated in 1913. Buildings erected in London for Australian banking houses and Canadian shipping lines and travel companies were instant drawcards. The European Headquarters of Canada's Grand Trunk Railway System and Grand Trunk Pacific Railway opened in Cockspur Street, on Trafalgar Square's western corner, in a building designed by Aston Webb (1909). Its open-plan office space (with murals by Frank Brangwyn) provided modern office accommodation that surpassed offices of most civil government buildings in London. Premises like these, that projected and connected Dominion members to Britons, anticipated the Dominion houses.

Immigration to Australia came almost entirely from Britain and close to a million Britons migrated to Canada between 1900 and 1914. It mattered to the rival governments of Australia and Canada that better information about their countries was available in Britain. The assertive publicity that each adopted reflected the intensifying competition to attract the migrants needed to develop their countries. They promoted the opportunities that their countries represented, as many of these migrants came from London, in shopfronts that were strategically selected for maximum visibility at key London railway stations, such as at Liverpool Street and Charing Cross. An advertisement (considered London's largest) across the entire eastern wall of Victoria House, 120 feet high, broadcast the message 'Go to Australia'. An oversized electrically illuminated message board publicising Australian achievement was positioned before the site of the new Commonwealth offices, concealing Australia House under construction.[30]

## Australia House: meaning

Commonwealth politicians' views about architecture serving nation-building purpose underpinned detail designed for the building. Exhibiting the resources of Australia, in order to promote Australian prosperity and the opportunities that Australia offered, was a chief function intended for Australia House. The High Commission was the Commonwealth's only representation abroad at the time. Instructions to the High Commissioner, former Prime Minister Sir George Reid (1910–16), were to sell the Promise of Australia. Architecture that reflected Australia's potential was needed. Australia House was charged with meaning from the outset. Its purpose was to project Australia, to reflect its scale and wealth of resources, to assert national influence. The consensus in Melbourne was that offices were required that offered dignity and efficiency, to serve the Commonwealth government and its defence and commercial needs.

Over the previous half-century, colonial resources were showcased at international expositions to promote the imperial project. Both Australians and Canadians quickly recognised that these displays strengthened a sense of community and national identity. New South Wales exhibited at the Exposition Universelle, Paris (1855) held in conjunction with the Melbourne Exhibition. The hyperbole of these expositions and their displays became part of the visual rhetoric that Australia House (and subsequent Dominion houses) employed to promote their countries. Showcasing their countries' resources became part of the self-conscious modernisation that Australia and Canada pursued.

Australia House was deliberately invested with an iconography that expressed Australian character. Its façade, faced with Portland stone for the upper elevations (meeting London County Council requirements), rested on a foundation course of Australian trachyte. It matched the Bowral trachyte of the Commonwealth Stone that marked the site at Centennial Park, Sydney of the official ceremony on 1 March 1901 of the Federation of Australia's colonies and the inauguration of its Commonwealth. National emblems were explicitly added to the building's classical theme. Decorative elements of the building held symbolic or referential meanings particular to Australia. Not a single fully rigged ship, representing the oceanic origins and links of Britain's empire, appeared.[31] Pillars of Caleula marble from New South Wales dignified the first-floor library and reading room, alongside carved Australian blackbean detailed to represent Golden Wattle, declared Australia's national flower in 1912. White Angaston marble from South Australia formed the twin half-circle staircases, symmetrically located either side of the central planning axis that led into the monumental ground floor exhibition hall (Figure 9.6). In expression, scale, and detail, the whole, rich interior composition with

**Figure 9.6** Interior, Australia House, Exhibition Hall, in Buchan (Victorian) marble, looking towards entrance. Courtesy State Library of New South Wales.

Australian marbles and timbers, stucco, and plaster showcased Australian wealth, both in raw materials and skill in their use.

Another point of distinction about the building was that multiuse spaces featured in Australia House. Unlike Whitehall's government buildings, shops and banking services along its ground floor façade catered to Australian customers. Selected commercial tenants with Australia-related interests occupied upper floor offices. Australia House was a centre for commerce and information, not only for administration. The library provided business information on Australia. The Great Hall displayed Australian products. The lower mezzanine housed a hall with a stage and cinema. Films promoting Australia were screened, which Pathé cameramen filmed at the behest of the Commonwealth government (which from 1909 recognised the propaganda value of film). The varied facilities that the building offered resembled the growing multipurpose use of office buildings seen in America, as were offered in Cass Gilbert's Woolworth Building, New York (1910–13).[32] The 'historicism' of decorative finishes both buildings employed cloaked the functional technologies which were included within them to streamline business efficiency.

## Australia House: impact

The building's impact in London was immediate. Its location adjacent to Kingsway was seen to demonstrate Australian progressiveness and represent its advanced policies. The eastern Strand and Kingsway had lain undeveloped for over a decade after slum clearance by the London County Council delayed its plans for modernising inner London. Australia House established the centrality of Kingsway–Strand as a prestigious business hub, midway between Westminster and the City, and hastened development of the neighbourhood's unoccupied sites.

The Dominion of New Zealand followed Australia's example by occupying leased premises on 413–416 Strand. The new building designed by Westminster architects Crickmay & Sons opened in May 1916. With a Strand frontage of fifty feet, its window-front promoted New Zealand products and opportunities to be found in a country populated by barely one million people. Clustered on the Strand, like satellites to the Commonwealth, were the offices for the governments for West Australia, Queensland, and South Australia, similarly displaying their state's wares in their shopfronts. Accustomed to their Agents-General customarily promoting their requirements, Australia's states resisted centralising in Australia House. The Western Australian Government moved its agency from Victoria Street to Savoy House, a converted five-storey building cornering Savoy Street on the Embankment side of the Strand. Its displays in the plate-glass window frontages, running forty-one feet along the Strand and sixty-five feet down Savoy Street, attracted attention. Queensland's agency occupied a ground floor showroom on 400–410 Strand, near the Adelphi Theatre, within what had been Gatti's restaurant, with a ground floor space of polished Aberdeen granite columns.

The office of the Agent-General of British Columbia was different from these conversions. The Canadian province, resisting the dominance of central Canada, had Cubitts erect a new building of 36,000 square feet over five floors (with a dormered attic) on a 100-foot frontage at 1 and 3 Regent Street. Here, Alfred Burr designed a display and office centre in Roman palazzo-style. Finished in Portland stone ashlar with a prominent entrance bay, it opened in December 1915. The building was notable for its ground floor exhibition space where British Columbian products were displayed.

### Shaping Dominion status?

Australia House was opened as Australia moved into the sphere of international politics, in the quickly evolving landscape of foreign relations during the first three decades of the century. The purposefulness that it took to build Australia House through 1914 to 1918 reinforced the impression it gave that Dominion Status (imperial unity) and autonomy could coexist. Britain's entering into war without consulting its Dominions tested loyalties. Direction for defence was undertaken by the British Cabinet. Dominion forces were put under British command. The Dominions proved a fundamental strength for Britain during the war. Australia House symbolised this as it stood unfinished into 1917. Its visible steel skeleton served as a reminder of the bonds of union within the empire, particularly (as time passed) of how much Britain owed to its Dominion partners in its unfinished business in the Fight for Right. In the course of the war, the Dominions developed a degree of autonomy with a right of direct reference to their own governments. Visiting prime ministers attending the cabinet meetings of the Imperial War Cabinet (1917–19) reinforced the importance of the Dominions. Australia, Canada, New Zealand, and South Africa were founder members of the League of Nations in 1919 (as was India, the League's only nongoverning member). Australia, New Zealand, and South Africa gained territory from Germany. Independently signing the Treaty of Versailles and joining the international community effectively ended their dependent Dominion status.

Alongside this reality, ambitions were strengthened to officially confirm London's position as the imperial hub. The war's end bolstered the empire movement. Britain gained from the war additional territory and population that made its empire unrivalled worldwide, with a quarter of the world's population. Imperialists believed the time was opportune to make London an imperial capital, sparing no effort to make London worthy of its larger significance as the heart of the empire.[33] Australia House was seen as an example of this (Figure 9.7). The *Times of India* reported that the Commonwealth commitment, made by a total population of less than five million spending a million sterling on their London headquarters, gave remarkable evidence from Australians 'of their sturdiness of spirit and of their whole-heartedness in shouldering the responsibilities of Imperial partnership as well as in enjoying its advantages'.[34] Press reports universally expressed admiration for Australia House's dignity and its prodigality in material and space. English architect Herbert W. Wills, editor of *The Builder* (1913–18), with wide experience abroad (including Canada, and New York with McKim, Mead & White), praised its distinctive display of rich detail. He stressed the decorous use of emblems from Australia and made much of the agreeable harmony of materials employed, such as was too seldom found. In the journal's verdict, 'We can call to mind few modern buildings of importance which have occupied their sites with such good results, both in themselves and to their surroundings.'[35] The dual significance of the centrality and importance of Australia House as a landmark building to both Australia and to London was recognised in the 1919 victory march. When allied troops paraded around the building, it stood as a dual symbol of its different identities, central foremost to Australian nation-building and to London's modernising, rather than the imperial imagination.

## Conclusion

Australia House was a conspicuous presence on the Strand. It connected the east end of the Strand to its western end (toward Trafalgar Square, to Whitehall and Webb's Admiralty Arch). It combined in the one assemblage a monumental building, a block of offices, and a gateway to the Aldwych and Kingsway. It was universally hailed as one of the most significant architectural features of London. It formed a striking and dignified object from every point of view, thought *The Builder*, which praised Australia House for giving an example to London.[36] But the journal overlooked the real example which Australia House gave in the immediate postwar period to the other Dominions. The strength of the building reflected their changed standing and recognition as sovereign states (as enshrined in the 1931 Statute of Westminster).

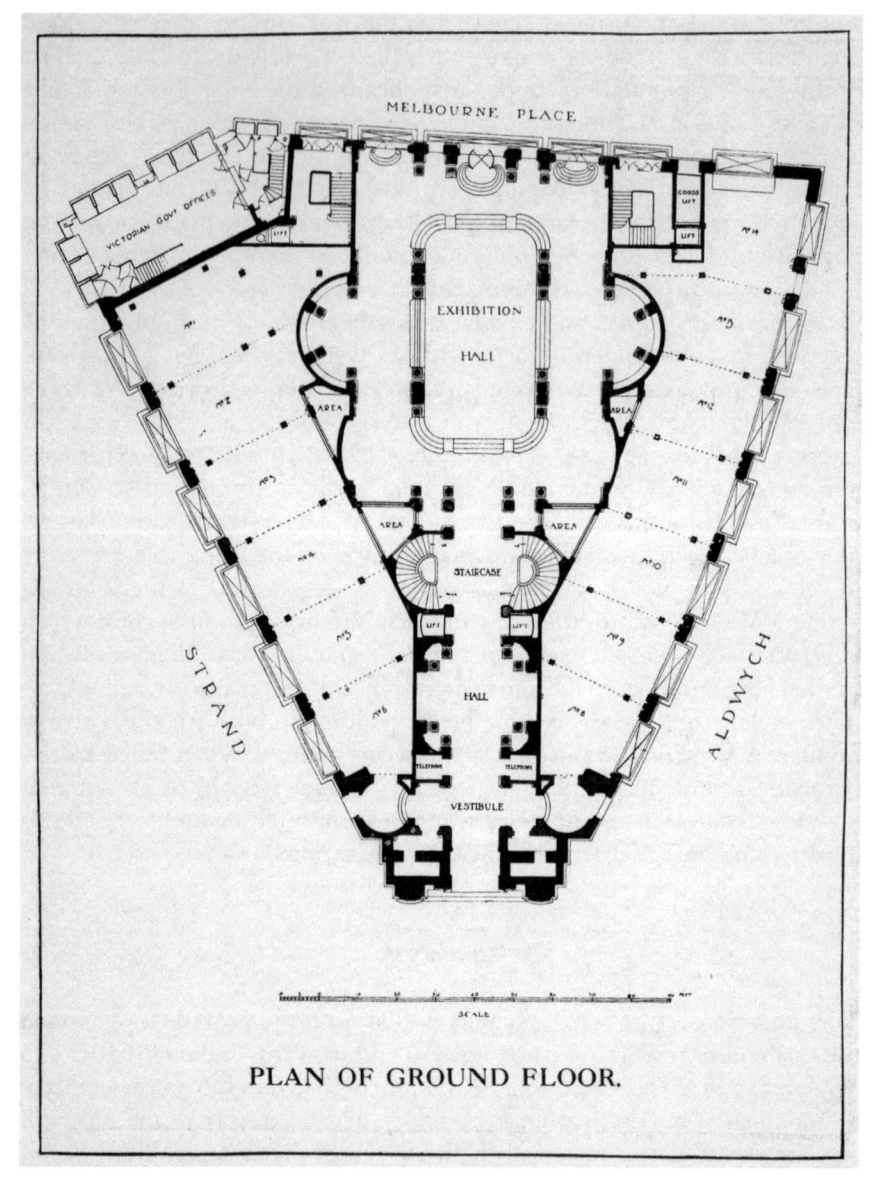

Figure 9.7 Australia House, ground floor plan (1918). Courtesy State Library of New South Wales.

To those in Britain who clung to the imperial ideal and to making London a city of empire, the Dominion houses were the most prominent architectural presence of 'Greater Britain' and so conveyed sense of imperial rule. If pleasing to imperial federationists, they were also about national advance (Australian, Canadian, even Indian). Rising nationalism matched two coronations (for Edward VII in 1902; George V in 1911) and Imperial Durbars (1903, 1911). Hence the Dominion houses represented a host of differentiated attitudes to empire that were closely related to domestic politics in the Dominions and associated visions of the future. Seen one way, they represented the 'Dominion Idea' (thought vital to underpinning a third British empire), and represented the essence of Greater Britain.[37] London County Council members (principally Sir Laurence Gomme, first Clerk of the Council (1990-14), saw Australia House as a building of imperial identity, as part of London's push to create 'the Empire City'.[38] Read otherwise, these Dominion buildings were 'National Houses' and, like Australia House, they were more about nation-building than about empire.

A 'Britannic' commonality might be assumed from the 'dominion uniformity' seen in these classically styled buildings, but the variety displayed in details within each declared their national character. If imperialists desired buildings with a dignity commensurate with empire and an imperial capital, the four settler Dominions, and even the yet-to-be Dominion (later Republic) of India, each insisted on representation in London with stateliness commensurate with their nation's importance. As buildings of identity, if dressed in imperial 'style', London's Dominion houses were more about national interests. Style and purpose intertwined with them, just as Dominion and imperial centre (London) were intertwined.

Uniquely, Australia House was the only purpose-built Dominion house to open while the term 'Dominions' still effectively applied. Canada's path to a High Commission building in London highlighted the rapidity of imperial dismemberment. In 1912, the erection of suitable offices in London for Canada's high commissioner and immigration staff was urged in the Canadian House of Commons. The prime minister, Mr Borden, said he favoured constructing a building worthy of Canada and the empire, and noticed the satisfactory effort made by Australia in this respect.[39] In 1925, Canada converted a building designed by Robert Smirke (1827) on Trafalgar Square, the heart of Britain's nationalism. In 1926, Britain upgraded the Dominions section of the Colonial Office to a separate Dominions office with its own secretary of state; Canada ceased using 'Dominion of Canada'. It opened a legation in Washington (1927), and Paris and Tokyo (1928). Canada's government, being most insistent to end the ongoing vestiges of subordination to the Mother Country, highlighted how the Britannic dream of Greater Britain was irrevocably changed.

Even imperial architect Sir Herbert Baker responded to shifting sentiment. Baker (with Alexander Scott) designed both India House and South Africa House for their governments (Figure 9.8). In both, as in Australia House, national emblems superseded iconography that communicated imperial power. Rather than highlighting imperial allusions, as Baker customarily did, he made play of national symbols (with Indian-inspired motifs and South African details). Baker's India House featured inlaid marbles, mural paintings, and carvings in rare Indian woods created by native craftsmen. Emblems of the religions, the provinces, and the states of India spurred King George V to remark: 'The building which contains them surely testifies to the unity of India in herself.'[40] He hoped that, 'The position of India House among those of her sister nations here in the centre of my capital, further symbolises the unity of the greater Commonwealth of which she is a part.' Events in India proved that two-fold unity would be impossible, with postwar resistance to surrender any degree of national sovereignty to any sort of imperial unity. In South Africa's building, spaces were designed to promote national products (with all the material brought from South Africa), and to pursue

**Figure 9.8** Herbert Baker, South Africa House, Trafalgar Square, London (1933), from *The Builder* (14 April 1933). Courtesy State Library of New South Wales.

national business. They included a cinema theatre, travel information bureau, visitors' reading room, and an exhibition hall. South Africans prided themselves on their 'national house', representing their Union that was seen as improbable less than thirty years before.

If Australia House, and the Dominion houses which followed it, manifested Britain's imperial reach, they did so in the empire's twilight. For Dominion members, their buildings expressed their moving away from political subordination to standing as equals. They symbolised the effective unravelling of empire that followed in the immediate aftermath of the war. As they opened, they reflected the strong and ever-growing instinct for independence that changing imperial affairs mirrored. The Balfour Declaration issued by the 1926 Imperial Conference of empire leaders declared the Dominions 'autonomous Communities within the British Empire, equal in status, in no way subordinate to another in any aspect of their domestic or external affairs, though united by a common allegiance to the Crown'.[41] At that conference and then in the Statute of Westminster in 1931, Great Britain created the British Commonwealth of Nations. With this, Britain divested itself of the burden of political rule. The loose association of self-governing countries were equal in status to one another but bound together by common loyalties.

Much later, in 1963, long after the term 'Dominions' held currency, the government of New Zealand, the last Dominion to adopt the Statute of Westminster in 1947, was usurped from the Strand by development plans for the building it leased. It built its tower block at Haymarket, just off the Western end of Trafalgar Square. A general-purpose office block, it effectively completed the ring of buildings erected by the former 'old Dominion' members, in the orbit of Trafalgar Square that Australia House began some four decades earlier. Much like the way that Webb achieved an imperial statement with his Arch in 1911, the Dominion buildings delineated what some regarded in the 1930s as an 'Imperial Precinct'. No longer on the outer perimeter (as at the Victoria Memorial), the proximity of their buildings to Trafalgar Square stamped this zone of central London with a character that evoked Britain's recent imperial past while they also mirrored the speed and scale of international change.

During the ensuing decades each of the Dominion buildings in London would play a unique role in projecting their nations, as they continue still to do. Exhibitions in the Grand Hall of Australia House promoted Australian products. That space and the building's theatre and library became venues for the social and business events that made the building become known as 'Australia's House' in London. It played a central role in the lives of countless Australians in London as well as Britons and others for whom the building became their portal to Australia.

## Notes

1. For different meanings that applied to the term 'Dominion' over time, see Peter C. Oliver, '"Dominion status": History, Framework and Context', *International Journal of Constitutional Law* 17, no. 4 (2019): 1173–91.
2. George Peel, 'The Nerves of Empire', in *The Empire and the Century: A Series of Essays on Imperial Problems and Possibilities by Various Writers*, ed. Charles Sydney Goldman (London: John Murray, 1905), 249.
3. G. A. Bremner, *Architecture and Urbanism in the British Empire* (Oxford: Oxford University Press, 2016), 126.
4. 'Sightseeing', *Daily Telegraph*, 6 December 1930, 8. Most are Grade II listed buildings on The National Heritage List for England (NHLE): historicengland.org.uk/listing/the-list.
5. Bremner, *Architecture and Urbanism*, 5.
6. John M. MacKenzie, 'Buildings of Empire, by Ashley Jackson', *The Journal of Imperial and Commonwealth History* 42, no. 3 (2014), 578. For Australia House in the context of London, see Eileen Chanin, *Capital Designs, Australia House and Visions of an Imperial London* (North Melbourne: Australian Scholarly, 2018). In recent literature, South Africa House has received attention in part because work on its interiors continued after its opening into 1938. See Frederico Freschi, 'The Fine Art of Fusion: Race, Gender and the Politics of South Africanism as Reflected in the Decorative Programme of South Africa House, London (1933)', *de arte* 40, no. 71 (2017): 14–34.
7. Examples include Roy MacLaren, *Commissions High: Canada in London, 1870–1971* (Montreal: McGill-Queen's University Press, 2014), 232–4. Carl Bridge, Frank Bongiorno, and David Lee, *The High Commissioners: Australia's Representatives in the United Kingdom, 1910–2010* (Barton, A.C.T: Dept. of Foreign Affairs and Trade, 2010). Roy Macnab, *The Story of South Africa House: South Africa in Britain, the Changing Pattern* (Johannesburg: J. Ball, 1983). For commemorative examples, see High Commission (Great Britain), *India House, London: Opened by His Majesty King George the Fifth, Emperor of India, July 8th, 1930* (London: Tuck, 1930); H. L. G. Pilkington and Sir Herbert Baker, *South Africa House Opened by His Majesty the King, Accompanied by Her Majesty the Queen, on 22nd June, 1933* (London: Office of the High Commissioner, 1933).
8. Bremner, *Architecture and Urbanism*, 12.
9. John M. MacKenzie, 'The British Empire: Ramshackle or Rampaging? A Historiographical Reflection', *The Journal of Imperial and Commonwealth History* 43, no. 1 (2015): 100.
10. MacKenzie, 'Buildings', 578.
11. Jane Loeffler, *The Architecture of Diplomacy: Building America's Embassies* (New York: Princeton Architectural Press, 2011); Ron Theodore Robin, *Enclaves of America: The Rhetoric of American Political Architecture Abroad, 1900–1965* (New York: Princeton University Press, 2014).

12 Iain S. Black, 'Rebuilding "The Heart of the Empire": Bank Headquarters in the City of London, 1919–1939', *Art History* 22, no. 4 (1999): 601.
13 Geoffrey Bolton, 'Money: Trade, Investment, and Economic Nationalism', in *Australia's Empire*, eds Deryck Schreuder and Stuart Ward (Oxford: Oxford University Press, 2010), 218.
14 Ronald Hyam, 'The British Empire in the Edwardian Era', in *The Oxford History of the British Empire: Volume IV: The Twentieth Century*, ed. Judith Brown (Oxford: Oxford University Press, 1999), 58.
15 John Hirst, 'Empire, State, Nation', in Schreuder and Ward, *Australia's Empire*, 151–4.
16 Stuart Ward, 'Security: Defending Australia's Empire', in Schreuder and Ward, *Australia's Empire*, 242–3.
17 Chanin, *Capital Designs*, 110.
18 Dave Muddiman, 'From Display to Data: The Commercial Museum and the Beginnings of Business Information, 1870–1914', in *Information Beyond Borders: International Cultural and Intellectual Exchange in the Belle Epoque*, ed. W. Boyd Rayward (London: Routledge, 2014), 259–82; Mark Crinson, 'Imperial Story-lands: Architecture and Display at the Imperial and Commonwealth Institutes', *Art History* 22, no. 1 (1999): 101–14; G. A. Bremner, '"Some Imperial Institute": Architecture, Symbolism, and the Ideal of Empire in Britain, 1887–93', *Journal of the Society of Architectural Historians* 62, no. 1 (2003): 50–73.
19 Chanin, *Capital Designs*, 40.
20 For example, see 'The Strand Site: Commonwealth Building', *Daily Telegraph* (London), 23 November 1907, 7.
21 Chanin, *Capital Designs*, 127.
22 As Herbert Baker expressed it in his designs, see *The Times*, 3 October 1912, 7–8. See also Jan Morris, *Stones of Empire: The Buildings of British India* (Harmondsworth: Penguin, 1994), 19–21; Jan Morris, 'In Quest of the Imperial Style', in *Architecture of the British Empire*, ed. Robert Fermor-Hesketh (Weidenfeld and Nicolson, 1996), 10–31.
23 G. A. Bremner, *Building Greater Britain: Architecture, Imperialism, and the Edwardian Baroque Revival, c.1885–1920* (London and New Haven: Paul Mellon Centre for Studies in British Art/Yale University Press, 2022).
24 S. D. A., 'Civic Design at the Royal Academy', *The Town Planning Review* 1, no. 2 (1910): 155.
25 Tori Smith, '"A grand work of noble conception": The Victoria Memorial and Imperial London', in *Imperial Cities, Landscape, Display and Identity*, eds Felix Driver and David Gilbert (Manchester: Manchester University Press, 1999), 21–39.
26 Peter H. Hoffenberg, *An Empire on Display: English, Indian, and Australian Exhibitions from the Crystal Palace to the Great War* (Berkeley: University of California Press, 2001), 275.
27 Richard Pomfret, 'Trade Policy in Canada and Australia in the Twentieth Century', *Australian Economic History Review* 40, no. 2 (2000): 114–26.

28 Chanin, *Capital Designs*, 111.
29 Andrew Dilley, 'The Politics of Commerce: The Congress of Chambers of Commerce of the Empire 1886–1914', *Sage Open* 3 (2013): 5.
30 'Australia's advertisement in the Strand', *Manchester Guardian*, 16 August 1912, 5.
31 As appeared in Herbert Baker's Dominion Columns, New Delhi (1931). See Bremner, *Architecture and Urbanism*, 116.
32 Gail Fenske, *The Skyscraper and the City: The Woolworth Building and the Making of Modern New York* (Chicago: University of Chicago Press, 2008), 6.
33 Lord Meath, 'London as the Heart of the Empire', in *London of the Future*, ed. Aston Webb (London: T. Fisher Unwin, 1921), 258.
34 Chanin, *Capital Designs*, 267.
35 'Australia House', *The Builder*, 15, no. 3936 (1918): 19.
36 'Australia House', *The Builder*, 15, no. 3939 (1918): 76.
37 John Darwin, 'A Third British Empire? The Dominion Idea in Imperial Politics', in Brown, *The Oxford History of the British Empire*, 64.
38 Laurence Gomme, 'Australia and the Island Site, Aldwych', *The Builder* 101, no. 3595 (1911): 357.
39 'Proposed Canadian Offices in London', *The Builder* 102, no. 3599 (1912): 91.
40 'The King's Plea for Indian Unity', *Daily Telegraph*, 9 July 1930, 12.
41 National Archives Australia CRS A4640, Imperial Conference 1926 Inter-Imperial Relations Committee, Report, Proceedings and Memoranda, Printed for the Imperial Conference, 1926, 3: www.foundingdoc.gov.au/resources/transcripts/cth11_doc_1926.pdf. Accessed 20 October 2019.

# 10

# Empire timbers: architecture, trade, and forestry, 1920–50

*Neal Shasore*

At the heart of the programme of the Royal Institute of British Architects' (RIBA) new headquarters at 66 Portland Place (opened in 1934) was the Florence Hall. Dominating the *piano nobile*, the space was deliberately designed to be multifunctional: it served as an examination hall, an exhibition gallery, and a banqueting facility. It was a space, therefore, at the very centre of Imperial British architectural culture: where its aspiring members were tested; where professionals' work was shown; and where its networks convened and politicked. An almost hallowed space, the Florence Hall evoked a basilica plan church: a tall 'nave' running its length, with lower 'side aisles', decorated splayed piers, and an ornamental ceiling, all intensely illuminated with different modes of natural and artificial light (Figure 10.1). There may have been no equivalent of an altar, but there was, at the climax of the plan, a metaphorical reredos made up of twenty relief panels, known as the Dominion Screen (Figure 10.2).

The panels were carved in timber by the London firm of joiners, Green & Vardy, to the designs of the sculptor Denis Cheyne Dunlop, and depicted the flora, fauna, industries, and peoples of the Dominions and India. The screen formed part of an Imperial iconography which ran throughout the RIBA's new headquarters, aimed specifically at emphasising a White Settler confraternity of architects drawn from the Federal Commonwealth of Australia, the Union of South Africa, the Dominions of Canada and New Zealand, and British India. This emphasis reflected the deliberate policy of supporting trade links between the semi-autonomous Dominions (recognised in the Balfour Declaration of 1926) and the United Kingdom through Imperial Preference following the Ottawa Conference of 1932.

The screen's panels were arranged in a matrix: along the horizontal axis, the individual Dominion nations – Australia, South Africa, India, Canada, and New Zealand;[1] and along the vertical axis, fauna, industries, peoples, and flora, from top to bottom. Sandwiched between stylised protea and springbok, waratah and kangaroo, lotus and elephant, maple leaf and

Figure 10.1 The Henry Florence Memorial Hall, 66 Portland Place (George Grey Wornum, 1934). Courtesy Architectural Press Archive/RIBA Collections.

beaver, silver fern and kiwi, were depictions of imagined (rather than necessarily observed) craft traditions, trades, and industries.

Such an ornamental scheme might seem an unexpected theme for a professional institute of architects, but the Dominion Screen implicitly connected architecture to, or rather situated it in, a wider political economy and ecology; a practice contingent on the wealth of the empire, derived from industrial enterprise, beginning with the extraction of its natural resources; and part of a wider visual and material culture which simultaneously fetishised indigenous craft and culture whilst being reliant on processes which erased them. In the South African section of the grid, as an example, one panel (Figure 10.3a) depicted a diamond mine set amidst a forest clearing (indicated by a stylised palm and fern in the foreground): it is likely to have been an abstracted representation of the De Beers Kimberley Diamond Mine and its 'Big Hole' pit – the distinctive headframe and chimneyed factory building are often featured in contemporary photographs of the site, and Table Mountain looms behind the mine shaft. The counterpoint to this industrial scene is a depiction of a bare-breasted figure – perhaps a Xhosa woman – pounding maize with a pestle and mortar (Figure 10.3b), with a seated child looking on as a hen pecks at his plate. Two Xhosa huts are made out in the background. In the New Zealand column, livestock

*Empire timbers: architecture, trade, and forestry, 1920–50* 275

**Figure 10.2** View of the Dominion Screen, designed by Denis Cheyne Dunlop (carved by Green & Vardy). Courtesy Architectural Press Archive/RIBA Collections.

**Figure 10.3** Details of the Dominion Screen showing the industry of South Africa (a *left*, b *right*). Courtesy Architectural Press Archive/RIBA Collections.

is represented by another hen and a calf contained in a pen, representing agriculture; and people and craft are represented by a Maori woman knitting a flax *kete*, adjacent to carved *pouwhenua*. And in the panels depicting Canada, a First Nations trapper, holding a gun in his right hand and fox in his left, grimaces as he navigates a snowy terrain with 'bear paw' snowshoes. The industry panel figures a moustached white Canadian poised with an axe to fell a tree. The stylised fronds in the top left of the panel suggest a species of pine. The stacks of logs in the background emphasise the theme of lumberjacking and forestry.

The Canadian lumberjack scene is all the more poignant because the screen for which it was carved was made from Quebec pine (*Pinus strobus*), also known as Canadian yellow or white pine, described in a contemporary handbook of timbers as 'easily worked', and 'well known for its suitability for pattern-making ... light building construction, joinery, interior finish, cabinet work and deck planking'.[2] This coincidence – of depicting lumberjacking (quite literally of pine), expressed in the extracted material – reinforces or makes manifest both the moment of extraction but also its transportation, crafting, and working into something else. In this sense it speaks to the concept of the reciprocal landscape identified by Jane Hutton, and the dialectic between 'site' and 'non-site', what she describes as the 'back and forth between the distant production site and designed landscape' in order to bring them 'at least conceptually, closer together'.[3]

Quebec pine was one of an almost infinite number of 'empire timbers' – woods grown overseas within the forests of the British empire – promoted by the British government and the timber trade to the domestic market.

Architects and those involved in the wider world of construction were among the primary consumers of these products, specifying their use in a range of buildings and projects in the United Kingdom. It formed but one strand of a wider trade policy debate, in which free trade was pitted against a belief in protectionism, essentially a reduction in multilateral trading through Imperial Preference, privileging products from the Dominions and Colonies in order to rely less and less on foreign markets and global competitors.

The Dominion Screen at 66 Portland Place – in its inextricably tied material, making and meaning – is a manifestation of the equally intertwined processes of Imperial forestry (and extractivism), trade policy, and architectural design and construction in the twentieth-century British empire. Its physical positioning at the heart of architecture's imperium – the RIBA's headquarters – shows how vividly, yet implicitly, this was understood by contemporaries. The screen was not merely decorative, but rather indicative, even representative, of architecture's profound implication in ecology and coloniality, as defined by decolonial thinkers such as Anibal Quijano and Walter Mignolo.[4] The nexus of modernity and coloniality points to the epistemic as well as economic, political, cultural, and indeed aesthetic attitudes which drove colonialism and Imperialism, and which indeed endured beyond political decolonisation. The empire timber campaign is a representative example of this endurance, as strategies to promote intra-imperial trade and forestry in the years after the First World War gave way to a conception of the Commonwealth in the decades after the Second World War.

We will return to 66 Portland Place and the RIBA later on; the Dominion Screen, however, serves as a useful framing device for this account of empire timber – an amorphous but essentially contiguous campaign – fostered by various departments, agencies, and bodies of the British government, as well as a number of associations, institutes, and commercial entities, to promote timber imports and cater to the domestic market, reducing reliance on foreign markets, in particular the United States and Eastern Europe export trade. This is not, however, a detailed economic assessment of the empire timbers campaign; it does not try to account in depth for any significant market shifts. Certainly, recent work in economic history has reaffirmed the profound effect that political commitment to imperial preference, cemented by the Ottowa Conference of 1932, had on trade; there was a significant growth in Imperial imports over the 1930s across many sectors and commodities. The timber market, however, remained largely dominated by cheap softwood imports from foreign sources, though anecdotal evidence suggests a growth in trade in more exotic hardwoods, in particular from West African colonies (namely Nigeria and the Gold

Coast), which were heavily promoted from the 1930s, alongside trade with the semi-autonomous Dominions, and especially Canada and India. The focus here instead is on the ways in which the empire timber campaign was supported by architects, and how the architectural profession and wider design community sought to give material expression to the principles of tariff reform and imperial preference.

This chapter stems from – and connects to – two concurrent discourses within architectural design and construction in the early twenty-first century, both stemming from climate emergency and its corollary of ecological collapse. First, the renewed emphasis on timber and timber construction as sustainable and inherently regenerative versus more carbon intensive and extractive materials and constructional technologies; timber is presented by some of its contemporary proselytisers as a panacea.[5] The historical dimensions of debates about timber have begun to be considered, but normally in relation to their longer pedigree in Modernist architectural discourse or in indigenous technologies of building. Recent scholarship in environmental humanities has detailed the long histories of modern forestry techniques rooted in imperial eco-development which are not often acknowledged in architectural discourse. Second, there is a growing body of critical thought and historical research on race, space, and architecture, as well as a maturing historiography on architectural/built-environment histories of the global south, and an understanding of extractive colonial and racial capitalism's influence over the built environment.

These have, as this volume has sought to show, omitted to consider how these dynamics played out in the production of built environments on the British Isles. Decolonial thought and its praxes have also been implicitly related to questions of race, space, and heritage: the Rhodes Must Fall campaign first in Cape Town and then in Oxford, alongside the Confederate monuments controversy in the United States, have drawn attention to the complex implication of space-making, building, and design in the British imperial project and enduring racial inequality, in the case of the US linked to long legacies of the transatlantic slave trade. In the public discourse these discussions have inevitably focused on individuals and discrete monuments rather than on more nuanced ecological and cultural entanglements. In order to explore decoloniality's potential for both architecture as an academic discipline and an epistemic formation, as well as a practice in the production of the built environment, architectural history must continue to emphasise the imbrication of built and natural environments: architecture relies on certain forms of land tenure and 'productive landscapes'; forestry and the timber trade are part of architecture's coloniality. We cannot seek to effectively 'decolonise' architecture (if that is indeed what we want to do, or are able to do), or more accurately, embed or bring into *re-existence* (paraphrasing Walter Mignolo) more ecologically harmonious interrelating built and natural environments, until we have a more comprehensive and lucid understanding of how architecture is historically and epistemically implicated in coloniality.[6]

Colonial trade and imperial eco-development have, of course, longer histories. The trade in mahogany in particular in the eighteenth century is one established case study.[7] The mid-nineteenth century saw the Museum of Economic Botany at Kew established in 1847 explicitly to stimulate interest in colonial woods, and then this was further catalysed by the development of more sophisticated forestry management techniques in India from the 1860s. The Economic Botany Collection acquired donations from aristocratic landowners but also exhibits from international trade shows, including the Great Exhibition and the London International Trade Exhibition. These donations led to the establishment of the Timber Museum and later, in 1910, the Museum of British Forestry.[8] As Kew increasingly focused on scientific research, methods of bureaucratic colonial organisation, developing trade policy, and political debate moved the emphasis on empire timbers away from Economic Botany. Kew became one of a number of bodies responsible for research into and promotion of empire timber, including the Forest Products Research Laboratory at Princes Risborough (1923), the Imperial Forestry Institute founded in Oxford (1924), the trade-led Empire Forestry Association and its *Journal of Empire Forestry* (1922), and the Imperial Institute who convened an Advisory Committee on Empire Timbers (1916). These formed typically twentieth-century frameworks for global imperial research and development to bolster commercial trade.

Moreover, twentieth-century architecture – particular interwar architecture, and architecture which was not necessarily modern or avant-garde – has been little considered where it may be useful to understand more mainstream attitudes and elements of a liberal consensus about the role of the architect and the means of producing architecture. I have argued elsewhere that this period was a critical one in the formation of the modern profession, irrespective of our taste for the stylistic eclecticism shown in design.[9] Katie Lloyd Thomas has articulated a 'proprietary turn' in interwar architectural practice – what she has called the emergence of the 'architect-as-shopper'. Architects were, in her formulation, 'commodity-brokers for the manufacturing industry', 'firmly in the service of capitalism'.[10] With a global network of supply chains, however, there were important colonial dimensions to the sourcing, manufacture, and distribution of materials and products within the construction industry yet to be discussed.

Though a continuous and contiguous campaign, there were nuances in the promotion of empire timbers at various moments in the early decades of the twentieth century. Debates about and promotion of empire timbers were often deliberately *re*newed, wilfully obscuring earlier attempts to develop the market, whilst rehearsing the same arguments – this is a reflection of market dynamics, and commerciality's appeal to the novel or original. Empire timber was caught up in the rhetorics of maturing practices of public relations, sales, and marketing, themselves responding to the vicissitudes of political and economic events such as postwar economic recovery, fears of a declining US market, and the move towards imperial preference. Moreover, there was a fundamentally different market for softwoods and hardwoods: softwoods – especially from Eastern Canada and British Columbia, promoted heavily in the 1920s – had potential for use in timber-frame construction, whereas hardwoods – in particular from Indian, Australian, and West African tropical species – were used more often for veneers, fixtures, and fittings. The maturing hardwood market was connected with the growing use of plywood in interior design and furniture-making.

The remainder of this chapter considers a series of 'episodes' in the campaign to promote empire timber by and for the architectural profession between 1920, the year of the Empire Timber Exhibition organised by the Department of Overseas Trade to coincide with the first British Empire Forestry Conference in London, and 1950, three years after the fifth British Empire Forestry Conference also held on 'home' turf, opening in London and closing in Oxford. These events were thereafter known as the British Commonwealth Forestry Conference, indicating a political shift in the postwar conception of empire. Oxford was chosen in part to celebrate the maturation of the Imperial Forestry Institute, whose establishment had been stimulated by the first conference, and whose building – the last case study in the chapter – was then being completed to the designs of Hubert Worthington on South Parks Road, on the periphery of the university's 'Science Area', not far from Herbert Baker's Rhodes House. Between these two landmark events – the first and fifth Empire Forestry Conferences – the chapter focuses on the presence of empire timbers at the British Empire Exhibitions at Wembley (1924–26) and Glasgow (1938) and between them the establishment of the Building Centre in 1932 which housed special displays of empire timbers, which in turn influenced the specification of Dominion woods for the RIBA's new building at 66 Portland Place. Empire timbers were ubiquitous in the built environment of interwar Britain, as we shall see. But the focus of the case studies included here are where forestry practice and research, promotion of intra-imperial trade, and a specific appeal to or implication of an architectural market converge; these moments, all of which were displays and exhibitions – variously temporary or more permanent – are productive opportunities to explore architecture's coloniality.[11]

## Market shapers: the Empire Timber Exhibition, Holland Park

The First World War had exposed Britain's reliance on the continental and US markets for a number of essential commodities for military and industrial purposes, among them timber. Wartime conditions had strengthened a powerful vision that self-reliance through imperial preference would protect Britain against such vulnerability. As a result, the government established a Forestry Commission in November 1919 under the auspices of the Forestry Act (1919). The Commission's charges included promoting education, undertaking research, and supporting forestry and timber supply, and as part of its initial investigations it sought to establish the extent of forestry resources across the British empire. Empire woods were considered an untapped source – the contemporary press noted that the empire 'embraces some 2,000,000 square miles of forest, and many of the chief timber trees of the world flourish within its borders'.[12] Whereas the United Kingdom derived about 10 per cent of its imported supplies of wood from the empire, it was estimated 80 per cent of its timber furniture was made from American oak.

The new Commission's first forays culminated in the first British Empire Forestry Conference held in London in July 1920, bringing together representatives of forestry and the timber trade across the empire.[13] Coincident with the conference, the Department of Overseas Trade – formed in 1918 to coordinate commercial trade and intelligence – had, since October 1919, been actively arranging a British Empire Timber Exhibition at Holland Park Ice Skating Rink.[14] Organised by a committee of senior figures in imperial forestry (including representatives from Newfoundland, South Africa, and New Zealand), it also sought to include representatives from the architectural profession and wider building trades, including representation from the RIBA and its rival professional body the Society of Architects. There was also an attempt to include Builders Associations from across the regions (including those of London, Cardiff, Liverpool, and York).[15] Its object, as the Exhibition catalogue set out, was to bring 'into more universal use the numerous though little known timbers of the Empire'.[16] There were stands organised by governments and administrations of colonies and Dominions: eighteen in total, including Canada, South Africa, and New Zealand, but also Trinidad, East Africa Protectorate, the Gold Coast, Nigeria, and the British North Borneo Chartered Company. India and Western Australia's stands housed the largest displays. Individual firms also exhibited, as did the Ministry of Labour and the Worshipful Company of Carpenters.

The trade exhibition was hardly spectacular – many of the displays were perfunctory. Guiana's stand, for instance, simply comprised largely rough sawn boards of various specimens. But in the larger Dominion displays, and indeed in the UK's exhibit, clearly greater resource was directed. In the Western Australian section, examples of York gum, largely made in the nineteenth century, were shown to demonstrate its durability in construction – there were paving blocks, posts, and rafters whose antiquity was emphasised in the catalogue. There was also a small panelled room of kiln-dried Jarrah replete with eighteenth-century style Jarrah furniture. Among the importers, the British Canadian Export Co Ltd showed Canadian kitchen dressers, cabinets, and refrigerators, including a 'mass production ready cut dresser' supplied for housing schemes and builders, made in Canadian birch and elm: 'This dresser,' it was claimed, 'is a vast improvement on the old type open dresser, and it combines practically every recommendation made by the Women's Advisory Committee on Housing and Reconstruction.'[17]

Though unremarkable in its mode of display – of poor attendance (it ran for eighteen days and garnered 6,500 visitors)[18] – the British Empire Timber Exhibition is significant for what it tells us about its perceived audience. That is partially revealed by the striking exhibition poster designed by the cartographer, typographer, and architect Macdonald Gill. Evoking a Tree of Jesse it comprises a tree trunk formed of intertwining yellow and white stems, opening out into branches gripping plaquettes showing the diverse uses of timber – in the centre, houses, but also furniture (beds, desks), fences, panelling, and flooring. Gill had produced a number of significant commissions for Frank Pick, then of the London Underground Electric Railways Company of London (UERL), including the 'London Wonderground' map ('Paying Us Your Pennies') and was part of Pick's design reform milieu.[19] It was through Pick that Gill gained the commission from Stephen Tallents of the newly established Empire Marketing Board in 1926, designing its emblem and a number of its posters. The Empire Timbers Exhibition's enlightened patronage of Gill, and its focus on design, construction, and finishing trades speaks to the close connection between design reform and strategies to promote intra-imperial trade seen later on in the decade through the activities of the Empire Marketing Board.

The other active architectural presence in the Empire Timbers Exhibition was the architect H. D. Searles-Wood (1853–1936) who chaired the General Purposes Sub-Committee organising the exhibition. Searles-Wood had a particular interest in constructional technology: he had served as President of the Concrete Institute and was a member of the councils of the Institution of Structural Engineers and the British Standards Institution. His interest in empire timber presumably stemmed from this element of his practice (he was not a particularly accomplished designer).[20] He certainly had given serious consideration to the use of Eastern Canadian softwoods in construction, spurred on by research produced by the Forest Products

Research Laboratory. Searles-Wood had also chaired the Imperial Institute's Timber Advisory Committee since its establishment in 1916; its remit was 'to consider the question of the wider utilization ... of new or relatively little-known Empire timbers, and to advise in connection with the work on timbers carried out'.[21] The committee published a regular series of reports on timber products from colonies and Dominions, a number of which were published in the *Bulletin of the Imperial Institute*. The committee played an active role in the long campaign for empire timbers: in 1928 it arranged its own exhibition to accompany the publication of its 'Descriptive List of Some Empire Timbers'.[22] Crucially the centrality of architecture, and architect-designers (a number of whom were connected to the late Arts and Crafts and the wider Design Reform movement) featured prominently in the exhibition: Indian timber doors designed by Sir Herbert Baker for India House, for instance, as well as examples of 'Australian blackwood silky oak' veneers and parquet flooring. The Imperial Forestry Institute in Oxford provided exhibits 'to illustrate the principles of silviculture, forest management, tree growth, and diseases and pest of trees'.[23] Architects were explicitly courted by the Institute to promote timbers through specification: a special lunch was hosted for members of the RIBA in May 1928, and the responsibility of the profession was spelt out in no uncertain terms: 'The ultimate ... reason why the Empire timber import was so small was that architects did not specify Empire woods in their professional practice. They were the final arbiters nearly always; they could recommend the woods to their clients and demand them from their timber merchants.'[24] This echoed concerns voiced by *inter alia* the *Financial Times* who, reviewing the Empire Timber Exhibition, bemoaned low attendance by architects, and an ignorance of, if not prejudice against, colonial lumber from the profession.[25]

The Empire Timber Exhibition was heralded by its organisers as the first such dedicated exhibition. This was clearly contestable: permanent displays of empire timbers had featured at Kew for decades, and were an established feature of international expositions, including at the Great Exhibition, the 1862 London International Exhibition, the Forestry Exhibition at Edinburgh in 1884, and the Colonial and Indian Exhibition of 1886.[26] It was, however, the first trade display backed by a formal and definitive policy established by the Forestry Act and Forestry Commission, and represented a nascent commitment from Dominions and colonies to cultivating a competitive market through the Empire Forestry Commission. Furthermore, the specific appeal of the exhibition-makers to the design professions and construction trades, and indeed the representation of the professional body in its organisation, shows the keenness of architects to shape the market for empire timbers.

## The British Empire Exhibition, Wembley

The British Empire Forestry Conference led to the establishment of two more permanent institutions directed towards commercial development and research and training. The Empire Forestry Association (EFA) was founded in 1922 'to federate in one central organization voluntary associations, individuals and corporate bodies engaged or interested in the growth, marketing and utilization of timbers throughout His Majesty's Dominions'.[27] Critically this voluntary body intended to move with greater agility and initiative than 'government-run business', perhaps belying an innate conservativism to forestry practice, mistrustful of an expanded state's capacity to shape the market. The Imperial Forestry Institute was established in 1924 as a training centre for forest officers, providing information and advice to a global practice of forest production. The institutional framework to support the promotion of empire timbers was developing.

As the debate about imperial preference continued in political circles, its advocates marshalled 'soft power' to promote the ideal of intra-imperial trade: these were, much like the EFA, not always direct governmental interventions. This was most manifest at the British Empire Exhibition at Wembley (BEE), held over two seasons between 1924 and 1926.[28] Trade and national pavilions provided an opportunity to showcase empire goods, including timber: 'The Empire Forestry Association hopes to utilize the British Empire Exhibition as a means of stimulating interest in this important subject, and to supplement the individual displays of the Dominions and Colonies by a central collection of hand samples.'[29]

Some minor controversy was aroused during construction of the exhibition site over the summer of 1923: despite the large amount of concrete infrastructure designed by the architectural firm Simpson and Ayrton with Owen Williams as consulting engineer, timber was used extensively for fencing and the set design for the pageant of empire held in the Empire Stadium.[30] It became clear, however, that empire woods had not been procured – it was first alleged in *The Times* by a disgruntled former official of the exhibition, that a colleague had suggested 'that it was impossible to get suitable timber for the Exhibition within the Empire, and passed round a sample of what he described as very inferior Canadian spruce':[31] 50,000 sq ft of Baltic timber was supposedly used 'to provide walls for decoration in the Stadium in connexion with the Pageant of the British Empire'.[32] The irony was clear: one of the most prominent expressions of the campaign to promote empire goods failed to abide by its own foundational principle, not only due to alleged ignorance of materials available, but also because of the inflexibility of a supply chain that could not deliver necessary product at speed.

It was true that postwar efforts to promote empire timber were not yet yielding material success. *The Times* reported that in the 1922 annual statement of trade, timber imported into the UK from foreign countries amounted to £32,512,634, whereas imports from the empire stalled at £4,808,383.[33] Despite this disparity, it was cheerily reported that 'the English market consumes large quantities of Empire-grown timber': though striking a more critical tone, it was warned that: 'It is not sufficient to know that large tracts of unexploited forest land exist in various parts of the Empire. It is far more vital to know that adequate facilities for the transport, shipment, and grading of the felled timber have been provided.'[34]

Unlike at Holland Park, there was no dedicated concentrated display of empire timbers at the BEE once it opened. Displays of UK and empire timbers were instead distributed across the various pavilions, including a number of quaint examples, such as the half-timbered Tudoresque building by the Federated Home Grown Timber Merchants' Associations and a Scottish 'village' hall in coniferous timber, decorated by Scottish artists for the Forestry Commission. In the Royal Pavilion in the UK Government Pavilion, English pollard oak panelling sat alongside Australian black bean.[35] Empire softwood's potential for construction was on display in the Canadian Section – there was bungalow in British Columbian timbers, including Douglas fir, red cedar, western hemlock, stika spruce, maple, and pine. The Burma Pavilion itself was crafted in timber by 'native' craftsman in teak and pyinkado, and featured 'finely panelled rooms', also in pyinkado, Burma teak, padauk, and haldu, along with scale models of 'famous buildings, shrines and woodwork from Rangoon and Mandalay'.[36] Africa, the *Empire Forestry Journal* noted, was somewhat of an unknown quantity, including timbers 'which have never been put on the world market, and their uses are in many cases unknown'[37] – it was not until the 1930s that the potential for the hardwood market in African timbers was more heavily promoted, though their presence at the Empire Exhibition in 1924 shows the voraciousness for new products and materials already in play at this time.

The success of the British Empire Exhibition was a clear demonstration of the efficacy of new propaganda and publicity methods in promoting intra-imperial trade. Often overlooked, there were significant links between its strategies of display and collective advertising and the Empire Marketing Board (EMB) established in 1926.[38]

### The Building Centre and 66 Portland Place, 1932–34

The EMB played a central role in the promotion of the empire timbers campaign. Established in 1926 by Leo Amery, and under the secretaryship of the pioneering public relations professional, Stephen Tallents, it championed the use of commercial art, posters, editorial, documentary film, and exhibitions to stimulate the market for Dominion produce: to 'bring the empire alive' for the consuming public. Artists such as Spenser Pryse and McKnight Kauffer produced notable posters for the EMB, as did Macdonald Gill, whom we encountered earlier, visualising for the public the networks of intra-imperial production, trade, and supply. There were notably posters advertising forestry: the Scottish artist Keith Henderson produced a series showing empire forests, labelled 'West African Mahogany', 'Australian Jarrah', 'A Teak Forest in Burma', and so on. These showed trees set amongst the flora and fauna of the forest in a state of unperturbed innocence; in the case of Burma, however, two mounted elephants are depicted in the thick of the forest, with a plush and verdant valley in the background, dragging teak logs. Extraction and production also featured in a poster by Ba Nyan (Plate 13), the Burmese painter trained in London, showing 'Timber Stacking': an elephant stacks a log atop a mounting pile of timber with a timber factory behind. The visualisation of supply and production was a common trope at the zenith of extractivism of colonial resource; significantly, as has been suggested, the institutions and protagonists of design reform were willingly enlisted to give it imaginative expression.

The EMB enthusiastically took up the cause of promoting empire timber, in particular to architects and the construction industry. Through a capital grant, it had extended the Forest Products Research Laboratory at Princes Risborough – 'at EMB charges to deal with Empire Timbers', as Stephen Tallents put it – seeking to establish a more rigorous regime of testing of new products.[39] There is a clear analogy with the Building Research Station and the ideal of research in architectural production.[40] A register kept at the Empire Marketing Board's offices attempted to provide a ready record of the use of empire timbers, in particular on government schemes promoted by the HM Office of Works or by municipalities. On Liverpool local authority housing schemes, for example, black spruce was used for roof timbers and general carcassing; the Office of Works used Douglas fir flooring for telephone exchanges at Kensington, Sutton, Colchester, and elsewhere, and indeed on the British Museum's Newspaper Repository at Colindale. Government clearly sought to set an example to wider industry, who readily took up the challenge: at a slight remove, Douglas fir was also used on panelling at the Pine Restaurant housed on the third floor of the Civil Service Supply Association's Department Store at 425, the Strand. The Friends Meeting House, Euston Road, used British Columbia western hemlock for the framing of the public hall, doors, and panelling, and at Ellis and Clark's Daily Express Building on Fleet Street, the boardroom, panelling, and doors were made of the same material. In 1933 the 'Buy British' Sub-Committee of the Forum Club – formerly the London Centre for Women's Institute Members – held an exhibition at their premises at 6 Grosvenor Place of 'Empire Timbers', in conjunction with the EMB. *The Times* architectural correspondent reported on the 40 'specially designed pieces of furniture and a display illustrating the use of Empire timber in panelling, flooring and sports accessories'.[41] Major firms of the period were represented, including Heal's with an Indian laurel wood cabinet, works by Betty Joel, and a special exhibit by Gordon Russell of Princess Elizabeth's 'Playbricks in Empire Woods'.[42]

The EMB was, therefore, active in cultivating an architectural market. Nowhere was this more clearly demonstrated than through its cultivated links with the Architectural Association's Building Materials Bureau – a permanent display of materials and proprietary products, curated by a former student, J. K. Winser. The Bureau was fast becoming a valuable service to AA members, digesting and standardising technical information about materials and proprietary products to facilitate better specification by architects for projects. By 1930, its collection represented 850 firms, responded to around 50 enquiries or visitors per week, and held a collection of materials catalogues, including a number of empire timbers. In its itinerant exhibition space at various properties on Bedford Square, the EMB had indeed sponsored a special exhibit for empire timbers. The EMB's campaign to promote empire timber was aimed at the popularisation of empire woods through 'the creation of an appetite by, and the education of, the public which would lead to a demand at present non-existent'.[43] A cornerstone of this campaign was to cultivate a sense of responsibility among architects and engineers to specify the use of empire timbers and to ensure their uses had been properly tested and the material properly treated.

By the early 1930s, the AA Building Materials Bureau was expanding and transitioning into a more commercial enterprise; inspired by similar institutions in New York and Berlin, it was re-established as the Building Centre in 1932. Supported by the AA's secretary, F. R. Yerbury, and a number of senior AA figures who served as the Centre's first board of directors, the project was bankrolled by the Gluckstein brothers who owned the contracting firm Bovis, underwriting the refurbishment of the former French Gallery on New Bond Street to provide it with a prominent site aimed at female consumers in particular.[44] Opened in autumn of 1932, the new Building Centre, housed across four floors designed by a number of its directors, included not only a display of empire timbers, but also displays of information produced by the Building Research Station and the Forest Products Research Laboratory about testing they had conducted on use, including the prevention of disease. The display itself (Figure 10.4) comprised fifty

**Figure 10.4** Empire timbers exhibit on the first floor of the Building Centre, photographer unknown (c. 1932). © Building Centre, London.

woods contained in a 'semi-circular display rack of the Empire Marketing Board, herein is housed in bookcase fashion a specimen of every Empire timber described in their recent handbook ...'.[45] Within the semi-circular floor space of the stand, one firm laid 'a fancy parquet flooring which shows the possibility of Empire woods for decorative floor covering'.[46] In addition, specimen miniature floors of hardwood strips were laid by Hollis Bros & Co, 'the well-known firm which has for many years devoted tremendous energy and solid hard work to the advancement of Empire woods on the floors of British buildings'.[47]

The British Empire Economic Conference (1932) – better known as the Ottawa Conference – was a significant milestone in the EMB's empire timbers campaign, buoyed by the formal policy adoption of imperial preference, despite ultimately leading to the EMB's obsolescence. Stephen Tallents prepared a proposal for the Interdepartmental Preparatory Committee in advance of the conference to demonstrate how tighter coordination in the promotion of empire timbers might work in practice. The memorandum is revealing in demonstrating how ad hoc arrangements had been. Tallents proposed a UK-based committee, probably attached to the EMB, with representatives of Canadian trade alongside the UK institutions involved in the testing and marketing of timber. The Dominion government would then institute a body in Canada to coordinate and cooperate with the UK committee. A group of 'Technical Officers' would split their time between the UK and Canada, liaising with supply and consumer sides of the market. Both governments would need to invest significant resources in the scoping of the market.[48] This sophisticated public relations scheme indicates a shift from the somewhat laissez-faire approach that had been taken in the 1920s. H. L. Stewart, writing in the late 1930s, perceptively commented that empire timbers were being promoted somewhat naively, first of all because 'timbers of undoubted merit created a bad first impression through being presented to the user in an unsatisfactory condition', and further failure was secured 'due to imperfect organization, by which zealous sales propaganda was allowed to outrun available stocks, with the result that the early favourable impression caused by shipments was entirely effaced by a reputation for unreliability'.[49]

This more coordinated way of thinking, and indeed the resolutions of the Ottawa Conference to focus on UK trade with the Dominions, was manifest both at the Building Centre, but also in the fitting out of the RIBA's new headquarters at 66 Portland Place designed by George Grey Wornum, who won the institute's 'Empire-wide' open competition in 1932. Wornum, an advocate for the use of wood in particular in interior design, had been a senior figure at the AA, serving as its president between 1930 and 1931, and sitting on the first Board of Directors at the Building Centre. Unsurprisingly, therefore, empire timbers were a prominent feature of the Portland Place building; clearly, Wornum's insistence not only on the extensive use of wood, but specifically on empire timbers grew out of this connection at the Building Centre.

There were other motivations too: the architect and Conservative MP Alfred Bossom had promoted empire timbers for use on the new headquarters to the institute's secretary, Ian MacAlister, having introduced him to Philip Cunliffe-Lister in April 1932 at a House of Commons lunch to promote empire timbers along with another architect, Arthur Knapp-Fisher. Cunliffe-Lister, then Secretary of State for the Colonies in the National Government, having served as President of the Board of Trade, was impressed by the 'clear evidence I had of the keenness of British architects to help Empire timber', and suggested that 'Empire timber could get no better advertisement than its presence' in the new institute building. Bossom, endorsing the suggestion, exhorted MacAlister to pursue the suggestion 'now that we have taken on this policy of trying to think of Empire, and with a little common-sense protection …'.[50] Bossom was actively promoting the use of softwoods at this time, announcing at his luncheon party that the London County Council had ordered over 900 'standards' of British Columbian timber for structural use in housing projects, including at Becontree.[51] Indeed the LCC was felt to play a significant role in opening up the market; through the stringent fire safety regulations under the London Building Act, it could determine which timbers could be marketable.[52]

The imperial dimensions of the architectural profession's organisation have still not yet fully been grasped. Certainly there was a centrifugal impulse: from the 1890s, the RIBA – having begun life as a fairly limited metropolitan club – had been actively federating with what it called 'Allied and Provincial' societies, in part to bolster its membership and strengthen its position as the leading imperial architectural institute. In 1934, the institute's centenary year, it had forty-nine allied societies, including four South African bodies, one in East Africa (modern Kenya), one in Rhodesia, seven in Australia, and one each in New Zealand, Canada, Burma, India, and Malay; these were represented in the governance of the profession through the institute's council, which saw itself as a professional parliament. As the Liverpudlian architect Bertram Kirby noted: 'we who are of the same race and who are accustomed to conduct our affairs under the influence of the same loyalties and ideals however infrequently defined, need hardly be surprised to find ourselves adopting similar policies and principles to those which have consolidated the British Empire'.[53] It is for these reasons, alongside the political and economic resolutions of the Ottawa Conference, that the White Settler Dominions – 'we who are of the same race' – were represented prominently at 66 Portland Place. It was the Dominions and the British Raj in India where trade and commercial links were most actively pursued, and this is reflected in the iconographical programme of Portland Place, rather than the various dependent colonies, protectorates, mandates, and informal trading colonies which comprised the rest of the extent of the British empire. We have seen this in the specific case of the Quebec pine Dominion Screen.

Empire timbers featured extensively throughout the building. Indian silver grey wood was used extensively, on the flooring of the Florence Hall, and in the furniture and fittings of the library. The sliding doors of the reception room on the first floor were veneered in walnut, teak, and laurel. English and Australian walnut, as well as Canadian maple, faced the walls and doors of the council chamber. Black bean, ash, and teak were used in the Jarvis Hall auditorium. All these woods were advertised by the EMB, and it seems clear that Wornum was keen to incorporate their use into Portland Place as a showcase. The *Evening News* reported that 'architects from all over the country who have been viewing their new temple during this week are making excited inquiries now about certain Empire woods and marbles', the latter an allusion to the red-veined black marble encasing the huge steel stanchions of the building frame.[54]

The relationship between the Building Centre and the RIBA's new premises at 66 Portland Place is a demonstration of the colonial and imperial dimensions of architecture's proprietary turn. The new headquarters building was intended as a subtle but deliberate permanent display of the institute's attempt to position architecture as part of a transnational professional service. The interior spaces of the new building quite literally framed their functions in empire timber, celebrating and acknowledging this absorption in a global network of supply. And yet, though often omitted from accounts of 66 Portland Place, the presence of empire timbers largely took the form of plywood veneers, a fact oddly concealed in contemporary discourse.

### Rise of the hardwoods: the British Empire Exhibition, Glasgow, 1938

Whereas hardwoods were considered a 'reserve of much promise' in the 1920s,[55] by the mid-1930s more and more hardwood products were coming to market. At Ottawa, efforts were made to 'ensure a greater degree of uniformity in standard specifications and trade practices' for hardwoods,[56] and this data was codified in the *Grading Rules and Standard Sizes for Empire Hardwoods* published in 1933.[57] Hardwood veneers were used extensively at 66 Portland Place as facings for plywood wall finishes.

With the winding down of the Empire Marketing Board in 1933, the campaign to promote empire timbers was taken up to a great extent by the Timber Development Association (TDA). The TDA had been established by the Council of the Timber Trade Federation in March 1934, essentially as its publicity committee. It had promoted competitions for design in timber, the results of which were displayed at the Ideal Homes Exhibition of 1936, and later a competition with the RIBA for farm-workers cottages held in 1938. Alan Powers has set out the TDA's role in promoting timber as a modern material.[58] The TDA's presence at the Empire Exhibition in Glasgow, held also in 1938, was another early success for its public relations campaign. It was claimed by the TDA's mouthpiece, the trade journal *Wood*, that 80 per cent of the exhibition was constructed in timber, including much of the amusement park, the wooden restaurant in the Tower of Empire, the Forestry Pavilion, and the Timber Development Association model village on the periphery of the exhibition site (Figure 10.5). The TDA's own pavilion was designed by Robert Furneaux Jordan, whom Powers establishes as 'the chief modernist spokesman for timber'.[59] The pavilion was built entirely of empire woods, using fifty-six varieties and demonstrating 'the practicability of timber construction on a large scale'. The pavilion housed horizontal bands of facing woods, illuminated by an upturned scull with concealed light fittings and 'hanging light-fittings of coiled plywood' (Plate 14).[60]

Hardwoods were promoted heavily; *Wood* included a special supplement on timbers from the Gold Coast. Bemoaning that land 'is still in the possession of the African, and domestic and agricultural pursuits are of more importance than afforestation', it was nonetheless celebrated that 'cultivation and extraction methods are being improved, and exports are steadily being increased'.[61] Much of the West African Pavilion was given over to the Gold Coast 'showing there the timbers available for export' arranged to 'show appropriate uses for floors, doors, wall treatment, furniture, display cabinets, and other fitments'.[62] The Nigerian section was also 'designed to draw attention to the decorative qualities of the native timber'.[63] Just as in Wembley, traditional construction and craftsmanship from Burma was celebrated: entirely constructed of wood, the 'low sweeping double roof is finished off with slates of teak, stained with red ochre in accordance with local custom' (Figure 10.6).[64]

## The Imperial Forestry Institute, 1950

Forestry, trade, and architecture once again converged in the conception and design of the Imperial Forestry Institute in Oxford. Established in

Empire timbers: architecture, trade, and forestry, 1920–50 293

Figure 10.5 The Timber Development Association's Pavilion, British Empire Exhibition, Glasgow (1938). Courtesy Architectural Press Archive/RIBA Collections.

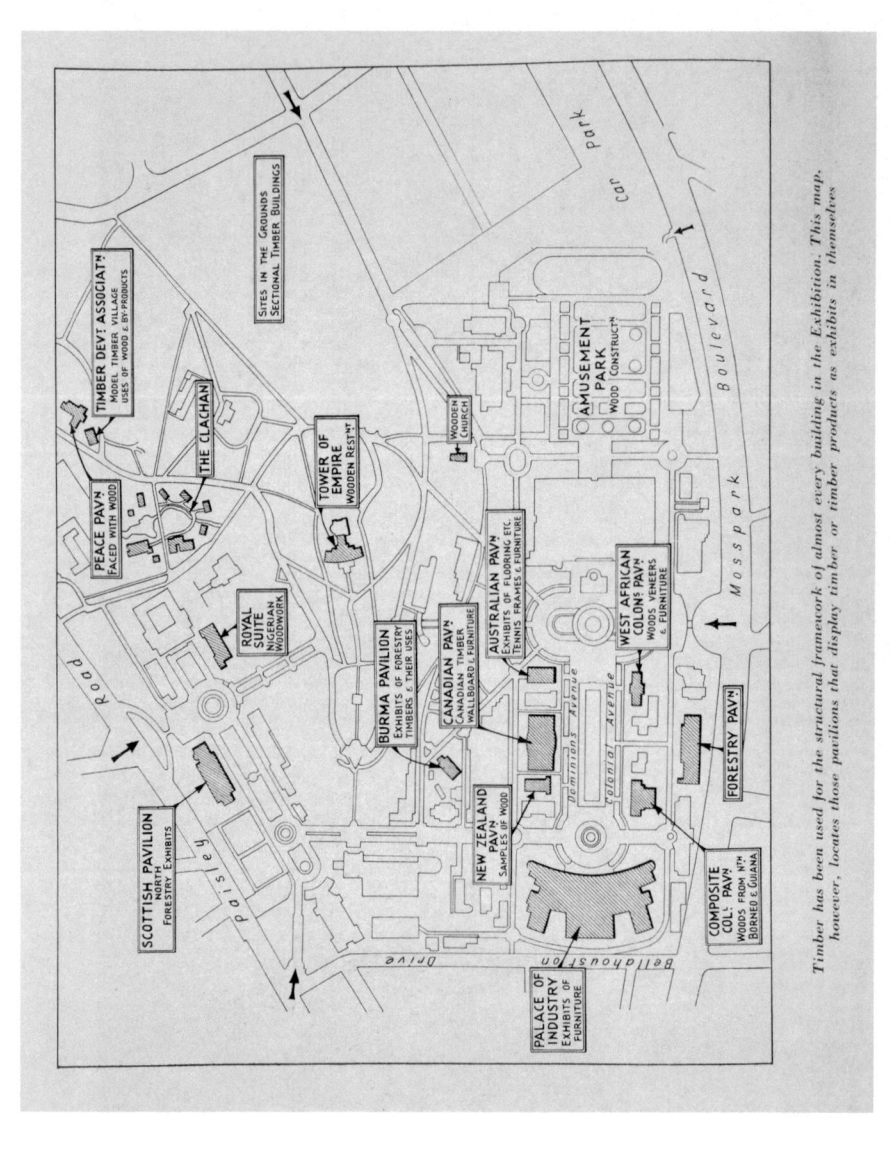

**Figure 10.6** A plan of the Glasgow British Empire Exhibition showing timber use across the exhibition site. Courtesy RIBA Collections.

Timber has been used for the structural framework of almost every building in the Exhibition. This map, however, locates those pavilions that display timber or timber products as exhibits in themselves

October 1924, it was intended as a 'central institution for the advanced training of forest officers and as a centre for research into the formation, tending and protection of the forest'.[65] It was connected to the Department of Forestry in the university, and indeed eventually merged with it in 1939. It had sought new premises in the early 1930s, bolstered by a £25,000 donation from the Rajah of Sarawak, and in 1934 a site was found in South Parks Road with designs drawn up by 1939.[66] It intended to bring together functions scattered across multiple sites, and there was an original intention to incorporate a large central museum. The building was designed by Hubert Worthington of the leading Manchester firm Thomas Worthington and Sons. Worthington had worked as an assistant in Lutyens's office before the First World War and had taught at the Royal College of Art in the middle years of the 1920s. In 1929, unusually, he was appointed as Slade Lecturer at Oxford and this led to many commissions for the university and colleges there, including the extension to the Radcliffe Science Library and a library at New College. A fairly pedestrian designer drawing on neo-Georgian and neo-Regency motifs, he was an architect who remained committed to the ideals of the Arts and Crafts and vernacular traditions in craft and building. As his friend the wood-engraver Margaret Pilkington recalled, he had 'an intimate knowledge of materials and methods of stone-cutting, wood-carving, and carpentry and he combined the care for such details with an understanding and appreciation of the skill of the men who worked under him'.[67] His loose use of classical vernacular with the rubbled ashlar made fashionable by Herbert Baker at Rhodes House was an architectural rhetoric to make almost absurdly parochial imperial institutions. Worthington too – in the Ruskinian tradition to which Pilkington alludes – demonstrates how discourse around craft and design reform were easily put in the service of campaigns to promote intra-imperial trade.

At the fifth Imperial Forestry Conference in 1947, partly held in Oxford, appeals were made for gifts of timber to be used in the new building. It was recorded that 'The response was most generous and 28 governments of the timber-producing areas within the Commonwealth sent choice samples of their forest products.'[68] Six merchanting firms also donated, such that all the interior fixtures and fittings could be rendered in empire timbers: 'The different species, with their great diversity of colour and configuration, have been excellently employed by the architect in the decorative treatment. Apart, however, from the aesthetic appeal of the lovely woods used, the interiors are of great value in forming a permanent exhibition of timber used in a "live" form in contrast to the specimen piece.'[69] Tellingly, despite the encouragement of experimentation in timber construction by the TDA, the Imperial Forestry Institute was built conventionally for the time: a steel frame, with masonry facings. In this regard, the commission reflects the growing emphasis on hardwood facings for interiors, rather than the promotion of softwoods.

The new institute building, opened in 1950, was arranged on an H plan. The entrance from South Parks Road (Figure 10.7) opened into a generous entrance hall panelled and floored in yellow birch, with a rock maple floor, gifted by the Canadian Lumberman's Association, surrounded by offices and committee rooms, including offices and laboratory space for the Forestry Commission. On the west side, the left foot of the H was the Rajah Brooke room (Figure 10.8), intended for exhibition purposes, fitted – incongruously given the connection with Sarawak – entirely in Australian woods, with veneer panelling of 'beautifully figured' Queensland walnut and contrasting mouldings in 'Queensland maple' and flooring in karri edged with Western Australian jarrah. The main lecture theatre, north-west of the site, and a 'bridge' with the Department of Botany building behind was faced in Western red cedar plywood with seating in hemlock. There were timbers from East, West, and South Africa, including relatively rare hardwoods like afara, avodire, iroko, and kokrodua, as well as timbers from the Caribbean, including blue mahoe for furniture and Central American cedar for shelving and cupboards. Timbers from India, the new nation of Pakistan, and colonial Ceylon also abounded: gurjun for laboratory

Figure 10.7 The Imperial Forestry Institute, Oxford (Hubert Worthington, 1950). © University of Manchester.

Empire timbers: architecture, trade, and forestry, 1920–50    297

Figure 10.8 'Logging scenes in Nigeria'. Courtesy Plant Science Collections, Radcliffe Science Library, University of Oxford.

benches and floors, Indian laurel for doors, padauk and Indian rosewood for furniture, and silver greywood for doors.

The Imperial Forestry Institute was in some senses a deliberately exotic interior, despite its conventional planning and institutional programme. The profusion of materials secured from colonial governments and commercial companies may have been impressive to contemporaries, but also, in some fundamental regards, represents and spatialises the ultimate limitations of the empire timber campaign; the triumph of the fairly limited hardwood market for decorative veneers, over any significant shift in softwood; the limited imagination for structural use, despite experiment and competition promoted by the TDA; the bland self-referentiality of an Imperial Forestry Institute bedecked with empire timbers. The architect served as shopper to the client, merely selecting from a seemingly unending variety of products, projecting a fantasy of flourishing intra-imperial trade.

Yet the Imperial Forestry Institute, and the framing of its spaces – to train generations of colonial foresters – has additional significance. It represents the University of Oxford's status as the centre of 'Imperial ecology', it is indeed in turn a manifestation of a particular conception of ecology as epistemically imperial and colonial.[70] We must also remember that the institute and its teaching methods – derived from nineteenth-century German forestry methods – was, paradoxically, held up for promoting 'responsible forestry', one which was conservative where needed and ideally regenerative, shifting the image of the 'British race', as the Prince of Wales described in 1926, with the 'unenviable distinction of being the most ruthless destroyer of forests in the world'.[71]

The university's establishment of the institute within its environs emphasises coloniality's presence in modern forestry, fundamental conceptions of the nature of ecology, and resource extraction for commercial trade. The production of architecture as we have seen, though sometimes with bland expression, made these entanglements materially manifest. These are as worthy of critical reflection, in the context of decolonial praxis and redress (called for by Rhodes Must Fall and other activist groups), as individual monuments to Rhodes, for example. These spatial and visual iconographies, as indeed RMF in Oxford's foundational statement declaims, require much further unpacking. Architecture played its role not just in the superficial design of the building's spaces, but much more profoundly, as we have seen, because it was conceived as providing a ready market for the products on display.

## Conclusion

In February 1939, the TDA's journal *Wood* published an article describing 'Empire Timbers in the Streets of London'.[72] Its author Donald Cowie demonstrated 'by a casual stroll through the streets of London not only how the use of Empire timbers has extended into practically every department of our lives today, but also how there is scope for still wider utilisation tomorrow'. He described paving in wood-blocks of Australian jarrah and Columbian pine, used since the nineteenth century but still maintained well into the twentieth century. Telegraph poles were made of tallow-wood jarrah or

Malayan keruing. Indeed, the article described the growing use of empire timbers in motor-vehicle production – noting that a 'very well-known motor firm, headed by a great Imperialist and philanthropist, has already placed several large orders for the beautiful coachwood, recently renamed "scented satinwood"'.[73] Cowie referred to pub interiors, with 'spiritous liquor, purveyed surely from vats or casks of New Zealand kaura', and panelling from Nigeria or British Honduras. As the perambulation continued, the author encountered empire timbers on the tube network – carriages fitted with Australian silky oak and Borneo cedar and Burma teak in the framing, and, at Moorgate, an escalator shaft panelled with different empire woods – 'Could Empire timbers have a better advertisement in the heart of the City of London?'[74] This was not unique to the tube network: London and North Eastern Railways (LNER) had ordered huge quantities of British Columbian fir in 1926 to provide sleepers across their network, and the shipping industry made similar commitments in order to provide a fillip to the empire timbers campaign.[75] A decade later, in 1937, for the King's coronation, the seating stands to accommodate an audience of 50,000 were erected by the Office of Works, again using Canadian softwoods.[76]

Empire timber was, so its promoters sought to emphasise, ubiquitous, and yet the campaign failed to make any serious market impact. Even as early as 1924, that bastion of Free Trade, *The Economist* sought to debunk the growing myth of empire timbers as a result of the BEE at Wembley: 'Dazzling reports appeared in the lay Press,' it wrote sardonically, 'of this wealth of the Empire's vast timber resources, especially those of Canada and India.'[77] And yet, through an analysis of Board of Trade returns it was observed 'how lightly we depend upon our overseas dependencies for our wood requirements'.[78] This was primarily because of the proximity of perfectly good sources of more local supply in Europe, and competition for imports from the largest imperial supply of softwoods, Canada, from its near neighbour the United States, who had more than decimated its own timber reserves.

For all the sylvan rapture of the empire timbers campaign – the promise of unending resource for extraction to serve the domestic market – in economic terms, it barely shifted the import market. It shows, significantly, the artificiality, even futility, of enduring coloniality, and architectural design's ability to mask, superficially, the fact by exaggerating display through public relations and advertising rhetoric.

Empire timbers tells us very little about architecture when considered as solely a design practice; rather, it reveals something about the production of built environments in the interwar years. It opens up a superficial contemporaneous understanding of supply and demand, low in economic impact, but high in terms of cultural capital. It was expeditious for architects to position themselves favourably in fostering expanding markets for new 'products'. Despite this, a conception of a limitless supply of source and variety in timber from the expansive forest estates of empire only serves to demonstrate an inherent extractivism to architecture's coloniality. That paradox was understood by contemporaries. The *Journal of Empire Forestry*, for instance, reflecting on the display of empire timbers at Wembley, recorded that: 'In the face of the display of what may appear to be unlimited timber resources, it is remarkable that we pay an annual import bill of approximately forty million sterling, of which only ten per cent comes from our Overseas dominions, whereas with efficient organisation a much greater proportion of our requirements could be supplied from Empire sources.'[79]

There is more to be investigated in questions of race and labour in the production of the built environment in the first half of the twentieth century in imperial Britain: Black African loggers, Burmese Mayanma craftspeople, and other forms of indigenous participation in forestry, the timber trade, and construction lurk just beneath the surface of architecture's conventional histories. Indeed, the myriad ways in which visual and material culture imagined global supply chains – in particular extraction and production, alongside labour – is really significant. It is recorded, for instance, in the photographs collected by the Imperial Forestry Institute and deployed in its teaching programme, conducted within those spaces, described above; it is contained in the romantic wood engravings of Canadian lumber in the pages of *Wood*; it is the economic basis of the dismal culture of colonial rule described in George Orwell's *Burmese Days*, in the wretchedness of the protagonist Florey, an agent of a local timber supply company who comes to see the futility of imperial rule.

There is more work to be done too in understanding architecture's coloniality, especially in the context of early twentieth-century Britain. The fundamental paradox of the empire timber campaign – of increasingly effective commercial rhetoric in promotion versus limited capacity to shift the market – shows that, at the so-called zenith of professional power, architecture's agency was limited, even if architects believed themselves to be not just 'shoppers' but shapers of products and markets within global Imperial networks of supply. If we wish to explore the implications of decoloniality and its praxes on architectural history, and indeed on architecture more generally, we need to think about these complex epistemic and ecological entanglements.

## Notes

1 In fact, the panels are removable, and are photographed in different configurations even at the time of completion.

2 Imperial Institute, *Descriptive List of Some Empire Timbers* (London: The Imperial Institute, 1928), 6.
3 Jane Hutton, *Reciprocal Landscapes: Stories of Material Movements* (London: Routledge, 2019).
4 *On Decoloniality: Concepts, Analytics, and Praxis*, eds Walter Mignolo and Catherine E. Walsh (Durham, NC: Duke University Press, 2018).
5 See, for example, Fran Williams, 'Over 90% of Concrete Used in Construction Could be Replaced with Timber'', *Architects' Journal*, 20 July 2023.
6 See Mignolo and Walsh, *On Decoloniality*.
7 Jennifer L. Anderson, *Mahogany: The Cost of Luxury in Early America* (Cambridge, MA: Harvard University Press, 2012).
8 Caroline Cornish, '"Useful and Curious": A Totem Pole at Kew's Timber Museum', *Journal of Museum Ethnography* 25 (2012): 138–51.
9 See Neal Shasore, *Designs on Democracy: Architecture and the Public in Interwar London* (Oxford: Oxford University Press, 2022).
10 Katie Lloyd-Thomas, 'The Strange Interloper: Building Products and the Emergence of the Architect-Shopper in 1930s Britain', in *Suffragette City: Women, Politics and the Built Environment*, eds Elizabeth Darling and Nathaniel Walker (London: Routledge, 2019), 110–35.
11 Harriet Atkinson has used Tim Ingold's idea of 'domains of entanglement' to analyse exhibitions during the middle decades of the twentieth century. See Harriet Atkinson, '"Lines of Becoming": Misha Black and Entanglements through Exhibition Design', *Journal of Design History* 34, no. 1 (2021): 37–53. See also Deborah Sugg Ryan, *Ideal Homes, 1918–1939: Domestic Design and Suburban Modernism* (Manchester: Manchester University Press, 2018).
12 *A Handbook of Empire Timbers* (London: Empire Marketing Board, 1932), 3.
13 J. M. Powell, '"Dominion over Palm and Pine": The British Empire Forestry Conferences, 1920–1947', *Journal of Historical Geography* 33, no. 4 (2007): 852–77.
14 See National Archives, Kew: CO 323/816/48, 'British Empire Timber Exhibition: Minutes and Resolutions of First Committee Meeting, held 16 October 1919', fol.386*ff*.
15 National Archives, Kew: CO 323/844/36, 'British Empire Timber Exhibition: Minutes and Resolutions of Fourth Committee Meeting' (4 May 1920), f.55.
16 'Empire Timber Exhibition: Catalogue of Exhibits' (London: HM Stationery Office, 1920), 10.
17 'Empire Timber Exhibition: Catalogue of Exhibits', 98.
18 'Empire Timber Show', *Financial Times*, 11 November 1920, 5.
19 See Michael T. Saler, *The Avant-Garde in Interwar England: Medieval Modernism and the London Underground* (Oxford: Oxford University Press, 2001). See also Caroline Walker, *Macdonald Gill* (London: Unicorn Press, 2019).
20 He was co-editor (with Henry Adams) of *Modern Building* (London: Gresham Publishing, 1921). See 'Empire Timbers from Home and Overseas for Building and Structural Purposes', *Journal of the Royal Society of Arts* (13 May

1932): 655. This review suggests that this informed his participation in the empire timbers campaign.
21 Empire Timber Exhibition Catalogue, xv. The Imperial Institute Advisory Committee was still active in the late 1930s and comprised twenty-three members including five architects, three of whom were nominated by the RIBA.
22 'Resources of the Empire', *The Times*, 4 February 1928, 9.
23 'Resources of the Empire', 9.
24 'Use of Empire Timbers: Plea to Architects', *The Times*, 24 May 1928, 5.
25 'London's First Forestry Exhibition', *Financial Times*, 10 July 1920, 5.
26 C. Cornish, P. Gasson, and M. Nesbitt, 'The Wood Collection (Xylarium) of the Royal Botanic Gardens Kew', *IAWA Journal* 35, no. 1 (2014): 85–104.
27 'Report of the Inaugural Meeting of the Empire Forestry Association', *Empire Forestry Journal* 1, no. 1 (March 1922): 3.
28 For an account of the UK Exhibits and the Palace of Industry as connected to this debate around trade policy, see Shasore, *Designs on Democracy*, ch. 1
29 'Empire Timber Resources', *The Times*, 1 June 1923, 11.
30 'Foreign Timber at Wembley', *The Times*, 28 July 1924, 8.
31 'British Empire Exhibition: Mr Donald's Protest', *The Times*, 18 October 1922, 14.
32 'British Empire Exhibition: Mr Donald's Protest', 14.
33 'Empire Forests', *The Times*, 29 July 1924, 42.
34 'Empire Forests', 42.
35 'Empire Timbers at Wembley', *Empire Forestry Journal* 3, no. 1 (July 1924): 53–4.
36 'Empire Timbers at Wembley', 55.
37 'Empire Timbers at Wembley', 55.
38 See Shasore, *Designs on Democracy*, 90–1.
39 See 'Prince Risborough: Forest Products Research Laboratory', *The Commonwealth Forestry Review* 50, no. 2 (June 1971): 178–80.
40 See Patrick Zamarian, 'William Allen and the "Scientific Outlook" in Architectural Education', *Architectural History* 64 (2021): 379–402; Mark Swenarton, 'Breeze Blocks and Bolshevism: Housing Policy and the Origins of the Building Research Station 1917–21', *Construction History* 21 (2005): 69–80.
41 'Exhibition of Empire Woods', *The Times*, 1 February 1933, 8.
42 'Exhibition of Empire Woods', 8.
43 'Empire Wood for Furniture', *The Times*, 7 September 1932, 9.
44 See Lloyd-Thomas, 'The Strange Interloper', and Shasore, *Designs on Democracy*, 164–6.
45 'New "Building Centre"', *Timber and Plywood*, 10 September 1932, 473. The handbook notes that similar specimens were issued to leading architecture schools: *A Handbook of Empire Timbers*, 56.
46 'New "Building Centre"', 473.
47 'New "Building Centre"', 473.

48 TNA, BT 55/47, Board of Trade Committee Papers, 'Ottawa Economic Conference: Inter-Departmental Preparatory Committee (1931), Possible Scheme for Promoting the Marketing of Empire Timbers – Notes by Mr Tallents', 1–4.
49 H. L. Stewart, 'Empire Development … The Marketing of Colonial Timbers', *Wood* (May 1938), 276.
50 RIBA Archive, New Building Committee Papers, Box 1, Folio 5: Suggestions regarding materials. Persons asking for appointments (August 1931–June 1932).
51 'Growing Use of Empire Timber', *Manchester Guardian*, 30 April 1932, 16; 'Empire Timber: British Columbia's Bid for English Market', *Financial Times*, 28 October 1932, 3.
52 'Fire-Resisting Empire Timbers', *Journal of the Royal Institute of British Architects*, 10 August 1935, 1050; 'Empire Timbers: Two More Approved by the LCC', *Financial Times*, 28 July 1936, 4. Proposals were submitted by the Imperial Institute Advisory Committee for iroko, African walnut, mora, crabwood, Andaman padauk, Queensland maple, Sekondi mahogany, pyinkado, pyinma, red meranti, and English ash.
53 E. Bertram Kirby, 'The Allied Societies', in *The Growth and Work of the Royal Institute of British Architects, 1834–1934*, ed. John Alfred Gotch (London: Royal Institute of British Architects, 1934).
54 RIBA Archive, Centenary Committee – Boxes, Press Cuttings, File B, *Evening News*, 7 November 1934. The article commented that Wornum 'had been studying Empire materials for many years, and knew a lot about them long before we became Empire-conscious'.
55 *Timber and Timber Products: Including Paper Making Materials*, ed. S. J. Duly (London: Ernest Benn, 1924), 14.
56 'Empire Hardwoods', *Wood* 2, no. 8 (1937): 237.
57 *Grading Rules and Standard Sizes for Empire Hardwoods (Square-Edged Boards and Planks)* (London: Imperial Institute, 2nd edn 1937).
58 Alan Powers, 'A Popular Modernism?, Timber Architecture in Britain 1936–39', *Architectural Theory Review* 25, no. 1–2 (2021): 245–66.
59 Powers, 'A Popular Modernism?'.
60 'Wood and the Empire Exhibition, Glasgow', *Wood* (May 1938), 247.
61 'The Gold Coast, Empire Exhibition', *Wood* (May 1938), 294.
62 'The Gold Coast, Empire Exhibition', 294.
63 'Wood and the Empire Exhibition, Glasgow', *Wood* (May 1938), 253.
64 'Wood and the Empire Exhibition, Glasgow', 253.
65 J. Burley, R. A. Mills, R. A. Plumptre, P. S. Savill, P. J. Wood, and H. L. Wright, 'A History of Forestry at Oxford University', *British Scholar* 1, no. 2 (2009): 239.
66 Oxford University Archives, UR 6/BG/FI, File 3, 'Department of Botany. Opening of the New Building by the Lord Rothschild (8 October 1951).' The Imperial Forestry Institute shared a building with the Department for Botany, conjoined by a lecture theatre and a garden quadrangle.
67 'Sir Hubert Worthington', *The Times*, 3 August 1963, 8.

68 'The New Building of the Imperial Forestry Institute', *Wood* (December 1950), 442.
69 'The New Building of the Imperial Forestry Institute', 442.
70 See Peder Anker, *Imperial Ecology: Environmental Order in the British Empire, 1895–1945* (Cambridge MA: Harvard University Press, 2002).
71 Anker, *Imperial Ecology*, 81.
72 Donald Cowie, 'Empire Timbers in the Streets of London', *Wood* (February 1939), 67.
73 Cowie, 'Empire Timbers in the Streets of London', 67.
74 Cowie, 'Empire Timbers in the Streets of London', 69.
75 'A Gigantic Order', *Manchester Guardian*, 13 January 1926, 9.
76 'Stands for the Coronation', *The Observer*, 17 January 1937, 10.
77 'Empire Timbers in the British Market', *The Economist*, 14 March 1925, 8–10.
78 'Empire Timbers in the British Market', 9.
79 'Empire Timbers at Wembley', *Empire Forestry Journal* 3, no. 1 (July 1924): 57.

# 11

# How to live in Britain: the Indian YMCA in Fitzroy Square

*Mark Crinson*

If you were a young Indian in the early 1950s and you were thinking about studying in Britain, you might well have turned to the British Council's guide *How to Live in Britain*. First published in 1952, and regularly revised and reissued until 1970, this slim volume covered everything from the cost of living, visas and passports, arriving in Britain, contraband, 'calling on "The Authorities"', and finding accommodation, to where to eat and drink, how to spend leisure time, and the right clothes in 'the so-called temperate zone'. It also gave copious advice on the intricacies of the 'habits and customs' to be found in Britain. Apparently, 'when British people are introduced to each other, they give a faint smile and say: "How do you do?"'. But, the guide warned students enigmatically, 'There is no answer to this question.' More hopefully, it advised that the weather was 'a useful topic with which to open a conversation with a stranger'; that, if invited out for a meal in someone's house 'it is ... customary to write and thank your host immediately you return to your lodgings'; and that 'while your national costume is always appreciated – and the more colourful the better – people are apt to be intolerant of men who adopt a flamboyant imitation of the British male attire'.[1]

Such advice may now seem quaint at best (and may well have done so to many even then), but it had a serious edge to it; indeed, within its job of providing information the guide barely contained its many anxieties. The student was to survive and hopefully to flourish, to study hard, and to return in good time to the home country.[2] And in the process she or he would have become a friend of Britain, a citizen of one of the members of the 'family' of imperial and post-imperial nations beginning to be called the 'Commonwealth'. So, comportment and adaptation to life in Britain were key. Here, in a country described as 'small' and 'overcrowded', it was essential that 'everybody tries to observe a clock-like punctuality and faithfully follows certain rules and regulations'. Students were warned that daily life, in this society still feeling the effects of the war, was 'harder and less formal than it used to be'. And in London these conditions were intensified, with more crowdedness, more distractions, and 'the fact that its inhabitants are all too preoccupied to spare much time for leisurely intercourse'.³

To fit into all this was to make accommodations in order to be accommodated, and this is also the theme of this chapter. What role, I want to ask, could new architecture play here over and above the mere provision of student rooms? Specifically, could it find spatial or figurative equivalents to themes like the ecumenical and the postcolonial? Architecture and guidebooks are different things, of course; they respond to different imperatives. But both in this case are about accommodation in its dual meanings: to provide lodging, and to adapt or to reconcile. The guide projected itself as eminently practical and even mundane. It advised potential students to find a college place before embarking for Britain, and to apportion their money carefully. To make accommodation was about situating oneself in a world of apparently strict controls, including the requirements of registering with High Commissioners, liaison officers, the Food Office (for ration books), and the National Health Service. Above all, it was about finding somewhere to live and negotiating the barriers to this in a war-damaged and still culturally defensive country. There were some university rooms and halls, of course, but there were also all the peculiar mores of lodgings: the rules of the house, getting on with the landlady, being your own servant, feeding meters, limiting hot water use, sending out laundry. There was also what the guide called 'participation in [a university's] club and social life', and here the Student Christian Movement and the Inter-Varsity Fellowship of Evangelical Unions figured prominently. But there were also – beyond universities – the British Council Centres for Overseas Students, the East and West Friendship Council, and the Victoria League ('promoting friendship between the British and other peoples of the Commonwealth').[4]

The guide's anxieties, if just beneath the surface, point to more evident concerns in government circles about the continuing idea of British imperial benevolence and, as part of this, about the myth of overseas students becoming ambassadors for Britain's role in the world. Broadly, what might potentially negative student experiences lead to?[5] Would colonial students, for instance, become disaffected by their experience of racial discrimination in Britain? Would they therefore mix with anticolonial and even Communist Party elements and return home radicalised to help lead their country's agitation against empire?[6] Or, in India's case, would they drive its post-independence resurgence but not in ways sympathetic to Britain?[7] Alternatively, would they stay in Britain, becoming interchangeable with the immigrants already perceived as a potential social problem?[8] And, during their student years, would they suffer 'doubts and anxieties ... mood swings of bewildering intensity', 'emotional strain', and depression, and even go off the rails and fail their courses?[9] Would they mix well with the British population but perhaps go too far – in the opinion of some natives, but equally of their own families back in India – and invoke the spectre of sexual involvement and even miscegenation? In all these areas the subject of colonial students was part of the more general topos of the time, that both the possibility and the actuality of decolonisation were the cause of 'syndromes and pathologies'.[10] Students might thus suffer 'brain fag' and 'overintegration', and, more damagingly for their hosts, these pathologies were symptomatic of a strong reaction against the metropolis.[11]

Nevertheless, despite all these fears, and a considerable amount of surveillance as a result of them, the actual provision of colonial students' housing was almost entirely left either in the hands of charities, religious groups, and philanthropists, or to the exigencies and whims of the market. The first type of provision had its problems – well-meaning benevolence sometimes being only the other side of the coin from a patronising demonstration of toleration or a kind of religiously or politically motivated attempt at recruitment.[12] But the other type, the private rental market, brought up the very real possibility of exposure to direct racial prejudice.

How to live in Britain was bound up with where to live in Britain, and this was becoming an increasingly acute problem as colonial student numbers soared in the postwar years.[13] Hostels and halls of residence specifically for colonial students were few and in great demand.[14] The British Council itself had a policy of encouraging association with British students and 'British people in their homes'.[15] So it was felt wise not to allow too many hostels specifically for overseas students and, where they existed, to advise their use only as a 'temporary necessity' and as a meeting place for nonresident students: they were a form of transition.[16] As the British Council planned it, students would be met on arrival and found accommodation in a 'transit hostel'. Arrangements would be made at the Colonial Office and British Council (India House, post-independent after August 1947, took over this responsibility for Indian students). Students would then take a series of introduction courses and guided group tours around London by members of the Student Christian Movement. Finally, students would find more permanent accommodation in lodgings or university halls of residence.[17]

What can thus be observed in the issue of overseas student accommodation, particularly for colonial and postcolonial students, is the tip of an iceberg. Not only were there all the continuing injustices and imbalances of colonialism, the rebarbative views of some of the British population, and the hardships of the still evident effects of the war, but there were also the new official policies of welfare and development, the need for new workforces that led to the migration of colonial peoples into postwar Britain, and the geopolitical dynamics of the developing Cold War.[18] And entirely submerged in all this was the fact that the postwar recovery of Britain, its new welfare state, and the rebuilding of its cities, was largely achieved via expropriations from the colonies in the form of loans.[19]

Becoming independent in 1947, India was an obvious addition to, but also a sudden absence in, the British state's concerns about colonial students. Once the initial doubts about Indian students even continuing to study in Britain had been alleviated, then it was thought that their potential disaffection would be less of an issue.[20] Instead, as India now figured in the more liminal position of ex-colony (it joined the Commonwealth in 1950) so its students became another means to the influence felt necessary in the Cold War.[21] As with colonial students, Indian student numbers increased exponentially in the postwar years and members of the British establishment were keen to accept invitations to address them.[22] The British Council's booklet was part of this gathering impetus of new welfare policies and new forms of Cold War propaganda within a different alignment of global relations. And into all this came the question of a new home for the Indian YMCA.

Founded in London in 1844, the YMCA was a Protestant lay organisation, a voluntary movement intended to promote philanthropy on a Christian and ecumenical basis. The Indian variant of this was set up in 1857; originally of North American provenance, it was well advanced in its indigenisation by 1910.[23] Its activities included intercultural education, physical education schemes, and rural reconstruction projects in India, and its charitable work with soldiers during the First World War had given it a 'remarkable global visibility' according to one historian.[24] In London, the Indian YMCA was one of several church and missionary societies that took an interest in students from the colonies: among them the Friends' International Centre, the Roman Catholic Church, the British Council of Churches, Toc H, and the Church Missionary Society. The idea of promoting itself as a social centre for Indian–British interactions dates back to the Indian YMCA's first London incarnation; such was the purpose of the Shakespeare Hut, a temporary building in Keppel Street, Bloomsbury, which after the First World War became the society's first hostel.[25] This was replaced in 1923 by the purchase of a row of Georgian houses at 106–112 Gower Street. When three of these houses were badly damaged by bombs in 1940, the University of London provided additional temporary premises in Woburn Square.

The YMCA was a global movement (the American YMCA would contribute substantially to the new building), but the Indian YMCA had distinctive features. For one thing, in India itself it was known, especially in the 1920s, to have sided strongly with independence movements in the subcontinent.[26] These political interests characterised the British-based Indian YMCA, if in a more inclusive or 'ecumenical' form. The hostel often hosted talks by nationalist leaders (Gandhi, Nehru, Tagore, B. R. Ambedkar, Annie Besant, and Mohammed Ali Jinnah) as well as British leaders and intellectuals (Conan Doyle, George Lansbury, Fenner Brockway, E. M. Forster, among them). In fact, if the hostel was to be a cultural centre for potential leaders then, in a sense, it had to be 'a sounding board of public opinion in Indian affairs'; it had to embrace, as Sir Abdul Qadir put it in 1938, the 'true nationalism' of unity among diversities.[27] (When independence came with partition in 1947, it was thus greeted within the Indian YMCA with distinctly mixed emotions.)[28] The Christian ecumenicism of the early movement had widened to include a multifaith ecumenicism. In the interwar period it mutated further into a secular and cultural ecumenicism that would have parallels with the Indian Constitution as drafted by Ambedkar and instigated in 1947. The cultivation of an enlightened constitutional, not traditional-social, morality was the keystone of this ideal of state ecumenicism.[29] All these intersecting and widening circles of ecumenicism were clearly vitally important to the Indian YMCA in how it understood and projected its role and identity in postwar London.

Institutionally, therefore, the Indian YMCA conceived of itself as much more than a student hostel. While the shaping of young Indian minds – the leaders of the future – was important, so too was the shaping of English minds: modelling their expectations, educating them in Indian matters, influencing their understanding of what was at stake in the relation between cultures. In these senses, the Indian YMCA had more in common institutionally with the Settlement movement in London's East End. Starting in the 1880s and reaching its peak in the 1920s, these were hostels (the most famous were Toynbee Hall, Oxford House, and Browning Hall) that brought middle-class volunteers to live and work among the poor of the East End.[30] Settlements could have philanthropic, religious, or social reformist motivations, but in all of them cultural events – performances, talks, sports, group visits – were critical to their activity. The Indian YMCA and the Settlement houses had many connections and similarities,[31] but there is no avoiding the inversion of Settlement practices that the former brought about by its very presence in London (and, decidedly, not in one of the city's poorer districts). The cultural elements of the mission – or, to put it more precisely, the combination of a form of new national projection with older means of proselytising – were made novel, often pointedly so, by the colonial and then postcolonial circumstances.[32]

The range of interests with a stake in the Indian YMCA, or wanting to be associated with it, was a result of what we would now call its soft power – both its philanthropical status and its position bridging cultures and religions. When it desperately needed a permanent new home after the Second World War, a building fund was launched in India and gathered donations from central and provincial governments as well as from the industrialist Tata family and the Maharajah of Cochin. Another fund was launched simultaneously in Britain, aimed at British firms with interests in India: ICI, Lloyds Bank, P&O, Imperial Tobacco, English Electrical Company, the Locomotive Manufacturer's Association, Boots, and the Britannia Iron Works, were all generous donors.[33] In addition, senior members of the British government like the Chancellor of the Exchequer and the Minister of Education, as well as the High Commissioner for India, were all brought in to support the application for a new building permit (permits in these postwar years being particularly hard to obtain until they were abolished in 1954).[34] The level and range of all these gestures of support indicate just how politically symbolic the new building was. The first design came in only a few months after independence was declared in August 1947.[35] It had been worked on simultaneously as the full horrors of partition were becoming apparent. Finished by 1953, the building provided shelter to Indian students regardless of faith and cultural identity.

Both sides, it seems, of the old imperial relationship, saw the Indian YMCA as an important expression of the new realignment. One can easily hypothesise their uncertainty about how that expression might actually work even as they were, simultaneously, keen to be in on the act. It helped that there was a felt sense of the shared endurance of the recent world war, embodied by the bomb-damaged Gower Street building (pictured, for instance, in a photographic vignette in a pamphlet celebrating the new building) and, as we will see, by the new surroundings in Fitzroy Square (Figure 11.1).

Ralph Tubbs was already working for the Indian YMCA, advising on repair jobs for the remaining Gower Street house, when he was commissioned to design the new building.[36] In some ways, and with some hindsight, Tubbs was an apt architect for his clients. As a member of the MARS Group (it was his flat in Essex Road where many of the group's informal discussions took place in the late 1930s), he declared early for Britain's modernist avantgarde. His Dome of Discovery would be, with the Festival Hall, the signal building of the 1951 Festival of Britain, and on a personal level marked Tubbs' place in what had become the modernist establishment. Unavoidable in its size and distinctive shape, the Dome was also strangely modest, as if shaking off any possibility of the usual grandeur of its type. As John Summerson wrote, comparing it with the 1924 Empire Exhibition, the Festival 'was not in the least like Wembley; it had taken to heart every one of the terrible lessons Wembley had to teach'.[37] It was some achievement for the biggest building of the festival to have achieved a lightness and informality, even a denial of axiality and monumentality. And to have done this in the face of the stultifying imperial

*How to live in Britain: the Indian YMCA in Fitzroy Square*     311

Blitz damage

**Figure 11.1** Destroyed houses at 106–112 Gower Street, London. Photographic vignette from *Commemorating ... Hostel*, 1953.

rhetoric of Wembley in 1924, was to put a marker down for what a post-imperial architecture might be.[38]

Whether any of this was registered by those who ran the Indian YMCA is not really the point, because Tubbs had been appointed architect for the new hostel before he designed the Dome; any such architectural response to imperialism was at best latent.[39] The key issue is that an ability to abstract or at least tone down pretensions to architectural grandiosity was already a characteristic of his work before the Dome of Discovery. And this brings us to issues of intent and authorship. Tubbs was the in-house architect in another sense beyond the fact he already worked for the Indian YMCA. In the absence of any archival documents that cast further light on the relationship, his views and design decisions must be regarded as also those of his clients. We can only imagine what he brought to the relationship and whether his clients had other ways of understanding his work; whether there were any contradictions or tensions. Was he their 'native informant' in a sense beyond the normal expertise of an architect, translating the norms and possibilities of the architectural culture to them, mediating their understanding? Did they instruct him in the orientalist elements that will be discussed later, or did he somehow impose them? Answers to these questions would only be speculations. In what follows, clients and architect will of necessity be treated as the same creative, agenda-setting, and organising entity.

In its stated purposes, the new Indian YMCA building would do much to complement *How to Live in Britain,* and to avoid some of the sources of the British Council's anxiety.[40] It would be a staging post, to some extent, providing a 'temporary home prior to finding permanent quarters' (hence the fifty-five single rooms on upper floors), and acting as an advice centre 'on first coming to this country'.[41] But it would also be a social and cultural hub. Indian students would be given a chance to socialise with other Indian students, as well as provided a place where they could entertain their English friends. Cultural facilities would be provided for the students and a wider public. The main provision would be on the ground floor with its dining hall and garden lounge looking out onto a paved courtyard, and in the basement with its assembly hall (named the Mahatma Gandhi Memorial Hall) seating over 300 for plays, concerts, and lectures. These facilities clearly expanded on what had been supplied at Gower Street, which had a restaurant and ran various cultural events.[42] The first floor of the new building was more specifically for the students, with a common room, library, and other social spaces. And located on the top floor, above three floors of student bedrooms, there was a flat and office for the warden and a sun terrace. Also at this level – well out of the way of the other forms of ecumenicism below – there was a simple square prayer room with a concrete dome in the form of a sail vault, lit by a glass oculus. A certain Gandhian gloss was put on all this with his words inscribed on the foundation stone: 'I do not want my house to be walled on all sides nor my windows to be shut. I want the culture of all lands to blow about my house as freely as possible: but I refuse to be blown off my feet by any of them.'[43] For all its messianic self-regard, this is another version of the ecumenical idea absorbed by the building.[44]

The University of London was directly involved in the move, seeing a chance to extend its estate by taking over the premises on Gower Street. In exchange, it agreed to acquire a site on the corner of Fitzroy Square, to the west of Bloomsbury. This might seem an unusual location for an Indian student hostel, but not for the reasons we may now associate with this remnant of the eighteenth-century extensions of the city. There were overseas students' residences further to the west – both Malaya Hall, in

Bryanston Square (acquired for Malayan students in 1949), and East Africa House (acquired for East African students in 1950) in Great Cumberland Place – but these, tellingly, were in Marylebone beyond Portland Place, rather than Fitzrovia. North of Oxford Street and west of Tottenham Court Road, Fitzroy Square was, by the late 1940s, caught betwixt and between. As a whole, Fitzrovia had never been regarded as part of London's West End; it was more a place of workshops (particularly for furniture-making and women's clothes), rooming houses, and offices. Neither as smart as Marylebone nor as academic as Bloomsbury, it was laid out without the many squares of those areas.[45] With its European immigrants it belonged if anything more to the liminal area of Soho to its south and had acquired a bohemian reputation by the 1940s, when the name 'Fitzrovia' was invented for it. In one historian's words, even Fitzroy Square had 'succumbed ... to a number of anonymous commercial hotels, private schools and bohemian artistic menàges', and this was more or less its state by the time of the Second World War.[46]

Indian students regarded the area as unsuitable for their hostel, and not because of any imperial associations with the Georgian square. Instead, it was 'full of pimps and prostitutes' or, in the more diplomatic language of committee minutes, it was 'not conducive to the moral well-being of the students'.[47] Either way, they demanded reconsideration.[48] Eventually, they seem to have accepted reassurances that the area was rapidly changing, though this was probably less to do with the idea that the new Indian YMCA hostel itself would effect this change and more related to the promised arrival of hostels run by University College London immediately beside it. In fact, as early as September 1949, Tubbs was showing how his design would relate to a 'Future College Quad' on the adjoining site (Figure 11.2).[49] The Indian YMCA building would thus become part of one side of a shared block of student residences, its rear terrace opening out onto a leafy open space (where Hertford Place had been), bordered by UCL residences.

Literally and symbolically, the Indian YMCA seemed to have arrived from elsewhere. '[It] takes its place in a London still pock-marked by its bombing of a decade ago', wrote one commentator.[50] And yet it also made a great effort to respect its architectural neighbours. Fitzrovia was certainly in transition, with extensive parts of it damaged or destroyed by the Blitz. The *Survey of London* volume for the area was published in 1949 and its pages are littered with references to the damage: '[Whitfield Street] has suffered severely from the air-raids during the war and most of the west side has gone from Windmill Street as far as Grafton Way', for instance, and 'the site between Grafton Way and Warren Street is almost wholly cleared'.[51] Two terraces by Robert Adam stood yards away from the site, originally designed by him in 1790.

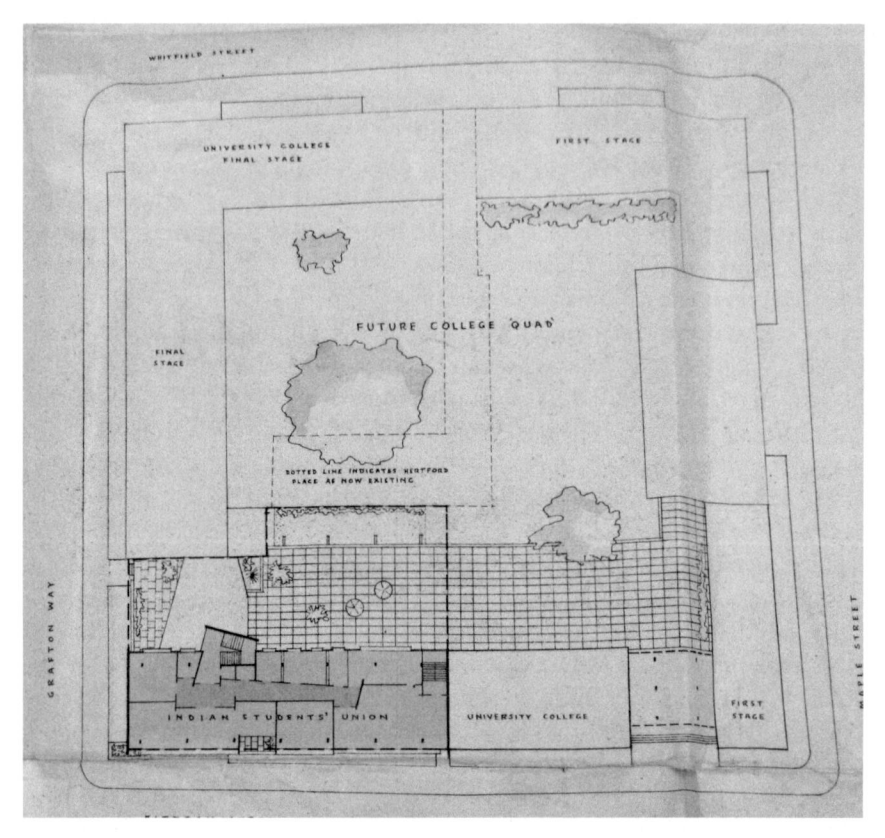

Figure 11.2 Ralph Tubbs, 'Future college quad', site plan (including first floor plan of Indian YMCA), 1949. Courtesy London Metropolitan Archives.

It was towards these Adam terraces that neighbourly respect was particularly paid. The terraces were badly damaged by bombing, while the site for the Indian YMCA, on the corner of Grafton Way and Fitzroy Street, facing onto the square from its south-eastern corner, was entirely cleared of its buildings. Surviving the war, and across Grafton Way from the Indian YMCA, No. 1a Fitzroy Square is one of Adam's houses of 'Palatine grandeur'.[52] Lifted up on an arched and rusticated ground floor, the façade brings Adam's composition to a conclusion at this corner with an imperious tripartite window crowned by a lunette reaching into the storey above. The house was hit by a bomb in 1940 and the third and fourth storeys lost most of their original ornament: the *Survey of London* described it as still 'gutted and roofless' in 1949.[53] All the beautifully carved Portland stone stops abruptly as the terrace turns its corner, so that a façade of brick faces the YMCA side with, still surviving after the war (though now demolished), a columned portico over the side entrance. The YMCA presents a stone face to this side of the Adam house, with three pierced panels the only concession to ornament. More pertinently, in terms of the first planning application for the new building, this end elevation 'picks up the line of stone on the south side of Fitzroy Square' (Plate 15).[54]

The south side of the square was also filled with an Adam terrace. This suffered even more severe damage, with the three houses of the central block almost completely destroyed.[55] The end house, nearest the YMCA, seems to have been relatively undamaged, its slightly projecting front fitted with carved Ionic shafts dividing the window and a short frieze of swags above. It is to the brick side of this house that the YMCA presents its main front, also in brick. The ground floor, with a wide stepped entrance, is mostly glazed, there is a large projecting window above, two floors with smaller windows for the student rooms, a final floor of student rooms connected by a balcony, and a roof garden and penthouse above that.

Aside from its immediate context, the models for the YMCA's combination of brick infill and concrete window frames were probably immediately prewar buildings like Ernö Goldfinger's terrace of three houses at Willow Road in Hampstead and Berthold Lubetkin's Highpoint Two flats in Highgate. Tubbs had been employed by Goldfinger, even making the working drawings for Willow Road.[56] The terrace's long projecting first floor window has a direct echo in Tubbs' first floor. Goldfinger expressed his desire for continuity with the nearby Georgian terraces, for a kind of affinity between the modern and the Georgian.[57] (This was in the form of continuing horizontal lines of façade division; the tall Georgian window remained decidedly *ultra vires* for modernists.) Highpoint Two was illustrated by Tubbs in his 1945 book *The Englishman Builds*, where it was admired for its 'dark recesses and light shadows [which] emphasize the subtle relationship of the forms and surfaces'.[58] As with Goldfinger, Lubetkin had used the argument that modernism was a logical continuation of Georgian architecture.[59] While lacking the complexly patterned compositions of Lubetkin's façade designs, Tubbs still played on four different window treatments, with two of them – the uppermost level of student rooms, and the first level of recreational rooms – both projecting to different extents out of the façade.

This supposed affinity between Georgian architecture and modernism was taken further by other British modernists. Relating to Georgian architecture was seen as a way of connecting to modernism something regarded as rooted in national culture, as well as for the claimed similarities between two architectures based on seriality and rationalism.[60] Tubbs reiterated some of this: 'Does not a Georgian square signify something of an attitude to life?' he asked, 'Do we not see reflected here some of the eighteenth-century belief in the dignity of man and also the resolution of the conflict between the claims of a complex society and the freedom of the individual?'[61] The self-regarding values are explicit – this is how 'the Englishman builds' – but, as we have seen, this same Georgian city was battered and under continuing threat (from redevelopment) at this time. Architectural historians like John Summerson, Nikolaus Pevsner, and the editors of the *Survey of London*, all expressed this sense of actual and potential loss. Summerson's book *Georgian London* (1945), researched in the war years, was considerably shadowed by destruction to its subject. As he wrote, with studied understatement, in the book's preface, 'the whole period has, of course, been somewhat unpropitious for a book of this sort. The subject-matter has been bombed from time to time.'[62]

The YMCA building's response to the neighbouring Robert Adam terraces was usually explained at the time as a piece of respectful contextualism. Here is Trevor Dannatt, writing in 1959:

> An important consideration of the design was to ensure that the form and scale of the building related successfully to the existing square … This has been accomplished by picking up certain lines of the old buildings in the new, by providing a Portland stone faced flank wall to the north end of the hostel so that the south side of the square is visually continued out of the square and by adding a certain weight to the skyline of the building at the corner, to carry the eye over the weak point of the square where the two roads lead out of it.[63]

The phrase 'picking up certain lines' of the old buildings probably refers to the coping of the new building, which continued the height established by the cornice in the Adam buildings. But it could also refer to other features. The YMCA mimicked Adam's distinction between ground and upper floors, the balance of vertical and horizontal elements on its façades. Its set back and largely glazed ground floor made some equivalence with the rusticated ground floors of the Adam buildings. The size of its student room windows was similar to the size of the attic windows over the road. But what Dannatt refers to as a 'certain weight' on the skyline is a curiously formalistic description, as is the idea that this volume helps punctuate the otherwise visually 'weak' junction. Dannatt is elaborating Tubbs' own statements here,[64] and what both are tiptoeing around is the anomaly of that 'certain weight', the fact that its domed, blank-faced shape is entirely different from anything else around it, as if one of Adam's shallow interior ceiling domes had thrust itself up through its roof. The dome houses a prayer room, a multifaith space that might otherwise easily be regarded as signalling the Indian YMCA's difference from its surroundings. This is not within the terms of a modernist contextualism based on abstractions of form, or at least it can hardly be contained by them at this time and in this place.

And there are other near violations of the contextualist code here. The long projection on the fourth floor (there is another one on the rear of the building) consisted of a balcony which the planning authority insisted on calling a 'verandah' because of its canopy and the fact that it was enclosed at its two ends.[65] To call this a balcony is to indicate a space only occasionally used in the hotter weather of the 'temperate zone'. To call it a verandah, however, is to associate it both with the year-round spaces used to moderate temperature in the 'tropical zone', and with a history of colonial incorporations of both language and building form.[66] The difference is telling, and the planner's insistence on naming this space 'verandah' is both a piece of pedantry and a way of conveying that something about the Indian YMCA must indicate difference. It's a kind of trap, of course, but one that has other bait in the building: the 'certain weight' of the prayer room is one, the pierced screens in the stone-faced wall possibly another. It is important, the architecture itself tells us, not to use the language of definite allusion or clear reference here. These architectural forms exist as just that – as forms. They clearly lack the explicitly orientalising thematics of an imperial culture; they are, one might say, at an angle oblique to such a culture but not entirely separate from it. Obliquity – literal and phenomenal – is, as we are seeing, one of the telling themes here.

From one point of view, the arrival of the Indian YMCA in Fitzroy Square is a form of mimicry. Its affinity-making between modernism and the Georgian city is a metonymy, a device 'against a mottled background, of becoming mottled',[67] or at least sufficiently 'mottled' as not to change the measure of decorum found around it. The elements of modernist-orientalism play along with this; as a 'certain weight', a piece of pedantry, an unfixable allusion, they are far from overbearing. But from another point of view the building's arrival has a double element of the paradoxical about it. The first paradox is the fact that this form of urban, contextual modernism was at least partly the product of émigré architects who had identified the Georgian as London's *genius loci*. The second paradox is to do with the new intrusion into Fitzroy Square being the medium by which the square returns to its older and better self. The hostel helps to repair, to cleanse, or at least to de-bohemianise its surroundings, and it does this through the arrival of a modernism that is also the product (and possibly the expression) of a no-longer colonial state, of the *Indian* YMCA. A good, even exemplary postcolonial subjectivity is here enacted, and it has as much to do with the shaping of English minds as of Indian leaders.

If the exterior expresses a sense of both deference and exemplarity in relation to its famous neighbouring architecture, then from within the building London looks as if it should be framed, turned into a set of views. The main front emphasises this with its concrete box frames around all the windows, but its most intriguing effects are to be found at the back of the building (Figure 11.3). Here a plethora of different window types and sizes express a range of nuanced relations between inside and outside. Some of this can be explained as an opening out of the interior, like a garden front, onto the collegial quad behind, a shedding of something of the besuited formality, the mottledness, of the elevations facing the more public Georgian surrounds. But there is more to it than that, and this is implied by the framed balcony (or is it a verandah-ed pulpit?) on the top level of the stair hall, and by the penthouse windows whose box frames angle them away from the Adam terraces. In this context, the simplicity of the individual student cell is deceptive because it is just one component of a greater complex of viewing conditions that includes the projecting balcony box (Figure 11.4). The theme of angled-ness or obliquity emerges further here (lower down, the canopy of the terrace and the upward-inclined long window of the assembly hall make it quite explicit), but it will become even more important as it gains figurative meaning inside. Here, on the rear of the exterior, it cannot help but hint at the ironic quality that mimicry inevitably brings with it.

Figure 11.3 Indian YMCA – rear elevation. Photograph by Reginald Galway, 1953. Courtesy Architectural Press Archive/RIBA Collections.

Figure 11.4 Indian YMCA – student room. Photograph by Reginald Galway, 1953. Courtesy Architectural Press Archive/RIBA Collections.

In the interior, many of the contrastive effects stem from the building's dual structure, switching between the lower storeys and the student rooms above the first floor. Where the former are freely planned around two rows of columnar supports, the latter accommodate cellular student rooms within a box frame construction.[68] It's as if one building has been placed on top of another, the change of structure embodying the change of function between reception and entertainment spaces below, and residential rooms above. (Again, the rear elevation is interesting here because, although there is a strong sense of one building mass sitting on top of another, the level where these masses meet is not actually the same as that where the structure changes.) Outwardly, the functional change of room types is apparent but not the different structures that had given point to it; only at the front on the ground floor are the columns exposed to the exterior, the long window of the dining hall conspicuously dodging around them.

The most spectacular, and at the same time the most curious, element in the building's design occurs inside and in the lower structure. Here the thematic of studied angularity is a sometimes subliminal and sometimes dramatic presence in many of the circulation spaces and in the assembly hall. The fulcrum for this is the splayed main staircase at the back of the entrance hall, which serves the assembly hall below. 'Here in this contemporary western architecture,' wrote one commentator at the time, 'the genius of ancient Indian civilization would thus find immediate emphasis and recognition.'[69] But again the commentary misses the subtlety, the play of abstracted reference in what is going on. As first built, the visitor would have encountered a balcony straight ahead on entering the building (this is now unfortunately screened off), which acted as a viewing platform onto the stair hall, establishing its spatial play as central to the public experience of the building's interior. It was originally intended that an Indian sculpture be positioned high on the far wall of this stair hall (Figure 11.5). Hung at eye level to those entering the building, spot-lit by a skylight, and with the wall intended to be painted grey-green, the sculpture would provide a further point of direction from the building's entrance, focusing the converging walls to either side.[70]

The reception desk was originally positioned in the far corner of the entrance hall to accommodate this axis. To descend down to the assembly hall meant turning back from the viewing platform and then turning sharp right down the angled stairs. These led to another foyer giving access to the assembly hall's gallery, and down again to the basement (Figure 11.6). To the right from that first viewing platform another set of stairs headed up to the student common rooms on the first floor. The assembly hall itself was announced by a tapered concrete fin rising the full height of the stair hall, and with two walls angled away from that entrance (from within the hall these walls are screened by two differently angled walls in front of them). Then, within the assembly hall itself, there is another askance wall hiding one of the far corners of the hall and, above the main seating, a gallery that cuts across one rear corner of the hall (Figures 11.7 and 11.8). The window range that gives onto a sunken garden is tilted up to catch the sunlight. Elsewhere, the angular theme was picked up, if more subtly, by a funnelled corridor at first floor (see Figure 11.2), by the angled walls facing the lift at every level, and on the roof of the building by a curious assemblage of walls at the entrance to the warden's flat. But it is this stair hall, with its abstract drama of multiple landing stages and inexplicable angles, that sets up the theme; every other iteration of it is like a ripple sent out across the building's spaces.

From the beginning, the building's public spaces were envisaged as 'a meeting place for East and West'.[71] The most obvious manifestation of this is the dining hall, still a popular eating venue in this part of London. From the outside this provides the Indian YMCA's shop window, its

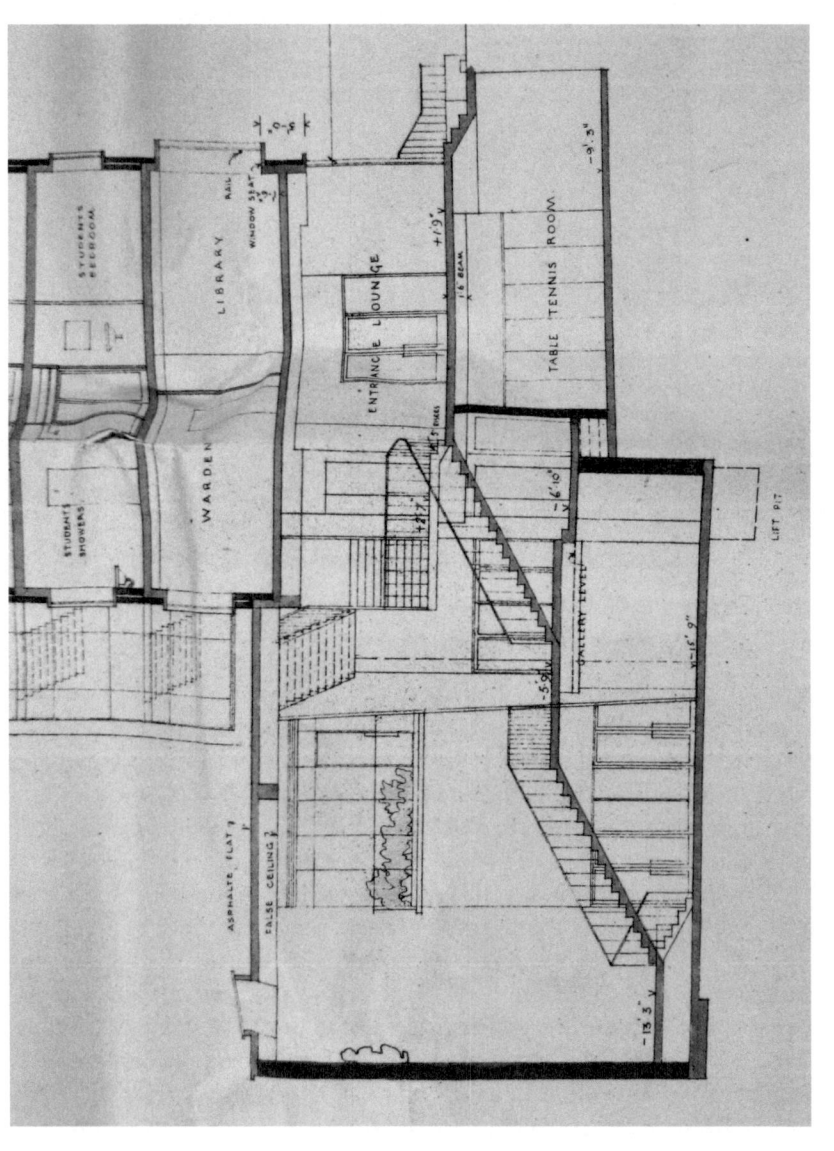

Figure 11.5 Stair hall, Indian YMCA – section. London Metropolitan Archives.

Figure 11.6 Stair hall, Indian YMCA. Photograph by Reginald Galway, 1953. Courtesy Architectural Press Archive/RIBA Collections.

most obvious enticement to the nonresident. Inside, it is positioned close to the entry, to the right and on a cross-axis with the axis focused on the stair hall (Figure 11.9). Originally, the dining hall was entered via a double door set at an angle to this cross-axis. But beyond this door the space is entirely rectilinear. The tables are set out in the window recesses and fill the main space; on a split level, the garden lounge offers a higher transitional space before the terraced garden, the threshold with the latter marked by a return of the angular theme in the form of concrete fins framing the doors. By locating the building's most actively used social space so that it spans front and rear a number of different kinds of areas are created, encouraging different forms of eating and sociability. It is ecumenical in a different way again, in this gregariousness and diversity, a kind of constructed conviviality around food that also has similarities with the Settlement movement mentioned earlier.[72] Of course, to place food – specifically Indian food, its making and sociable consumption – as one of the key elements in a 'meeting place of East and West', also has an element of playing to expectations. Architecturally, the dining function

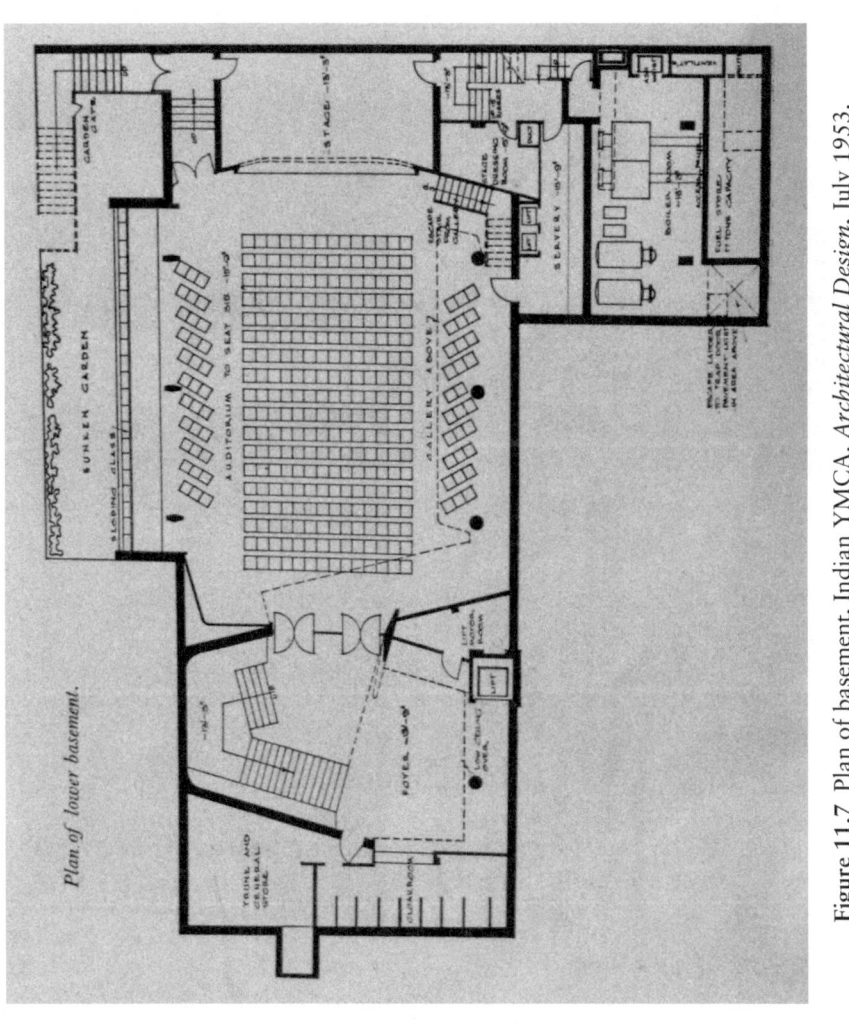

Figure 11.7 Plan of basement, Indian YMCA. *Architectural Design*, July 1953.

Figure 11.8 Assembly hall, Indian YMCA. Photograph by Reginald Galway, 1953. Courtesy Architectural Press Archive/RIBA Collections.

complements the spatio-spiritual rhetoric of the design elsewhere as well as providing an alternative logic.

The idea of a meeting place was, then, more than just to do with the functions of particular spaces. One writer (probably Tubbs himself) explained:

> It has been the deliberate policy of the architect to break up the usual lines of perspective with walls out of parallel – just as in a painting where the perspective is deliberately ignored, this gives a certain air of mystery, which it is felt was in keeping with the aesthetic of the East.[73]

The latter part of this statement is all-too obviously orientalist (it would be interesting to know how the clients understood it), but there is something interesting here nonetheless. Its combination of two narratives – the modernist and the orientalist – is notable for the entire lack of a figure (ornament, say) or figuration (historical reference) for this, and its entire dependence instead on the bare abstraction of 'walls out of parallel', of 'mystery'; orientalism simply is not woven into the material and formal fabric of the building, it is not recognisable without being conjured up by the verbal claim. What we have is a post-Cubist modernism where

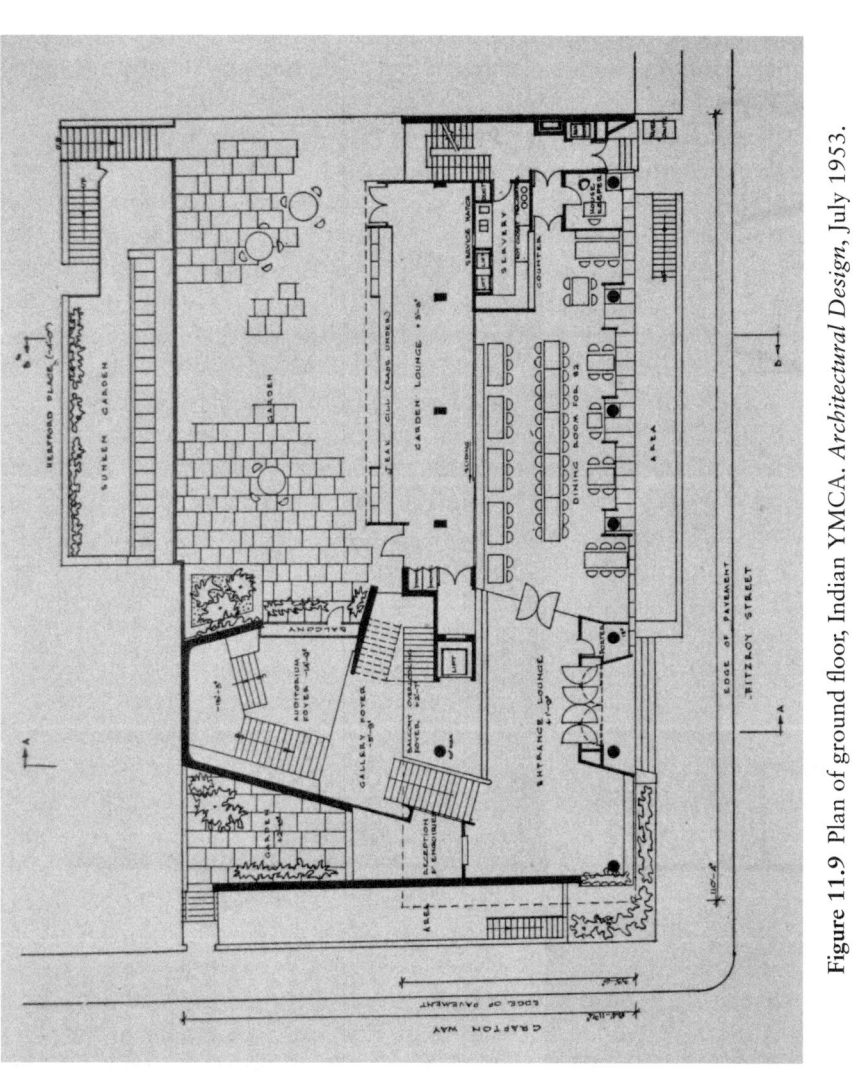

Figure 11.9 Plan of ground floor, Indian YMCA. *Architectural Design*, July 1953.

'walls out of parallel' evince not just a post-Cartesian sensibility, but what might be called an 'inverted colonial action', a self-reflexive affinity with what was generically deemed not of the West.[74] It would be easy to miss the reflexivity and condemn the orientalist association, and certainly the trope is at best a lazy one. Elsewhere, colour took over this associative job: the intended scheme, according to Tubbs, would have 'colours which have become traditional in India ... mauve and gold, dark green and pale blue'.[75] Whether such associations work is questionable, the point rather is that the spaces here seem freshly expressive – controlled, surprising, subliminally effective, and intriguing (perhaps that is what 'mystery' is). Obliquity, again, seems a good term for it. Modernism is the means for a kind of emptying out of orientalism, and what stands in for it is the oblique, the angle as counterpoint or counter-plane. This is evidently related aesthetically to, and pre-empts, Tubbs' design for the Dome of Discovery at the Festival of Britain, with its great fin-buttresses and its oddly positioned stairs and escalators (Plate 16). Arguably – speculatively – these might be understood in terms of an emerging post-imperial sense of national identity; just as the Dome's exhibits tried to re-cast imperial exploitation into the benevolent form of scientific discovery, so the design of the Dome took on the equivalent architectural rhetoric and attempted to redirect it. 'Mystery' of course is just as problematic as 'discovery', but in both the Dome and the Indian YMCA what is being signalled by such terms is this process of un-fixing, of abstracting and making askew the forms both of mimicry and of authorisation.

The Indian YMCA building was certainly one way of modelling 'how to live in Britain'. But its central architectural lessons were nuanced: a kind of orderly deference, a measured obliquity, even a heterotopic ecumenicism. The centrality of dining used food to establish different terms on which hosting and being hosted could be negotiated. National costume was not worn here, at least not by the architecture, but instead there was a modernised version of older themes – abstract, allusive, and near-subliminal. Orientalism, banal and remaindered, becomes just another abstracted ecumenical ingredient. Though it faces a square in which the historic national costume of neoclassicism is a damaged, socially compromised, yet still incontestable presence, there is to be no 'flamboyant imitation' here. The YMCA must be temperate *and* tropical. The visitor enters the oblique, the angled passage or stairs, into the warm coloured 'mysteries' of its spaces. The building opens itself out, mannerly yet curious, to its host city; it accommodates the student to this city, but it also accommodates the city to the student, condenses it, makes it into part of the hostel's ecumene. Out of all this the architecture wants to produce the healthy, the syndrome-free, the truly postcolonial student.

## Acknowledgements

I especially want to thank J. P. F. X. Fernandes, General Secretary of the YMCA Indian Student Hostel, and his staff for their very helpful support for my research. Thanks to Shaun Theobald for his many generous and perceptive comments. I have also benefited from the discussion of the paper at the symposium 'Liminal London', held at Birkbeck in February 2020 and organised by Jo Cottrell and Alistair Cartwright.

## Notes

1 British Council, *How to Live in Britain – A Handbook for Students from Overseas* (London: The British Council, 1952), 12, 29–31.
2 There certainly was great awareness of students' potential role as political leaders: A. T. Carey, *Colonial Students: A Study of the Social Adaptation of Colonial Students in London* (London: Secker & Warburg, 1956), xi. Indian students' experience is marginal to Carey's book, presumably because they were no longer 'colonial'.
3 British Council, *How to Live in Britain*, vii–viii.
4 British Council, *How to Live in Britain*, 36.
5 Such anxieties were the reason for setting up a Political and Economic Planning group (an independent research body) to study the situation in 1951, finally reporting in 1956: Political and Economic Planning, *Colonial Students in Britain* (London: Political and Economic Planning, 1955). The report does not, of course, concern itself with Indian students. On colonial students in postwar Britain, see A. J. Stockwell, 'Leaders, Dissidents and the Disappointed: Colonial Students in Britain as Empire Ended', *Journal of Imperial and Commonwealth History* 36, no. 3 (September 2008): 487–507.
6 On colonial students' own experiences of racial discrimination, see *Disappointed Guests – Essays by African, Asian and West Indian Students*, eds Henri Tajfel and John L. Dawson (Oxford: Oxford University Press, 1965). On fears of Communist Party links, see Sumita Mukherjee, *Nationalism, Education and Migrant Identities: The England-returned* (London: Routledge, 2010), 104.
7 There was some evidence by the mid-1950s that Indian students educated in Britain were positive about the former heart of empire, but this may not have been so clear in the immediate post-independence years. See John Useem and Ruth Hill Useem, *The Western-Educated Man in India* (New York: Dryden Press, 1955). See also Edward Shils, *The Intellectual Between Tradition and Modernity: The Indian Situation* (The Hague: Mouton, 1961), 79–81.
8 Paul B. Rich, *Prospero's Return: Historical Essays on Race, Culture and British Society* (London: Hansib, 1994), 153–65.
9 A. S. Livingstone, *The Overseas Student in Britain* (Manchester: Manchester University Press, 1960), 4; Amar Kumar Singh, *Indian Students in Britain*

(New York: Asia Publishing House, 1963), 94–101. One study thought that Indian students 'react acutely to stress and recover easily when reassured'. See J. C. Read, 'Psychological Disturbances in Students from Overseas', *Medical World* 90, no. 1 (1959): 21.
10 Jordanna Bailkin, *The Afterlife of Empire* (Berkeley: University of California Press, 2012), 7.
11 For 'brain fag' (supposedly found in West African students) and over-integration (found in West Indians) see Bailkin, *The Afterlife of Empire*, 119–24.
12 Sheila Kitzinger, 'Conditional Philanthropy Towards Colored Students in Britain', *Phylon* 21 (Summer 1960): 167–72.
13 Political and Economic Planning, *Colonial Students*, 1.
14 Stockwell, 'Leaders, Dissidents and the Disappointed', 492–3. There was a major protest in 1951 about accommodation in the largest of these, the Hans Crescent Hostel: Stockwell, 'Leaders, Dissidents and the Disappointed', 498.
15 Political and Economic Planning, *Colonial Students*, 41–2.
16 Political and Economic Planning, *Colonial Students*, 183–4.
17 Political and Economic Planning, *Colonial Students*, 41. For the negative experiences of one student who was inducted like this, see J. Ayodele Langley, 'Through a Glass Darkly', in *Colour, Culture and Consciousness: Immigrant Intellectuals in Britain*, ed. Bhikhu Parekh (London: Allen & Unwin, 1974), 34.
18 Bailkin has an excellent summary of all this. Bailkin, *The Afterlife of Empire*, 1–22.
19 Edmund Dell, *A Strange Eventful History: Democratic Socialism in Britain* (London: Harper & Collins, 1999), Chapter 7.
20 Indian YMCA archives, London: YMCA Minute Book, vol. VI, May 20, 1947.
21 Bailkin, *The Afterlife of Empire*, 100, 108, 113, 116–18, 120.
22 *Commemorating the Opening of the New YMCA Indian Students' Union and Hostel* (London: YMCA, 1953), 1, 3.
23 For a short history, see Harald Fischer-Tiné, '"Unparalleled Opportunities"': The Indian YMCA's Army Work Schemes for Imperial Troops During the Great War', *Journal of Imperial and Commonwealth History* 47, no. 1 (2019): 102–4.
24 Fischer-Tiné, '"Unparalleled Opportunities"', 102. On its rural reconstruction projects, see Harald Fischer-Tiné, 'The YMCA and Low-Modernist Rural Development in South Asia, c1922–1957', *Past and Present* 240, no. 1 (August 2018): 193–234. On physical education, see Harald Fischer-Tiné, 'Fitness for Modernity? The YMCA and Physical-Education Schemes in Late-Colonial South Asia (circa 1900–40)', *Modern Asian Studies* 53, no. 2 (2019): 512–59.
25 See, for instance, *With Indian Students in London, being the Sixteenth Annual Report of the Indian Students' Union and Hostel* (London: YMCA, 1935), 4–5.
26 See, for instance, H. Hobbs, *Indian YMCA and Politics* (Calcutta: Hobbs, 1927). For a recent, modulated view on the Indian YMCA's anti-imperialism before and during the First World War, see Fischer-Tiné, '"Unparalleled Opportunities"', 116–17.
27 *YMCA Indian Student Hostel ... 1920–2010* (London: YMCA, 2010), np.

28 Indian YMCA archives: *Annual Report*, June 1947–May 1948.
29 Arundhati Roy, 'The Doctor and the Saint', introduction to B. R. Ambedkar, *Annihilation of Caste* (London: Verso, 2014), 45–6.
30 The best accounts are still of individual Settlement houses. For instance, see Asa Briggs, *Toynbee Hall: The First Hundred Years* (London: Routledge & Kegan Paul, 1984); Standish Meacham, *Toynbee Hall and Social Reform, 1880–1914* (New Haven: Yale University Press, 1987).
31 Gandhi, for one, understood the Settlements' significance. During his 1931 visit to London, he spoke at Oxford House and stayed at Kingsley Hall, both East End settlement houses. See Kathryn Tidrick, *Gandhi – A Political and Spiritual Life* (London: Verso, 2013), 253. It would be interesting to trace the relationship between the Settlement movement and Gandhi's ashrams.
32 'National projection' was a term of the 1930s. See Stephen Tallents, *The Projection of England* (London: Faber & Faber, 1932).
33 *Commemorating*, 3–4, 11–12.
34 Indian YMCA archives: YMCA Minute Book, vol. VI, 16 September 1949. Elain Harwood, *Space, Time and Brutalism: English Architecture 1945–1975* (New Haven: Paul Mellon Centre for Studies in British Art, 2015), 119–20.
35 Indian YMCA archives: YMCA Minute Book, vol. VI, 16 December 1946.
36 Tubbs was working for the Indian YMCA in December 1946. See Indian YMCA archives: YMCA Minute Book, vol. VI, 19 December 1946.
37 John Summerson, 'Introduction', in *Modern Architecture in Britain*, ed. Trevor Dannatt (London: Batsford), 19.
38 For more on the post-imperial elements of the Festival of Britain, see Mark Crinson, *Modern Architecture and the End of Empire* (Aldershot: Ashgate, 2003), 109–16.
39 Tubbs did not obtain the commission for the Dome of Discovery until late 1948. See Hugh Casson, 'Period Piece', in *A Tonic to the Nation – The Festival of Britain 1951*, eds Mary Banham and Bevis Hillier (London: Thames & Hudson, 1976), 78.
40 'A hostel is not only cheaper but gives security, relief from loneliness, and, above all, it eliminates that spectre of colonial student life, the intolerant or grasping landlady'. See Carey, *Colonial Students*, 77. I am not concerned here with the extension to the hostel added in the early 1960s for female students, also designed by Ralph Tubbs. This led to part of the rear of the original building being hidden and a significant change to the foyer.
41 'Union and Hostel for Indian Students', *Architectural Design* 21, no. 5 (1951): 127.
42 *Commemorating*, 1.
43 Quoted in 'Indian Students' Hostel', *Building* 28 (August 1953): 294.
44 On Gandhi and Jesus, see Tidrick, *Gandhi*.
45 Ann Basu, *Fitzrovia, The Other Side of Oxford Street – A Social History 1900–1950* (Stroud: History Press, 2019). In his foreword to Basu's book, Nick Bailey explains this pattern of development: 'while the Bedford Estate to the east and the Cavendish-Harley Estate to the west managed to maintain substantial

control over the use and repair of their properties, the Southampton (Fitzroy) Estate soon lost interest well before the first round of leases began to expire in the mid to late nineteenth century'.

46 Nick Bailey, *Fitzrovia* (London: Historical Publications, 1981), 39.
47 Quoted without source in *YMCA Indian Student Hostel ... 1920–2010* (London: YMCA, 2010), np; Indian YMCA archives: YMCA Minute Book, vol. VI, 21 June 1948.
48 Indian YMCA archives: YMCA Minute Book, vol. VI, 19 July 1948.
49 London Metropolitan Archives: GLC/AR/BR/06/080555, drawing marked ISU/FS/9. Tubbs was in contact with Hector Corfiato, the architect for the University of London.
50 'Indian Students' Hostel', *Building* 28b (August 1953): 294.
51 London County Council, *Survey of London – Volume XXI Tottenham Court Road and Neighbourhood* (London: London County Council, 1949), 30–1.
52 John Summerson, *Georgian London* (London: Peregrine, 1978 [originally published 1945]), 138.
53 London County Council, *Survey*, 54–5.
54 London Metropolitan Archives, GLC/AR/BR/06/080555, letter from Tubbs to the LCC superintending architect (Robert H. Matthew), dated 16 September 1949.
55 Nikolaus Pevsner, *The Buildings of England – London, Except the Cities of London and Westminster* (Harmondsworth: Penguin, 1952), 338.
56 Charles Knevitt, 'Obituary – Ralph Tubbs', the *Independent*, 6 December 1996.
57 Nigel Warburton, *Ernö Goldfinger – The Life of an Architect* (London: Routledge, 2004), 38, 81.
58 Ralph Tubbs, *The Englishman Builds* (Harmondsworth: Penguin, 1945), 65.
59 John Allan, *Berthold Lubetkin – Architecture and the Tradition of Progress* (London: Artifice, 2012), 174.
60 Elizabeth McKellar, 'Populism vs Professionalism: John Summerson and the Twentieth-Century Creation of the "Georgian"', in *Articulating British Classicism: New Approaches to Eighteenth-Century Architecture*, eds B. Arciszewska and E. McKellar (Aldershot: Ashgate, 2004), 35–56.
61 Tubbs, *The Englishman Builds*, 73.
62 John Summerson, Preface (dated August 1945), in Summerson, *Georgian London*, 9.
63 Dannatt, *Modern Architecture in Britain*, 212.
64 A very similar text appears in 'YMCA Indian Students' Union and Hostel', *Architect and Building News*, 204, no. 1 (July 1953): 64–5.
65 London Metropolitan Archives, GLC/AR/BR/06/080555, LCC superintending architect (Robert H. Matthew) recommendation dated 16 March 1951.
66 Anthony D. King, 'An Architectural Note on the Term 'Verandah'', in *The Bungalow: The Production of a Global Culture* (London: Routledge & Kegan Paul, 1984), 265–67.
67 Homi Bhabha, 'Of Mimicry and Man: The Ambivalence of Colonial Discourse', in *The Location of Culture* (London: Routledge, 1994), 85.

68 This is best seen in section, 'Indian Students' Hostel, London', *Concrete* 49, no. 8 (1954): 248.
69 'YMCA Indian Students' Union and Hostel', *Architect and Building News* 204, no. 1 (1953): 69.
70 'YMCA Indian Students' Union and Hostel', *Architectural Design*, 23 July 1953, 180.
71 *Commemorating*, 4.
72 I am grateful to Shaun Theobald for the phrase 'constructed conviviality' and for encouraging me to think more about the dining function within the building.
73 'Union and Hostel for Indian Students', *Architectural Design* 21, no. 5 (May 1951): 129.
74 'Inverted colonial action' is from George Kubler, *The Shape of Time: Remarks on the History of Things* (New Haven: Yale University Press, 1962), 108.
75 'YMCA Indian Students' Union and Hostel', *Architectural Design*, 23 July 1953, 183.

# Index

accommodation 18, 61, 62, 63, 218, 260, 305–7
  hotels 240, 257
  hostels 307, 329 n.40
Act of Union 54–5, 78, 100, 101–5, 110, 113, 120
Admiralty Arch 12, 223, 257, 265
Africa 7, 17, 79, 156–7, 169, 174–5, 180, 219, 221, 224, 227, 231, 264, 277, 280–1, 285–6, 289, 300, 313
  Nigeria 239, 277, 281, 292, 297, 299
  West Africa 79, 102, 157, 169, 180
  West African colonies 277
agency houses (Scottish), East Asia 196
agricultural improvement 200, 202–3
  Highland Clearances 201
Allen, Brian 162, 166
America 65, 59, 83–4, 87, 95, 130, 132, 134, 136, 140–1, 145, 171, 209, 263, 308
  American Federal Government 65
Anglocentrism 128, 132–4, 143
Anglo–Irish 10, 29, 142, 144, 145
Anglo–Saxon 103, 104, 251
architects 6, 18, 65, 73, 103, 108, 113, 132–6, 139–40, 145, 208, 210, 220, 239–40, 257, 263, 273, 277–9, 281, 283, 286–7, 291, 299–300, 317
  Baker, Sir Herbert 268, 283
  Belcher, John 224
  Blomfield, Reginald 132
  Bryce, David 210–11
  Burr, Alfred 52, 264

  Campbell, Colen 133, 140, 171
  Colcutt, Thomas 229
  Cooley, Thomas 108
  Dance, George (the elder) 167, 170
  Dance, George (the younger) 168
  Gandon, James 108, 142
  Gibbs, James 140
  Gill, Macdonald 282, 286
  Goldfinger, Ernö 315
  Graham, James Gillespie 210
  Gwynn, John 141
  Hargrave, John 112
  Hawksmoor, Nicholas 135, 157, 167
  Herbert, Henry 171
  'Heart of the Empire' 224
  Jacobsen, Theodore 157, 161, 165, 167–9, 171
  Jones, Inigo 135, 166, 171
  Jordan, Robert Furneaux 292
  Kent, William 133, 135, 140,
  Lovett Pearce, Sir Edward 128, 131, 136–7
  Lubetkin, Berthold 315
  Mackenzie, A. Marshall 257–8
  Morris, Roger 171
  Morrison, Richard 103
  Morrison, William Vitruvius 110–11
  Murray, William 114
  Paine, James 133
  Palladio, Andrea 132, 136–7
  Pugin, Augustus 221
  Richardson, A. E. 132, 139
  Rogers, Richard 16, 155
  Ross, Alexander 209
  Searles Wood, H. D. 282–3

Shaw, R. Norman 253
Simpson and Ayrton 284
Smirke, Robert 267
Smithe, T. Roger 239
Soane, John 168
Taylor, Sir Robert 133
Thomas Worthington and Sons 295
Tubbs, Ralph 18, 310–16, 324, 326
Vanbrugh, Sir John 134, 138, 257
Ware, Isaac 133
Whichcord, John 226
Wills, Herbert W 265
Wilson, Charles 208
Wittkower, Rudolf 128
Worthington, Hubert 18, 280, 295–6
Artisan and Labourers' Dwellings Improvement Act (1875) 86
Asia 16–17, 156, 161, 169, 173–7, 181, 194–6, 198, 201, 219, 221, 227, 230–1
Asian population 219
asylums 80, 101, 105, 233
  Royal India Asylum 233
Australasia 7, 59, 197
  New South Wales 199, 254–5, 258, 260–2, 266, 268
Australia 199 224, 238, 248–57, 259–65, 267, 269, 273, 280, 290
  Canberra 260
  Federation of Australia's colonies, The 262
  Gold Coast 277, 281, 292
  Queensland 252, 263–4
  South Australia 262–3
  Trans-Australian Railway 250–1
  Western Australia 250, 263
  *see also* Commonwealth, Dominion

Balfour Declaration 269, 273
banks 224–7, 242
  Bank of England 11, 167, 224, 242
  Bank of Ireland 131
  Bank of New Zealand 224, 226, 227
  Lloyds Bank 310
  Oriental Bank 224
Bernera Riot 201

Bevington Street scheme 91–4
Black Lives Matter 1, 156
Blitz, The 313
Board of Trade 252, 290, 299
Boer War 223
Bonnerjee, Womesh Chandra 233
Booth, Charles 227, 231, 233
Boson, John 167, 170
Boyle, Richard (Lord Burlington) 132, 135, 138–9, 140, 145, 166–8
Britannia 144, 161–2, 174, 227
Britannia Iron Works, the 310
British Poor Law Commissioners 105
British Army 58, 68
British Canadian Export Co Ltd, the 282
British Council 305–308, 312
British Council of Churches 308
British Crown 155
British Empire Exhibition 13, 280, 284–5, 291, 293–4
British Empire 142, 269, 276
British Fisheries Society 6, 53, 68–73
British India 193, 231, 273
British Isles 2–10, 13–14, 19, 53–6, 66, 133, 139, 143, 195, 278
British Library 155, 158, 161, 181
British Raj 291
British Standards Institution 282
Buckingham Palace 222–3, 257
Building Centre, The 8, 280, 285, 287–91
Building Research Station 286–7
Bulletin of the Imperial Institute 283
bungalow 236, 238
Burlingtonian classicism 168
Byrne, 'Dandy' Pat 88–9
Burma Pavilion 285

Canada 53, 61, 70, 201, 248–52, 257, 259–61, 264–5, 267, 270 273, 276, 278, 280–1, 289, 290, 299
  British Columbia 264, 280, 285, 286
  government offices 257, 258
  House of Commons 267
  Canadian Lumberman's Association 296

Canada (*cont.*)
  Nova Scotia 7, 63, 70
  *see also* Commonwealth, Dominion
Caribbean 10, 173, 221, 231, 296
  Barbados 177
  Jamaica 11, 171, 193, 239
  slave plantations 193
  *see also* slavery
cathedrals 96
  Canterbury Cathedral 167
  St Paul's Cathedral 12, 157, 163–4, 222–4
  *see also* churches, religion
carpet 172–3, 181
cellar housing 80–6
Central America 171, 296
ceremonial space 221–3
chain stores 235–7, 310
Charter Act, the 158
Chevalier de la Tocnaye 141
China 169, 172, 178, 196–7 201, 204, 206, 210, 212, 219, 227, 231
  Canton 169, 194, 199, 200, 202, 204
  China trade 16, 178, 194–8, 200, 205, 207–12
  Chinese imperial Authorities 202
  Imperial China 208
  Macau 194, 199–200
  Shanghai 194
chinoiserie 173
cholera 84–5
churches 94, 119, 308
  Church of Ireland 101–4, 119–20
  *see also* cathedrals, religion
Civil War (1922–23), 115, 116, 118
class 82–3, 89–91, 108, 145, 220, 224, 228, 231, 233, 236, 239
  lower middle-class 220, 228, 233
  middle-class 80, 88, 113, 220, 228, 231, 233, 239, 309
  working class 80, 155, 228, 233, 236
coinage, coins 130, 168–9, 178, 208
Cold War 307–8
Colonial Office 236, 252, 267, 307
colonial trade 13, 227, 279
  British North Borneo Chartered Company 281

East India Company 10, 16, 69, 155–89, 196, 199, 204, 227–8, 230–1, 233
Dutch East India Company 174, 177–8
opium 195–7, 199, 202, 207–9, 212
Royal African Company 69, 157, 168, 180–1
sugar 156, 172, 229–30
tea 156–7, 164, 173, 196–7, 206–8, 212, 227, 229, 235–6
Trade Enquiry Offices 252
trade monopoly 196–9
trade-led Empire Forestry Association, the 279
United Company of Merchants of England Trading to the East Indies 157, 176
*see also* intra–imperial trade
colonialism 1–8, 14, 33, 39, 53–6, 59, 66–7, 70, 103, 169, 277, 307
*see also* colonial trade, decolonisation
commercial space 224–8, 240–2
Commonwealth 249–51, 256, 257, 261–5, 277, 295, 308
  British Commonwealth of Nations 249, 269
  Commonwealth of Australia 249, 273
  Commonwealth Offices Building 257
  Commonwealth Stone 262
  Victoria League 306
Company of Royal Adventurers Trading to Africa 157
Confederate monuments controversy 278
Connolly, Laurence 88
Conolly, William 130, 141
Corinthian columns 212
Coromandel screens 172
cosmopolitanism 221, 231, 242
court housing 80–81, 84–86, 93
courthouses 100, 103–104, 108–12, 114–16, 118
Cowie, Donald 298

cowrie shells 156
Crickmay & Sons 263

De Beers Kimberley Diamond Mine 274
Declaratory Act (1782) 130
decolonisation 11, 248, 277–8, 298, 300, 307
Defoe, Daniel 163–4, 178
Department of Forestry 295
Department of Overseas Trade, the 18, 280–1
department stores 240, 242
Deptford Dockyard 66, 170
Disraeli, Benjamin (British prime minister) 194, 198, 222
Docklands 155
Dome of Discovery 310–11, 326
Domestic space 220, 228–36, 238–9, 242
Dominion 17–18, 144, 164, 197, 248–69, 273, 277–8, 281–4, 289–291, 300
  Dominion Government, the 289
  Dominion houses 17, 248–9, 260–1, 267, 269
    Australia House 17, 248–50, 256–69
    Canada House 249
    India House 249, 268, 283, 307
    New Zealand House 249
    South Africa House 12, 249, 268–9
Dominion Screen 274–7, 291
Doric order 166
Downey, Archbishop 'Dickie' 96
Dublin 15, 31, 100, 101, 105, 108, 112–13,129, 131, 133–5, 139–44, 236
  Custom House (1781–91), The 80, 132, 142
  Dublin Castle 15, 105, 110, 142
  Four Courts 15, 108, 116–17
  House of Commons 143
  Kilmainham gaol 115
  Parliament House 128–45
  Royal Dublin Society 141
  Stillorgan House 139

Duncan, Dr W. H. 80–4
Dunlop, Denis Cheyne 273

East Africa House 313
East India Docks 155
East India House 155–80, 240
East India trade 170
East Indiaman 170, 180
Economic Botany Collection 279
ecumenicism 308–9, 312, 322, 326
Edward I 65–6
Edwardian baroque 13, 221, 223, 256
Egypt 219, 224
Empire Exhibition Wembley 13, 280 284–5, 310
Empire Forestry Association 279, 284
Empire Marketing Board 18, 282–6, 289, 292
Empire Timber Exhibition 280–3
England/English 5,14,16, 31–33, 43, 53–5, 59, 67, 82, 95, 102, 126–38, 123–5, 172–3, 177–80, 202, 213
English Heritage 9, 10, 193
Europe 1–2, 8, 12, 29, 55–6, 63, 65–6, 72, 90–1, 95, 103, 131, 139, 142, 178, 209, 219, 222, 229, 231, 259, 260, 277, 299, 313
Exchequer (Britain) 29, 197
Eyre Estate, the 230

Father Nugent 83, 88
Faulkner, George 142
Festival of Britain (1951), the 310–11
fever 82, 83, 85, 88
First Opium War (1839–42), the 194, 202
First World War 92–93, 95, 219, 223, 250, 277, 281, 295
floating hospitals 83
Florence Hall 273, 291
Foreign, Commonwealth, and Development Office 181
Forestry Act (1919), the 281, 283
Forestry Commission, the 281, 283, 285, 296, 178, 180

fortifications 53, 65, 105–6, 174–6,
    forts 3, 14, 34, 35, 43, 53, 57–8,
        60–1, 63, 67, 70, 73–4, 161–2,
        175, 176, 178, 180
    Fort August 61, 64
    Fort George 53, 63–7, 70, 73
    Fort St George 175, 178
    Fort William 61, 64
Forwood, A. B. 86, 90
Foucault, Michel 176
Foundling Hospital 161–2
Free State Government 116, 119
free trade, imperialism 196–198
Fry, Elizabeth 113

Gaelic 41–2, 46, 68, 89, 145
Gandhi 240, 309, 312
gardens 17, 35–9, 44, 59, 222, 229–31,
    235–6, 242
    Kew Gardens 235, 279
gated communities 229, 231
George II 60, 65, 168, 171
George III 117
Georgian (affinity with Modernism)
    315–16
Georgian Britain 66, 128
Georgian Ireland 101, 103, 142
Germany 136, 219, 264
Gladstone, William (British prime
    minister) 198
Gluckstein Brothers 287
gold 168–9, 172
gothic 221, 224
Great Exhibition (1851) 12, 228, 279,
    283
Great Exhibition of the Works of
    Industry of All Nations 228
Great Famine (1845–52) 101–2, 113
Great Fire of 1666 166
Great Northern Railway 231
Green & Vardy 273, 275

Hanoverian regime 139
Harford, Austin 89, 90–3
Hayton, David 130, 141, 145
Henderson, Keith 286
High Commission, the 261

Highlands 3, 6, 9–10, 14, 53–74
    Highland Gaels 61, 68–9, 72
    Highland Jacobite army 68
    Highland Society of London, the 68
HM Office of Works 286, 299
Holland, Henry 157, 168
Hong Kong 194, 197, 199, 206, 209,
    211, 239
    Causeway Bay 197
    East Point 197
Hope, Dr E. W. 91
House of Commons (Britain) the 130,
    290
House of Lords 108, 130, 135–6
Houses of Parliament 218, 221, 239–40
Housing Committee 90, 91, 93

imitation 305
    see also mimicry
imperial government 220, 223, 225
Imperial Institute 12, 229, 252, 256,
    279, 283, 295
imperial space 219–21, 228, 241
Imperial War Cabinet 264
India 18, 59, 102, 136, 155–78, 197,
    204, 222, 224, 229, 231, 236,
    240, 264, 267–8, 273–81,
    290–1, 296, 299, 306–10, 326
    Bombay 161, 174, 201, 204, 240
        Tellicherry 174, 178
    Calcutta 174, 176, 200, 227,
        229–31, 236–7, 239–40
    Indian Constitution 309
    Indian Empire 228, 229
    Indian nationalism 309
    Madras 161, 174–5, 178, 227, 229
    see also Commonwealth, Dominion
India Office, the 158, 240
infrastructure 4, 16, 53, 57, 59, 63, 73,
    96, 105 116, 197, 250, 284
    bridges 53–67, 200
    railway infrastructure, 116
    roads 14, 33, 35–6, 38, 53, 57,
        58–63, 67, 73, 106, 155, 200,
        233
        Commissioners for Highland
            Roads and Bridges 63, 67

Scotland Road 86, 95
  see also fortifications
informal empire, 194–5, 219, 224
inn, the 41–2
  Weem Inn 61, 62, 66
inner empire 3, 6, 7, 11, 13–5, 19, 36, 39, 54, 78, 101, 195, 213
Insanitary Property and Artisans' Dwelling Committee 86, 89–90
international exhibitions 220, 227–9
intra–imperial trade 277, 280, 282, 284–6, 295, 298
Ireland/Irish 4–16, 29–39, 42, 44, 54–6, 78, 82–3, 87, 100–20, 129–34, 138–42, 144–5 221, 231, 233
  Ahascragh (Co.Galway) 119
  Armagh (Co.) 34, 108, 113
  Association for the improvement of Prisons and of Prison Discipline (AIPPD) 113, 114
  Carlow (Co.) 110–12
  Cork (Co.) 100, 101, 116
    gaol (Co. Cork) 100–1, 112
  Dáil (the Irish Parliament) 116
  Ennis (Co. Clare) 104
  Fermanagh (Co.) 145
  Hibernia 36, 144
  Irish courts 116
  Irish famine 79, 80, 82, 83–4
  Irish Free State 96, 100, 133
  Irish Georgian Society 134
  Irish home rule 78, 87–8
  Irish National Party (INP) 88–93
  Irish Parliament House 128, 134, 139, 140
  Irish Poor Law Workhouse 107
  Irish Prisons Act of 1810, the 12
  Irish Public Works Loan Act 108
  Irish Republican Army (IRA) 115–19
  Louth (Co.) 109, 113–15
    Dundalk (Co. Louth) 109, 114–15
    gaol 114–15
  Monaghan (Co.) 110–11, 119
  Shannonbridge (Co. Offaly) 106
  Sinn Fein 89, 95
  Society of United Irishmen 130

St Patrick's Day 87
Tralee (Co. Kerry) 101, 110–12
Trim (Co. Meath) 112
Tullamore (Co. Offaly) 116–19
Viceroy 102
Wexford (Co.), 116
Irish Sea, the 79, 131, 133
iron 59, 60, 86, 238
Italianate classicism 114–15, 138

Jacobite Rebellions 53, 59, 63–4, 67, 68–9
Jacobite Uprising 57
James, John 157
Japan 197, 231
Jardine, Andrew 206
Jardine, Joseph 205
Jardine, Matheson & Co. (Formerly Magniac & Co.) 194–8, 200, 202, 204, 206, 212
Jardine, Robert 206–7, 210–11
Jardine, Skinner & Co. (Calcutta) 199
Jardine, William 194, 196, 198, 204, 207, 210, 212
Jejeebhoy, Jamsetjee 201
Jingoistic imperialism 220
Jupp, Richard 157, 168

Kauffer McKnight 286
King Charles II 157
King George V 256, 268
Kings House 62
Kingsway 223, 263, 265
Knox, John 69

La Roche, Sophie Von 164
lacquerware 172–3, 178
Lambert, George 161, 167, 173–8
Latin America 219, 224
Leadenhall Market 163
League of Nations, the 264
Leoni, Giacomo 166
Lipton, Thomas 235–6
Liverpool Building Act (1842) 85
Liverpool Sanitary Act (1846) 82, 84, 85
Liverpool, Lord 108

Lloyd's of London 155–6, 168
loans from colonies 308
lodging houses 81, 82, 84–5
London 16–17, 58–9, 66, 68–70, 86, 113, 128, 132, 135–6, 139, 140–2, 145, 155–78 193, 198–9, 204–7, 218–42, 248–69, 279–83, 286–8, 290, 298–9, 305, 307–9, 313–17, 320
   Aldwych 223, 249, 253, 256, 257, 265
   Bayswater 230–32, 238
   Blackwall 164, 170
   Bloomsbury 308, 312–13
   Charing Cross 61
   City of 155–92, 166–7, 219, 224–8
     Customs House 164
     docks 219, 227
     London Bridge 163–4, 222
   County Council, London 218, 223, 257, 262–3, 267, 290
   Ealing 221, 233
   Earl's Court 227, 229
   East End 309
   Embankment 222, 264
   Fitzrovia 313
   Fitzroy Square 18, 310, 312–15, 317
   Greenwich 157, 170, 248
   Hampstead 221, 231, 238
   Holborn 221
   Kensington 221, 228–30, 238–9, 252, 286
   Kew 235, 238, 279, 283
   London and North Eastern Railways (LNER) 299
   London Building Act 290
   London Commercial Sale Rooms 227
   London Underground 282
   Poplar 155, 227
   Shepherds Bush 252–6
   Strand, The 222–3, 249, 252–3, 256–7, 260, 263–5, 269, 286
   Thames 66, 132, 155, 164, 170, 176, 218, 222–3, 227, 236, 238
   Trafalgar Square 11–12, 222–3, 249, 257, 260, 265, 267–9
   West End 166–7, 218, 223, 228, 239, 241, 242, 313
   Westminster 15, 63, 101–2, 105, 129, 133, 138, 140–1, 163–4, 166, 199, 209, 219, 221, 239, 241, 249, 263, 265, 269
     Westminster Abbey 12, 58, 68, 222, 240
     Westminster Bridge 222
   Whitehall 13, 102, 105, 134–5, 219–22, 240, 263, 265
long eighteenth century 54, 143

MacAlister, Ian 290
Machiavelli 56–7
Mackintosh & Co. (Calcutta) 200
Magniac & Co 200, 204
Maitland, William 166
mansion flats 17, 236, 239, 240–1
Mansion House 167, 170, 224, 226
maps, mapping, mapwork 177–9, 225, 228, 233–4, 241
marble 58, 62, 161–2, 171, 173, 212, 256, 262, 268, 291
Marble Hill House 171–2
MARS Group 310
Matheson & Co 16, 194, 196–9, 200–13
   Matheson, Alexander, 194, 198, 201–4, 207, 209
   Matheson, Hugh 199
   Matheson, James 194, 198–201, 204, 208–9
Melvill, Robert 70, 72–3
Metropolitan & District Railway 222
Metropolitan Board of Works 218
migration 219, 221, 227–8, 231, 233, 236, 239
mimicry 317–18, 326
   *see also* imitation
Ministry of Labour 281
Moll, Herman 178–9
money laundering 193–4
monument 42, 53, 59, 60, 63, 100, 133–5, 142, 163–4, 212, 278, 298

museums 228–9
  British Museum 228
  Horniman Museum 229
  Museum of British Forestry 279
  Museum of Economic Botany 279
  South Kensington Museum (later Victoria & Albert) 228
  Timber Museum 279

nabob, 10, 16, 193–4
Napoleonic wars 108, 219
National Health Service 306
National Trust 11, 134, 193
nationalism 89, 235, 249, 267, 309
Navigation Act (1779) 130
Nelson's Column 11, 222
Neville, John 114–15
New Treasury Offices 222
New Zealand 224, 226–7, 249–50, 256–7, 263, 274, 299
  Maori 276
  New Zealand Loan & Mercantile Agency Company 226
  *see also* Commonwealth, Dominion
Nicholson, William 170
Nine Years War 31, 27
North America 54, 59, 64, 240, 308
North Britain 14, 53–74
Nugent, Father James 83, 88

O'Connell, Daniel 104, 108
O'Connor, T. P. 89–91, 96
O'Higgins, Kevin 116
O'Neill, Sir Phelim 43
obliquity 317–18, 324, 326
orientalism 312, 317, 324, 326
orthodox classicism 132, 138
Orwell, George 300
Osterley Park 172
Ottawa Conference of 1932 273, 289–90
Oxford 239, 278–80, 283, 292, 295–6, 298
Oxford House 309

Paddy's Market 94
painting 161–3, 173–8, 180, 268

Palladianism 15, 128, 132–6, 138–40, 142, 157, 166, 168–9, 171
  Anglo–Palladian 131–3, 139
  Irish Palladianism 133, 138
  Irish school of Palladianism 136
Palmer, James 113
Palmerston, Lord 194, 202
parliament 178, 180
Pathé 263
Pearcean 135
Peel, Robert (British prime minister) 108, 222
philanthropy, 87, 194, 308–9
planned villages 68–9, 70, 72
  *see also* town planning
Plantagenets 55
postcolonialism 1, 8, 12, 18, 56, 118, 120, 140, 250, 306– 9, 317, 326
  *see also* colonialism, decolonisation
postwar Britain 18, 307
Prince William Augustus 65
prisons 112–16, 118
  Newgate Prison 132
processions 220, 222–3
Public Record Office 116–17

Queen Victoria 222–3
Queen Victoria Memorial 257
Queensberry House 166

racial prejudice 68, 81, 96, 278, 306–7
Ralph, James 168, 170
Rand Lords 193
Rebellion of 1798 100, 130
Redmond, John 44, 90–1
religion 30–1, 44–6, 55, 95, 101–2, 114, 201, 268, 309
  Anglican 96, 113
  Catholic 45–6, 83, 87–96, 119, 130, 144, 308
    Catholic Emancipation 10
  Christian 29
  Protestant 31, 42, 44–6, 80, 87–8, 95, 102–4, 106, 111, 116–17, 119, 120, 129, 138, 141, 145, 308
    Protestant Ascendancy 129, 138
    Protestant missionaries 102

religion (*cont.*)
  Quaker 113
  *see also* cathedrals, churches
remitted wealth (from colonies), 195, 207–13
Renaissance 33, 65, 96
Rhodes House 13, 280, 295
Rhodes Must Fall campaign 278, 298
River Tay 14, 59
Robber Baron 193
Roman imperial (limes system), 60–1, 63
Roman palazzo (style), 264
Rome 29, 53, 56–8, 74, 96, 135, 223, 256
  Roman Empire 53, 56–7, 140, 221
Roscoe, William 79
Royal Academy 157, 200
Royal Arsenal 221
Royal Exchange 10, 163, 224
Royal Hospital for Seamen, Greenwich 157
Royal Institute of British Architects (RIBA) 18, 136, 239, 273, 277, 280, 281, 283, 289–92
Royal Irish Constabulary police barracks 119
Royal William Yard 66
Rysbrack, John Michael 161–2, 166, 173, 174, 178, 181

Said, Edward, 213
Scotland/Scottish – 3, 4, 6, 9, 14, 16, 53–74, 80,
  Annandale 207
  Ardross 201, 203, 207, 209, 210
    Ardross Castle 203, 210
  Attadale 202, 207
  Balintraid 203
  Barony of Corrie 206
  Castlemilk 205–7, 210–11
  Dalmore 203
  Delny 203
  Dumfries 206–7
    Lochmaben 212
  Easter Ross 203

  Edinburgh 62, 65, 70, 140, 200, 206, 283
    Merchiston Castle school 206
  Galloway 207
  Glasgow 11, 13, 236, 280
    Empire Exhibition 291–94
  Inverinate 202
  Island of Lewis 200
    Lews Castle, 200, 207–9
  Lanrick Castle, 204–5, 207, 210
  Ledgowan 202
  Lochalsh 202, 207, 209
    Duncraig Castle 203, 207, 209
  Merchants 194–213
  Ross–shire 207
  Scotia 144
  Scottish Gaels 9, 56–7, 65, 68, 70, 73
Scots Baronial (style) 208–10
Scott, Samuel 161, 173–6, 178
sculpture 161, 167, 170, 173, 227–8, 320
Second World War, 277, 309, 313
settlement movement 309, 322
Seven Years War 53, 61, 70
Shelter Neighbourhood Action Project 95
Shepherd, Thomas 171, 173
ships 63, 84, 85, 156, 161, 164, 170–7, 204, 262
slavery 156, 183, 193, 213, 224
  slave trade 5, 11, 12, 13, 79, 84, 156, 170, 172, 177, 193, 219, 224, 278
  *see also* colonialism, colonial trade
slum clearance 86
Society of Architects 281
Somerset House 132, 166–7, 257
South Africa 59, 229, 248, 250, 264, 268–9, 273–4, 276, 281, 290, 296
  Cape of Good Hope 157, 173,
  Table Mountain 274
  Union of South Africa 273
  *see also* Commonwealth, Dominion
South America 169, 231
space, production of 12, 219–20, 241, 242

St George's Circus 222
St Helena 161, 173–4, 177 183
St James's Palace 163
St Martin's Cottages 85
Statute of Westminster 249, 265, 269
street improvements 218, 232–3, 239
street names 233–5
  Gower Street 308, 310, 312
  Granby Four Streets 95
  Leadenhall Street 16, 156–7, 159, 161, 164, 166, 227–8
  Liverpool Street 261
  Queen Victoria Street 224, 226
  Savoy Street 264
  Victoria Street 239, 240, 241, 253, 263
stucco 171, 231, 263
Student Christian Movement 306–7
student pathologies 307
students as ambassadors 306
suburbia 220, 229–38, 242
Summerson, Sir John 96, 128, 133–4, 139, 167, 310, 316

Taipans 16, 194, 198, 206
Tallents, Stephen 282, 286, 289
temperate and tropical zones 317, 326
tenement housing 90, 91, 94
Thackeray, William 100, 236
Timber Development Association (TDA) 292–3, 295, 298
*Times*, The 222, 259, 265, 284–5, 287
town planning 223, 241
  planned towns 53, 57–8, 67, 68–9, 70– 4
  *see also* planned villages
Treasury Building 135
Treaty of Nanking (1842) 202

Treaty of Versailles 264
Trench, Dr W. 85
Tudors, the 6, 14, 31, 55
typhoid 84–5
typhus 83–5

Ulster Plantation 6, 33, 36, 42, 46
universities 10, 202, 204, 298, 308, 312–13

Verandah 236, 238, 241, 317, 318
Vertue, George 161–2, 167
Victoria House 252–6, 261

Wale, Samuel 157–8, 166–7
Walpole, Robert (British prime minister), 166, 171
War of Independence (1919–21), 115–16, 118
warehouses 155, 157, 163–4
Webb, Aston 223, 257, 260, 265, 269
Westenra, Henry 110–11
Whiggism 128, 130, 142, 240, 263, 265
wood 64, 172–3, 178, 276–300
  mahogany 172–3, 181, 256, 279, 286
  maple 285, 291, 296
  oak 59, 60, 170, 281, 285, 299
  timber 18, 62, 65, 157, 257, 262, 274–99
  walnut 291, 296
workhouses 15, 90, 101, 105, 107, 120

YMCA 18, 308–27
Yrisarri & Co. (Macau) 200
Yrisarri, Xavier 200